CHRISTIAN HERITAGE COLLEGE

2100 Greenfield Dr.

El Cajon, CA 92021

Hippies, Drugs and Promiscuity

HIPPIES, DRUGS AND PROMISCUITY

By Suzanne Labin

Translated by Stephanie Winston

Arlington House   New Rochelle, N.Y.

Library of Congress Catalog Card Number 70–189375

ISBN 0–87000–156–6

MANUFACTURED IN THE UNITED STATES OF AMERICA

Contents

Hippies, Drugs and Promiscuity

1

Young "Heads" at Night

I had to get to the bottom of it.

During my last tour around the continent of cybernetic beauty shops, market analyses, air conditioning, and "vitamin-enriched" food, I had stumbled, to my amazement, on troops of emaciated pilgrims with long scruffy hair framing unwashed faces that sometimes sported multihued designs. This new breed of mendicant friars—enveloped in old Indian ponchos, weighed down with anklets, neckbands and amulets—wandered, feet bare, in the service of a new religion of Love. The pupils of almost every one of these avatars of the New Age were dilated, and their gaze was vague and blank, because they had not yet emerged from their last encounter with one of the hallucinogenic drugs.

These were the famous hippies, the flower-children of America. They were all wearing protest buttons, found by the thousands in the shops that serviced their world, along with all sorts of curious, often erotic objects in screeching colors, and psychedelic posters of a strange beauty. The buttons read, among other things:

> STUDYING CAUSES CANCER
> LEGALIZE DRUGS
> DOWN WITH BRAS
> CURE VIRGINITY
> LONG LIVE SEX

So here, right in the heart of the country that has pushed prosperity, hygiene, and efficiency just about as far as they would go, a subculture had exploded for whom the values of antiprosperity, antihygiene, and antiefficiency were pushed about as far as *they* would go. Mysticism and drugs had been elevated into a new religion, pulling the group back into the darkest recesses of its primeval past, while at that same moment, in the same country, Cosmic Man was programming his electronic brains to conquer the moon. This was an extraordinary paradox, and I decided that the hippie phenomenon was worth an investigation.

For a year I read all that the aboveground press has had to say on this new kind of protest movement, as well as a number of scientific studies dealing with it. One set of statistics, from the Los Angeles Bureau of Narcotics, particularly caught my attention: drug arrests had increased, for just the year of 1967 and for just the city of Los Angeles, 56 percent for adults and 130 percent for minors. In California as a whole, arrests grew from 7000 in 1964 to 37,000 in 1967; and I think we can assume that the people who have actually been arrested are an insignificant fraction of the people who actually use drugs. But, after I spent one night in a police station, this abstraction of numbers took on a human reality that shook me profoundly.

A Police Station in Hollywood

I had believed that during the night a police station would hum softly with a diluted, somnolent kind of life. What I found, however, was the febrile kind of animation that must dominate General Headquarters while the battle rages outside. In the West Hollywood district alone, sixteen patrol cars and four detective cars leave the station every few minutes to make their rounds and return periodically to report. The offices are full of harassed people who man the radios, and every five minutes or so the main door opens to admit one or two new wrongdoers, accompanied by two husky cops.

This time it may be a drug-pusher whose face is strained with the effort to disavow the incriminating merchandise he is hiding on his person. Next it's a drunk, still under the influence, who yells, makes a scene, then collapses sobbing. Now a truckdriver who had taken one too many and ran someone down, next a housebreaker—furious at being caught—who snarls "shut your mouth" at the drunk, and shut his mouth he does. There's a placid prostitute who, finding herself in the more or less respectable atmosphere of the police station, takes on the airs of a chaste young damsel. There's an "intellectual" hippie who "knows his rights" and shouts "I'll bring charges against you!" at the cops, until another "shut your mouth" from the would-be burglar has the same calming effect on him that it had on the drunk.

When I first came in I noticed, in the room to the left of the main hall, two men behind bars, and I felt that same pinching at the heart I always feel when I see human beings in cages, because they seem to me to have been reduced to beasts and—worst of all—to have been reduced to that state by other human beings. While the main door swung back and forth in that constant rhythm and new candidates for the human cages made their appearance, an impassive policeman, oblivious to the insults of the newcomers, took inventories of the possessions of the preceding batch. The prisoners waited, dulled after their initial, and useless, cries of rage, to be taken to the section appropriate to their particular misdemeanor; there was a section for drunks, for drug-users, for women, minors, major crimes, etc., all of which were properly posted on the plan on the entrance wall.

But soon enough my pity for these beings whom life had bruised gave way to something infinitely more painful. A tide of veritable children who had been picked up drifting alone through the night, most of them carrying drugs, swept in through the heavy front door escorted by two policemen.

From time to time, I went out on rounds with two plainclothes detectives during their tour of hippie clubs on Sunset Strip, Los Angeles' famous "street of joy." On each occasion, when we came back to the station the cells up front had been emptied of their previous occupants, whose faces I had come to know, and replaced by a new group twisted by a private drama that spurted out of eyes inflamed like cheap red wine. The women and young people—from whom, at least, the policemen had nothing to fear in the way of active attack—were kept under guard in the waiting room or questioned in the offices. I saw at least a dozen young people, practically children, wise as statues.

Pockets Full of Pot

California's curfew law makes it illegal for a minor of less than eighteen years to walk in the streets after ten o'clock unless accompanied by an adult. But here it is one o'clock in the morning, and I am treated to a rare spectacle: an invisible but implacable tide, each wave leaving in its wake a group of kids beached on the underground reefs of the nocturnal life of the big city. First, two skinny boys, then a mini-couple, then three young girls. The oldest girl (all of fifteen) was appealing in her short dress that outlined her pubescent breasts and left her frail shoulders bare; it's hot in Los Angeles. The two other girls, sloppily dressed, with straggly hair, combined the typical awkwardness of their thirteen years with the eternal beauty of healthy cheeks. They looked like schoolgirls, not streetwalkers. And they were schoolgirls. They wouldn't give their parents' addresses, and pretended not to know where they lived. They lied openly and with aplomb. One of them sniffed, "My mother? If you know where she is, tell me: I'd like to know!"

The boys seemed more shaken. Confronted with superior force, they could have no recourse to coquetry, that powerful weapon in the female armory. One of them, near tears, gave his mother's address. He was fourteen years old, from Quebec. In Canada, paternal authority is not dispensed with quite so gaily as in the United States, and he was afraid of parental recriminations. The young Americans, on the other hand, couldn't have cared less. The police told me that half the time when a family is called down to the station to pick up their wayward girl who had run away and been picked up smoking marijuana, their response was, "Well, she's sixteen; she's old enough to know what to do." The alternative behavior is to send the girl to a psychoanalyst. In consequence of which, the girl would go back to her home, go back to her drugs, go back into the arms of the police, back to her parents, back to the psychoanalyst, and on around again forever.

In the United States, the "runaway" problem amounts now to a national tragedy. In San Francisco, before 1965, there were no more than five or six cases a month. Today, photos sent to the police cover whole walls from the floor to the ceiling, fifty times more than there were five years ago. This fact alone, which shook me to the roots, proves that we are dealing here with an epidemic. In cases where the kids have been recovered before the necessary few weeks it takes to adopt the hippie style of dress—rags and naked feet—they generally are found comfortably dressed and shod, well-fed and armed with plenty of money. They seem more spoiled than mistreated. They left home, mostly, because of a scolding, or out of romantic fantasy, or from a taste for adventure, not to mention a simple wish to be "in," up-to-the-minute, incapable of resisting the unprecedented publicity attendant to the wandering hippies. Most of the time, they were not angry at their families.

A woman attendant searched the girls. Every one of them, like the boys, was found carrying marijuana cigarettes ("joints") wrapped in toilet paper and stored in little metal boxes that in more innocent days carried beauty creams or throat lozenges.

I struck up a conversation with the young Canadian boy in French, and told him he could speak freely with me since no one else at the station understood our language. He was a sweet boy, timid and polite, sniffing back his tears. It is the first time, he told me, that he has spent a night in jail. I asked him to tell me the story of his day; he is not likely to forget it.

He lived with his older sister and his mother in a house that he had no wish to leave, because he was loved there. But one night, coming back home from a friend's birthday party, he felt moved instead to wander Hollywood's streets of pleasure and neon all alone. Nothing much so far. But then someone "laid some grass" on him, and things began to get sticky. In the United States these days, marijuana spreads faster than the eye can see. Whereas in the old days drug-pushing was a business plain and simple, it's become now a form of proselytizing, or perhaps—since very often the drug is given away free—there is some deliberate attempt to pervert youth. In any case, the United States can congratulate itself on holding the world's record for the youngest recorded victim of heroin poisoning: Walter Vaudemer, seven-years-old, found dead from an overdose in a Harlem apartment.

The Psychedelic Scene on Sunset Strip

I took a tour with the detectives around Sunset Strip or, as it should more aptly be called, the Strip of Rising Hell, and went into a hippie discotheque. The band was so loud that my eardrums hurt. Against a background of strident discords drawn with the paroxysmal intensity of thick-muscled throats from brass instruments, rose the hoarse, hysterical cries of a girl singer who writhed like one possessed while drawing her long hair all down the length of her serpentine arms. She twisted herself around like a worm, then threw her shock of matted hair over a face that no longer had eyes or mouth, just a voice, the voice of a madwoman straining through a madwoman's hair.

While I stood there fearing that at any moment my eardrums would tear apart or my brain explode, my eyes were assailed, pierced, wounded by an orgy of luminous and lurid images that glanced over me, then brusquely went their way before I could even grasp them. Before I had quite taken in the face of the young woman, her mouth wide open, a gun drawn by a gangster flashed full in my eyes; a horse galloped over me; then a very beautiful nude young girl, strolling through a garden of Eden passed before me, only to be immediately superseded by a shipwreck in a demented sea. And always, all the time, piercingly superimposed over all these images, was the open-mouthed face of that young girl whose face and expression stayed tantalizingly out of reach. My optic nerves were at the mercy of ten projectors all throwing out their images onto various places on the dark wall, no single picture lasting longer than a lightning flash, but just as blinding. The pictures were sometimes violently colored, sometimes somber, but always superimposed on one another, clashing, colliding, torturing.

"Torture" is the right word, particularly for a discotheque a journalist friend had taken me to a year before. It was even more Dantesque than the dive on Sunset Strip. My head, under the triple aggression of optic, auditory and psychic poundings, was going into shock; I couldn't bear more than ten minutes of this fury. I left, at the end of my strength. My companion told me that no newcomer he had ever brought to this discotheque had been able to last more than fifteen minutes. "But," I asked, "how can the regulars tolerate this hell for a whole night?" "Because," he answered, "they are all stoned [high on drugs], which deadens the perceptions."

Meanwhile, back on the Strip, it took a while before I could make out, in the darkness, the shadows in human form that jerked in cadence. It took me yet another while to realize that this sight had to do with what, in other times, we would have called dancing. They were packed together and they were the most solitary dancers in the world. Each one of them undulated to his own private beat. Even if a female happened to be facing a male—which was not always the case—no one actually danced with a partner. Everyone for himself, and the devil for all. No one even paid attention to the horror-show fireworks that flashed on the wall. They looked at their feet moving in rhythm, and no girl smiled at any boy, nor any boy at any girl. There was nothing to see, nothing to touch, nothing to desire. These moving, twisting, crouching phantoms were all wrapped, on their lower parts, in shapeless pants, covered in the middle by too-large Indian vests whose fringes seemed to move to their own independent beat, and wrapped on top by long hair that, propelled by the incessant movement of its owners' heads, also seemed to take on its own propulsion. These were shadows without bodies, without necks, without sex—just shadows consecrated to absolute movement within absolute noise.

In another place on the Strip, egocentric exhibitionism had been carried to a further point of refinement. The dancers were perched on a platform raised above the surrounding tables. Here too everyone danced alone, absorbed in himself, ignoring his partner, but this time the dancers could watch themselves on a closed-circuit television setup. I saw a black thing, black from head to foot, thrust a leg into the air, lower its bottom to the floor, get up again, throw an arm out into the night that surrounded it, and start all over again, and again. The thing was bundled, in spite of the heat, in a large, long-haired fur jacket. At the end of its legs perched two slippers, also long-haired fur. The skin of its hands and face was jet black, and its hair was long and straight, except for a crinkly top. I said to the detective, "Did you see that black woman with the straight-haired wig? You'd say she was a sorceress doing a satanic dance during the Middle Ages."

"That's not a black woman," he answered, "it's a black man, and he doesn't go back to the Middle Ages, but to the caves. He's in a primitive trance, dressed in the skin of the beast he's just sated himself on."

I went back to the West Hollywood police station, took a look at the new faces behind the grilles, and a shudder crawled up me. One of the prisoners, unusually well-muscled, whose face was still covered with blood from some slash, truly had a beast within him. His hairy arm, like that of a huge, evil ape, was wrapped around the bars. Had he put his arm outside the bars to wrap it around the throat of a nearby policeman who was writing out some report? No, he was reaching out to grasp the telephone that the homeland of electronics had not failed to place, on a little table in front of the bars, at the disposition of its criminals.

A Little Child Shall Lead Them

I went farther back into the station and came upon a small, slender boy with finely traced features, a girl's soft skin, and big chestnut eyes with dilated pupils that made them seem even larger. I went over to talk to him, but before I'd even opened my mouth he said, "Are you from the narks?" I made him repeat his question, my English not being up to hippie slang, but I finally understood that he wanted to know if I was a narcotics detective. I laughed and informed him that I was just a French journalist inquiring into the hippie phenomenon. My accent (alas!) convinced him of my good faith, and he began to open up to me. In fact, none of the detained youths that I approached in the United States responded to my questions with rudeness or bad grace. Perhaps a person suddenly caught in the net of the law clutches at anyone who shows interest in him.

The boy was sitting at a table strewn with the evidence of his wrongdoing: a dozen marijuana cigarettes wrapped in yellowish paper, some acrid-smelling "roaches" (butt ends of the joint), some hemp seeds—hemp is the plant from which the drug is derived—and a very long knitting needle whose function was, one might think, to prick little girls' behinds. The young delinquent made me understand, however, that a knitting needle made a nice, handy, and indeed legal (since knitting is not against the law) little weapon, with which he had himself jabbed the nose of his arresting officer. And finally, there were the rose-colored capsules of LSD; one of the most dangerous drugs known, as it can, among other things, damage the brain cells and the chromosomes that carry the genetic heritage from one generation to the next. Our young man had had his LSD in his pockets. He told me that he "dropped acid" regularly, to go on "trips" that would last about twelve hours.

"Aren't you afraid of hurting yourself?" I asked.

"Oh, everybody turns on."

"No, not everyone, just the kind of people you go around with, and that's a tiny fraction of all the people in this huge country. And this tiny fraction is killing itself."

"Kill yourself with LSD or alcohol, what's the difference? Why is 'society' so anxious to save me from drug-poisoning, while they don't give a damn if I get cancer from tobacco?"

"Because tobacco does its work only over a very long period of time, and no one is sure of its effects anyway, whereas the danger of LSD is immediate and certain. Besides, society *is* doing things about alcohol and tobacco."

"Well anyway, what does the Establishment care about *me!* What's one person more or less out of the billions of people cluttering the earth?"

I was tempted for a minute to quote him Kant's categorical imperative: "Act so that the principle that guides you could become the rule of action for all." If everyone took LSD, the human species would have had it. But I was afraid that an argument based on the premise that the human race is worth saving would not go far with this budding nihilist, so I tried another tack.

"It seems to me that society ought to protect the lives of young people until they have acquired the judgment to decide their courses for themselves."

"Oh sure, keep them healthy and strong until they're twenty, and then send them off to die in Vietnam . . . I'd just as soon have a good time while I'm waiting."

"And you couldn't have a good time without destroying yourself? There are so many things to do, my goodness! Traveling, lectures, learning about the world, movies, the arts, sports, girls. . . ."

"Sure, but all that costs money. My mother is poor, she's a waitress at a soda fountain. I don't want to be like her."

Meanwhile, a policeman had brought over the most damning bit of evidence—a witness to the human tragicomedy of our time: a school notebook filled with the earnest, labored handwriting of a child. In the first few pages my young nihilist pusher had listed, in alphabetical order, the names, addresses, and telephone numbers of his clients. On another page he had recorded, in different color inks, the selling prices, according to their quality, of marijuana, LSD, and methedrine (an amphetamine stimulant). His bookkeeping records were farther back: the month's intake and outgo, with a big blank in the LSD section, and this regretful reflection: "I could have taken in seventy-five dollars if I hadn't dropped so much myself!"

I was stunned. Seventy-five dollars' worth of LSD! At $4 per dose, he had tripped almost twenty times in one month! This was suicide. The names and addresses of some wholesalers took up another page, and still another listed the names of prospective new clients to contact, new fields to conquer. At the end of the book, scrawled across a fresh page in a bold ascending slant, our little Napoleon of the drug scene had written: "I must expand my empire."

He didn't want to finish his life selling sodas like his mother. This was perfectly fine, I told him, but had he just applied the talent for organization, the energy and ambition revealed by his notebook to selling shoes, or newspapers, or something else, he would surely have become a Rockefeller. But now his prospects for prosperity were distinctly somber. His crime was not minor; if he wanted to ruin his own life that was his business, but he was taking others along with him. He was a trafficker in death, and he would have to spend several years in reform school where his talents for commerce would dry up.

"Ugh, I'm sick of everything," he answered. "I'm just one big question mark."

They came then to take him to his cell. His globes of eyes rolled backward for a quarter of a second; his talk with me had made him forget for a while where he was. He stood up with the look of one whose footing had fallen away from him—a look I've never been able to forget —and said to me, "It's done me good to talk with you." Then he walked with heavy steps into the destruction of his life.

He was fifteen.

Drug "Escalation" Among the Young

This parade of drugged children took place on a Friday just like any other Friday in just one section of just one American city. If you add up all the evenings in all the big cities, hundreds of thousands of teenagers have been tasting the forbidden fruit. And more and more of these young potheads are "escalating" into hashish, the famed drug of the *Thousand and One Nights*. Both drugs are refined from hemp, but hashish is a more concentrated resin of the hemp *(Cannabis)* plant, and therefore more toxic than marijuana. They are escalating as well into LSD, STP, mescaline, the amphetamines, and heroin. For kids of thirteen on up, drugs have become the focus of extracurricular activities. The school kids gargle out the vocabulary of the initiated: "pot" or "grass" for marijuana; "acid" for lysergic acid (that is, LSD);

"speed" for methedrine; to be "stoned" or "high," that is, under the influence of a drug; to be "busted," picked up by the police; to "trip," to go on a hallucinatory voyage. They know they need three to four draws (or "tokes") on a joint to "take off," and that each joint costs about 60 cents. When I asked how they got hold of the drug, they all replied that it's very easy, that people would approach them in the streets, in school, in drugstores. Marijuana is so cheap because it's so accessible; the plant can be cultivated in your kitchen window. When I was in San Francisco, they arrested a hippie who had grown 200 plants of this "grass" in his own backyard.

The detectives told me that three years ago, three police cars would patrol the West Hollywood district on weekend nights. Now there are twenty cars, complete with two-way radios and forty armed officers. And the police are still stretched thin, despite a five-fold increase of personnel in three years.

The detectives went out again for another nocturnal sally through their district, and again I went with them, more and more wrought up by my descent into hell. I felt like a 20th-century Orpheus crossing the River Styx to search out, and bring back to the light, a beloved being too soon departed. And the new kingdom of Pluto was this fantastic world where humans gifted with reason voluntarily embraced madness, a world that I discovered, little by little, beneath the skin of the world that we have been pleased to call "reasonable." I had, however, to confess in my heart of hearts that I in no way risked the danger that stalked Orpheus, since I made my exploration flanked by two strapping men who, in the reasonable world, functioned as detectives. However, a certain perfume of danger did float around me; I had to sign a paper absolving the police of any responsibility should something untoward happen to me as we made our nocturnal rounds.

Stoned-Soul Schooldays

Once, in an elegant section of Los Angeles, I met a wealthy lady in obvious distress who told me that she had begun to notice that her sixteen-year-old daughter was troubled, and then more and more despondent. With all the scruples that American mothers seem to feel, she had not dared to question her daughter, and both of them became more and more unhappy. Finally, the young girl confided that two of her fellow students had been pressing her without let-up to "trip" with them, and while she resisted they acted as if she were a stupid drip of a girl who was depriving herself of earthly paradise by keeping to silly bourgeois rules. In the end, she gave in.

The mother, horrified, went to the principal of the school, one of the most prestigious in the city. He told her he knew quite well what was going on, but that he could do nothing. He knew that marijuana and LSD, along with goodness knew what else, were stashed away in the kids' lockers. The mother insisted that, at the very least, the pushers be exposed and punished, but the principal replied that that would create a scandal, which he wanted to avoid at all costs. The mother had no choice but to withdraw her daughter from the school, and send her away to boarding school.

Here is an account from another mother, from New York, who told me that her daughter had come back the day before from an outing with her friends and announced:

"You know we smoked grass. I'm still stoned, but don't be scared. I'm completely out of it." My mouth hung open. My daughter is fourteen years old. When her father remonstrated with her she said, "I would really be a creep if I didn't smoke with the other kids. Everybody does it now, you don't understand anything." Then, looking at us both, her pupils huge, she said, "Try it yourselves, you'll see, it's sensational, and then we could smoke pot all together."

The child was not being insolent. She had been brainwashed by the underground press which advises frequently that kids get their parents to try marijuana or LSD so they can see for themselves that it's not as terrible as all that; that in fact it's "sensational."

These encounters with American mothers left me even more stunned than my visits to the discotheques. It's true that certain authorities cover up drug use or just let it pass. And the parents confess they don't know what to do. A whole flock of questions swirled in my head, in no order, violent and fleeting, like that carnival of gargoyles in the hippie nightclubs.

First, is it true that the hippie movement is more significant than any other wave of protesting youth known to history? Or instead, is this just a vast but transitory explosion of indolence, of eroticism, and of a kind of affected deviltry? Or, even more simply, are we all being intoxicated by journalistic sensationalism? But I have seen them, these hordes of lost children who have no equivalent throughout history; never before have feverish hands of less than fifteen years reached out for drugs. And I know that never before now has the disintegration of an established order been linked with the use of mind-twisting drugs.

And what is the responsibility of this "new way," which sees no merit or spirit in anything but a revolutionary pathos, however hollow it may be? Is it not ridiculous to speak of revolt and "liberation" when everyone is free in a society that has almost eliminated the ancient shame of poverty? Is there anything really to fight for, except for the "liberation" of sex, neckties, and long hair?

Or, on the contrary, are we dealing with a more profound revolution that intends to deliver the body, the mind, and the imagination from the heavy constraints that have heretofore bound them; constraints as heavy as those that weighed down, in other times, the disinherited classes? Is it so terrible that, after the time of revolt against the social order, a new revolt, against the human organism itself—sacrosanct up till now—should show its head? Are we heading into a biological and psychical revolution infinitely more profound than any of the political and material revolutions of the past? Is it extreme daring or extreme foolishness that claims to ameliorate man's brain through chemistry? Is it grandeur or perversity to transgress the natural frontiers of the senses, and to blur the boundaries between reason and madness?

Is the whole human race threatened by these new drugs that carry the user into a delirium of ecstasy, and from delirium into stupor? Is America the powerful, as she conquers outer space, risking the moral and physical decay of her youth? Or will she give birth, as the hippies believe, to a revolution whose consequences are incalculable?

And what about certain leftist political organizations? Have they fallen into step with the new whirlwind so as not to be left behind? Or is the movement being encouraged by hostile political groups? Why do these young people, self-styled pilgrims of liberty, denounce a democratic society that has allowed them unrestricted horizons; why have they chosen a path that turns men into things? In any case, is it not possible that these political forces—which *have* fallen into line with the hippie movement, whether out of "follow the leader" or a wish to exploit them for political ends—will be left behind by the strength of hippie nihilism?

And the police—so maligned by the hippies—the new Satan. Are they not, quietly and without fuss, carrying out thankless but precious work? Is it not the police, in the end, who will save these new little "dead souls," our children, who wilt in a false paradise?

But by what right do we try to forbid them access to these charmed paths? We may believe that they are setting out into premature decay, but *they* are looking for a way to expand their consciousnesses. Does not each person have the right to use his own body as he wishes? Which is good, which is evil? What is truth, what is falsehood?

I had to write a book about it, and here it is.

What can the young do with themselves faced with this sad American version of the planet? The best ones, the most sensitive and aware, drop out of this society. They wander over the body of the nation, looking their elders straight in the eye. They wear long Biblical hair, and set up communities right in the midst of the slums. They make pilgrimages to Big Sur and live naked in the forests questing for visions of nature and meditations. They are recreating Gardens of Eden in the heart of the great cities of the "straight" world, as if these cities were deep in the forests.

The flower-children profess that it is possible to recreate islands of pastoral tranquility in our century of missiles in the center of the most fevered cities, and to develop a civilization that is not based on the consumption of goods, in the kingdom of abundance itself, simply by dropping out of conventional society in order to set themselves up into primitive communities that live on drugs, love, and macrobiotic diets.

The hippies themselves believe that they spearhead a social revolution without precedent in history. One of them wrote:

> People like us are the biggest scare the straight world has ever known. We are affecting people through art, music, language, style, thought, the shape of civilization, and through the simple fact that we have dropped out of everything. When our kind of people decide that a society has become useless, we can't be dismissed. (*Toronto Globe & Mail*, August 19, 1967.)

The editor of the *Oracle*, a hippie journal, has exclaimed: "The hippie movement is far and away the most unique, the most extraordinary, and the most revolutionary in human history." These views, obviously, spring from devoted followers of the movement. But you never can tell what surprises a particular mystique may have in store when it captures the imagination of the young. Thousands of articles on the flower children have already come out, thousands of documentaries and interviews have filled up television, thousands of nighttime places have their own psychedelic light shows, hippie enclaves are springing up like mushrooms in all the big cities, in San Francisco, New York, Yorkville (Toronto), Mexico City, London, Amsterdam, Paris, Munich, Kabul, Katmandu, Goa, Tokyo.

Hashish, LSD, and the amphetamines aren't restricted any more to the hippie world, they are spreading as fast as long hair in the universities and the schools of the whole world. It can no longer be denied that we are in the midst of a social revolution; and it is vitally important to question whether this is a fad that will vanish as it came, or if we are indeed attending the birth of the "age of hallucinogens" predicted by the high priest Timothy Leary.

San Francisco: Hippie Cradle

The "hippielands," hippie oases in the midst of big cities, are attracting more tourists today than Disneyland. But whereas American movies were born in Los Angeles, hippiedom first saw the light of day in San Francisco, a city that stretches sensuously like a bather whose arms enlace with mini-seas out along the hilly forms of the Pacific coast. The boys and girls who fill their veins with drugs have chosen to live out their fantasies in this fascinating city.

Penniless hippies invaded the streets of Haight Ashbury, near the Golden Gate Bridge, and installed themselves in old Victorian four-story houses divided into apartments large enough to sustain a whole community, and cheap enough, denuded as they are of the super-comforts (air conditioning, garbage disposals) demanded by modern America. Haight Ashbury was once a quarter of solid, respectable citizenry, but when the multitudes began to invade the area, the burghers left to build the futuristic creations that line the shores of the Pacific. In the 1950's the gingerbread houses were taken over by the protesters of that time, the beatniks, and then the buildings were invaded in their turn by the hippies.

At first, there were the "drop-outs"—ex-students who had already begun to experiment with drugs in their universities, and then left all that for a life of freedom. Next came the runaways, children less than sixteen years old who had abandoned their families in response to the calls of the hippie press that circulated from hand to hand in the schools. During 1969–70, many hippies, frightened by the resurgence of crime and commercial drug-pushing (as opposed to the friendly drug exchanges of yore), fled Haight Ashbury to camp around the Berkeley campus of the University of California, some thirty miles from San Francisco proper. All at once, Telegraph Avenue was turned upside down. The "straight" tradesmen, the restaurants, and the respectable bookstores frequented by professors have been partly pushed out by the garish new boutiques that make their way on eccentricity. And located as they are right in the bosom of the university community, the hippie colony extends to the students a permanent invitation to give it all up and come join them.

It has been estimated that there are 50,000 hippies in the San Francisco area. They stuff themselves five to a room sleeping on mattresses set up side by side on the floor. All of these Victorian houses have a front stoop with six or eight steps, and at any hour of the day or night these steps are occupied by bands of hippies who sleep, chat, or smoke marijuana, and disport themselves in curious clothes.

The Clothing of Protest

Haight Ashbury and Telegraph Avenue have taken on a hurdy-gurdy air of carnival that would be very hard to imagine in Paris. Boys wear long manes of hair like the druids of ancient Gaul. They are dressed like gypsies, like cowboys, like hobos, like Indians, in gaucho costumes with Argentine ponchos. I have seen kids in Civil War uniforms, or in their great-grandfather's old frock-coats, or in Navy uniforms bought at I know not what third-hand store, but whose golden buttons have been replaced by new ones reading, "Draft beer, not students," "I am an enemy of the state," "Make love, not war."

Some of them have adopted the stripped-down style of Hindu holy men, wandering barefoot with a simple white cloth flapping between their legs; others display Oriental sarongs imprinted with Malay designs. A few of the more extreme have come up with fluorescent vests, or a dueling outfit à la Errol Flynn, or a shirt fashioned from an American flag. Occasionally someone will wear a hat: a top hat or a stovepipe of the last century, an Arab fez, Hindu turban, opera hat, tarboosh, fur toques, outsize sombreros, Indian feathers. But these masqueraders do not wear the faces of carnival: they are grave—conscientiously defiant of the straight world.

The girls' outfits range from long gypsy skirts to blue jeans pulled so tight over the buttocks that one waits for the rip of a splitting seam at each movement to miniskirts that apparently arouse no particular response in anyone even though, in this case, the said buttocks are already practically open to public view. Many girls wear Hindu saris, especially when they are at home with their hippie "families." I spoke to a pretty blonde heiress of eighteen, who whipped up confections from her grandmother's old laces. Some of them go around in mangy furs, following the precept, "If you can't eat it, wear it."

Hippies of both sexes bedeck themselves in long strands of many-colored beads, bracelets, gypsy earrings. They wear headbands of multicolored ribbon, and pink, green or blue sunglasses. Colors play a large part in hippie fashion; not only are they pretty in their ordinary state, but when you are tripping, colors take on an inexpressible richness and voluptuousness. The hippies confess themselves powerless to articulate the delights of their hallucinations except by vague terms like "marvelous," "fantastic," "sensational." The only verbal responses they can make with any precision have to do with colors, which ravish them: "Oh, this intense blue, dazzling, it's alive, this blue . . ." they repeat in ecstasy. But a color can also make them freeze in horror: "Oh! That red, that spurt of blood, that purple clot is suffocating me!" they moan.

Since they cannot, try though they may, live on a permanent diet of LSD, they construct a psychedelic world around them: a debauch of colors in their clothes, their eyeglasses, their posters, their lights, the multi-colored flowers they affix to their cars, and the motley designs with which they tattoo their bodies. These are the essence of psychedelicism. In the Avallon in San Francisco, the go-go girls plaster their faces, shoulders, and arms with brightly colored fluorescent designs. A clever entrepreneur can make his fortune from this culture of kaleidoscope. Every day, in the hippie press, there are ads like this:

> Going naked? Cover your body with psychedelic love signs, instant tattoos. Eighteen fluorescent tattoos, red and green, for one dollar. Box 612, Mill Valley, California.

Other ads tout sensuous tattoos, or savage ones, or obscene ones, or tattoos that can be seen only under ultaviolet light.

The little bells that the hippies wear at their wrists, ankles, or necks, are similarly designed with an eye toward expediting the "takeoff" on the "trip" with the piercing tinkle that accompanies each of their movements. Some of them paste a brilliantly reflecting metal disk onto their foreheads which throws rainbow reflections into the eyes of their friends. This kind of thoughtfulness toward one's neighbor comes from the same source as the giving out of flowers; the generous flower-children strive to offer others the same psychedelic pleasures that they themselves enjoy.

These costumes represent their only statements of principle or philosophy. Their feathers and headbands express their identification with the original purity of the Indian tribes. Their saris and turbans are so many *hommages* to the mysticism of the Hindus. The young girl who passed me one day wearing a wide-brimmed hat decked with long streamers that covered her face was a walking affirmation of her faith in the occult sciences. By wearing these absurd clothes, the flower-children intend to signify that the modern world is absurd. A pirate costume bears witness to a sympathy with those people who live outside the law. Those boys and girls who appeared in the streets of London and on the Isle of Wight in the costumes God gave them are simply putting into practice their faith in the way of nature. But at the same time these costumes symbolize philosophical attitudes, they also demonstrate the particular secret neurosis of the wearer. According to the manner of dress, one can distinguish the exhibitionists, the fools, the adventurers, the narcissists, the powerless ones, the new breed of conformists, and the long stream of the dissatisfied ones of the world who pretend to be, even if just for a few days, people they are not.

Protest Buttons

All through Haight Ashbury new boutiques have sprung up to sell all these curious clothes, records, and protest buttons. The button industry has become one of the most flourishing in the hippie economy, dispensing wisdom like

> NIRVANA NOW
> LEGALIZE DRUGS
> CURE YOUR VIRGINITY
> IF IT MOVES, PET IT

The counters of the stores are laden with paint for tattooing, amulets, sandals, hashish or opium pipes, pornographic photographs, paste jewels, underground newspapers and magazines, colored chalks, sacred masks, and incense. Psychedelic posters whose brightly colored pigments somehow manage to blend mellowly into one another cover the

walls. Their subjects, sometimes simple and innocent, sometimes anguished, are the dreamstuff from the kingdom of drugs. Every little spot
of vacant wall left over has its tacked-up message. The whole swims in
music: rock, African drums, pop songs.

The first hippie boutique in San Francisco opened in 1966. Since
then at least forty more have joined the ranks, including a huge combination drugstore-café-restaurant-perfumery-grocery-bookstore. It is
open day and night, including Sundays, and always crowded with
flower-children come to ease the imperious hunger aroused by
marijuana, or to make a connection with their local pusher. But the
thing that really distinguishes this drugstore from any other is its
psychedelic decor. Its walls are covered with mirrors that reflect giant
apothecary bottles filled with translucent viscous or fluorescent colored
liquids, while strips of cellophane dangle from the ceiling. The whole
scene has the glaucous feel of an aquarium. Here and there strange
mobiles, perpetual motion made concrete, slowly cloud your mind.
Here too, as in all hippie places, the scent of incense is pervasive.
Incense is an important part of the psychedelic rites, but it serves as
well to disguise the acrid and immediately recognizable odor of
marijuana from the police.

When the crush reaches its frantic peak, just as it begins to get
dark, the dour-faced drug-pushers begin to shove their way through the
hippie masquerade and the mob of gawkers, along with the merchants
of porn selling their photographic wares, and the preachers of all the
little sects and subsects—each with his obsession or his grain of madness—who never miss any occasion to spread the true word. The new
priests of the hippie church distribute pamphlets advocating the use of
drugs as a religious sacrament. In the bustle, you push against the
new-style beggars—twenty-year-old boys and girls of good families—
camera-snapping tourists in sightseeing buses, members of the motor-
cylce gang Hell's Angels, "straight" reporters doing their pieces on the
movement, television cameramen, roving hotdog vendors, plainclothes
detectives, nervously excited "respectable" people coming down for a
little thrill, soldiers on leave looking for easy gives, homosexuals, narcotics agents, full-fledged criminals, and anguished mothers looking for
their missing children, not to mention the political agitators propagating their own particular brand of salvation: pro-Vietcong, or pacifist,
or terrorist, or all three at once like the Black Panthers. There are

whites and blacks and yellows and Indians, go-betweens, middlemen, pimps, Mormon missionaries or soldiers from the Salvation Army. . . . And on every streetcorner, a long-haired youth hawking one of the hundred "underground" publications—all of which specialize in sex, drugs, astrology, Hinduism, agitation for the legalization of marijuana, condemnation of the war in Vietnam, denunciations of "police terror," and erotic classified ads—at the top of his voice.

During the hot time of the year all is roses for these children who float in mysticism through a crass, materialistic world. The sun gives them leave to thumb their noses at the consumer society. But when the chill comes, they huddle on their front stoops against each other as shields from the glacial wind from the Bay, paralyzed with cold under their filthy blankets, snuggling up with their cats to keep each other warm. They breathe in the smell of cat fur while they smoke grass underneath the covers. The body of one hippie, a boy named Chob, was discovered by another flower-child in search of his cat. Winter is a rude awakening for runaway children. They dream of heat that will warm them through, and of the fragrant cooking in their mother's house, so they give in and ask Daddy for that check that will see them home again. They go back, but they go back with curious scars on their bodies and in their souls; their drugged heads may never quite get back together again, and there is that file in the San Francisco police station. . . .

Drugs as Religion

The hippie churches, which I discovered during my explorations around Hollywood, are one of the most curious phenomena of the movement. The regular hippie places, which are licensed bars, are liable to regular police inspection—which they receive, once or twice a night—whereas a "church" could only be entered with a warrant. So whatever genuine religious feeling may have inspired the establishment of these psychedelic churches, this relative freedom from police interference didn't hurt. The one I saw in Hollywood had once been a very large store fronting on the street. It was called "His Place," and it was open only from nine o'clock at night till morning. In the big display window, a huge, brightly lit Christ reposed on his cross, and various texts of the new faith were set out. The police could not enter it, so

I left the detectives who escorted me there, and crossed the threshold by myself.

What a spectacle! At the entrance a crowd of bearded, barefoot, and long-haired hippies, dressed in baroque costumes, encircled a tall receptacle hissing out steam, not from holy water, but from coffee, free to all. There was a "No Smoking" sign on one side, and another group of hippies stretched out on the floor. Way in the back a music lover banged loudly on a piano. Always, always that noise. On the wall, psychedelic posters and propaganda. In the middle of the church, a giant black cross lay flat on the floor. Couples, lolling at random on top of and around the cross, spoke to one another in low voices, or slept, or cuddled, or copulated. Everything was bathed in an unpleasant half-light.

These couples enlaced on the cross were, in fact, iconoclasts. They had returned to the ostentatiously sacrilegious anticlericalism that created such a furor in 19th-century Europe. This movement had disappeared during the 20th century, first because the clamorous atheists began to recognize that they inflamed, rather than discouraged, the faith of others, and then because, as they traveled more widely, they experienced the multiple forms faith assumes among the human race; and finally, the movement died because a general climate of tolerance finally prevailed in all the democracies. And now, smack in the 20th century, in the country that is most respectful of the forms of organized religion, when we shall soon, perhaps, encounter other civilizations beyond the earth whose ways of life and thought we cannot dream of, a vast iconoclastic movement was born in the United States.

Actually, the adherents to this old/new order deny that their practices are sacrilegious. They propose that love in all its forms, spiritual or physical, would not shock Christ, who was, at the same time, love and love made material. The act of flesh should not be offensive to the one who created it. To love one another while lying on the cross is all the better to serve the Saviour.

At the back of the storefront church, there was a certain amount of movement back and forth from the toilets. There was a staircase there, leading to the second floor, with the message, "No noise. Whisper only." What could be up there? Perhaps people were dreaming their drugged dreams? I had barely set foot on the first step when the guardian of the High Place, half-Messiah, half-propagandist, stopped me.

"What is your religion?" he asked. "Catholic," I answered.

"And do you think that's enough to make you a Christian? Christ said that in order to be faithful to him, neither rituals nor priests were needed."

So there I was, being instructed on the soul and the afterlife, while being invited to desert my established church. In order to become a true Christian, I had only to study the material he gave me and come every night to "His Place." I nodded agreement to get rid of him and tried to go upstairs, but it became apparent that my interlocutor had no intention of letting me go so easily.

I noticed, as I noticed throughout my whole inquiry, that the proselytizing missionaries of the different hippie communities did not wear beards or long hair or extravagant clothes. And I believe that they did not use drugs either. They had to keep cool heads in order to inflame the greatest number of prospective converts. Once again a question that had haunted me subterraneanly flared up: Is the hippie movement entirely spontaneous? Or has it been infiltrated by other forces who seek to exploit it for their own reasons?

I had stayed there long enough, still never making it up the stairs. The detectives, who had waited for me, breathed a sigh of relief when I emerged unscathed. I went back there the next day during the day, but "His Place" was closed. I would never have a chance to investigate the mysteries of the second floor, because that same evening I left Los Angeles.

"His Place" was not an isolated case. A whole forest of these new, extravagant religions has already sprung from the hippie tree, and they see themselves as functioning, legitimate churches, not just as symbols of the flower-children's purely verbal "religion of love."

The Constitution protects freedom of religion, but up till now it has not seemed necessary to define precisely what a religion is. The weight of history and tradition has seemed to delineate the term clearly enough. But now the hippies have made up new and baroque cults in which prayer is conducted in hallucinogenic stupor, where communion is sanctified, not with a wafer, but with a sugar cube of LSD, and in which the god Sex is the object of worship. The hippie churches have indeed evoked their constitutional right to drugs in the practice of their religion, and the issue has been carried to the Supreme Court, which has studied the matter with attention and care. The intellectual scrupulousness of the American juridical system is truly extraordinary.

In an article published in 1968, the glossy hippie review *Oracle* (an apt name) discussed a recent decision of the Supreme Court to affirm the right of Mana, an Apache Indian from Denver, to use peyote —a Mexican cactus with hallucinogenic properties—in the sacraments of his church. The Court based its decision partly on the fact that this drug had from long tradition played an important role in the church's rites. The *Oracle*'s resident legalist/theologian explained that this decision of the Supreme Court constituted a binding precedent for recognizing the constitutional rights of the hippies to use marijuana and LSD in the rites of their new religions, and he offered to send a pamphlet on the subject, written by himself, without charge to anyone who asked for it.

The key to the matter, said the *Oracle*'s oracle, is to declare publicly, *and in advance*, that sacramental drug use would take place:

> It will be enough to write on a piece of paper headed "Declaration of Faith" that you take LSD regularly, where you take it, with whom, where your church is, and that you add that there is no intention to take the drug for profit or for pleasure, but for the elevation of your being. *And you will have created a religion.* The sad thing is that our hippie brothers never do these things in time. If you don't make your rituals and your reasons clear *ahead of time*, before you're arrested, the law will get you. But if you take these precautions, they can't do anything.
>
> And I repeat: this declaration of faith is valid without restriction. For example, you could write, "My religion is me and my woman. We use LSD to attain a higher plane of lovemaking. Our temple is our bedroom. We have a little candle that we burn above our bed, to the greater glory of our God. We pray before and after copulation." That's a religion. . . . The only condition is that you have solemnly written out your declaration of faith, in advance, on a piece of paper that you sign and seal in an envelope, that you address to yourself and don't open. So if the police make a bust, you open the envelope, and you're covered by the freedom of religion clause in the Constitution.

The *Oracle* journalist tells us that several hundred religions based on LSD and transcendental eroticism have been founded this way in the United States. Many others since then have subjected this legal counsel

to even greater refinement, while assembling great numbers of followers—as Timothy Leary had done—or by giving their new temple some
external correspondence with religion as it has heretofore been understood, like the storefront that has unleashed Christ on Hollywood.

In Honolulu and on the other islands of the Hawaiian paradise,
where the god of the flower-children shines every day of the year on
warm sands and coconut trees, the impending hippie invasion was
stopped cold by a law insisting that each new arrival have at least $50
in his pocket.

But California is still the goal of pilgrimage, and San Francisco is
its Mecca. After the first World War, when a young man rebelled
against his family and society, he departed for the debaucheries of
Europe. His father, in those days, with stern tone, would direct him
to the West, young man . . . to California, to test his mettle against
that harsh land where one could make his fortune and purify his soul
through work. Today the young rebel from New York or Chicago runs
to California to "expand his consciousness." And his father, in these
days, tries to persuade him to refresh his soul in the museums and
purifying values of old Europe. But the hippie would rather congregate
with his fellows under the psychedelic sun of California.

Greenwich Village

In New York, the world capital of the consumer society, the
hippies gather far away from the skyscrapers and the bright lights, in
an old quarter still strewn with buildings from the last century beribboned with those dreadful iron fire escapes. This is Greenwich Village,
with its newer and even more "groovy" annex to the east, the East
Village (once the Lower East Side, the haven for immigrants).

The hippies ramble down the length of Macdougal Street or along
St. Mark's Place, or perhaps stretch out alongside the waterless fountain in Washington Square. I recall two youths with long wheat-colored
hair, anemic faces, and large blue eyes, lounging against the fountain
waiting for a rich customer. These are hippie prostitutes, not too
different—except for their sex—from the prostitutes of the "straight"
world. Some runaway kids, obviously from the provinces, bundled up
in too-large high school sweaters, came slouching toward these gods of
beauty with looks of envy. They sported flowers behind their ears and

protest buttons in their buttonholes, but they had already lost the
swagger of novice rebels confronted as they were, alone and miserable,
with a ferociously indifferent hip world, the warm family exasperating
in its solicitude far behind them.

In the Village, the "straight" world is in constant friction with its
resident hippies. There are huge, screechingly new buildings that have
encroached on the genteel preserves of the old houses. Elsewhere, there
are the flower-children, "spaced out" in the transcendental kingdom of
drugs, who dispute a piece of sidewalk on St. Mark's Place, at midnight,
with two old sots floating in the outmoded kingdom of Bacchus. Shops
that haven't changed in fifty years sit cheek by jowl with Italian pizza
stands, Chinese or Puerto Rican restaurants, barbershops whose proprietors are enraged at having their customers blasted out by the hippie
discotheques. There are schools of belly-dance or yoga, and psychedelic
stores. And the skin flicks dear to old-style lechers are being driven out
of business by the very contemporary pocket theaters that show the real
thing, or by the movies that turn everyone on together.

Greenwich Village is no longer the haven of peace it was for the
groups of writers and painters during the thirties, who came down there
in self-exile from the frantic life of the skyscraper city. The Village has
become the most commercialized place in the world, in which the life
of the artist or of the mind plays a minimal role; a place in which the
only thing that bears weight is militant eccentricity or provocative
eccentricity; the eccentricity you can buy at the corner drugstore.

Business Is Business

The Village has been commercialized by the clever craftsmen
quick to hawk whatever gimcrack is "in" this week. The Village has
been commercialized as well by the new brand of shopkeepers whose
hippiedom stops short with the hippie get-ups and long hair. These are
capitalists in the good old American tradition scorned by the flower-
children who've adapted their style to the new era, but whose energies
are devoted to the same old conquest: money.

The "head shops"—the name is derived from the term "pothead"
applied to a regular marijuana smoker—draws in its clientele by providing a communal bulletin board. Do you want a guitarist? Looking for

a runaway? Need a place to stay? The head shop puts up notices for anything, like this one: "Need six square feet of your floor to lay down my sleeping bag. Can pay $8 a week." The proprietor, Jeff Glich, twenty-six years old, is the king of the drug accessory market, like the famous perfumed cigarette paper that camouflages the smell of marijuana. Jeff disports himself in the appropriate love beads and bells, but does not go so far as to renounce the quest for filthy lucre. He started his "head shop" in May, 1966, with $300 worth of merchandise on consignment. By the end of his first year, his store was worth $100,000, and by the end of 1969, after having opened several branches in Manhattan and elsewhere, his enterprise was valued at over a half-million dollars.

The "Print Missa," the large poster and button store in San Francisco, put out a financial statement claiming a gross of $1000 per day—nearly a half-million per year (*Congressional Record*, November 6, 1969).

The "Electric Lotus" is something else altogether. It sells yoga wisdom. All day long, in a meditation chamber at the back of the store, the acolytes chant "Hare Krishna, Hare, Hare. . . ." It is not unusual to see them joined by businessmen whose furrowed features mark them as from the straight world. Their nerves stretched tight by the strains of commerce, they come in from time to time to don the white cotton robe of the Hindus and be soothed. They sit on the floor with legs crossed in the lotus position and chant with the harsh voice of someone at forced labor who is about to have a heart attack, "Hare Krishna, Hare, Hare. . . ." The true believers put on psychedelic glasses through which they view a world like a palette of deformed rainbows, and deformed differently for each eye, since each of the two prismatic lenses is different from the other in size and color. This is one way to "take off" on a paradisiacal "trip" without ever leaving the business section. Devoted to the needs of a clientele in a hurry, even in the midst of the hymnasts to indolence, the Electric Lotus has developed a "basic hippie kit": a glass bead necklace, an Indian headdress, tiny bells, incense, artificial flowers, a colored balloon, and a love charm—everything you need for two dollars. The drive toward mass consumption seems just as urgent among the hippies as among the bourgeoisie.

The "straight" businessmen in the community, to meet the competition, have learned that they have to cater to the hippie trade. So, for example, a "delicatessen" adapts into a "psychedelicatessen." Along with the usual delicacies, they also offer incense and dried, grated banana skin which is very much like marijuana in texture and smell. The hippies are thrilled to buy something they believe is a drug, but as it is not, the straight storekeeper can play to the hippie without drawing down the wrath of the police.

The lights of old Broadway have opened up to the psychedelic world. Discotheques like Cheetah offer "sound and light" shows of brutal intensity—brutal in their decibel level and intensity of light, but relatively restrained when it comes to sex. Some compromises have to be made with the world of the straights, after all, as that's still where the big money is.

Even the churches (the real ones) in Greenwich Village have joined the parade. The dissonances of jazz emanate from the old Saint-Mark's-on-the-Bouwerie, which bears a large plaque in memory of all the Vietnam dead, whether American or Vietcong.

Let us also not forget the "Peace Eye Book," a Village bookstore. It is a distribution center for the underground press of the East Coast; a group of publications that specialize in sex, civil rights, revolution, and drugs. Its classified ad section is truly spectacular:

> Nice boy with clean balls would like to meet sweet girl wishing to make love.

> Man of 48, straight exterior, hippie interior, wishes acidulated [that is, under LSD] sex with a woman, without hangups, who is hippie inside and out.

Among the most significant organs of this press is the *Avatar* of Cambridge, Massachusetts, the home of Harvard. The *Avatar* is illustrated with flowing, convoluted Oriental-type engravings upon which are superimposed half-esoteric, half-prophetic bits of poetry in all the characters and all the colors imaginable in all possible geometric variations: in round, in triangle, in zigzag, in oblique angles, in crosses, in waves —in brief, unreadable. It is this journal that announced the prediction that mass consumption of hashish and LSD was at hand. Let us also mention the *East Village Other*—EVO for short—which publishes mad, giant telegrams like these:

A GOVERNMENT OF HATE IS IN POWER
LET'S DECLARE THE MARTIAL LAW OF INDIFFERENCE
SIRENS, BLOOD, BUTCHERIES, BOOTS WILL HOLD BACK
THE FINAL REVOLUTION OF ORGASM
GUERILLAS OF LOVE STRUGGLE EVERYWHERE
BLACKS AND LATIN AMERICANS ATTEND MOLOTOV COCK-
TAIL PARTIES AGAINST
THE C.I.A. Signed: WORLD INTERGALACTIC BRAIN

I leafed through the *East Village Other* which, starting out as purely hippie, has taken on a militant leftist coloration; then there is *Kiss* which proclaims itself "a pornographic magazine on sex and drugs only," *Marijuana Review*, the *Underground Review*, and *Inner Space*. The more political publications are *Graffiti*, *Guerrilla*, and *Ramparts Magazine*—bitterly anti-American all.

The owner of "Peace Eye Book," Ed Sanders, himself puts out a journal whose four-letter-word title helped it to catch on immediately. At the beginning he sent it out only to a confidential, selective mailing list, but when the list of subscribers grew to include celebrities like Allen Ginsberg and a good dozen university professors, Sanders decided to go public. The police then stopped its distribution on moral grounds, but that did nothing but create a cause célèbre, so that once the ban was lifted, Sanders went on to make a fortune.

In Washington, the long-haired ones have set up their turf in Georgetown and around Dupont Circle. After dark you can pick up a capsule of LSD for $4.

It's more on the industrial Atlantic Coast, rather than on the sun-drenched Pacific, that the hippies seem dirty. I saw a group wading with naked feet in the mud of a rainy New York morning, with jeans the color of mud, as was the texture of the skin of their malnourished, drugged faces. I marveled that these streets without trees or flowers, these repellent tenements, these cheap luncheonettes, these grimy stores unrelieved by any flair or style, could seem appropriate places to the flower-children in their pursuit of universal love. Somehow, in their search for a higher truth and absolute beauty, these kids had left any critical sense far behind them. That which they had found was, in reality, a hippie ghetto; a ghetto that was just as despairing as the hellish black ghettos uptown.

Where Do They Come From?

Scratch the grime that covers a hippie, and chances are you will uncover a young person of good family who once went to college and had a car. They belong, for the most part, to the middle or upper-middle classes. I met the son of a Dallas judge, the daughter of a Senator from Michigan, the offspring of a Chicago minister, and a young lady who was just waiting to turn twenty-one, when she would inherit several million dollars. *Marijuana Review*, a magazine that served as a worldwide clearing house for drug information, told the story, in its December, 1968, issue, of "Mountain Girl"; a girl who left her parents, both of whom were professors in a first-rank university. Then there was the huge brouhaha in the regular press over the savage murder of Linda Fitzpatrick, a wealthy girl from Greenwich, Connecticut, whose nude body was found with that of "Groovy," her boy companion in misfortune.

Curiously enough, there are very few black hippies. Blacks form a substantial part of the Haight Ashbury population, and they are quite at ease with these young whites who have left old prejudices far behind, but still, I would guess that there are hardly sixty genuine hippies of color in all of San Francisco.

As I see it, this stems from the fact that most white hippies are people who have gone through the whole bourgeois scene and come out on the other side, whereas blacks, for the most part, never really had access to this world, and this is where their aspirations lie. In the international congresses that I have attended, I have noticed that the blacks (perhaps in reaction to the primitive conditions of their native Africa) tend to be most demanding when it comes to the comfort of their rooms, are most reluctant to share their rooms with a fellow congress-goer, and are most concerned that others should not fail to notice that they are accompanied by a private secretary. Unlike the Latin Americans and Asians, who theoretically share with them the same revolutionary doctrine, the blacks, even the Marxists, have no intention of "dropping out" of consumer society. They intend to profit from it to the fullest. Do not Marxists, they rationalize, fight for the amelioration of the conditions of life? The black has not yet become an intellectual Talmudist willing to immolate himself on the altar of his principles. He has not, in general, lost touch with his natural instincts, whereas white and yellow people, whose senses have been smothered in the cotton wool of a life that is too cerebral, feel the need to reach themselves artificially with dope. The average black is fortunate enough not to need the hallucinogenic paradise of LSD. He has the physical and emotional energy to release himself through dance or through love. The white, pinned for years before television screens that spoon-fed all his sensations, aspires to a voluptuousness made easy. To gulp down a capsule of LSD, to smoke a pipe of hashish, to inject himself with methedrine—that's all the energy the white hippie needs to achieve ecstasy.

A survey conducted at Washington University in St. Louis, published in *Trans-Action* in December, 1967, reported that the majority of hippies come from the urban middle classes. There are many Jews, very few blacks, and no known people of rural background. The survey established that very few hippies come from broken homes. Among the drug users, very few had ever engaged in sports or led student activities.

Your Career in Begging

The hippies, like great lords, detest work—fortunately for them, their philosophy is congenial with natural inclination. It is part of their function to live parasitically on the rest of society. *Noblesse oblige.* But unlike the nobles, they never stop biting the hand that feeds them.

They usually get by for a while on the little capital they take with them from home, and then on the checks good old Dad is always glad to provide just for the happiness of an occasional long-distance appeal, collect, from his prodigal child.

But, to help the hippies cut the tie that binds for good, "free stores" have been set up that distribute free food, clothes, and medicines. These organizations, backed by affluent liberals, still don't quite fill the bill. Rents in the big cities are high, even sharing ten to a room. Birth-control pills are expensive too, as well as inoculation against venereal disease. Above all, drugs are ruinous. And bail, when you've been busted, comes very dear. There's even gas for the flower-stickered VW bus; the hippies, who condemn the society that produces automobiles, don't really like to have to walk very far. So very quickly, the checks from home and the free stores don't provide enough, and it becomes necessary to take up a profession.

Begging is the least tiring. The flower-children stand out on the street and beg without embarrassment, with their usual gentle courtesy. There is a curious irony in the fact that the hippies, who aspire to change society into something utterly new, have been conducted by their own principles into a path as old as man: beggary. And in the richest country in the world, at that. These young men and women in the full strength of their years stop passersby with "Give me a dime." If I take a photo, the charge is twenty cents. Outstretched hands are as prominent now in the hippie quarters of America as in the most verminous places in India.

Some of them live in fantasy. "I'm a human robot, put a quarter in my box and I'll sing for you," one of them said. A passerby tossed in a coin and the boy began to sing, to the melody of "Cielito Lindo":

> Folks are free in Haight Ashbury
> They can live and be what they wanna;
> Wedding cakes give stomachache
> So the hippies take marijuana.
>
> High, high, high, high
> It's no dishonor;
> Phony matrimony's a lousy life,
> If you need a wife, marry Juana.

The police try to chase the begging hippies away, but highly sophisticated as they are, they have devised a thousand ploys. For example, one hippie couple worked it so that while the boy was begging, his girlfriend would stand next to him taking notes. If they were stopped by the police, the girl would show her notes to them as proof that they were conducting a sociological survey as to the reactions of the public on being solicited!

But the competition, the bitter competition for the hand-outs, plays cruel havoc among the flower-children, and the resources of the street aren't enough. They soon learn that survival on the street, unless supplemented with money from home, requires something more than eternal love. So, in the last extremity, they will look for work . . . highly irregular work, of course. Many of them go to work for the Post Office. The lowest wage paid by the government for a thirty-two hour week of not too tiring night work is $500 a month. Since a hippie can live on $40 a month, one month's work will do for the rest of the year. That's why the major employer of the world's hippies is the Post Office, which is to say, the U.S. government. The barefoot, long-maned mailman has become an integral part now of San Francisco folklore. But in Washington, the Post Office drew the line at naked feet and Indian feathers. In fact, they required not only shoes, but uniforms, while beards were permitted to wave freely. The director of the Washington Post Office pleaded for understanding:

> Hippie mailmen at the doors of foreign embassies would create far too poor an impression of the Postal Service. . . . They wear anything imaginable, from bearskin jackets to mechanics' overalls. It seems to me that it is entirely inappropriate for a representative of the United States government to appear in public in such attire. (*Montreal Star*, January 31, 1968.)

The question has been raised as to why, in the name of God, the American postal service has engaged such scruffy representatives of *la vie bohème* to carry the sacred mails at all. Federal law forbids discrimination on racial, religious, or social grounds. The hippies take the qualifying civil service examination like everyone else, their scores are invariably high, and nothing in the rules mentions that curious personal appearance makes one any less worthy to deliver the mail. But the director of the Washington Post Office, reactionary though he may be called, finally put limits to such tolerance.

A second career in great demand among the hippies—that is, in relation to their feeble wish for any career—is hawking the underground press in the streets. Other hippies work part-time in psychedelic craft work. One group in New York, called "Image," composed of thirty hippies from the Mid-West, makes panels of silk imprinted with psychedelic designs. Others are salespeople in the hippie boutiques. But the most profitable enterprise, although the most risky, is dealing in drugs. The hippie who has not turned his hand to this at some time or another is rare. Often a single dealer can support a whole hippie community. New candidates for dealing pop up all the time; credit in the drug market is easy—no prior investment required, plenty of return.

Homosexual Prostitution

For the hippies of both sexes, there is still another lucrative and simple calling: prostitution. But as in all things hippie, this activity is essentially amateur; at least for a girl, who will offer her charms in exchange for a roof for the night or drugs, with no taint of the systematic professionalism of ordinary prostitution. This privilege seems to be reserved for men. The hippie press is full of offers of people for sale, four out of five of whom are men:

> Caucasian, 31 years old, impeccable manners, wishes to sell his body and soul for the good life with a rich lady. (*Berkeley Barb*, November 23, 1967.)

> Exuberant hippie, 25 years old, male, nice, bored with work, needs a warm woman to love, pamper, support him. (*Berkeley Barb*, October 26, 1967.)

> Discreet man, accomplished in the strange and bizarre and in French culture, will satisfy all your desires, your wildest dreams." (*Los Angeles Free Press*, November 12, 1968.)

> Beautiful boy offers his services to lonely, bored, neglected, frustrated, curious, adventurous women, whether young girls, married women, or widows. (*Berkeley Barb*, October 30, 1967.)

From a girl:

> I will do anything, absolutely anything, for money. Write Susi, Box, xxx, what you will pay. (*Open City*, September 14, 1967.)

But it is homosexual prostitution that really fills the classifieds. There are hundreds of ads every week, and I must repeat a few, for otherwise no one would believe their audacity:

> Tall man, thin, *professional*, good looking, seeks intimate relations with a married or unmarried man. (*Berkeley Barb*, November 23, 1967.)

> Omnisexual male wants a lot of money. Any offers considered. Call telephone number xxx. (*Berkeley Barb*, December 1967.)

There are any number of requests from young people for an older man with whom they can "explore the reality of the senses and of the beyond [that is, the drug heaven]."

A Caucasian *professional* wishes to meet a dominant man of any race and take my pleasure in being his slave.

Homosexual prostitution has become such a galloping disease in the United States that Congress has investigated it. The *Washington Post* published the personal account, picked up from the *Congressional Record* (November 6, 1967), of a hippie named Bill.

> I make my living by having sexual relations with men. It's not unpleasant. I don't think I'm a freak. I would prefer to be bisexual so that I could dig anyone, man or woman. I usually pick up my clients in Market Street [San Francisco], which is where I started out. I've tried other things too, but prostitution is my steadiest source of income. I also take drugs. I have three serious clients, of whom a psychology professor at Berkeley pays me $60 to have intimate relations with him under LSD. . . . I haven't read anything for the last few years, because it's very painful to read when you're on drugs, but I love the philosophical discussions I have with my professor.

Sixty dollars is a lot to pay for a sexual encounter, but it's little enough I suppose when you realize that the professor is paying his partner to commit three breaches of the law: prostitution, homosexuality, drugs.

The rare hippies who know how to play a musical instrument will very often join a rock group, some of which have become extremely well known, like the Grateful Dead and the Jefferson Airplane.

The intellectuals among them may write for the underground press. And the ones with aptitude for promotion have produced some spectacular shows. This latter group works very hard, and can make a great deal of money. They may be hippies on the outside, but their souls are capitalist. One of these entrepreneurs started a "rent-a-hippie" service. Just as geishas are rented out for the evening in Japan, so hippies could be rented to lend a certain picturesque tone to otherwise respectable gatherings. One "rent-a-hippie" ad charged $25 per evening. If the hippie can play the guitar or create psychedelic tattoos for the merrymakers, there is a $10 supplemental charge. And the ad concluded, "No party can be a success without its hippie."

Hippies have set up their own employment agencies. One staff member of the "Hip Job Co-op" told me, "We could find 200 part time jobs for people every day, but we don't have enough takers, even though very few of these jobs require any particular special skills. The hippies have to understand that they have to make a little effort if they want to maintain their independence." But in fact, all these agencies are knocking themselves against the stone wall of the hippie philosophy, expressed in the commandment, "Thou shalt not do anything unless you want to. . . ."

The hippies are worshipers at the altar of indolence. A whole literature has developed around the theme of how to live for nothing. The *Los Angeles Free Press* has published a series of articles called "How to Survive in the Streets," which was then reprinted in a widely distributed *Hippie Manual*. This catechism teaches everything you need to know to live off the fat of the land in the big cities: where and how to pick up food, clothes, medicines, a roof over your head, and free legal counsel. It lists the places and hours when the big wholesale markets pass out whatever is left in their stalls; where and when meat is distributed free; cooking schools where, after classes, elegant dishes are given away; the names and addresses of various charities. The most famous of this latter—the Diggers—have opened "free stores" that have signs on the walls like "Everything you see is yours. Take your choice." I found clothes, books, magazines, suitcases, used records. A girl, who looked like a short, round spinning top, came in one day lugging a heavy sack on her back. She stood in the middle of the store and called out, "Chow!" Hippies who looked as if they hadn't eaten in a week threw themselves on her sack, filled with greasy little cookies.

This kind of hippie charity is extremely precious to them, and permits the majority of the flower children to survive. But still and all, thumb their hippie noses though they might, they know that if they really get into trouble the straight world is there with its hospitals and clinics for people on bad trips, for girl-mothers, for hippies with venereal disease, not to mention all the other places the hippies can go for help. Straight Americans are generous. "When we would go into the streets," recalled Susan Atkins, one of Charles Manson's "family," "we wouldn't have to ask for anything, people would just give it to us. People would bring us baskets all filled up." Every morning the hippie volunteers make their calls, sack in hand like Buddhist monks, to the merchants, restaurants, and supermarkets of the neighborhood, and they never come back emptyhanded.

Killing Time

They go to bed very late at night after they've smoked their marijuana, listened to some records or been to a psychedelic show. They talk, they turn on, they make love, and they are still sleeping when the sun is high in the sky. But in the afternoon the hippie world begins to come alive, with hippies strolling in the streets and in and out of their shops. When they are tired of walking they sit down, on the sidewalks if the police will let them, and chat desultorily while watching the passersby, occasionally putting out their hands for money. They talk about their sexual adventures, their drug experiences, their troubles with the police. Drugs, police, sex. Sex police, drugs. Endlessly.

In fact they are always waiting for something to happen. . . .

Because they are bored. Once the forbidden fruits have been tasted, once the novelty and excitement of "freedom" have worn off, they drag around woefully; what could be longer than a day when there is nothing, absolutely nothing, to do: neither work nor study nor cooking nor reading, nor even washing your face. To lift the pall of ennui, they vainly search for something, anything, that will cause a little excitement. And they constantly give themselves and each other the illusion that they've found it by calling everything—a flower, a toy, an alley cat, a can of sardines—"groovy." "It's groovy, man."

And what else do they do?

They stand in line. Like all other underdeveloped peoples—and essentially the hippies have devoted themselves to creating an enclave of underdevelopment in the most developed country in the world—they kill time by waiting. They stand in line for their hippie shows. They stand in line in front of the Diggers' trucks waiting for a bowl of free stew.

And what else do they do?

They exist.

The Festival Days: Be-ins, Love-ins, Smoke-ins

Given this general weight of boredom, the great hippie festival days take on an air of historical importance. People talk about them for weeks before and after. Naturally, even the hippie population—feeble in initiative though it be for the most part—produces a breed of promoters who periodically come to the surface to organize the most extraordinary gatherings: combination village fairs, local dances, company picnics, religious processions, Boy Scout camps, mystical initiations, communal drug participations, nudist camps, brothels, and political conventions. Some of them have marked watersheds in hippie culture. They are called "be-ins" or "happenings"—meetings of a large group of people where something happens—half ritual, half festive.

The first be-in was in San Francisco, in the Golden Gate Park, on January 14, 1967. A mob of longhairs estimated by the police at 20,000, and by the hippies themselves at 50,000, assembled there. They sat on the grass, burned incense, played their pipes, guitars, and drums, while rock music blasted out of the loudspeaker system. They ate hot dogs and drank the free Coca Cola. They picked all the flowers out of their beds to give to passersby. The guru hierarchy made its appearance, including Allen Ginsberg, who led a Hindu chant that curled itself around the whole day: "Hare Krishna, hare, hare. . . ." The famous organist Pig Pen, whose eccentric sweater is worn by thousands of hippies, was there; and then there was Timothy Leary, the pope of the movement, who launched his slogan that would be heard 'round the world, "Turn on, tune in, drop out."

On June 21, 1967, the famous Grand Canyon love-in—planned to coincide with the summer solstice, venerated by the Indians—took place. This qualified as a monumental event in hippie history. The festival began at sunrise with a mystico-religious ceremony. The organizers, admirably thorough, had prepared maps giving directions to the site, programs for the events of the day, camping information, and even "what to do in case of a bust." The *Los Angeles Free Press* and the *Oracle* announced that the flower-children would be smoking marijuana in defiance of the law, and the police girded up for war. The Colorado authorities called two-day seminars for 150 police officers on crowd psychology, riot control, and arrest procedures. And when they found out that 5000 girls and boys intended to perpetrate a public love-in, which might lead goodness knew where, they applied to Washington for the back-up assistance of the National Guard. The nearby highway patrols were also placed on alert.

At Seal Beach in California, 3000 followers of the god of love paid him tribute to the rhythms of tambourines made from garbage-can lids.

There was another love-in in Central Park one Easter Sunday. The girls surrounded the policemen chanting, "Love, love, love"—which did not make the cops feel very loving. At the University of Michigan, a kiss-in was organized. Nearly a thousand students kissed one another for hours, breast against breast, in the full view of all, to protest the expulsion of two of their fellows who had prolonged a goodnight kiss in a bedroom longer than the officials had thought was absolutely necessary. Another love-in brought 10,000 hippies to a ranch near San Diego. The organizers had hired their own private guards to forestall interference by the local police. The flower-children painted everything, including themselves, brilliant colors: their legs, their faces, their VW buses, their tents, and even the bushes. There was a burst of wildly colored kites. At night, they lit up Chinese lanterns of all colors. There were three mystical love ceremonies designed to carry the crowd to the "heights of sensual intoxication."

These public manifestations of love began to catch on in Europe. For a love-in on Britain's Isle of Wight in the summer of 1969, a very beautiful couple started things off with a flourish by making love in full daylight before 100,000 people.

In other "happenings," called "smoke-ins," the participants gather specifically to take drugs together. During the smoke-in organized by Ken Kesey, most of the hippies were in a constant state of drugged bemusement, helped along by the free distribution of grass and incense.

The hippies have developed very intelligent gambits to frustrate the "narks," and keep them from making arrests during these illegal smoke-ins. They begin the day by burning incense or by smoking dried banana skin, which gives off the same bittersweet odor as the cannabis plant. If the police move in, provoked by the smells, they are confused and withdraw shamefacedly to general laughter. But in the afternoon, the participants seat themselves down in rows, and the people in the back begin to smoke marijuana quite openly. The police cannot push through the ranks of festival goers to reach the malefactors in the back without provoking a general riot, so they pretend that they don't see anything. In this way, the Tompkins Square (East Village, New York) smoke-in of July, 1967, began with a call for a mass banana smoke-in. The publicity posters for the gathering read, "Bring musical instruments, drums, bells, flutes, joints [marijuana cigarettes]. . . . Forget paranoia. Make music together. Tompkins Square at ten o'clock." They danced, they sang, they smoked banana skins. When the crowd had reached a thousand, the marijuana came out.

The account of the big party as written up by the *East Village Other* of August 8, 1967, took pains to point out:

> By 8:00, hundreds of joints appeared everywhere in the crowd; a sweet haze rose skyward. Then anonymous benefactors in back of the regular seating threw handfuls of joints into the air. The crowd cheered and surged. When two regular blue-clothes police waded in, people started applauding. The cops shrugged their shoulders, turned around, until they left the park. . . . Until 10:30, marijuana, in huge quantities, appeared not only in front of the bandshell, but all over the park, among groups listening to guitars or conga drums. Clearly, just about everybody on the Lower East Side wants to smoke openly, without fear. . . . Everybody was smoking—not banana, but real, free grass. People turned on. . . . The hip, grass-smoking poor of the ghetto—"hippie," Puerto Rican, black—can ignore police hasslement, if they're together. The cops aren't going to bust 3000 people, or molest a crowd made up from all groups—not with rioting going on all over the country. . . . Together the people here are even capable of resisting the laws—like the laws against grass.

The spectacular Woodstock Festival in Bethel, New York, in August, 1969, during which more than 90 percent of the 400,000 participants openly smoked marijuana and grooved on rock, may have been the greatest occasion of all. It was chilled and muddy, but there were only peace and good will, and many people—not all of them hippies— thought that a new "age of love" had truly dawned. That illusion was broken brutally four months later, in December, 1969, when the Rolling Stones brought their "message of peace" to 300,000 young people at Altamont, near San Francisco. Marijuana, LSD and other drugs were sold freely in the name of "freedom from taboos" and "hatred of war." But by the end of the festival, three people were dead and many more had been injured.

3

Hustling Hippies, Guru Hippies, Mystic Hippies, Plastic Hippies

It has been estimated that there is a floating population of 500,000 hippies in the United States. There are probably no more than 100,000 full-time hippies, but during sunny weekends, the influx of weekend hippies may swell their number up to a million. The hippie Mecca, San Francisco, shelters around 30,000 full-time hippies, about 100,000 occasional hippies, and for the major festivals and celebrations of love, San Francisco can call upon up to 200,000 of them. (*Information and Documents*, January, 1969, American Embassy, Paris.)

The hippies can be broadly classified into several different groups. The most amiable, the people who began the movement, are the flower-children. They distribute smiles and flowers to passersby, and are always gracious, even to the police who arrest them. I have visited some of their "families," as they like to call the people they live with, and as I left there would always be a sweet "Come back soon," even though I belonged to that straight world that they had dropped out of. They dream of a totally free society, inspired by universal love and the complete sharing of all resources, but they have no concrete ideas on how to realize such an ideal world, and are not particularly interested in developing any. They don't even have the intellectual curiosity to discuss, just for fun among themselves, possible solutions to the problems they see. They just yawn and go to put on a record that "wipes them out." In the face of difficulties they react anxiously, with no will to fight. They are carefree utopians, easily influenced, and they still believe in fairy tales. They are indolent, allergic to all sorts of work whether intellectual or physical, contemplative without interest in doctrines of any kind. They aspire to serenity and to sensual pleasure, that's all. They can afford to be gay and sweet because they are troubled by no personal ambition or by no sense of moral duty. Marijuana makes every day a holiday, and they play and laugh together.

The mystic hippies take more powerful drugs—opium or LSD—to better open the way to eternal truth, and in the hope of seeing God face-to-face. They love to proselytize and to talk about their ecstasies or about the new world they are creating. They are pantheists, meta-naturists, animists. The staunchest among them march proudly in clothes that recall the robēs of the apostles. With their long hair, their naked feet, and their smooth high foreheads, they resemble Christ. The beauty of some of these heads of Apollo was striking, as well as the extreme ugliness of some of the others, emaciated, toothless, wrinkled, already old before they were thirty. These are the impenitent addicts —whether emotional or physical—for whom the ultimate mystery lies in their drugs, and in whose veins runs inexorable death.

The flower-children and the mystic hippies belong to the "full-time hippie" class, as opposed to the part-time, or "plastic" hippies about whom we shall speak further on. And among these full-time hippies, we can distinguish between the street hippies and the stay-at-homes.

The street hippies, or "street people" as they are often called, who have no fixed place of residence, no particular end in mind, no particular attachments, are the most pitiful. They quickly become real bums, derelicts, who sleep on door stoops when the weather is nice, and crouch in a corner of an abandoned building when it's bad. This kind of person is utterly immature now, and probably always will be. He is an eternal babe-in-the-woods, who stays untaught because he can't stand to learn. He is game for any sort of tomfoolery with drugs, no matter how dangerous, out of ignorance, stupidity, depravity, or bravado. He will shoot one drug into his veins and gulp another into his stomach at the same time, when their effects are contrary—one, say, a depressant and the other a stimulant—and completely disorient his already feeble judgment. He will deal in hard drugs (heroin and other opium derivatives), steal, become a homosexual prostitute, anything for some "bread." In a wild moment he will strike out physically, or even kill. He can keep neither woman, love, friend, or job. He doesn't know what he wants, but he will protect himself fiercely from what he doesn't want: any authority of any kind, whether from his parents, his teachers, the government, employers, or even from his peers. That's why he can't tolerate life within a hippie community. Incapable of gathering himself together sufficiently to achieve anything, he will bend his violent energies toward the destruction of others like himself.

Among the street people, the most poignant spectacle is the "teenyboppers": children from twelve to fifteen who have escaped from the shelter of their parental homes, and from any other hippie or straight shelter that might have taken them in. It should be pointed out that over the years that the hippie movement has been in existence, the median age has fallen lower and lower. At first it was young people in their early twenties, college students mostly, and they attracted teenagers—kids from about sixteen to nineteen. This example from their immediate elders magnetized these very young children. It was mostly kids of this age that I met at that police station in Hollywood. It has been estimated that, during the summer, there are some 25,000 teenyboppers in San Francisco alone (Haight Ashbury Research Project, San Francisco). These young runaways, to whom the police devote their major efforts in an attempt to return them to their home, want to be like their elders but, being so young, they have absolutely no prudence when it comes to using drugs. They exceed the drug limit guidelines published in the hippie press, and it is among these children that the most tragic incidents occur. Some of them are exploited by the drug dealers, who use them as shills: the kids will approach people in the streets and sell them drugs at retail. And indeed, the kids are apt pupils; it's surprising how quickly these persons of tender age catch on to the tricks. When they are arrested, they are often more stoic than their elders, and it is considerably more difficult to get them to divulge information about their sources.

The girls are a pitiful sight. They are ugly, with their sunken cheeks and greasy hair. They give up a little of their youth with each sleepless night that they pass in those discotheques of hell, with each sunny day that they spend sleeping off the preceding night, with each LSD trip that destroys their vital cells, with each skipped meal, with each junky concoction they throw into their stomachs, with each bug they pick up from a casual sexual encounter.

But these street girls go practically unnoticed next to their more flourishing sisters, the weekend hippies or plastic hippies. These are Daddy's girls from the Bronx or New Jersey who come downtown to play at hippiedom on weekends. These "plastic" (in every sense of the term) hippies are pretty, because during the rest of the week they dine on good steaks, and wash their hair in fragrant shampoos while they bathe in sweet-smelling oils.

The plastic hippies of both sexes have plenty of money to spend —Daddy's money—in the stores of psychedelia. On week days they go home to swim in the backyard pool, and they put on shoes for driving around in one of the family cars. For better or worse, they keep going to school—and more for the worse than for the better. During the summer vacation they fly off, without telling their parents where, to San Francisco or Greenwich Village to taste the charms of adventure and easy love. They take drugs without any particular enthusiasm, just to "make the scene."

Unfortunately, alas, these idyllic adventures have their dark side. Instead of meeting the prince charming or the flower-girl their underground magazines have promised, the weekend hippies find themselves face to face, without defense, with all the flotsam that drifts the streets of great cities: sexual deviants, swindlers, perverts, drug addicts, gangsters, the deranged, and criminals who prey upon the innocence of the flower-children. And they find an infernal sub-world underneath the flowers where they can be mugged, raped, or killed.

Stay-at-home Hippies

These crimes throw the world of the hippies into turmoil, and lead many of them into the protection of their own communities—or rather, as it pleases them to term themselves, into hippie "families." These hippies who settle into their own kind of homes are more emotionally mature than the wanderers, as proved by the fact that they can rouse themseves to earn the money required to support a permanent roof over their heads. Among these stay-at-home hippies, there are two main branches: those who set up communities within the cities, and those who establish "communes"—a kind of tribal community in the country.

The tribal, or commune, hippies must be taken seriously. They aspire to create a new civilization, and they have had the energy to act on their theories. Many of them have been to college, though they usually left school before they qualified for any profession. Within their tribes, they share all the domestic, artisan, and field work. Other groups have come together on the basis of one particular enterprise: to bring out a newspaper, some sort of theatrical activity, music, creation of a new church, launching some sort of craft works. They are alert and intelligent, and they formulate their philosophy with assurance. Some individuals, living as they profess to believe, have renounced all thought of personal success "in the world," choosing to act with and for their "families." But others, having once tasted some success, don't have the strength of character to stay in the shade, and they begin to act like movie stars, relishing the admiring gaze of the crowd. Personal ambition does not always stay renounced.

And then there are the "yeah-yeah" hippies, the dandies of the movement. They love hippie clothes, as long as they are elegantly tailored in fine fabrics. They have inserted themselves into hippie culture because it offers them numerous occasions to savor the delights of narcissism. The "yeah-yeah" males have a tendency to dye their hair platinum. I saw one glorious creature display himself on Sunset Strip draped in a cape of mauve silk studded with sea-green disks, booted in black lacquered boots that went up to his knees. Their heads are empty, but their material needs are great. Sooner or later they will go back to the straight world, to which they are bound by the umbilical cord of money.

The hippie hustlers are the least numerous among the movement, but they have the largest influence. They have glued themselves onto the movement like oysters onto a rock. They imitate the hippies, mimic them, take on all the accoutrements—long hair, beads, argot. But they only play at hippiedom for what it's worth to them. The hippie businessmen are found among this group. They own the hippie boutiques and the psychedelic discotheques à go go, they run the enormous underground press (the journalists themselves being true hippies), and the large-scale drug dealers are found among their number.

But not all professional hippies are potentates. There are low-caste ones as well: the confirmed "heads" who do the hippie thing to provide themselves with easier access to drugs and also, should they be arrested, to profit from the free legal aid available to hippies.

The "political hippie" class—as they are designated with contempt by the flower-children, who are afraid that this group is trying to exploit them for partisan political ends—should also be classified with the hustlers. These political hippies invariably belong to the extreme left: communists, especially pro-Chinese and Castroites, anarchists, terrorists, New Left. They are very mature, activist, clever, capable. Their feet are on the ground, and there's an organizational plan in their heads. They display all the hippie attributes, but they wash in private and, while they make a show of strong support for drug use, they don't take it themselves.

Beatles and Hell's Angels

I have already spoken of the terrible motorcycle gang Hell's Angels. In fact, they stem more from the family of "beatles" than from the hippies proper. On this point, it seems appropriate to analyze the ties among and the distinctions between these two groups.

Beatles and hippies demonstrate the same contempt for the sexual mores and general bourgeois systems that dominate the straight world, the same predilection for vagabondage, Oriental mysticism, drugs. Both groups wear unconventional clothes and long hair. Here the resemblance stops.

The beatles stem, in general, from the lower-middle and working classes, whereas the hippies are mostly middle- and upper-middle. The beatles are thinkers who have launched ringing manifestos; the hippies are anti-intellectuals who have formulated no genuine statement of principle. Their sole professions of faith are contained in the kind of Hindu chants, hippie poems, and button slogans that pervaded the great Golden Gate picnic in January, 1967. The jazz of the beatles is cerebral and cold, the hippies' rock music visceral and burning. The dominant color in beatle painting is black, while the hippies live in an orgy of polychrome. The beatles deny the existence of God, and the hippies worship him in the person of his avatars. The beatles, raised in relative poverty, condemn physical deprivation, while the hippies have contempt for the "good life," and preach renunciation. The beatles are prone to use force and the Hell's Angels, with their roaring motorcycles, sow terror the length of the Pacific coast. The hippies, who are tender as lambs, preach nonviolence and love for mankind.

For the most part, the Hell's Angels are older than the hippies. They are superior to them in muscular development, as well as intellectual development, and a special kind of aura surrounds them. Very reticent, they snap at anyone who annoys them with questions. Their women, who wear leather gear, are tough and hard. When they stop off together for hamburgers, they park their cycles in battle formation —ready to take off for action at a moment's notice. They go to the big hippie festivals looking for trouble and, according to the flower-children, it's the Hell's Angels that have given the movement such a bad name.

The political hippies, on the other hand, have forged an alliance with these shock troops. According to the *Congressional Record* of November 6, 1967, the political activists called in the Hell's Angels as a line of defense against the police. This is why the political hippies have tried to effect a rapprochement between the main body of hippies and the Angels. On August 11, 1967, *Open City* published the following:

> A little band of cyclists outlawed in Los Angeles, but active there nonetheless, came to the aid of hippies molested by the police. A melee ensued during the course of which the police arrested forty demonstrators. So an alliance was forged between the two groups which is the way it should be, since both groups smoke pot, drop acid, take meth, and they have a common enemy: the fuzz. Up till now, the hippies have been afraid of the Hell's Angels because of their violence, but from now on it is up to our press to make them understand that they need the Angels for defense against the cops.

The chief of the Oakland branch of the Hell's Angels, Ralph Barger, with eyes like laser beams, runs the "Galloping Geese," the most fearsome band on the Pacific Coast. Ralph and the editor of *Open City* got together to discuss ways of bringing the hippies and the cyclists together "to make common cause in the street warfare that the establishment is waging against its dissenters" (sic). Barger reproached the hippies for their naiveté in the face of the brutal nature of the human condition, and he put down their gaudy, effeminate showiness:

You don't have to wear kooky clothes to be an outlaw. I'm one. I'm always ready to battle the fuzz. And for that I don't need to be a raunchy dirty motherfucker. I've done everything I can to keep my "Galloping Geese" physically and mentally clean.

And he concluded, addressing himself to the venerators of love: "We don't love you, but we don't need to love you to hang together with you."

The credit for the rapprochement between these two antithetic movements must be laid at the door of the political hippies.

Hippie Gurus

We have left for last the high caste—the Brahmins among the hippies—the "gurus." They are not, properly speaking, "leaders," for the egalitarian hippie philosophy recognizes no such. The term "guru," in its original sense, designates a Brahmin versed in the great Indian religious books, the Vedas, and now, in India, has come to mean the philosophical master or religious chief of a community.

The hippie gurus, like their Indian examples, owe their standing, first, to their spiritual illuminations, with the important difference that the Hindu gurus attain this state of grace through prolonged fasts, while their "now" followers come to grace through drugs; and second, they gain prestige from their denunciation of the materialist society that surrounds them, and to their exhortations to renunciation. But our hippie gurus are quite some way from the asceticism of their Hindu brothers, who roam the banks of the Ganges, almost nude, with no other possession than a little blanket. With a few exceptions, the guru hippies lead the soft life of the consumer society that they denounce, but at least their life of ease is carried out in a properly psychedelic manner; that is to say, filled with color and magical objects. I've visited some guru lodgings, and they all have a large meditation room illumined by a soft light filtered through windows covered with rice paper. The walls are covered with Hindu tapestries and vivid paintings. Their rugs are crazy-quilts of brightly colored fabrics, and there is hardly any furniture, as in a Japanese house. Instead, soft puffy cushions are strewn on the floor, along with statues of Buddha, huge vases filled with artificial flowers, and perpetual-motion mobiles whose wiry arms bear little featherweight disks that shine in the light like wavelets on a sunny sea. An agreeable odor of incense fills their rooms, with a background of soft music that floats like a light breeze through a mountain valley. These guru hippies have cars, telephones, the newest gadgets. "When I trip into the magic world of LSD," one of them told me, "I like to look at my color TV." They travel on planes, going to lectures where straight people pay high prices for the pleasure of hearing themselves called mental retardates and "sexual impotents." In brief, the gurus avail themselves of all the commodities and inventions of the established order in order to discredit and demolish all the commodities and inventions of the established order.

The erotic poet Allen Ginsberg, who is nearly fifty now, as is Timothy Leary, is one of the most famous gurus. Ginsberg's head, face and chest are entangled in mats of dense black hair. He prides himself that his beard has not seen a razor, nor his head a scissors, for many, many years. He loves to spend his time in the company of young people and, say his admirers, call upon their sense of mysticism; upon their gullibility, say his critics. Among his hippie flock, Ginsberg puts on mystic ceremonies like this Hindu "mela":

> It began by chanting a special mantra. It is an incantation designed to avert catastrophes. Then we made a purificatory procession around the Polo Grounds to exorcise the demons and the Evil Eye.

Are these sincere convictions, or an exploitation of the naiveté of his young disciples?

Then there is Allen Cohen, editor of the elegant psychedelic review *Oracle*, who has lived in San Francisco since the arrival of the first flower-children. And there is also the famous troubadour Bob Dylan, whose every performance earns him his weight in gold. The writers in the hippie pantheon are Jack Kerouac, Norman Mailer, Alan Watts, author of *The Way of Zen* and *The Book*, and William Burroughs, who wrote *Naked Lunch*, which was banned at one time. Burroughs writes that he sought hallucinatory visions by "chemical manipulations of the senses," but that he found himself caught in a trap, and abandoned drugs altogether. But he still fights the good fight for sexual freedom.

And finally there is the novelist Ken Kesey, author of *One Flew Over the Cuckoo's Nest*. He was arrested twice on drug charges, and fled into Mexico. From there he sends paranoid letters back to the United States, writing about his wild flights, his hiding places, his disguises, his hashish dreams, his women, his drug experiences. One of his letters, written in the third person, parodies "straight world" comments on his doings:

> Thus, this young and beautiful boy—think of it, he was 33—happily married to a pretty woman and the father of three magnificent children—was a drug fiend. He ran away to escape arrest, having committed three felonies and God knows how many misdemeanors. . . . Not too long ago this handsome athlete was a sportsman of national renown. Today, he wouldn't be able to do six pushups. Not too long ago he had a handsome balance in the bank. Now it's all his poor wife can do to scrape eight dollars together to send him in Mexico. He, who was listed in *Who's Who* and had been invited to give lectures before such select audiences as the Wellesley Club, can't even organize meetings now against the war in Vietnam. What could have brought a man so full of promise so low in such a short time? . . . "Dope," he answered.

There is also the very mysterious Stanley Owsley, the grandson of a Kentucky Senator, who struck it rich from the manufacture and distribution of LSD. Before the drug was declared illegal in 1966, Owsley decided "to light up the world" by acid and by psychedelic rock. He is known to have financed the successful San Francisco rock group The Grateful Dead, whose leader, Jerry Garcia, is so hung up on LSD that he's called "Captain Trip." At thirty-two, Owsley had acquired a million dollars, and was called the "Henry Ford of psychedelia." The hippies tell so many stories about him that it is hard to tell where reality ends and legend begins. He is reputed to manufacture the purest LSD with the best equipment and the best chemists in the United States, and there is a rumor that he is going to put out a super-hallucinogen that he will call FDA; a barb at the Food and Drug Administration.

These gurus are at the top of the heap, but there are inferior castes as well. For example, there is a strange person called Galahad who came to Greenwich Village from New Orleans in 1966, bringing nothing with him but his own twenty years and his powers of seduction. He learned quickly that life in a big city without a roof over one's head and without money is hell. He rented, for $35 a month, a decrepit apartment in a disintegrating East Village building, and later took over two more apartments in the same deplorable condition as the first one. He converted all three into dormitories, covering the entire floor surface with mattresses for 70 sleepers. On weekends, he could squeeze in some 100 people who had nowhere else to go. His people would roam Broadway, bringing back the leavings the restaurants threw out. Galahad and his friend Groovy themselves begged in the streets to pay the rent on the three apartments.

The High Priest of LSD: Timothy Leary

The arch-guru of the hippie brotherhood, Timothy Leary, calls for a special section all his own. The credit—or the discredit—for the incredible blossoming of hallucinogens must, in large part, be laid at the door of this long-haired, robed, sandaled former university professor. He was discharged from Harvard for giving LSD to his students, but far from being shaken, the professor loudly justified his actions on metaphysical grounds, which brought him considerable publicity, and whipped up public curiosity about his discoveries. For some people Leary became the devil, for others a demi-god, and the Leary cult began.

The weekly *Avatar* published an issue with a picture of Leary-as-Christ on its cover, wearing a crown of thorns, a white robe over his shoulders, and a long-chained cross on his chest. Another magazine showed him as Buddha, his body, ornamented with an Indian pendant, radiating a supernatural red light, his navel proudly prominent. In the *New York World Journal Tribune* (January 20, 1967), he appeared worshiping at an altar where a flame burned, with his hands clasped in a saintly fashion. Other pictures had him as a prophet holding his eyelids open with two fingers; then as a tightrope walker in a skintight leotard that displayed his muscles from the front, from behind, from a three-quarter angle, and obliquely, no doubt providing many women with a psychedelic turn-on. *Cavalier* (July, 1968) reported on one of his lectures at Town Hall in New York with huge close-ups, first of the upper part of his face, then of the lower part; then there were intimate views of his mouth and teeth, and lastly a picture of one eye upside down, suggesting that he was in a state of stoned bliss. One of his disciples, testifying before a Senate committee, affirmed that Leary was the Messiah. *Look*, in 1967, showed him dressed as a Brahmin, preaching from a platform overlooking an audience so vast that their heads seemed to be as close and tiny as beans on a plate. Underneath the photo, this caption: "The high priest of LSD, Dr. Timothy Leary, spreading the word before a huge assembly of young apostles." It was to this assembly, fallen under the spell of his charisma, that he formulated the creed of the new religion:

> All the followers of my path must, in order to reach spiritual discovery, make one hallucinogenic trip per week with LSD, and every day with marijuana. They must search for inner ecstasy at every opportunity. . . . They must abandon their families and society as soon as possible.

Another song of this male siren:

> I am not disturbed that great numbers of young people are setting out to explore their consciousness [Understand that this exploration is under drugs]. Buddha, after all, also searched for a way to expand his consciousness, he also fled away from, dropped out of, his society. True, there are statistics that say that 20 percent of American students take marijuana and LSD. But there's another statistic that really ought to make the "straight" world tremble: That is that 51 percent of all Americans are less than 25. I consider that an even greater menace for the middle-aged whisky drinkers who are going through an intellectual, as well as physical, menopause. . . . I am convinced that the present generation of young, under 25, Americans is the most sophisticated, the most intelligent, the wisest and holiest generation since mankind began.

Flatteries more appropriate to a candidate for office than to an educator. For these young people, after all, have not yet contributed anything to the society that has given them so much, materially and spiritually. And society's gifts have been offered to them with a generosity never seen in other cultures or in other times. The tender loving care lavished on these young people is something *truly* new in the history of humanity. And I am glad. But in return, rarely have young people carried ingratitude and contempt for their elders to such a pitch. And

I am sad. They forget that their ancestors, who did quite well in a world where they had to expand their consciousnesses all by themselves, include Confucius, Buddha, Socrates, Archimedes, Phidias, Galileo, Copernicus, Michelangelo, Shakespeare, Molière, Rembrandt, Newton, Mozart, Lavoisier, Bach, Kant, Beethoven, Pasteur, Chekhov, Tolstoy, Proust, Rodin, etc. There are legions of artists and thinkers who have enlarged humanity's consciousness without LSD, not to mention the scientists who invented the steam engine, penicillin, anesthetics, electricity (without which there would be no psychedelic light shows), and, indeed, LSD. Today's hippies could never have discovered their wonder drug, since they are not spending much time these days in research laboratories.

Timothy Leary also wrote in his address to parents:

> I am the father of two young children, and I am concerned with their education like all parents. And I have never dictated to my children what they should or should not do to their nervous systems; but I have told them what I have learned myself during my researches with the hallucinogenic drugs . . . I have made it clear to them that I prefer that they smoke marijuana rather than cigarettes, or drink alcohol, both of which are toxic and addictive substances. . . . I say to all parents who are disturbed that their school-age children take psychedelic drugs: there is nothing you can do to prevent it, neither by coercion or threat. If you would like to persuade them, to teach them, then first learn more about the drugs than they know themselves. . . . Why don't you make this agreement with them: "Let's read books together that deal with drugs. Let us speak with people who use them and, after two or three months of preparation, let us make a decision together based on our knowledge of the facts." And, if your knowledge of the facts suggests it, go on a "trip" with your children. I am an old-fashioned father. I much prefer that my children go through strange experiences in my company than behind my back. . . . And instead of finding your children cause for lamentation and trying to imprison them, listen to them, support them, and share the drug experience together.

Demagogy and intellectual naiveté pierce every one of the sentences of this text. It is evidently not true, could not possibly be true, that Leary has never dictated to his children "what they should or should not do to their nervous systems." He has molded 90 percent of this system when, like all parents, he taught his children to keep away from fire, taught them not to defecate in the living room, not to bite and scratch their playmates, not to roll in the mud; and when, later, he trained them not to count on their fingers, made them go to bed, or had them read a certain book. Also, Leary contradicts himself in the next phrase, when he states that he would rather that his children indulge in marijuana rather than tobacco or alcohol. To pretend that he is more "liberal" than other parents because he is content to make his preference "clear to them" is pure hypocrisy, because he knows perfectly well that the minds of young children are not yet formed enough to reason maturely, and that their behavior is based above all on the example of their parents; so that, when parents adopt a certain mode of conduct, they influence their children more strongly than through a hundred lectures.

Most likely Timothy Leary has pondered more, not less, than the average person over the training of his children, for he lives an intellectualized life.

Going on with Leary's text, the "scientific" counsels that Leary gives to parents to guide them in the matter of drugs sound like the spiel of a snake-oil salesman among the yokels: "Read about drugs, talk about drugs, experiment with drugs. . . ." By setting parents to thinking about drugs, the temptation to use them will, Leary hopes, become irresistible, and once parents have tasted the forbidden fruit, their authority will dwindle, their judgment grow dim, and their will evaporate . . . to be replaced by Leary's influence over the minds of their children. This would be betrayal indeed! Is it not sensible, rather, to follow the counsels of reputable physicians who urge that young people be kept away from drugs? This is, is it not, one of the functions of science—To research and experiment so that those who follow can start where the last researcher left off, and not have to go through the same experiments again? Does each father personally have to circumnavigate the globe to prove to his child that the earth is round? Or take strychnine in order to announce that it is a poison?

After his siren songs, Dr. Leary takes on the role of visionary prophet to break down any lingering defenses: "We have entered the psychedelic age. A psychedelic revolution is under way. Nothing can stop the march of the hallucinogens."

Who is this Messiah to whom we owe, in good part, the epidemic of drugging and flight that swirls through the young?

Timothy Leary is the only son of a strict Catholic family. His

2

The Sense Revolution in the United States

One of two main themes stands out in most writing about hippies: the enthusiastic apology or indignant morality. The apologists see profound significance and romantic hue in the hippie lifestyle. They deal only with their positive characteristics: the spontaneity with which they confront the "hypocrisy" of the bourgeois world; their love for mankind, as opposed to what they see as a general atmosphere of aggression that pervades the United States; their disinterest in the money-thirst that they say has driven their elders. The moralists, on the other hand, can deal with nothing but the negative side of the movement: violence, crime, the venereal diseases that plague the hippie ghettos. The moralists are irritated by their sexual extravagance, their long hair, their eccentric dress, their dirty feet, the mania for drugs, and, above all, by the fact that the hippies are parasites on a society that is willing to support them, albeit reluctantly, while they never deal with the fact that they could not exist except by society's grace.

It is impossible not to take sides, and I make my side clear in my conclusion, but only after an honest discussion of the problems involved. And so that my readers might come to their own personal determination of the matter, in this first part of the book I just set out, in as objective a way as possible, the acts, ideas, rituals, and hallucinogenic experiences that collectively constitute the "hippie culture." In the second part, I will discuss the validity of the protest of the flower-children, and I will try to answer the many questions I have posed in the preceding section.

Who Are They?

Where does the word "hippie" come from?

Some people say it derives from the word "hep"—up to the minute, "in the know"—that was current during the thirties. Others see it as an evolution from the fifties' word "hip" that had to do with the blue jeans skinned tightly over the hips of the beatniks—or "hipsters"—current then. Today the word "hippie" signifies boys and girls who have fallen away from their families, schools, and professions, and have abandoned traditional values in favor of a life they have chosen for themselves, whose basis is a return to the essential wonder of existence, and whose aspiration is the attainment of cosmic consciousness through drugs.

Like all revolutionaries, the hippies reject the traditional values of the established order, but, unlike other revolutionaries, many reject violence as a means of overturning that order. Unlike the communists, they refuse to discipline themselves and organize themselves politically. Unlike atheistic Marxists, they are profoundly mystical and believe in a whole pantheon of gods and prophets, from Christ to Buddha to Timothy Leary. The hippies also differ from the beatniks in that they are encumbered neither with their aggressive ideology, their menacing air, nor their intellectual pretensions. The hippies are gentle, modest, smiling, always ready to tell you that they love you. They worship love, the sun, doing nothing, and flowers—from whence the term "flower-children."

But they are distinguished, above all, from all other protest movements present or past, by their systematic usage of mind-bending drugs. They suck in chemical substances like mother's milk, whether to pleasure the senses, to be lifted to unknown ecstasies, or to penetrate swiftly into the hidden truths or to mystic visions of God.

It is not useful to act as if the hippies are simply the young devil-may-cares that curdle the blood of the bourgeoisie. Their press proclaims that they have done much more than just liberate themselves, they have squarely abandoned the old society in order to create another culture, another style of life that erases all acquired values, all taboos. They are drop-outs from the "straight" world, deserters from the social contract. The poet Allen Ginsberg, one of their luminaries, describes it like this:

father, a sea captain of Irish origin, intended his son for the sea. "I am, in any case, still in navigation," he said, holding up his capsules of LSD. Tim went to West Point, and must have done something dreadful there because for nine months his fellow cadets kept him in a kind of social quarantine: no one could talk to him, and no one would sit next to him at meals (*New York World Journal Tribune*, January 29, 1967). This cruel exclusion must certainly have marked him profoundly, and may well be at the root of his eagerness to "drop out" and preach the same to others.

In any case, as early as his West Point period—perhaps as a way of avenging himself on a society that had rejected him—Leary threw himself into esoteric readings and mystical introspection. He concentrated on Oriental philosophy and Yoga, and left West Point for the University of Alabama where he took his degree in psychology. In 1942 he entered the army as a psychologist.

Sixteen years later, fate tapped Leary again. In 1958, while on vacation in Spain, he had an "extraordinary experience."

> One day I got an atrocious itching on my scalp. Something incredible. I couldn't stop scratching till I bled. It was total insanity. My mind blotted everything else out but the itch. Then my face swelled until I couldn't see. Huge red blotches covered my skin, and then the whole thing went down to my ankles and I couldn't walk. I wasn't sick, I had no fever, it was a wave of something mysterious in my body, a psychosomatic experience—corporeal and spiritual at the same time—like a snake that moults its skin and moults its soul at the same time. I knew then that I would not go back to the United States.

Anybody else would have gone to a doctor and no doubt learned that there was a perfectly ordinary name for Leary's attack, and that there was a cure for it, but Leary's mystic spirit preferred to see the mark of destiny. In fact, he did go back to the United States, which should have proved to him that his interior voice was not in touch with the cosmos, but he never seemed to make the connection.

At thirty-eight he joined Harvard's Center of Personality Research, and he would probably be there now if he hadn't gone to Mexico. In August, 1960, at a friend's villa in Cuernavaca, he was lounging around the swimming pool when someone offered him a bite from a "sacred mushroom"—so-called for the fantastic colorful visions they induce. Having nothing better to do Leary accepted and

> I had never taken a drug before, and I was carried into a state of unimaginable euphoria, but I already knew that I would devote the rest of my life to the study of drugs. . . . Suppose that three hundred years earlier I had been a doctor who diagnosed diseases by examining my patients' tongues. And suppose that one day someone brought me a microscope and said, "Look at that blood cell." It would have seemed gigantic, and astonishing. In a very similar way, those sacred mushrooms showed me that everything I had perceived before was just a superficial construct of my tribal mind, and that everything was actually infinitely more grand, more wise and incredibly more beautiful than it seemed to our crude senses. The hallucinogenic drugs create nothing, they don't impose. They simply reveal the things that exist, but that have been up till now invisible.

Back in the United States, Leary set up and directed the International Foundation for Internal Liberty, and he began to experiment with small doses of LSD on prisoners in a Massachusetts penitentiary. His idea was to substitute a spiritual liberty for the physical liberty that the prisoners had lost. It was a stunning failure. The prisoners threw his drugs at him; they preferred to have their bodies outside the prison gates than have their minds outside their bodies.

But Leary was not discouraged for long, and went on with his experiments. From May to October, 1961, he gave psilocybin to student volunteers at Harvard. The "old crabs" at the university—as he called them—cracked down on him and made him promise to give up experiments on humans, but he could not resist the temptation and began them again in secret. In 1963, Leary crossed the line. After two years, having fed some 400 of his students with 3500 doses of psilocybin, he began to give them LSD, a much more dangerous drug. He and his disciple Professor Richard Alpert—who has since written a book called *Be Here Now* in which he outlines his eventual break with Leary, his abandonment of drugs, and the new, rich path his life has taken— were censured by their colleagues at Harvard, and dismissed from the teaching staff. It was the second time in Leary's life that an "establishment" institution had expelled an irritating foreign body from its ranks. He swore to bring down this society that he detested.

He went to Mexico, where he set up a "Center of Psychedelic Training." He charged $200 a month for this "training," which con-sisted of drugging his clients on LSD. But Mexico expelled him, so he set up shop in Antigua and then Dominica, two British possessions from which Her Majesty quickly deported him. Stripped of flock and altar, Leary would no doubt have disappeared into oblivion had rescue not arrived in the form of a twenty-seven-year-old millionaire, William Hitchcock. This banker, who liked to take LSD because it made his green dollars look red, gave Leary an estate in Millbrook, New York. So Leary became a potentate in a vast palace of sixty-four rooms, equipped with every convenience, set in the midst of acres of fields, forests, hills, plains, brooks, lakes, ponds, bridges, trails, a river, chalets, camping grounds, and a trailer.

The trailer served as residence for the Hindu community of Shri Ram Ashram, while the Gate House was headquarters for Arthur Kleps, High Priest of the New American Church. And the main house of sixty-four rooms—"Leary's Lair," as they called it in Millbrook—was home for thirty or so people and their six children, and the seat of Leary's Castalia Foundation for psychedelic research. Theory didn't get very far, but "practical application" bubbled on merrily, especially on weekends when the hosts and their guests carried out their "disinterested research" on the wings of LSD.

The community practiced a mélange of communism, vegetarianism, macrobioticism, and Christianized Hinduism. Oriental spiritualism floated in the air mingling with juniper incense and hashish smoke. The women, dressed in vivid saris, sailed like queens among disheveled men and their drugged dogs. Apparently LSD was given to seven-year-old children at Leary's Lair, and to a ginger-colored French poodle. On certain nights, Leary would wear a long white robe and would proceed, like a Druid, to consecrate marriages. I was fortunate enough to run into a hippie who had spent a season at Millbrook and who described to me the ceremony he attended: The couple, dressed in the Oriental manner, knelt near a fireplace and Leary sat down facing them. A turbaned Indian recited a poem in Hindi or Urdu. Then, after a pause, Leary took a candle, brought it close to the face of the bride, and asked, "Why do you want to get married?" "To have a child," she answered (nothing very psychedelic about that). Another pious pause, and then Leary brought the candle close to the face of the groom and asked, "Why do you want to get married?" "To turn on, tune in, and drop out."

In December, 1965, Leary was arrested in Laredo, Texas, for having illegally brought marijuana from Mexico into the United States, and in March, 1966, he was sentenced to ten years in prison, which he appealed. In April, 1966, his Millbrook castle was searched by the police, who found drugs in the bedrooms. Leary was arrested once again, and this time he could have received, as a previous offender, a maximum sentence of thirty years in prison and a $30,000 fine. Astonishingly enough, the high priest of LSD was prosecuted only for infraction of the marijuana laws, with no mention of the fact that he had given LSD to more than a thousand persons—a figure he proudly offered himself—including some 69 ministers of various persuasions, and for having taken it more than 300 times himself. But at that time LSD was a comparatively unknown chemical discovery, and it had not yet entered the register of forbidden drugs. It wasn't until February, 1966, that Congress passed a law declaring its manufacture, possession and sale illegal.

In April, 1966, a drop-out medical student was arrested in Brooklyn for cutting his mother-in-law's throat with a kitchen knife. He explained that "I've been flying high for three days on LSD." But this didn't stop Leary, in June, 1966, from singing the drug's praises to a colloquium on LSD in San Francisco. The prophet announced that two million doses would be distributed in California during June, 1966. He compared the LSD trip to a religious pilgrimage, the LSD upheavals to religious ecstasy, and the LSD panic to a spiritual crisis.

On September 19, 1966, Leary announced with great fanfare that he had founded a new religion: the League for Spiritual Discovery (LSD, for short). Leary hoped, with his League, that his legal appeal would succeed on the grounds that he was no longer a simple drug-pusher, but the high priest of a religion that incorporated the drug into its sacred rites. The next day, September 20, he celebrated the first public service of his new religion in a large New York theater. On September 23, the charges against Leary stemming from his second arrest the preceding April were dropped. American justice was caught in the trap of drug-as-sacrament. The announcement that the charges had been dropped raised a storm of indignation, but it was a triumph for his followers.

Leary was arrested a third time, on October 12, 1966, for having carried drugs from Canada, but he was released once again. The hippie press had so successfully created an aura of sainthood around this new Messiah, that the police simply didn't dare to lay hands on this man who, feeding on his own madness, described himself as a mystic, an alchemist, a guru, and the great prophet of the century.

Leary was in no way chastened by his various brushes with the law. He continued to conduct the rites of his church, which incorporated Indian ragas, Papuan laments, guitars, trumpets, tom-toms, jazz, blues, rock, and Wagnerian choirs. Converts in San Francisco had 20,000 membership cards for the League printed up, and proposed to distribute them throughout the country, but Leary was afraid that this kind of publicity would attract damage suits by people who had been injured physically or mentally by LSD. He stuck to his single church in New York, recommending, however, that his followers set up their own churches all over the country. On this advice, Leary's disciple Arthur Kleps founded the New American Church in Florida. The "host" of the cult, Leary has written, has both its legal and psychedelic justifications. Psychedelically speaking, an LSD trip is more enriching when you concentrate on something beautiful, like God. And legally, when a police officer arrests a member of a religious community for taking LSD, he can plead that he was practicing the organized rituals of his religion (*Los Angeles Free Press*, December 16, 1966). Leary counsels each hippie community to retain a lawyer, and to file a request to create such a church.

But the winds have turned. On March 16, 1967, Dr. Marmon Cohen and two other physicians demonstrated irrefutably that LSD causes the brain cells to deteriorate and damages the chromosomes. There is a definite danger that regular use will induce schizophrenia or that a woman will bear deformed children. Dr. Cohen has demanded that the authorities take urgent measures against this poison. It was a lightning bolt. Public opinion waxed furiously against the least step, gesture, or word of Leary. The winds of panic blew through families, who ran to seek out their runaway children in the hippie ghettos of New York, San Francisco, or Los Angeles. Even Leary's partisans were shaken. Only Leary himself, imperturbable, continued his proselytism for acid. He declared at a press conference, not without a certain deliberate provocativeness, that "the only truly dangerous drugs are nicotine, alcohol, and tranquillizers." Some allies in strange quarters came to his aid. A Dr. Ditman, a professor at the University of California, affirmed in the *New York Times* of March 17, 1967, that LSD "is a very valuable tool in the fight against alcoholism, with no dangerous side effects." A biochemist, Alfred Prince, maintained that Dr. Cohen had made his accusations without proof, whereas he in turn was accused of having done no research. Passions were unleashed. Throughout the land no one talked of anything but hippies, marijuana and LSD.

Dr. Cohen's assertions were, alas, only too true. Full page microphotos of LSD-damaged chromosomes broke all over the country. It was Leary's fall from grace, helped by Dr. Donald Louria's revelations in the *Washington Post* that, in the last 18 months, 130 LSD trippers had been brought to Bellevue Hospital in a sorry state. Dr. Duke Fisher stated that the majority of LSD users were college and high school students. It was learned that children fourteen years old, under the drug, believing they could fly, had thrown themselves from windows to crash on the ground below. These betwitched children, enchanted by a poisonous potion, had to be saved.

On April 8, 1967, a survey conducted at Princeton gave substance to Dr. Fisher's statements: 15 percent of the students at that university acknowledged having taken the drug. But how many did not acknowledge it? In the state colleges in the San Francisco area, more than 35 percent of the students openly admitted to having experimented with the drug, and meanwhile, the number of runaways kept mounting. The police marshalled their resources to find these young fugitives, first doubling, then tripling, then quadrupling their forces. The Beatles, who by singing the praises of LSD, had done much to popularize it, decided to abandon drugs and seek ecstasy through Yoga. Meanwhile, every day more and more hippies turned their backs on their erstwhile high priest; they had become afraid. There had been too many bad trips, too many voyages to hell.

Leary's back was to the wall, and he could only repeat his contention—a cliché by now—that no legal institution could control a person's right to his own nervous system, any more than the state could regulate virginity. But in vain. By the beginning of 1968, Leary's star had faded. He stood accused, through his own words, of frivolity, irresponsibility, and megalomania. People remembered that even though the hippie press had suggested doses limited to 250 micrograms per trip, Leary early on counseled doses of 500 micrograms. Leary casually said one day to a reporter, "I hope no one has taken me too seriously." "Well no, I haven't," the journalist replied, "but I don't know what the thousands of boys and girls who have left everything behind for you would say to that, Uncle Tim."

And some of them are dead.

In March, 1970, a Federal court upheld Leary's initial conviction for carrying marijuana from Mexico to Texas, and sustained as well the ten-year sentence he had received. He had hidden the grass, by the way, in a snuffbox tucked into his daughter's underclothes. The Federal judge in Houston declared that Leary was a "menace to society." Handcuffs around his wrists, he was brought to a prison in Santa Ana, California, to await sentencing on another drug charge, and the sky has neither fallen on his judges' heads, nor has Texas erupted into civil disorder. Leary's day was over.

But perhaps Leary's madness had a method in't. Richard Goldstein, the young *Village Voice* critic, expressed strong distaste for the spectacle of Leary-as-merchandise:

> Timothy Leary's prose comes out in mass-circulation magazines about two times a week on average. His records are sold all over the country. He has written introductions to books on drugs the way the Japanese produce tin Statues of Liberty. His press conferences were held in the best clubs. Now he runs a church in the second largest theatre in New York. On Tuesdays, he organizes nighttime fun and games. His shows, with lines that any promoter would be proud of, tour the country at $5 a ticket. The networks spend half their time interviewing him—pure gold in his pocket. His "testimonials" are everywhere, he organizes his "acid culture weeks," and his books sell like there's no tomorrow. Madison Avenue has capitalized on the hippie style. Acid art has edged out pop art. All of which means that, up to and including "psychedelicious candy stores," Leary's enterprises have attracted massive publicity. His Castalia Foundation at Millbrook had been registered as a nonprofit organization and paid not one penny of taxes on all its revenues and donations. Leary is a tax-free rich man. The time has come for this guru to draw the line between revelation and commercialization.

So, treason was in the air, the fall was imminent. The psychedelic religion of Timothy Leary would die, like so many others before it, because the moneychangers were not driven from the temple of the Castalia Foundation.

4

A Kaleidoscope of Drugs

From earliest times men have known of, and absorbed, substances that induce strange, captivating, or fearful psychic states that transcend the senses' normal limits. These substances, called "drugs," can be divided into three major classes: the hallucinogens, which will evoke visions that may or may not be based on reality; the stimulants, which, though they may also provoke hallucinations at very high doses, mainly serve to spur physical and mental energies; and the calmatives, whose essential function is to relieve the anguish of the human condition and slip the user into a state of waking dream. (This is an especially important chapter for parents.)

THE HALLUCINOGENS

Hashish and Marijuana

Marijuana, called "grass" or "pot" in the argot, is the ground-up leaf and flower of a hemp plant that grows in hot countries, whereas hashish is the resin, and therefore more concentrated, of that same plant. The active substance in both marijuana and hashish is an alcohol called cannabinol (from *cannabis*, the Latin name for the hemp plant). Today this substance is produced synthetically, under the name "Delta 9." Hashish contains two to three times more cannabinol than marijuana, and the intensity of its effects is therefore two or three times stronger.

Hashish and marijuana reach the wholesaler in the form of flat, brownish cakes with a penetrating odor of leather, earth, and musk. The wholesaler breaks up the cakes and mixes them with ordinary tobacco, ready for smoking in cigarette or pipe. They can also be dissolved in drinks or baked into cookies or, very popularly, brownies.

Four or five "tokes" on a "joint" will send the smoker off into a euphoric paradise.

The hemp plants cultivated in very hot countries—India, Mexico, Morocco, etc.—are the richest in cannabinol. Nothing easier than to cultivate this hemp and, beginning with the raw resin exuded from the female flowers, to extract the "poison of delight." Even fans in the cities can grow the plant on their balconies or in kitchen gardens. There are clandestine plantations in France. This ease of cultivation and extraction explain the low price of marijuana, the "poor man's opium." In France, one joint, which can "send off" a half dozen people, costs no more than 60¢, and many hosts now offer marijuana to their guests along with the peanuts and potato chips.

Hashish is the most ancient drug still in current use. In 2130 B.C. the Chinese emperor Shen Nung described in detail, in a pharmaceutical treatise, the culture of the plant and its effects. In the true spirit of science, however, he *proscribed* its usage "to induce false happiness," while he *prescribed* it in minute doses to combat rheumatism, malaria, constipation, and "women's troubles." The Chinese by and large followed the wise counsels of their emperor, but the Hindus absorbed the "poison of delight" in great quantities.

Cannabis consumption spread quickly throughout the Orient, and the *Thousand and One Nights* is filled with references to "hashish eaters." The famous Hassan-Ibn-Sabbah, whom the first Crusaders called "The Old Man of the Mountains," fed it in enormous amounts to the young men he employed to secretly kill all his enemies. The appellation "hashishin," or "taker of hashish," that was applied to these young killers is the origin of our word "assassin." The Crusaders introduced the drug into Europe, along with the word "assassin." The Indians of Mexico, where the plant also grows profusely, discovered the drug independently and smoked it well before the arrival of Christopher Columbus. It was the invading Spaniards who gave it the name "marijuana."

What are the effects of hashish on the body and the mind? It is important, in this case as in all the other drugs we shall discuss, to distinguish between short-term and long-term effects.

The short-term effects have two phases: first a period of euphoria, and then the somnolent stage. During the euphoric stage, which can last two hours, the smoker is exalted, gay, talkative, though his words may be, but are not always, disjointed. He laughs for no reason, his pupils dilate, and later he becomes very hungry and very thirsty, but he often cannot work up the ambition actually to go get himself something to eat or drink. For, differently from alcohol, cannabis infuses the mind with an energy that cannot be translated into action. The smoker rapidly loses his sense of time, but he has the impression that his senses have become sharply acute, and that he can perceive things with extraordinary sensitivity. "The eyes," Baudelaire has written in his *Paradis Artificiels*,

> can see into infinity. The ear can perceive sounds, in the midst of however great a tumult, that are ordinarily almost indistinguishable. The objects around one slowly, successively, take on singular appearances. Then come the transpositions. Sounds turn to colors, and colors contain music. A very common sensation to the hashish-smoker is to *identify himself with the objects.* You are the tree, the bird, the wall. By a curious kind of substitution, you will feel yourself evaporating and it seems as if the pipe, in which you are gathered together and packed down like tobacco, *is smoking you.*

After two hours or so, the mental excitation dies down and the drugged person enters into a vague, troubled, often sad state of consciousness, marked by the abdiction of all will and the confusion of forms and distances. In the United States, more and more motor accidents are due to people driving in this latter stage of the drug process. "But the day after," Baudelaire writes,

> the terrible day after! All muscles weak, tired, the nerves stretched almost to breaking, a nervous wish to cry, the impossibility of applying oneself to any concentrated work; you learn cruelly that you have played a forbidden game. Your hideous surroundings, stripped of the illuminations of the night before, have the look of the melancholy debris from a party.

But above all, there are the terrible effects of the day after the next day—the long-term effects. It is true, as its defenders affirm, that hashish leaves no demonstrable organic changes. But what becomes of the regular smoker after several years? Alcohol also wreaks no visible change in the body after ten or twenty bouts of drunkenness. Yet, drop by drop, in secret, the way water forms stalactites in caves, after years, alcohol ends by ravaging the body and annihilating the mental faculties. In this long-term sense, cannabis can be even more destructive than alcohol. Several years of *regular* use will suffice to dissolve the will into a state of permanent lethargy. And, Baudelaire remarks, "can it be said that a man who is totally unsuited to action is 'well,' even though his body shows no apparent damage?" And who can say that the brain remains intact? There have hardly been any microcellular autopsies done on long-term hashish smokers, but it is common knowledge that their memories fade.

Prolonged use of marijuana and, particularly, hashish, destroys the ability to take action and, besides that, it renders the person asocial, irritable, violent, and sometimes murderous. Hassan-Ibn-Sabbah's "assassins" became assassins under the repeated influence of the drug. And the band of hippies, mesmerized by Charles Manson, who carried out the absurd and hellish butchery of Sharon Tate and six of her guests in her Beverly Hills villa, were hashish smokers. The outbursts of rage, assault, rape, suicide, and other crimes committed by beings who had once seemed reasonably stable can no longer be reckoned up.

The abuse of cannabis also causes chronic bronchitis, asthma, and hypoglycemia, an abnormal lowering of the blood sugar level. The drug is not addictive—or, as the specialists say, it does not give rise to physical dependence—in the sense that the body of a marijuana smoker suffers no ill effects if he stops using the drug. But it is difficult to stop because he is caught in the psychic need that he feels. One can say, therefore, that he falls into "psychic dependence." And besides that, once the door has been opened, the user may be led to experiment with other, stronger, more dangerous toxic substances.

Peyote and Mescaline

Peyote is a small Mexican cactus whose seeds, dried and ground to powder, form a hallucinogenic drug used for centuries by the Indians to bring on religious ecstasies. Some Indian religious groups use it as part of their rituals. The active substance in peyote is mescaline, a powerful alkaloid that can now be synthesized. It is sold as a powder, as pills, or in solution. As it is very bitter, it is taken with highly sugared tea or coffee, or fruit juice, or gulped down in pill form. The peyote trip to ecstasy costs considerably more than hashish or marijuana: somewhere between $4 and $6 a trip.

Mescaline is the "intellectual" drug. It had especially seduced the English novelist Aldous Huxley whose descriptions of its effects, in his book *The Doors of Perception*, played a crucial role in infatuating artists and writers with this drug. According to Huxley, peyote's short-term effect is a trip of four to eight hours to the beyond of consciousness, during which, in his words, "I was seeing what Adam had seen on the morning of his creation—the miracle—moment by moment—of naked existence." There is some hallucination; one sees geometric forms, draperies, and magical architectures evolve in fairyland colors on one's interior screen. But this is not the essential thing. The essential thing is that one discovers that the objects that surround him have a texture, a weight, a coloration, a vibration, that so-called "normal" perception hardly suspects, and which give the universe "the glory of absolute beauty and the beauty of absolute glory." (I must say that I experienced this glory myself, without hallucinogens, when I faced the Himalayas and the Andes.) "Above all," Huxley wrote, "the colors hold you in fascinated silence for long minutes." If your companions speak to you, you can answer coherently, but you prefer to be silent and regard the nail of your big toe, which becomes the jewel and the emblem of "surreality." Huxley recognized that the mind, in the case of mescaline as well as cannabis, becomes incapable of any positive concrete activity. And the spatial senses (distance, volume, sequence, etc.) become disturbed and are in some sense displaced by the enormous weight of the "naked existence" of each object.

The "coming down" is less distressing than with cannabis, and the return to normal sensations is akin to coming out of a sedative. The long-term effects are still little known, because peyote is in considerably less common use than the other drugs, and its adherents talk less about it. There seems, however, to be little doubt that here too systematic and prolonged usage will lead to a lowering of vital tone, and to grave psychic troubles, which may have something to do with the impassive mask of the American Indian.

Let us recall that peyote has played an important strategic role in the diffusion of hallucinogens in the United States, because the Supreme Court has authorized its usage among the Indian tribes, on the basis that peyote formed part of the traditional religious rites of these tribes. The hippies claim that what is allowed to one group cannot be withheld from another, and hence the startling growth of religious sects that we have discussed earlier.

The Sacred Mushroom and Psilocybin

Psilocybin is the active substance in a "sacred" mushroom indigenous to Mexico that produces effects analogous to those of peyote. This mushroom is eaten almost nowhere else but in Mexico, but its historic importance is secured through the fact that one of this species converted Professor Timothy Leary to his life of hallucination.

LSD

In 1935, a Dr. Hoffmann, a biochemist at the Sandoz Laboratories in Basle, Switzerland, was experimenting with ergot, a dark-red mushroom that lived as a parasite on rye, and had almost decimated the rye crop during one particularly humid summer. He extracted a substance from that mushroom which he recognized as lysergic acid and, to study its polymerization, he mixed it with another substance, diethylamine. He gave the name Lyserg Saure ("acid" in German) Diethylamine to this combination, or LSD for short. Then other work claimed him, he pushed his mixture into a cupboard, and came upon it again five years later. Not remembering precisely what the liquid was, he tasted a drop on his finger, as chemists will do. A half hour later, bicycling back home, he fell into extraordinary visions, "mad and sublime." "Any sound, that of a passing automobile for example, induced images and colors in me that corresponded to it, while they changed ceaselessly like a kaleidoscope." Thus was born the most astonishing and most dangerous hallucinogen of our time.

Now LSD—which is absolutely odorless, colorless, and tasteless— is manufactured in pills or capsules that sell for $4 to $5 each. Each pill or capsule contains on the average 250 micrograms of lysergic acid, a sufficient quantity for a twelve- to fourteen-hour trip. Even though the price for one dose is low enough to permit very widespread use, LSD is, in relation to its weight, the most expensive substance in the world; one gram, containing 4000 doses of 250 micrograms each, is worth \$12,000 to \$16,000. The underground manufacturers of LSD do not sell in quantities of less than 500 doses at a time, with a 200 percent markup, and the retailers distribute the drug with another markup of 200 percent.

Since "acid" is undetectable to the senses, one person can administer it to an unsuspecting victim in, say, a glass of water. Or some hippies, as a little graciousness to a friend, will send an "acid letter;" that is, they will put a little on the stamp and say at some point in the letter, "lick the stamp." The word "acid," once innocent enough, has taken on a new and formidable resonance in the United States.

The LSD trip can produce a limitless range of types of fantasy, but the most characteristic effect, on a "good" trip at any rate, is an incredible intensification of sensations. Not only do sounds take on color, but it feels as if a blindfold has been lifted from your eyes. Everything becomes more brilliant, more precise, weighted with infinite details of infinite significance. Translucent substances become gems that revolve while reflecting the most vivid, unexpected colors. One can discern each note, each chord, each vibration in a piece of music, whether it be Bach or the Beatles; one becomes Bach himself, one surpasses that, *one is oneself the music.* Pure energy itself seems perceptible, vibrant, and filled with color. The sense of touch becomes acutely sensitive, each pore of the skin senses each cold or hot droplet of the shower as if it were a sensual bullet. Hallucinations can even be tasted. The user's face is pale, going from calm to terrified in turn, happy or strained, at peace or anxious. The pupils are dilated, temperature and tension level high, and he trembles with cold or sweats with heat. Sometimes he feels that he is no longer in his body at all, and keeps his limbs in the same position for hours.

LSD brings subconscious states or drives to the surface, with a richness and intensity that are held to be more revealing than a hundred sessions of psychoanalysis. The user grasps the vanity of rules, the absurdity of constraints, the hypocrisy of the attitudes that the "straight world" adopts. The most mystic among them insist that they have seen God. Others tell of the incomparable ecstasies experienced during sexual intercourse under acid: "Every cell of your body," writes Timothy Leary, "makes love with every cell of your partner's body, during a whole night without intermission. . . ." LSD is clearly a virtual psychic atom bomb.

One of the characteristics of acid, unlike marijuana or peyote, is that its visions are unpredictable. Its devotees affirm that these trips are marvelous, indescribable, but all too often the tripper voyages into a land of horror filled with Dantesque hallucinations of hideous dead, spurts of blood, monsters, howls. The terrified "head" may, bursting with hysterical screams, run out into the street to save himself. LSD has provoked even more terrible events than hashish, including the dreadful affair of eighteen-year-old Linda Fitzpatrick, a rich little girl from Greenwich, Connecticut, who was found nude, with her hippie friend "Groovy," their heads savagely broken, on the cement floor of an East Village boiler room. The crime was committed during an LSD party by a man on a bad trip.

But the good trips can end tragically too. There are numerous cases of young people who, believing themselves to be great-winged birds, take off into the air from a building's upper story, only to crash down onto the pavement. Others disrobe and run nude through the streets. Still others, believing that their bodies have become spirit, have run out on to highways, and been crushed.

But, above all, it is the "morning after" that is devastating. Its long-term effects appear to be in direct proportion to the intensity of the hallucinations during the period of intoxication. There is no more "psychic dependence" than under mescaline or cannabis, but as noted before, it has been definitely established that LSD can damage the chromosomes. Timothy Leary himself has counseled pregnant women not to take the drug. The mental faculties can disintegrate to the point of incurable insanity, and the regular user can almost certainly look forward to chronic anxiety, instability, and schizoid tendencies.

The gurus, trying to temper the avidity of some of their young followers, recommend that no one set off on LSD without the constant support of a "guide." These guides are mostly hippies, experienced in handling drug reactions, who, like modern-day Florence Nightingales, generously and patiently stay with and help the tripper for twenty-four hours. Nonetheless, tragic accidents have multiplied to the point that the magazines that had most enthusiastically praised the marvels of the LSD paradise are beginning to change their tune, some even counseling that LSD be avoided completely. But four years of irresponsible publicity have already made their ravages among the credulous young.

Let us add that the dangers of LSD can directly menace the entire social fabric. About a quart of LSD poured into the water reservoirs of a city the size of Paris would throw the whole city out of commission for twelve hours, making the city easy prey for any kind of invader.

STIMULANTS

Amphetamines

The amphetamines, chemical products whose principal immediate effect is to whip up the physical and mental energies while deadening the appetite, are well known in their relatively benign common forms as euphoriants, stimulants, "pick-me-ups," etc. This is the pill, available at any drugstore, that a student will take before an exam to enable him to study all night and then perform at top level the next day, or an athlete will take one for an extra lift before the big game. In fact, these stimulants do not so much increase energy as they suppress fatigue, which is very dangerous for the body in that brain or muscle fatigue is the body's alarm signal indicating that rest is necessary, if the cells are not to become, in a sense, poisoned. To systematically suppress this defense is to poison the organism irremediably. Indeed, in experiments, dogs that have been kept from sleep for four consecutive days die. Under amphetamines, the unconsciousness of fatigue together with the loss of appetite lead the subject to exhaust himself for days without sleep or nourishment. He wastes away rapidly and will die unless sleep—the body's final line of defense—just overcomes him like lead after about the third or fourth sleepless day.

With a stronger dose than ordinary of the drug, one crosses the line from "stimulation" to "drug-taking" strictly speaking. Among the amphetamines, the current favorite is "methedrine," called "speed" in the argot, or "meth," or "crystal," from its crystalline appearance. Benzedrine and Dexedrine are also in favor, along with other variants of the amphetamine family. Methedrine is called "speed" because it acts so much faster than the relatively slow-acting hallucinogens. Also, the amphetamines are extremely cheap, one dose costing perhaps 40 cents. This is the drug-of-choice for the "plastic hippies"—the ones who play at liberation on weekends—and also for musicians who have to perform every night. Most true hippies, who confine themselves to hashish or LSD, refer to the amphetamine-takers, derogatorily, as "speed freaks." But even some of the real hippies will "pop" an amphetamine pill as a kind of appetizer to the main course, the true hallucinogens. By priming themselves with "speed," which does indeed speed up all reactions, they can enter into hallucinogenic glory immediately after taking the LSD or whatever, without marking time through the ordinary half-hour to hour waiting period. But even the hippiest journals counsel against this dangerous recipe.

Amphetamines at very high doses provoke strange, fleeting, uncoordinated—but always violent—visions connected to the user's physical and mental state at that moment. These are not true hallucinogenic trips. Usually one form will impose itself arbitrarily over another without rhyme or reason. The user can't stop talking, like certain drunkards. He feels invigorated with unexpected power—above all, sexual power. Indeed, some drugs, in high doses, will induce orgasm without sexual contact. These several hours of super-intensity and super-power are usually followed by long hours of depression during which the user will say, write, or hear the same things a hundred times. Ordinarily an amphetamine trip has more to do with violent sensation than with visions, leading quickly to physical exhaustion, though only rarely does the trip become filled with terror in the LSD manner.

The immediate effect—which can last two or three days—is, in the great majority of cases, euphoric—"groovy," as the hippies say—especially in the high that immediately follows absorption. The long-term effects can be even graver than with LSD. The amphetamines are not physically addictive, but they can provoke an irrepressible desire for a constant flow of new experiences. One great danger is that the subject, becoming very "nervy," seeks to calm himself through narcotics, and turns toward heroin. Prolonged usage of "speed" provokes delusions of persecution which lead to permanent paranoia, and weaken the muscles to a state that can be treated only in a hospital. Brain cell damage occurs, and the metabolism breaks down. The amphetamines, particularly if absorbed by direct injection into the bloodstream, are the serpent's apple in the psychedelic Eden. Even hippies sometimes wear buttons saying "Speed Kills."

One hippie guru wrote in the *Oracle*: "For the last two years, meth has carried my spirit up to paradise, while it destroyed my body." Yes, speed kills, even faster than heroin.

THE MAXI-DRUGS

During the last few years, new and more and more powerful drugs, of unknown composition, have been reaching the drug public. Only recently did analysts discover that they are, for the most part, an explosive mixture of hallucinogens and stimulants.

One of them, DMT (dimethyltryptamine), which exists in a natural state in certain West Indian plants, was easily synthesized. It produces, grossly magnified, the effects of LSD and methedrine *combined*, but with a fantastic blinding intensity that lasts no longer than half an hour.

STP, or DOM (methyl 34 dimethoxy-phenyl-alpha-methyl-ethylamine) combines mescaline with an amphetamine. It is called STP in homage to a commercial gasoline additive; like the original STP, the drug "puts a tiger in your tank." Under its real name, DOM, the drug has been used to treat certain mental illnesses, but somehow it seeped out from the secret vaults of respectable pharmaceutical houses into the underground. Five to ten thousand capsules were distributed free during a great San Francisco "love-in." DOM trips—some of which are "super-Biblical," but most of which are hellish, filled with death and agonies, though always in living color and always marked by "the direct communion of the person with things"—can last several days. I have read descriptions of DOM trips that made my hair stand on end.

Ten DOM trips are quite enough to send a person to a hospital forever, a human wreck. The first few cases to come to a hospital were treated with chlorpromazine, a common antidote to regular LSD bad trips, since the doctors did not know they were dealing with something different, and the results were ghastly. The chlorpromazine aggravated, sometimes mortally, the "explosions" in the brain. The hippie gurus have publicly rejected the use of DMT and DOM.

THE MINI-DRUGS

As there are maxi-drugs, so there are mini-drugs, with which the very young initiates generally take their first steps into the hazy world. The formulas for numerous mini-drugs circulate in their more-or-less clandestine press.

They very often begin with belladonna, which can be bought at any drugstore. The Italian ladies of the Renaissance—that is, the "donna"—used to put some of this substance in their eyes so as to make their eyes more beautiful—"bella"—by dilating the pupils. The hippies have discovered that this ancestral elixir, taken on an empty stomach, produces the sensations of which they are so fond. However, if the drug is used regularly with constantly increasing dose, it will lead eventually to madness and death.

Dried and ground banana skin is totally inoffensive, for the good reason that it contains no drugs. But it also produces no ecstasy, except perhaps through autosuggestion. This has not stopped the hippie press from working up a whole publicity campaign about it to make the kids believe that they have entered the precious and forbidden kingdom of drugs, and to inspire them to penetrate it more deeply.

Freon gas, used to fill up balloons, procures a very satisfactory range of drunken vertigo, followed by an agreeable kind of swooning. The hippie press recommends it for children from ten to fifteen years. During the great hippie gatherings, ballon sellers distributed free bottles of pressurized gas to people standing in line. They would take several sniffs, lie on the grass for a few minutes until the delicious swoon had passed, and then go back to stand in line. One child, eight years old, died in Central Park from the excessive expansion and chilling this gas caused in his small lungs.

Other delights can be found by sniffing some brands of model airplane glue, insecticides, lighter fluid, ether, household products like naphtha, and amyl nitrite, found in every drugstore as an asthma remedy, no prescription needed, about 20 cents a tube. You break the tube, breathe deeply, and take off on a ten-minute trip filled with undulating iridescent forms, and even accompanying music. After which, your head starts to spin, and you slump to the ground to recuperate.

NARCOTICS

Narcotic drugs include the barbiturates, the opiates, and cocaine.

Barbiturates

The barbiturates, hypnotics and calmatives of the nervous system, are the active ingredient in sleeping pills. They are made up in yellow or red capsules, from whence the name "yellow jackets" or "red jackets." At the medical dose, they can be found in all drugstores at a very low price, sometimes without a prescription. But even if a prescription is needed, most people who want barbiturates can find a prescription somewhere, even if they have to write it up themselves. Barbiturates are often used, to ill effect, in combination with amphetamines or with alcohol to achieve a "high"—though I think "low" is actually the more appropriate term. Once a person has started taking barbiturates regularly, he can never stop; a physical addiction is created. Many fatal accidents or suicides have followed the consumption of these dangerous drugs.

The Opiates

These drugs, of which the principal ones are opium, heroin, and morphine, have been so well known for centuries that there is no point in discussing them at great length.

Opium, an extract from the opium poppy, is smoked, while its derivatives, heroin and morphine, are powders that are dissolved and then injected into the bloodstream. These drugs are very expensive, though the price has gone down in recent years, ever since China and Turkey threw massive amounts onto the world black market. Even so, one dose costs anywhere from $10 to $16. The opiates induce such a grave physical dependence that, if the user does try to go off the drug, he suffers atrociously and goes into convulsions that can even lead to death. So disintoxication generally proceeds by reducing the doses little by little, under medical surveillance, like the "drying out" of an alcoholic. In general, a heroin addict can break the habit only by isolation and forced withdrawal. And of those who accept such a treatment, only around 15 percent are really cured.

At the beginning of the 19th century, the Englishman Thomas

de Quincy, a writer of great talent who had been addicted to opium for some twenty years, wrote his *Confessions of an English Opium Eater*, an admirable description of the effects of opium, rich in human perception and almost scientific in its observations. One does not "trip" with opium. Its principal "virtue" is to dissipate all sense of anxiety, of guilt, or of inferiority, and to plunge the smoker into a "divine" calm of the mind and of the senses, a long delicious reverie in which one sees the beings and the places that one knows in a new light, haloed with wisdom, with charity, with sweetness. Certain reveries are sad, filled with funereal scenes, nostalgic returns to the past, but this never degernates into scenes of horror. The opium addict, over the long term, retains his ability to think, but only in a poetic and contemplative fashion. He can do no creative work, he becomes incapable of analytic or deductive thought, he totally loses the power and the taste to undertake whatever might be. Most historians agree that widespread use of opium is at the root of the centuries-long slumber of Chinese civilization.

Cocaine

Cocaine is an alkaloid extract from the coca leaf, a shrub that grows in the Andes. It is essentially a local anesthetic, an analgesic, and a calmative. Cocaine addicts, who are becoming more and more rare, rarely take "coke" by injection. Its immediate effect is a sensation of great well-being, but over the long term its dangers are even greater than those of opium: insomnia, tachycardia, loss of appetite, delirium, disappearance of the moral sense, dementia, suicidal, and homicidal drives. It is the pitiless betrayer-drug par excellence; you pay for the short sweetness it grants by the blackness that it leaves behind.

The hippies are afraid of cocaine, by and large, as they are of all the opiates. For the most part, these drugs are out of bounds for the hippie world, though there are a few people who can't break the terrible escalation into the addictive drugs; especially for those in search of a few moments of interior peace from the terrifying eruptions of the hallucinogens and stimulants. That is why, for the first time in history, use of these soporific drugs—heretofore reserved to adult fringe groups —is spreading out more and more widely among our educated youth.

A DRUG IS A DRUG IS A DRUG

We still don't know the exact physiological mechanisms that provoke these strange sensory and spiritual exaltations. The chances are that they modify the chemical makeup of the neurons of the brain, which we know are extraordinarily complex, subtle and sensitive, as well as the levels of sugar, carbonic gas, and other constituents of the blood. These distortions of the extremely delicate physiological equilibrium are sufficient to induce the bizarre hallucinations discussed in the preceding sections. But, without going further into the complex biology of it, one can disengage, by statistical observation alone, several traits that all the drugs have in common that justify classing them as more or less violent poisons.

First, the euphoria that they produce, the famous "artificial paradise," is always short and always has its price, in the long run, with the corrosion and disorganization of the body.

Next, the regular user almost always grows dependent on his drug —whether physically or emotionally—to a point of tyrannical passion that dominates the individual in every area of his life.

Above all, all the drugs, in the long run, sap the will and the power to reason—the two principal pillars of all civilization—to the point of destroying them. If there is no power positively to reflect upon the universe, and then will to act upon that reflection, there is no more creation, there is no more true culture; and if, as the hippies claim, drug use should become universal, there will be no more civilization.

5

The Hashish Trail

Ever since the Western countries have begun cracking down on hashish and its users, the hippies have started to emigrate en masse toward the countries that accept their curious ways with more equanimity. The Americans and Canadians take the highway to Mexico where marijuana appears on every street corner. Then, since they are affluent —even though hippies—they cross the Atlantic and join their European counterparts who have themselves begun to follow the golden way of cannabis. There are two principal paths: one takes the traveler across the Mediterranean to North Africa, especially to Morocco, where marijuana is called "kif," and the other goes through Eastern Europe to Turkey—a difficult passage—and then on to Afghanistan, the haven of felicity for the lovers of "ganja," cannabis' name in the Near East. But their guiding star, the source of all well-being, is India, where "Indian hemp" has been known as the source of happiness under the name "bhang" for centuries. Recently, however, when the Indian authorities began to block this emigration of longhairs, the star swerved on its path toward the little kingdom of Nepal, the only country in the world where restaurants offer cannabis on their menus.

The Guiding Star: India

More than 100,000 American hippies have wandered into India so far, supplemented by their fellows from all over Europe, and from as far away as Australia and New Zealand. It has become a true diaspora.

Why do they gather at Benares on the banks of the Ganges, or at Delhi, or at Goa? Because India, for centuries, has been a land of hippiedom without even knowing it. This country, with its frozen caste system, has been the crucible par excellence of irrationality, the blessed land of indolence, of long manes blowing in the breeze, of mysticism, of prophets, anchorites, and other ascetics who, through their fasts, their self-lacerations, yoga and drugs, have made a guiding principle out of the release of the soul from the prison of the body—at least, that's what they've always said, and the hippies believe it. India is the fabulous world of the psychedelic jewels—emeralds and rubies—of the sandaled brahmins, of the gurus wrapped in sheets, and of the untouchables dressed in dirt thick as an elephant's hide. Each hippie has no trouble aligning himself with the caste of his choice, from the most verminous, if poverty is where his heart lies, to the most religious if he chooses mysticism.

In this universe where the profane mingles with the sacred, and where the sacred swims in fairyland, the hippies have unearthed an obscure sect, the Tantrics, in whom, with wonderment and pleasure, they see themselves mirrored best of all. The Tantrics were, in effect, the hippies of their day: they protested against the "materialism" of the 6th-century Hindu "establishment," they claimed complete sexual liberty for themselves, and recommended drugs as the way toward the heights of being. They "dropped out" of their "straight" world, seeking refuge in the Himalayas to live the life of their choice. This is why so many hippies run to Nepal to see the Tantrics' descendants, of whom they believe themselves to be the reincarnation.

The hippies go to India ostensibly in search of "Eternal Truth," but they do not, in reality, carry these particular researches very far. I have not very often seen them seated drinking in lessons at the feet of the wandering gurus or the Brahmin philosophers, or meditating at their sides. But I've seen a lot of them, on the other hand, sitting on the terrace of some café on Janpath Avenue watching the people go by, or stretched out on park lawns, dressed like coolies in costumes of a heavy yellowish cotton that was once white, drinking in the sun like lizards. In fact, the real hippie Grail is the sun, the star of indolence, the Supreme Philosopher, always inspiring, helpful and hospitable. Thanks to the sun, one can live on love and cool water, without shoes or coats, with a loincloth around the hips and a few handfuls of grains or fruit. The most recent wave of hippies has headed for Goa, the old Portuguese colony, with its beach of Calanguta, one of the most exquisite and peaceful in all India. The other beaches are battered by monumental, and often dangerous, waves. At Goa, one can sleep for nothing in the soft, downy mattress of golden sand, in the dappled shade of the palm trees, and live on fruit plucked from the trees.

But this enchanting beach has also been the scene for hippie tragedies. I saw one myself: a tragicomedy. Two long-haired Swiss had lent $150 to two French flower-children, on their statement that money from home would be arriving any day. The French boys quickly ran through the money, lavishing it on food and "grass," and, the money from home never showing up, they had decamped without notice. The Swiss boys ran into them by accident and thrashed them so vigorously that the police had to intervene. On this occasion, the police discovered that the Swiss were carrying revolvers, heroin, and hypodermic needles, and they promptly found themselves behind bars, while the French boys, back on the sand in the sun, drank their health.

The hippies come to India also because it is a very appealing country in spite of, or perhaps because of, its poverty and squalor. It is so easy to share when one has nothing. It is easier to spend a sleeping-bag night on the floor of a poor Sikh's overcrowded room, than in the apartment left vacant by a rich Londoner on vacation. Consider also this major point: India is the only country in the world where one can live without paying for any lodging. This is always the most onerous expense for an impecunious traveler. One can, in effect, sleep for free in the Hindu temples, or in the Moslem mosques, in the public gardens, or in doorways, or even, like everyone else, on the sidewalks. In Calcutta, there are one million Hindus who are born, live and die in the streets, even during the torrential rains of the monsoon. What's a few thousand hippies more or less?

In certain areas in the south, the hippies live in caves like troglodytes, or like the Buddhist monks of the Middle Ages who transformed the grottos of Ajunta and Allora into little museums, with frescos, colonnades, statues, and rooms carved right out of the rock. But the hippies have not marked their passage with works of art to delight their posterity. I am afraid that tin cans will remain the sign that "hippies were here."

Finally, the hippies can spend the night in free shelters that are available to the religious pilgrims, shelters without water or electricity, where men and women lie side by side on the floor, but at least protected from the frost.

The Great Turkish Waterloo

However, comparatively few of those who launch themselves along the hashish trail actually reach India. They drop off or get mislaid en route. The way is long and full of pitfalls for these child-men who set out for unknown lands, paying heed neither to the season of the year, nor to stopping-off places, nor to their wallets.

In November, 1969, preparing to set off for a trip around the world, I spent considerable time at the Institut Pasteur for vaccinations, and at various embassies applying for visas. At all of these places I ran into a considerably larger number of hippies than in preceding years. I spoke to them in English, since all the hippies I had known of had been American. But when their faces turned blankly toward me, I realized that they were French, and not just from Paris, but from the provinces. Everyone was pilgrimaging to India by thumb.

One young man from Corsica had set out all alone on his great adventure with his entire worldly goods—$160—in his pocket, a beautiful brown head of Louis XIV-style hair, and dreams of ecstasy in his pipe. He had no map, was completely unfamiliar with the route, and winter was beginning. Another traveler, waiting, along with the hippies and me, for his visa to Afghanistan, remarked that the Turkish highways would be filled with snow, often impassable, that the boy would be in grave danger from cold and hunger, and that he would do better to wait until spring. But no, our Corsican, strongheaded as his fellow-countryman Napoleon, would leave right away should hell (not to mention himself) freeze over, magnetized like an ancient Crusader by the call of an irrepressible faith. His shepherd's star was Benares and its gurus who sit, immobile, on the banks of the Ganges, lost in an interior floating that they call "meditation." But the Indian government—socialist though it may be—had tried to stem the tide of penniless tourists by ordering that no one be granted a visa unless he possessed a round-trip airplane ticket. So the young Corsican had come to ask for a visa to Afghanistan, a more open country, from where he planned to cross over into India in some illegal way.

So the new pilgrims of hashish leave from San Francisco, from Quebec, London, Paris, Munich, Amsterdam, Stockholm, etc., for the country of the wise men. They cross through Yugoslavia and through Greece, but 70 percent of them never get through Turkey, their Waterloo. The hippies arrive in Istanbul at the end of their resources; their little nest egg dribbled away faster than they could have imagined on little nothings, "parties," and drugs, which are still expensive in Europe. So they collect their remaining pennies and blow it all on a cablegram begging money from their parents. But often the money doesn't come right away, they get into debt, and go to ask help from their consulate which offers to send them back home. These are the cases where all's well that ends well. But the other hippies, the ones who still have money, are swindled, robbed, even killed by the Turkish thieves; the girls too, but not until they have been raped. The classic strategy is to graciously offer the hippie a drug, and then while he's stoned, to relieve him of everything he has.

One flower-child from the south of France, whom I met in Kabul, Afghanistan, recollected his trip through Turkey as if it were a nightmare. He had hitchhiked there, as elsewhere; and as fewer and fewer respectable travelers were willing to pick up someone in filthy clothes and hangdog look—a look that wandering hippies acquire quickly—he had managed to flag down an occasional truck. The truckdrivers, by and large, welcomed him as a diversion from the weary monotone of miles, and he only had to stand them to a round of drinks to be even. But in Turkey, things didn't take such a sociable turn. The truck drivers demanded that he pay them a fare but the French boy, so nearsighted that you could hardly see his eyes through his glasses, answered that he didn't have a cent. So the two Turks seized him, beat him up, searched him and finding, indeed, no money, had to be satisfied with his knapsack and wristwatch. But it was his knapsack he missed— hippies aren't interested in what time it is. "Six Eyes" (six instead of four, because his glasses were so thick)—as he was called, applied for help at the French Embassy but they replied, harassed by thousands of hippies in dire straits in Turkey, that they were neither a charitable institution, nor a tourist agency, nor a placement office, nor a bank. Six Eyes swore that he would never set foot in Turkey again, but would head home through Iran, Iraq, and Syria, and from there he would ship on board some vessel as a cabin boy to get to Greece. But somehow he ended up in Kabul and there he stayed, waiting for a money order from France that never came. . . .

Afghanistan: First Stop on the Hashish Trail

Out of the 25 percent or so of hippies who make it through the Turkish ordeal of fire, only about a third of those actually arrive in the promised land. These are the happy members of the British Commonwealth—Britons, Canadians, Australians, New Zealanders—who need no visa to enter India. On foot, hitchhiking, by bus, they cross the immense deserts of Persia and Pakistan and, during that long march, a new contingent falls by the wayside, felled by fatigue, hunger, sickness, or drug overdose. When at last they reach the Temple of Gold in Amritsar or the tower of Kutb Minar in Delhi, supposed to be the most perfect in the world, all the germs they have been pleased to pick up en route have had plenty of time to ripen and multiply into magnificent hepatitises or dysenteries or syphilises. Some of the travelers, at the end of their long journey, ask to be repatriated; for some others, the grinding trip is just too much and they die; none of them take care of themselves. Barely half of the Commonwealth hippies who make it to India arrive safe, much less sound. As for the other drug pilgrims who cannot find the precious visa, they go back toward the snowy mountains of Afghanistan where they finally find a place to rest.

The capital of Afghanistan, Kabul, is their haven of peace, first of all because at last they have stopped traveling; next because, in spite of the cold—Kabul is 1800 meters above sea level—it is easier to live there than in Turkey or Iran because lodgings and food are cheaper, and drugs more plentiful. Let us not forget that drugs and long hair are the two badges of hippies, just as the cross and the sword were the Crusaders' badges. Now, in Afghanistan, hashish is semi-open. Contrary to the statement of the *New York Times*, which said that "Afghanistan has no law against the use or sale of the drug," this country is a party to the 1961 UN International Convention against drugs. Because of this, it cannot authorize either commerce in or consumption of hashish. To prove that the two cultures do not mix, I shall tell an incident that happened in the famous Keyber restaurant in Kabul—a huge cafeteria, where Afghans and hippies sit side by side.

My eye was drawn by an especially eccentric group of hippies wearing round felt hats that looked for all the world like chamberpots, and clad in the rags worn by all derelicts since the time of Hammurabi. I presented myself to them, saying that a hippie I had met in Katmandu had asked me to look for an English boy named X, to return some money to him that he owed. Right away they invited me to sit at their table, all of them saying amiably that they were the moneylender but none of them really expecting me to believe it, and offering me sections of oranges. The hippies never eat anything without sharing it with their neighbors, even if they don't know each other. I went up to the counter and came back with a plate of little cakes, which I put at the disposition of the community. Our friendship was sealed. It was at this table that I met "Six Eyes," the victim of the Turks. He practically exploded with the joy of being able to speak French at last. He did not have one more penny and had just joined the ranks of the fly-by-night hippies, picking up a grapefruit quarter here, a cake there, elsewhere a morsel of cheese or a piece of bread, and this kind of catch-as-catch-can arrangement had provided him with his necessaries for the past three weeks.

A Canadian boy with a lively eye, dressed like a pirate fallen on evil days, with a large cutlass that gave him a grim air dangling from his hip, asked me if I "had already smoked"; he was talking about hashish, of course, since he could not possibly mean anything else. When I answered no, he took a little chestnut-colored ball, resembling glazed glass, out of his pocket; he held the flame from his pocket lighter under it and pressed it with his fingers until the little ball crumbled into something like the consistency of large grains of dry sand. He mixed this "hash tobacco" up with regular tobacco, and rolled it all up into a cigarette. During this whole operation—I should say, this rite—all diversion ceased while the others regarded the whole thing with a religious attention. A whisper of communion passed around the table.

The Canadian lit up the cigarette, sucked in two large drags, and then began to circulate the "joint," beginning with me. I declined, explaining that I don't smoke anything, even regular cigarettes. He insisted, "Then at least just sniff up the smoke. Suck in hard." As a politeness to these people who had been gracious to me I did so, and then passed the cigarette to Six Eyes who inhaled, as fast as he could, four enormous draws; it wasn't until later that I understood that this was much more for the joy of packing in as much as he could of something that was free, than from the wish to get high. Six Eyes passed the cigarette on to a giant English boy, a sort of super-tramp, who gave it in his turn to a smaller English mini-tramp, and then on to an American affluent-tramp, who gave it to a Hollander with a beard and a beat-up guitar. So the joint came back again to the Canadian pirate, and then he handed it to me once again. This time, out of some mysterious premonition, I shipped it directly on to Six Eyes instead of fiddling with it and inhaling the smoke as before. No sooner had he brought the joint to his mouth than two waiters in the café threw themselves upon him, ripped the cigarette out of his hands, smelled it and shouted, "It's hashish! We're going to call the police!" They hauled him up by his shoulders, lifting him out of his chair, and pushed him out the door, without even giving him a chance to collect his goatskin jacket. Decidedly Six Eyes had been born under an unlucky star. He had been beaten by the Turks, and it was upon him that the Afghan wrath fell, when it wasn't even he who had made the cigarette!

I was surprised, and told these new-style vagabonds that I had just come back from Nepal, where hashish was open and, on the basis of articles I had read in the French and American press, I had believed that the same was true in Afghanistan. The Canadian pirate retorted mischievously, "If the waiters had come over a second earlier, it's you who would have been shipped off to jail; the joint was in your hands. . . ."

I broke out into a cold sweat. On the comfort scale, Afghan prisons hovered around absolute zero.

Forbidden Without Being Exactly Forbidden by the Grace of Allah

During the next few days, while meeting with members of the Afghan Ministry of Foreign Affairs and with the Minister of Information, I carefully avoided the Keyber incident, asking only whether hashish was in fact legal in Afghanistan. Both replied with a categorical "No."

However, I must admit that Afghans have a tendency to make flexible accommodations with the will of Allah. It is not permitted to take a drug in a public place, but vigilance is really so casual that I once saw, at another table at this same Keyber, a girl "shooting up"; that is, injecting something into her veins. And Six Eyes, who had been *definitively* barred from the Keyber forever, was back with a group of friends two days later. I noted especially that hashish and opium are consumed with complete freedom in all the rooms of all the little fleabag hotels where the police never come and there are no controls whatever. No matter who you are, no matter what time it is, anyone can walk into any one of these rooms during the twenty-four hours out of the twenty-four that the party goes on, just by turning the doorknob. The owner of the hotel, in order to check on how many beds have been taken and how much space there is left on the floor, will drop in from time to time, and each occupant will bring a crew of friends with him or receive visitors. There's a continual coming-and-going that considerably facilitated my investigations. I asked one hippie if he would show me his room, he pleasantly agreed, and we entered a room smothered in smoke and stuffed with people eating watermelons, sitting on the floor, playing guitars, and passing around a pipe whose bowl was swathed in a damp cloth.

Six Eyes took me to the room in the Hotel Fez where he had his little corner. It was so small that nothing else would fit in it but its three jammed-together beds. On two of the beds, two young Germans with long straight blond hair were stretched out languidly. They wore Oriental robes with three loops of beads around their necks, amulets and bracelets, and smoked a concoction of their own devising: a mixture of hashish, opium and aspirin, at the end of a tube two meters long which plunged into a retort half filled with perfumed water. It was the famous water pipe, or hookah. Their beardless, blue-eyed faces and their flamboyant attire contrasted oddly with something grave and asexual in their faces that made them look like hermaphrodites. They spoke very slowly and courteously, and seemed not at all disturbed by my intrusion. The room was filled with thick smoke for, in addition to their hookah, they were burning incense. It was metaphysical and unbreathable. I told them I had just come from Nepal, and one of them asked me if there were beautiful bazaars. "Oh, it's not the bazaars that make Nepal fascinating," I answered, "but its pagodas, its animal sacrifice, its population, so nonchalantly pagan, carrying out their business—like in the Middle Ages—on the temple steps." But this didn't seem to hold the attention of our languid hermaphrodites, who returned to their pipe, sucking in, at the same time, ecstasy and a small, dry tubercular cough. They explained to me that the smoke was passed through the water to rid it of irritants to the lungs. They very politely let me take a photo of them as they smoked. I will never forget their voices from beyond the tomb, their dragging speech, their beauty carved-in-stone, and their perfect civility.

In Afghanistan, then, drug consumption is for all practical purposes open in the hotel rooms, even the communal ones. As some rumors have it, the hotels are owned by important people whose profits are not to be disturbed. According to other rumors, the authorities' tolerance stems from the fact that, for centuries, the dervishes—one type of holy man—were hashish eaters, so that the Afghans, who are very much practicing Moslems, could hardly make a crime out of something that their own holy men found sacred.

I was told that there is a lucrative sideline attached to the drug traffic. Certain hippies had been approached on the streets by peddlers who would whisper that they could buy a large quantity of the drug at a nearby tavern for a very low price. The hippie would run there and buy enough to resell later when he had come to a country where hashish is much more expensive. But the peddler would keep the Customs Bureau up to date on his transactions, so that when his hippie customers tried to leave Afghanistan, the customs people would confiscate the drug and expel the offender from the country. So that way the peddler made a double profit: the money from the original sale, and an informer's fee from customs. It is clear that the juridical and moral drug situation in Afghanistan is a tangled web indeed.

The hashish available there is of excellent quality, which is to say that it is black and "breaks up right away." One gram costs about 2 cents, while in France the average charge is 50 cents—ten to twenty-five times more. A smoker doesn't need more than around five grams per day to keep himself perpetually stoned, a state that can be achieved in Afghanistan for the modest sum of 10 cents! The drug is readily available in the markets, grocery stores, and drug stores. Some druggists also carry on a lucrative sideline trade, without prescription, in opium, heroin, and fairly low quality brand-name amphetamines. So it's clear why the hippies have been flocking to Afghanistan as opposed, say, to surrounding countries like Lebanon, which has begun to punish drug traffickers more and more severely. In Turkey, one can be sentenced to thirty years in prison, or even be subject to capital punishment. While I was in Iran, a country that already counts some 200,000 drug users of various kinds among its population, the press announced that one drug dealer had been executed. So Afghanistan remains, along with Nepal, one of the rare drug sanctuaries.

Also, in 1968, a new law brought an end to the old system whereby all strangers had to be registered—a system that had effectively made Afghanistan as closed to the outside world as old Japan. Afghanistan decided to open its doors to attract tourists to this picturesque but little-known country with its Greco-Buddhist art, the two giant Buddhas sculptured out of rock, the Oriental bazaars, the feminine forms behind the midnight blue veils floating in the wind, the deserts on which Biblical camel caravans file ringed with overhanging mountains, the great Mosque so blue that one could almost believe it is heaven itself congealed in mosaics and arabesques. . . . And then, to the chagrin of the Tourist Office, the people who flocked through these newly opened doors were indigent hippies. A bed in a communal room costs them 30 cents a day; 20 cents to sleep on the floor, 15 cents if the hotel furnishes neither mattress nor cover. In a tavern, a meal of rice and mutton, not bad, costs 20 cents, a cup of tea included. Adding up all expenses, including drug money, a hippie can live in Kabul in reasonable comfort for $1 to $1.40 per day (a regular hotel room, in excellent accommodations, costs around $8 to $14 a day). But even so, this indigent tourism adds its bit to the Afghan Treasury, for no one knows how the hippies manage to do it, but they always find money to live. In fact, they do it so well that these enemies of the consumer society, in fact, consume more per capita than the average native. In comparison with the almost rocklike sobriety of the rather poor Afghans, the hippies must seem like lavish playboys.

Many Afghans are disturbed by the dangerous example these Western youths offer to their own young people. "The West," a director of the Ministry of Foreign Affairs, who spoke an elegant French, told me, "has always been the symbol of culture, of enterprise, of civility, of power, of artistic splendor for us. And now we have the children of this West in the streets of Kabul: dressed like tramps, stretched out on tables, begging in the streets, scornful of learning, spending full-time on drugs or, at best, guitars. We have the impression that the marrow of your civilization is rotting. Excuse me for speaking so frankly. The sons of our more prominent families have traditionally had only one aspiration: to go study in the brilliant West. Now they don't want to go any more, and besides, their families—in whom the traditions of good breeding, of order, and of respect for the traditional ways are still very much alive—agree that their children should not go off into your world of perdition. The hippies have turned our youth away from the West."

Beyond Misery: The Hotel Noor

One does not need much imagination to grasp the ambiance of a low-class hotel in a country so underdeveloped that there is neither railroad, nor public restrooms. I went to a neighboring hotel, the Bamyan, to visit the room of the Canadian pirate group I had met the evening before at the Keyber. There were five unmade beds covered in dirty sheets and, in the middle, a stove whose chimney pipe exited through a hole in the window. Wood has to be brought in from outside. The Canadian, he of the piercing eye, blew on the fire to get it started. the hippies from next door, who had no stove, came in to warm up. This made ten people in a room of sixty-five square feet. The two Britons— the maxi and the mini—were seated on their respective beds in their coats and tramp-style hats. The others hung around dreamily, leaving any initiative to the Canadian. After taking care of the fire, he prepared and passed around a pipe of hashish. I needed steel in my spine to refuse it: first, my urge finally to try it, to see what all the fuss was about, had begun to get the upper hand; and second, I wanted to seal the bonds of friendship by joining my friends in their ritual. But I held fast, and excused myself by saying that I had a cold. The two English boys coughed without stopping, but they didn't miss their turns on the pipe.

A hippie's first impulse is to proselytize for his drug. It is perhaps in this respect that the movement differs basically from classic drug use. In the old days, the drug takers, at least in the West, hid their vice out of shame, and besides, opium and heroin are expensive. But for today's hippies drugs are not a vice, but the doors of initiation into an enlarged interior life, and a badge of independence from "narrow-minded" laws. So drugs satisfy, at the same time, their metaphysical yearnings and their sense of rebellion. And since marijuana, LSD, and the amphetamines don't cost much, they can freely share these drugs among one another.

The Canadian brought me a grayish powder that he said was hashish. "Put it between your lower lip and your gum," he told me, "and let it melt. Come on, try it." I pulled back, he insisted, put a good quantity in the palm of my hand and said, "Okay then, just keep it in your hand, play with it, look at it, sniff it. You'll see, it's a groove." I was dubious, but I did study the powder, intrigued. It didn't look like hashish. Then the Canadian gave a quantity to the maxi-Briton who, as amenable as he was corpulent, set it right away in between his lower lip and his gum as ordered. I asked him what it was, but he shrugged his shoulders in ignorance.

I asked whether they were long-time friends, supposing, since they shared a room, that they had been traveling together for months. "For four days," he answered. And here he had just taken in a substance into his body offered by someone he hardly knew, coming from God-knew-where, containing God-knew-what, and hadn't even asked what it was! But I had found that this was one consistent characteristic of the hippies: they would offer themselves up for any experience, whatever effect it might have on the nervous system, the most delicate part of the body, and do it existentially, on the basis of a casual encounter with someone they did not know. The intimate entanglements between them gave them confidence, and they were credulous and curious as little children. The drug dealers profited from this openness by offering their roommates powdered heroin until they had been hooked. So they manufactured their own, very lucrative, clientele.

Suddenly someone knocked on the door and came in before anyone answered. It was the hotel manager, who asked how many empty beds were left. One, the hippies answered. Upon which a little Japanese prince charming, hardly sixteen years old, came in behind him. He had the smooth white skin of a young girl, his face framed by a mane of jet-black hair. He was thin in his skin-tight bluejeans, underneath his big cowboy hat ornamented with a lanyard that dangled under his chin. He sat down gently on the empty bed and smiled a circuit around the room with little mouse's teeth. They asked him the regular questions: Where did he come from? Where was he going? What did he do? He came from Tokyo, and was on his way to Switzerland by bus. That was sufficient information; now they could go back to the real matter at hand, their drug. The delicate Japanese boy undid the large leather belt that encircled his slender waist, and drew out a little wallet slipped in between his pants and his belly. Then he went out and came back an hour later with provisions, grapefruit, candy, bread, putting them on the ground at the disposition of everyone. He knew the customs.

Six Eyes threw himself on the food. Then the "ganja" cigarette made its circuit again, while the Canadian—who, someone whispered to me, was really an American AWOL traveling under a Canadian passport—offered to trade I don't know what in exchange for the ivories the little Japanese prince was carrying with him to sell in Switzerland.

On my return from a trip to Mazar-i-Sharif, I wanted to visit the Hotel Noor, which I had been told was an earthly Purgatory but, too nervous to go alone, I went to look for Six Eyes. I knocked on the door, a voice from beyond the tomb bade me enter, and I saw the two hermaphrodite Germans stretched out—perhaps they hadn't moved in the last two days? They explained to me, in voices somewhat more fogged than before, that the French boy had disappeared two days ago, and that the hotel manager had confiscated his possessions as he hadn't paid for the room (20 cents per day). While they were, as always, courteous, they seemed somewhat impatient this time. I understood that their opium/aspirin mixture had carried them into an advanced state of reverie, and I left. These two did not leave their rooms again; they had definitively drawn down the curtain between the world and themselves.

I found Six Eyes at the Keyber. He had—with the intention of scrounging something to eat—harpooned an Adonis with wavy brown hair, feet bare in spite of the cold weather except for light sandals, and an embroidered goatskin jacket. He was practically a neighbor, a French boy from Cannes, but as beautiful as Six Eyes—from Marseilles—was sickly. He came from a well-to-do home, whereas Six Eyes was the son of a laborer and a domestic. Six Eyes sought no other goal in life than fun with his buddies, whereas the boy from Cannes had some sense of the artist. I asked them both if they would go with me to the Noor. The hippies, who never have anything to do, always jump eagerly at any new little adventure. A taxi carried us to the Noor, while I thought about our approach. Should we ask for a room? My "straight" look would not give much support to our request. A hairy young man going back to his room at the hotel rescued us. I asked him to let us visit his room. Something new was happening in his life too . . . he agreed at once.

And they had spoken to me of Purgatory! As far as I could see, this was Hell itself. An absolutely bare room, no mattress, no blanket, no water, no dresser, no curtains, was occupied by six boys who kept going in and out. One of them, wearing a bright red felt hat that hid his face, crouched in front of a cylindrical stove, whose flames he stared at steadily through the open grate. A French boy, tall and strong, wearing a long mauve scarf that fell to his knees and a vicious look, played the flute while standing up against the wall. There was also an American from San Francisco, a Swedish boy with little bells around his wrists and ankles, a Chinese boy, and a Japanese from Tokyo. We chatted standing up since there was nothing to sit on, and in English. The room's only ornaments were the obscene frescos and drugged murals painted on the walls by hippies passing through.

I was going to take a photo when the big French boy in the mauve scarf stopped me. He had just come from nine months in a French prison for some drug affair, and didn't want anyone to recognize him. The Adonis from Cannes, in a confiding mood, let us know that he too had just come from two months in prison on the same charge.

I said to Mauve Scarf, "Your fairy godmother marijuana must have carried you into unnameable ecstasies, for you to have gone to prison for her. I would like you to describe for me as concretely as you can your experiences under the drug."

"It's impossible," he replied.

The Adonis, more intellectual, added, "The only way to convey the sense of it is through philosophic or poetic analogy. Can you describe *concretely* the experience of orgasm, or even the taste of a ripe and fragrant peach, or the quenching of a great thirst, or the delight it is to feel your naked body penetrated by the rays of the sun, to someone who has never known these things? The same goes for drugs."

Outsiders, on the other hand, have told me that they have tried this or that wondrous substance at one time or another, and just got sick for their trouble, or else were overwhelmed by sleep. For "ecstasy," practice is required.

None of these young people have any sort of project for the future, any kind of ambition. They live for each hour as it comes, and consider themselves the wiser for it. I would ask what they plan to do later, how they will make out when their families aren't around to help them, and they would invariably reply, "How do you expect us to know what we're going to be doing in ten years, when we don't know where we're going to be a month from now. And besides, we don't give a damn. . . ." "As for me," said the American from San Francisco, "the only thing that bothers me is how to get enough money to have a good Christmas next week."

Six Eyes told me that he had wanted to get to New Caledonia, but that he had been stuck in Kabul for lack of money. He was looking around for handouts from various French organizations, but so far in vain. I asked him what he was qualified to do. Nothing! He had never followed any course of study, no kind of apprenticeship, but he had been told that well-paying work was easy to come by in New Caledonia. He despaired now of ever getting there.

During all this time, the hashish pipe made its tour, and the figure under the red hat still hadn't moved. It seemed unconnected to everything going on around it, it wasn't even curious enough to toss a glance at the visitors. It seemed as if it didn't even hear us. The Adonis was the only one to have some aim in his life. He was going to Indonesia because there was still a form of truly "authentic" wood sculpture there, and there still existed, on Bali, a folk art not yet "corrupted by civilization." He wanted to "soak himself in a pure and true artistic atmosphere. . . ."

"I know Indonesia," I told him. "I've visited sculpture workshops in Djakarta and Djojakarta, where the most famous Hindu temples are. I bought a beautiful piece in the port of Surayaba—filled with rats, by the way (the port, not the piece.) I've browsed among the art stores on the island of Bali, famous for its pretty sinuous-armed dancers, its naked-breasted village girls, and its monkey dances. Every tourist takes home some Indonesian sculpture. Believe me, in Bali you'll find as commercial an art colony as ever existed in Greenwich Village." I thought of Baudelaire's line, "Children who find beauty in everything that comes from far." Or, more prosaically, "Just because the names are Oriental— New Caledonia, Bali, Java—you think you are returning to the pure sources of art. You don't realize that our civilization has left no virgin place on earth." Nonetheless, I encouraged the young boy from Cannes to go to Bali because at last I had found, before my very eyes, a hippie who aspired to do something with his brain and with his hands.

The red-hatted form finally got up, but still without saying a word. It wandered through the room without seeing anyone. Suddenly, I saw its face and realized that it was a girl. She lived here with these six boys. "Is she sick?" I asked. Mauve Scarf answered no, and then I asked whether she was tripping on LSD. "No, no, she's thinking. . . ." I could draw out nothing more, but this girl was visibly under the spell of some evil drug, or else she had already lost her mind. One of them told me that she would sleep with each boy on demand, absent in this occupation too as in all others.

Mauve Scarf asked me if I could get him a blanket. The hotel manager refused to lend him one, saying that the hippies would sell it for drugs. The Swedish boy asked me if I could get him a little flask of perfume. These were so many disguised forms of begging. Whatever they got, they would sell.

I asked the Japanese boy to tell me about the hippie movement in Japan. He told me that there are several "underground" periodicals, like the *Shinjuku Sutra*, distributed clandestinely in the university and sold in the street by students.

The editor of the paper is a Chinese who lives in Japan, and his associate is an American who calls himself a "natural wanderer, with no permanent residence." He came to Tokyo to found this branch of Sutra, which is already popular in the U.S. But the most popular thing in Japan is the amphetamines. People became used to them during World War II, when the military authorities would give them to fliers and soldiers who might have to go several days without sleep. After the war, the surplus stocks were sold on the black market, and the civilian population began to dope themselves up. There was violence, murder, and the powers that be got more worked up than over Hiroshima. Our hippies prefer opium to hashish. Opium comes to us at a good price from Communist China, by way of Hong Kong or North Korea. Peking distributes as well throughout Malaysia. I have learned that there are 35,000 opium addicts in Kuala Lumpur.

There is also the Zero Dimension group, to which I belonged, that provokes one incident after another. Its leader, Kato, wears an American Indian kind of headband. According to him, man can reach the true essence of things through pornography. The philosophy of the Zeros is worked out in a manual of 5000 pages [I wondered idly how many pages would have been required if the group had had a hundred, or a thousand, dimensions]. The basic idea is that the profound nature of things cannot be perceived except by those who fix their attention on things that most people think are filthy, vulgar, and disgusting. We militant Zeros hardly let an hour go by without thinking a dirty thought or doing something crude. When we take the subway, we carry some pornographic book and consult it solemnly as if it were a prayer book. One of my Zero friends, who is slight, clean and well groomed as if he were a bank employee, pastes vicious, obscene and disgusting handbills on public walls. A whole squad of police does nothing else but tear them off. He says that art that pleases most people is sabotage, because it reinforces the confidence of the society in itself. Another Zero, Hijikata, organizes "happenings" of naked dancers cavorting on the streets of downtown Tokyo. He has them pretend to make love, and bombards them with lights of swooping zeros. The cops come in jeeps and throw tear gas, which turns the whole scene into a riot.

A third Zero, Adachi, has made a film whose heroine has no vagina. A boy, who knows nothing about her deformity, is in love with her. In her urgent desire to make love like everyone else you see the nude girl, slender as a doll, writhe painfully around her suitor's useless member. That's porno-tragedy. It is that same Adachi who threw Coke bottles from the roof of a skyscraper to express his hostility toward "voyeurs." In consequence of which, a crowd gathered right away at the foot of the building, only increasing the number of voyeurs.

Everyone burst out laughing. "I have to put Tokyo on my itinerary," Mauve Scarf said.

Unlike the majority of hippies, the Chinese boy from Honolulu possessed intellectual pretensions, political convictions, and an extraordinary gift of gab. His hair was respectable length, and I never saw him draw on the pipe. He was a relentless debater, and he started up with me right away, guessing correctly that I would give him more response than the drugged mollusks that haunted the naked room. His eyes sparkling, his little heart-shaped mouth asmirk, he lit right into me:

They say that Asia's problems are caused by overpopulation. Nothing could be less true. It's the Western monster that devours all the fruits of the land. With his cars, his newspapers, his advertising, he sucks up all the resources —oil, forests, coal, minerals—from all the rest of humanity. It's not that the Indians and Chinese have too many children, it's that the United States steals their natural birthright from them. Take the case of automobiles: they pollute the air we breathe, they devour the combustibles that we must have to keep ourselves warm, there are more people killed on the road than were ever soldiers killed in all wars combined, they aggress against all the world all the time. That's the enemy of man!

"How did you get to Kabul?" I asked.

"Hitchhiking."

"Well then, you have done your little bit to pollute our precious oxygen, and to run down passersby."

He smiled his doll's smile and answered:

"If there hadn't been so many cars in America, I wouldn't have had to leave my country to come breathe the comparatively pure air of Kabul."

Point one for him. He carried on, with a voice loud enough for the others to hear:

"The West has destroyed humanity with its incessant wars. There are hundreds of millions of casualties that can be laid at the doorstep of the white man's instinct toward aggression."

"Haven't you read the history of your own China? Don't you know that some of the Han kingdoms spent centuries slaughtering each other? And Genghis Khan . . . he wasn't Western! And besides, you can kill millions of people even without war: just by police repression and concentration camps. . . ."

"Oh yes, I know what you're talking about. But Communism itself is an evil that springs from the West . . . Karl Marx, Lenin. . . ."

He was talky and sparkling as a Latin. I've never seen such a voluble Chinese, who are ordinarily circumspect and discreet. However, he had played devil's advocate for nothing. The other hippies in the room had not felt called upon to interject one word into our conversation. They hadn't even listened. The subject didn't interest them. What subject, O heavens! What subject interests them?

The Art of Survival

Of all the hippies who wander the hashish trail, the Americans are most numerous, followed by the Germans, and then by the English, French, Dutch, and Scandinavians. There were also a few Australians, New Zealanders, Swiss, and an occasional Italian, Finn, and Asiatic. I saw no Latin Americans. All these hippies had come to the Orient to escape their bondage from the "code" of the "straight" world, and its concern for money. And *voilà*, there they were caught in new bondages, new codes, new concerns: the first one being the need to scrounge enough pennies to see them through the next day.

To this end, they devised every conceivable strategy. The American hippies would gather in front of the American Embassy in New Delhi and call out "bakshish, bakshish," the Hindu beggar's term for alms. They would forget their war to the death against the Establishment long enough to penetrate into the embassy's cafeteria and munch on its decadent delicacies. So many American hippies would find their way into that well-stocked, air-conditioned chamber, that the ambassador had to close the premises to them during regular meal hours so that his own staff would have somewhere to sit down (*San Francisco Examiner*, January 20, 1970).

Most of the Americans would send SOS telegrams to their parents, but once aid had been received, the parents would hear no more until the next time. There were positively lines of hippies waiting at American Express to see if their checks had come. Some of them played a clever little trick that could double their take. First they had the check changed into traveler's checks whose numbers they would note down right away. They would sell these in the black market, at a higher exchange rate than the official one. The next step was to go back to American Express, claim that the checks had been lost, and—since the hippie had made a neat list of the check's numbers—American Express would give him a new batch. Then, when the black market purchaser of the original checks would go to change his money, the checks would not be honored. Usually nothing more was done about it, as the check buyer was just a petty black marketeer, but even if anybody had wanted to do anything, our hippie con man was already far away, probably in some Himalayan smoking den.

The European hippie is no less bereft of imagination. In Kabul, one flower-child from the Mediterranean area falsified student identification cards, selling them to fellow hippies, which gave them access to canteens and other services reserved to university students. He was caught, though, and had to pay a $200 fine. Quite a few hippies sell their passports to a front office for one of the Asian Communist countries always on the lookout for identity papers their secret agents can use. A hippie can get $100 on this little deal, and then go to his consulate to claim the loss. Others would sell their blood. One pretty girl, whose picture I saw, sold blood so frequently, under several different identities, that she died. A lot of the kids sold the return airplane tickets that their parents had sent them.

One young Swedish girl managed, telling one wild story after another, to borrow 5000 afghans—that is, $70. Her father had to fly in from Sweden to pay back the money, without which his little girl would have gone to jail. Some hippie crooks sell fabricated antiques. Practically everyone will prostitute themselves at one time or another, whether homosexually or heterosexually, without a second thought, but basically they hang on to their amateur status. But most of the kids make their bread by begging. To preserve their image, they try to imitate the malings, the afghan religious men who, for centuries, have, in beards and long hair, asked for charity. But in return, *they* pray for your soul. The malings have great professional integrity, and they really do pray. The hippies have become international malings, but your soul holds their attention only for the time it takes them to turn the corner.

The hard-shelled ones deal in drugs or in the contraband arms traffic. They are often stopped at the frontiers, and the customs people know all the hiding places, all the little tricks. While I was in Kabul, there was a great to-do about a hippie who had hidden his hash under the enormous plaster cast of his "broken leg." Photos of the guilty leg were published throughout the Afghan press. One American hippie, who was kind enough to offer me a selection between the hashish and opium he had stashed in his pocket—both similar in their brown, pasty form, but with distinct odors—did business in Oriental rugs. His only problem was obtaining false certificates of antiquity so they could be brought into the United States duty free.

The heroin habit is ruinous and imperious, and addicts are capable of anything. They need up to $60 a day, and they do not hesitate at violence and theft to get it. Some local pharmacies serve as "drops" for the hard drugs. I was told to keep my eye on my handbag and my photographic equipment. But in fairness it must be said that many of the flower-children would never steal or beg. The boy from Cannes said to me, "Those are two things that, try as I may to free myself from all bourgeois prejudice, I could never do." But a certain percentage of the classic kind of international thief was let their hair grow and donned some beads, becoming indistinguishable from the mass of hippies. And among the real hippies, alas, there is a growing group of what I call "amoralists"—I do not say "immoralists," but "amoralists"—who have lost all sense of good and evil. This group, unlike the rebels we have been discussing, could not care less about a new morality. They have no morality. It is undoubtedly true that each generation, in all times and all countries and all social levels, has had its small percentage of such amoralists. Remember Manon Lescaut, that lovely girl who did evil as she breathed, with a perfect grace and total innocence? Today she would be an accomplished member of this recent breed of flower-child.

In Switzerland, where I spent the holidays in Valais on my return from Iran, I met a young apprentice workman with hair down to his shoulders. I invited him to come talk with me after his day's work. His case is typical of this kind of hippie amorality. His father, a mason, and his mother, a housekeeper, made life difficult for him because he refused to cut his hair. At dances, the "straight" boys would provoke him into fights out of jealousy that the girls were drawn to him with his Tarzan hair. Most of his buddies couldn't hold out, and had given in, but he would not. And yet, he didn't seem to be a hard-nosed person. He didn't like trouble. He had no political ideas to speak of either. He read neither books nor newspapers; he didn't like reading, and he hated school. He didn't ski either, no sports were fun for him. There were only two points on which he seemed to be more or less firm: first, he did not want to go into the army, and had decided to skip out shortly before they would call him. Where? No idea. With what? He didn't know. And wouldn't his parents be upset? So what. They'd get over it. Secondly, he did not want to work, and he said so straightforwardly. He did not want to learn a trade. His father had forced him but just wait, he'd soon call his own tune. He had a holy horror of being bound by the work day: in the shop from eight to twelve, then two hours for lunch, then work again from two to six. So what did he like to do? Nothing much, except hang around with his friends and play the guitar.

"How did you hear about the hippies up here in your mountains?" I asked.

"From hippie musicians and other Americans here on vacation."

I told him about the hippies in the United States or in the Orient that beg and steal. He laughed, a little hesitantly.

"Do you think you could beg or steal?" I asked, expecting a firm rejection of the idea.

He smiled. No, it wouldn't bother him at all. Just last summer he and some friends had begged their way around Spain. And they were picked up for stealing. He was even in prison for three days. He had to borrow money from the Swiss consul to get out, telling him that he had lost his wallet. The consul had believed him. He was a sucker. Well, that's life.

I have related this little slice of contemporary life first, to show how the epidemic has spread everywhere; and secondly, to clarify the flower-child mentality a little. All the ingenuity that a regular person will devote to succeeding in life and supporting a family, the hippies put to the service of surviving from one day to the next: who to "touch" for this evening's dinner? What con game to get a visa against the rules? How to slip through society's repressive nets? What game to get your residence permit renewed? If you don't have one, how to hide? Where to pick up a few cents for a night's room? Where to find drugs? How to shake off someone you owe money to? Where to scrounge a pair of shoes when it's cold? How to con a "square" into lending you his bathroom so that, at least once, you can take a bath in hot water?

... A hippie's day—when he's not stoned—is spent insuring his survival for another day without working or studying. Some people call it a life free from enslavement, responsibilities, rules; I call it the life of a dog.

The Fairytale Kingdom: Nepal

The lucky ones who manage to get a visa for India—false, if need be—or the even luckier ones from the British Commonwealth who don't need one only stay in Kabul for a few days. They cross through Pakistan then, and on into the Promised Land. According to the *Revue de Médecine de France* (December, 1969), 100,000 hippies had entered India by that date.

India is humanity at its most basic, an ocean of misery, of pageantry, and of free movement where everyone strolls at his own pace, lies down where he wishes—including, of course, on the sidewalk—dresses as his mood takes him, or doesn't dress at all—like the naked holy men I saw leading demonstrations against the slaughtering of cows. Each citizen practices the religion that pleases him, wears his hair as long as he feels, paints his favorite cabalistic signs on his face, walks barefoot as long as his callouses hold out, only works when it suits him, floats through hours, days or years in a void of meditation, and begs as naturally as he breathes. In this world, the hippies are just fish come back to the water. They shock no one, no one insults them, or even looks at them oddly. The Hindus incorporate them effortlessly as they would any other act of nature: the trees, rocks, gods, the monsoon—all things that can be tied by no rules, so must just be accepted.

Though the masses may accept every mode of being and of nonbeing, the government has enough to do with its own rootless populace to shoulder responsibility for these new ones who fall on them out of the sky and create a thousand new insoluble problems on top of their usual hundred-thousand-old insoluble problems per day. There are not enough hospitals for the natives, not enough housing, not enough prisons, and there is an immense, an unfathomable excess of beggars. So, what to do with sick hippies, penniless hippies, drug-dealing hippies, or begging hippies? What to do with all the self-made outcasts when you have millions and millions of real ones to deal with? How to endure a situation in which facsimiles of the poor sponge off of the real poor? Are not these affluent slummers an insult to the truly miserable beings dying around them? But above all, above all, the hippies carry with them the virus of drugs—a new affliction for the Hindu world on top of all the rest.

Until two years ago, hashish was open in India. Up till then, only a tiny fragment of the population had indulged in it, and they had done no proselytizing. Now, all of a sudden, the hippies invade and smoke their hash in public, offering it to their Hindu neighbors in restaurants and hotels, and to the well-brought-up young girls they meet. The risk of corrupting Hindu youth—already so close to the abyss as to hardly matter—seemed so imminent, that the Delhi government declared hashish illegal. From that time on, any hippie so foolhardy as to let himself be caught with the drug faced two years in an Indian prison, compared to which a prison in America, or even France, was positively a Sing Sing Hilton. This past year, there were some 100 hippies in the jails of Mrs. Indira Gandhi. Moreover, once a hippie's visa had expired, out he went.

So the Holy Land rejected its children. Where to go from there? The word passed from ear to ear: to Nepal, of course! To that kingdom of legends where there are more temples than houses, more holidays than work days, and more mountain peaks than inhabitants. To Nepal, where you can stay forever without a visa. To Nepal, whose ways of life are even more inviting than in India. To Nepal, where the sun shines every day, but its heat does not enervate. To Nepal, where drugs are totally open. To Nepal, where adults enjoy eternal childhood.

So it was in December, 1966, that the fairytale capital of Katmandu which, like Sleeping Beauty, had slept tranquilly with its 200,-000 people in the green cradle of the Himalayas, was surprised awake by 200 hippies, come from the ends of the earth, to respond to the call, "Christmas in Katmandu!" The visitors were dressed for carnival, with flowers in their hair and guitars in their hands. And their Holy Grail was nothing more than to find a place to talk and laugh and play music and smoke ganja and talk and laugh. The Nepalese were enchanted.

The most marvelous thing about Nepal was the ridiculously low cost of drugs. One ounce of hashish—that is, 28 grams—cost $1.40, or 5 cents a gram. For 20 cents a day, one could, like a grand lord, invite all comers to ecstatic parties right in any public place, which did much to cement the friendships among the followers of the grand drug crusade.

Hash Coming Up!

I went one evening, accompanied by an Air France stewardess, to the Cabin Restaurant. Not here the standard restaurant scene of flowered tablecloths and candles on the tables. The Cabin is a hole in the wall, all wood, with no other ventilation than the entrance door, studded with raw wood tables on the beaten earth floor, surrounded by benches piled with uncombed youth. The waitress, who was carrying a baby in her arms—her own baby—seemed about fifteen years old. She was a pretty little Nepalese girl who smiled at everyone, even if they didn't order anything. About a quarter of the hippies just rooted themselves there for the evening, without ordering, just for the pleasure of drawing now and again on the hashish pipe that circulated round and round, never stopping. And they coughed, coughed as if to cough up their souls.

The menu at the Cabin was unique. My mouth open, I read the dessert list: hashish cakes, ganja candy, marijuana pudding, etc. I asked the waitress, who jabbered a pidgin English, whether this was just pretend. No indeed, these delicacies were the real thing. Wouldn't I like one?

My neighbor at the table, an Englishman, lit up a huge pipe whose short stem he had wrapped with a damp rag. He took in three draws, and passed the pipe on to a girl with a shock of golden hair, who sent it in her turn to a young Nepalese, and so it went for the rest of the evening. I read a notice from an English-language Nepalese newspaper, placed so all could see it, "Anyone possessing an export license for cannabis, ganja, hashish, telephone . . . etc." This was the promised land indeed.

The golden-shocked girl was a tall, slender American. She had put her embroidered goatskin vest—a gift from a Kabul merchant in gratitude for an hour of love in the "French style"—on the back of her chair. French love, at least, had not been devalued like the franc. Her gypsy blouse gave a clear view, on either side of the inevitable beads, of two very *there* and very well-set breasts. Her Andalusian dancer pants traced out buttocks that were firm, but thin from too many skipped meals. Her head reminded one of a goat, like her vest—a pretty goat, with large white teeth, and eyes enlarged by malnutrition and cannabis. Her braided, silky hair looked like the wool of golden merino sheep. She talked and talked under the euphoric beginnings of a hashish high. She told about a night when she made love high on mescaline.

Everything in the room went in waves, even the bed and the naked boy beside her. It was "groovy." She had felt like she was on a ship in a rolling sea: pitch and roll, roll and pitch. And at the top . . . it made her sick, and the boy tried in vain to bring her round. It wasn't "groovy" any more. The next time she tried it with LSD, it was supposed to be "out of sight." She had already tried opium, but that was as blurry as if she'd been wrapped in cotton wool.

"Try speed then," said the hippie at her side. "It's a blast."

"Hey, that's an idea. But what about the new super-high drug? The tiger-in-your tank stuff?"

And the conversation would have gone on in this vein for hours if I hadn't interrupted to ask the goat-girl what had brought her to Nepal. She directed a look of universal love my way, offered me her pipe of ganja and a flower, and composed a vast open-heart smile. A hippie is a hippie wherever he, or she, may be. Then she answered, with no hesitations:

"I'm here because Nepal is far enough away from my folks that they won't come after me and drag me home. In the United States, I lived in Kansas City with my father, mother, and little brother. I ran away several times, first to Greenwich Village, then to Sunset Strip, and then to Haight Ashbury. But always my mom would be crying after me, begging me to come back. She would have me looked for for weeks, she would send information about me and my picture to the police all over the place, she would force my dad to take the car and come look for me, and in the end she always found out where I was. And then, oh God, what scenes!"

"Did she scream at you?"

"Oh, no. If she had insulted me, I would have had good reason to tell her to go to hell. She would cry, oh God, would she cry. She would cry and say she was dying, and Daddy would back her up. 'You wouldn't let your mother die! And your little brother, who calls for you every day.' And on and on like that. He couldn't care less about me, that brat. But in the end she would make me cry with that old family stuff, and I would go back. Then once back again, still carryings on. How to have peace and quiet for a twelve-hour LSD trip? Mom would come knocking at the door of my room at mealtimes, she'd ask if I was sick, call up some draggy doctor that I didn't want to tell anything to. . . . And my little brother would come banging on my door. At night,

I had to be back home by one o'clock. Talk about prison! Couldn't possibly sleep with anyone. And they wanted me to go to a psychoanalyst. If he had been young and groovy, maybe, but they landed on some old dumbo. He wanted me to tell him all the dirty little things I only tell my best friends. I wasn't going to talk to that square about anything but grass, LSD and mescaline. And he, he didn't know anything about drugs. But *nothing!* He was an ass. And he was supposed to be a doctor. Those shrink sessions bored me so that I thought I'd die. So I gathered up this and that, and everything my parents had deposited to my savings account for when I got married. And there again you see how the straights are! As if you have to be a certain age before you're old enough to know how to spend money. Mother, she's fifty, but without Daddy she wouldn't know to come in out of the rain. She couldn't even travel by herself. Or even buy a hotdog, for Christ's sake. She's a drag. Me, *I* know how to spend money."

"How much did you take?"

"Eighteen hundred dollars."

"But that's a fortune for a hippie!"

"Well, there's not much left now. I've been traveling around the world now for two years, and it goes. And there was a bastard in Istanbul who lifted my bag and a good piece of the bread with it. A good thing I had hidden the rest in my bra."

"I thought the hippies were against bras."

"That's true, and mostly I don't wear one either [and to prove it, she opened her blouse to let me see for myself]. But going through Turkey, where the men are like rams in heat, I thought I needed a little protection."

"Are you going to ask your parents for help?"

"Hardly. It's been two years now since I've written them. They don't know where I am. If they did, it would be just like them to fly over here and try again."

Then she turned to the young Nepalese boy, who had been puffing away all the time, and said, "Come on now, can't you pass the pipe? There are other people here too."

"When your money's gone, what will you do?"

"I'll worry about that then. I'm going to Goa. Because here in Katmandu, you have to pay for a place to sleep. Isn't that ridiculous? To have to pay to eat is bad enough, but to pay for sleeping is just idiotic. Do you pay to breathe? A crappy room costs sixty cents a day, but you can sleep in the Globe dormitory for twenty cents and, when the cafés close, you can spend the night on one of the tables for ten cents. But that's still too much money to pay just to exist for eight hours. In Goa you can sleep for nothing."

A Dutchman had just sat down at the next table. His naturally ruddy countenance, lit up by a lantern, had faded into pallor, and his young cheeks were already furrowed by a hard life. His curly brown hair was brightened by a multicolored crested hat, and he held a guitar. I was enthralled, he was the reincarnation of Franz Hals "Joyful Lad with Guitar." He was dragging a straggle-haired, half asleep girl after him, wearing a disordered sari. I asked them questions, but only the boy replied. He told me that he had tried every drug, that he had been doped on methedrine for two years, but that he had felt the rats of death nibbling on his innards, and had had the strength of will to stop in time. If not, he would have died for sure (an experience, I thought, that was waiting around the corner for his already ruined companion).

The golden goat-girl interrupted.

"Like my buttons say, 'speed kills.' That's why, outside of marijuana, which isn't a drug, I just take the big one, acid. I look at myself in the mirror, and I'm weaving from the top of my head to my feet like a snake. My hair weaves too, I don't have to go to the hairdresser anymore."

And she exploded with laughter. She was stoned now, and anything could make her laugh. But the companion of the Dutch youth still hadn't said a word. She didn't have the strength to hold her head up; it fell down onto the empty table in front of her. She had ordered nothing. She must have been broke. I offered her something to eat. Finally she opened her mouth to say, in a gravelly voice, "I'd rather have a pipe."

The Dutch boy had met her just a few days before. She was trying to stick with him, but she wasn't very appetizing any more with her greasy hair that fell over dull cheeks. He got around by drawing pictures of Hindu gods on rice paper. He tried to sell me some. The Nepalese waitress came to announce, smiling, that they were going to close. A bitter odor of hashish bathed the little room. And the baby that she held in her arms breathed it in day after day. His little face already looked wizened and old—older than the face of his child-mother.

The "Lodges"

I was told that I shouldn't miss the "lodges"; that is, the flop-houses that housed the hippies and the most destitute Asian travelers. I decided to begin with a visit to the "Tibetan lodge," the Globe, where the ganja-smoking Tibetan muleteers stay. The Globe's walls bore photographs of the Dalai Lama, the exiled God-King of Tibet, and of Mahendra, the king of Nepal. The Globe was, so to speak, elegant, with its plastic tableclothes covering its eight rectangular wooden tables. Then I went to another little restaurant the size of a handkerchief, with four bare wooden tables. No portraits on the walls this time, but jackets and gourds of traveling Tibetans. I ordered a hot lemonade, a main dish, and a dessert. It was delicious, and cost 60 cents. The waiter was a tiny ten-year-old Tibetan boy, sharp at taking orders and negotiating the service. Between waiting on tables, he put his hands in his pockets and whistled with a superior air. But he kept a sharp eye out, and never let a hippie leave without paying. It was he who, in a high, clear voice, reeled off the drink orders to the owner who filled them, and no one had ever managed to sneak one behind his back. This Tibetan orphan, who spoke snatches of English, was so adorable that a British family had begun proceedings to adopt him.

I went in to another Tibetan bistro. There also, a nine-year-old boy served the customers until midnight. A muleteer from Lhasa invited me to buy something—supposedly from Tibet, but actually made in Nepal—from his knapsack. A hippie with tousled red hair, his shirt open to reveal his hairy chest on which a gold chain sparkled, was moved to ecstasies: "How beautiful it is! What a shame I have no money." He coveted worldly goods, just like his opposite number on the other side of the "straight" fence; he was just as much a consumer as they, but had deflected his desires away from cars and refrigerators to Oriental knickknacks, from mechanical gadgets to paste gimcracks.

I saw two hippies, not like the others, dressed in voluminous black monks' robes with very wide sleeves, sitting at a bench near the door. One of them pretended to doze, but spoke Italian in a low voice to his companion. Then he cast a rather furtive eye on the coatrack behind him, where the hippies' goatskin jackets and knapsacks hung. Both of them bore the faces of Calabrian bandits playing at being monks. I watched them. The one who was supposed to be sleeping squinted at the group around him from underneath his eyelids. Something was afoot, no question, but then they left quickly. They were Mafia types wrapped up in hippie clothing. An hour later, just as the little café was closing, a hippie started looking in vain for his guitar, which had fled with the two monks.

I went out too and in the dark night (the streets are not lit in Katmandu) I heard shattering music, toward which I walked. It was a Nepalese lodge filled with hippies smoking hashish. There were some twelve tables. I have to admire once more the way our world can turn the forces that may one day overturn it into a source of profit—at least until the revolution. Trade has flourished along the hashish trail just as it once prospered along the old routes of pilgrimage. Its clientele is gaunt and marginal to be sure, but even so, these nomade can put a few pennies into the pockets of stay-at-home entrepreneurs; the flight of one group is a windfall for another or, looked at another way, the scorn one group has for money generates money for another. Far from having divorced themselves from the consumer society, the hippies have just added a new, if peripheral, dimension to it.

In among all the other hairy, scruffy, and beribboned hippies, I noticed a well-shaven young Chinese with short hair, wearing a good European-style overcoat, who took no turns on the circulating pipe. After a moment, he rose and sang the song of Mao:

"The young Americans don't want to live in their own country any more. Their country is hell, that's why they come to Nepal and to China. . . . Viva Mao!"

"It's the eye of Peking," someone whispered.

I asked a well-built Australian if there were many hippies in Australia. He took offense at my question:

"What do you mean by 'hippies?' We aren't hippies."

"Flower-children then?"

"Even less; we're human beings. Why do you call us hippies?"

"I didn't mean to deny that you are human beings, but it's just that man has always had collective names for the different kinds of groups that evolve on the basis of a common race, or origin, or religion, or philosophy. Thus the whites, the blacks, the Jews, the surrealists, etc. Tell me the name that you want to be called, and that's what I'll call you."

"Call us human beings," he repeated stubbornly, unable, no doubt, to think of a good name.

"But the 'bourgeois' you talk about all the time are human beings too. How do you distinguish yourselves from them?"

I had engaged before in two other discussions of this kind. They protest the term, but can't find another that suits them.

I saw a fine-featured, bearded little man wearing an enormous fur hat. He sat quietly amid the roar, saying nothing, ignoring the hashish pipe, and making mental notes. Was he, more clever than the Mao mouthpiece, the "eye of Moscow?"

I went out on to a large square bathed in night. I could make out the shadow of a large tent that the hippies had raised in the middle of the square, which was in the heart of town. A cow and a dog wandered about. I was alone, and a little frightened. A car whooshed by, sounding its horn. The cow, frightened, ran away, knocking against the tent. The dog barked. No one moved. Everything was black. And under their tent, the hippies took trips into the country of nowhere.

Himalayan Refuge

Responding to the increase in drug-caused incidents, the Nepalese authorities have begun to—I won't say become alarmed, that's too big a word for such an insouciant little country—but to make a few light regulations governing their visitors, like limiting the time of residence permits. Once again, a place that had seemed to be a final refuge was closing its doors just a mite, and who knew what might come next. But resourceful always, they realized that if they just moved out a little way from Katmandu, perhaps to the area around Patan, the city of a thousand pagodas, or to the large palace-and-temple village of Bagdhaon—I say village rather than city, because temples are set right amid farming land—the police would not bother to come after them. The Nepalese police had not yet acquired the manhunting reflex. If the hippies didn't cross their paths, they weren't going to cross the hippies'.

I took an excursion to the temple of Swayambunath, a half-hour's car trip from Katmandu, where a colony of Tibetan lamas passed their time in prayer and begging alms from tourists. Groups of hippies had attached themselves to the lama colony, and I couldn't take three steps around the temple before running into three hippies. One of them told me that his little group made their home up in the mountain.

"May I come with you? My taxi will take us."

Thrilled not to have to make the journey on foot with a pack of provisions on his back, he agreed, and the other two hippes came with us just for something to do. We followed a sandy path running along the foot of the mountain, and after twenty minutes, the hippie pointed out a small hut clinging to the top of a steep hill. That was it. The taxi could go no further, and the ascent on foot was hard. They pulled my arms, they pushed me. . . . I thought I would never get there! Fortunately, I didn't have to, because two thirds along the way, on the green-apple carpet of a mountain meadow, we came upon my escort's companions: four long-haired boys sitting facing the Himalayan peaks that were just being gilded by the fine gold of the setting sun. It was magnificent. One of the boys—a handsome Danish youth with hair of the same fine-spun gold—wore earrings and the saffron robe of a Buddhist monk, leaving one shoulder nobly bare like an ancient Roman. His three companions were Americans. They were eating oranges, and offered us some. There was no woman with them, neither here on the meadow or up at their little house. Did the beautiful golden-haired one take on that role? I asked questions, to which it was mostly this youth who replied, with a serious air, all the while rolling his long hair into a chignon. Was he afraid of catching it on the branches of a tree? Or did he fear to let his hair be caught by an indiscreet camera?.. . . The discussion turned to religion. For him, God had neither name nor attribute. He believed in reincarnation.

"And if you were reincarnated as a banker?" I asked mischievously.

His face stayed grave.

"Do you read?"

"No."

"Do you play a musical instrument?"

"No."

"Do you watch television?"

He laughed finally, with his companions. "Our color TV is here" he said to me, waving his hand out toward the red-gold crown resting on the brown peak of the old mountain. "Every day we come down to watch this sight."

"And what else do you do?"

"We take drugs, and contemplate our interior life."

"And don't you find this life monotonous?"

"Less than making cars on an assembly line. Or than taking the subway in New York, where no one laughs. Here we are calm and happy. We are never bored."

Several minutes later, I learned that they planned to go to Goa, the enchanting beach to the south of India. "People say it's groovy." They talked about their itinerary, the places they would visit en route.

. . .

"But aren't these peaks, glowing like your most beautiful drug trips, enough for you? My friends, let me tell you that, despite your superhuman efforts, you'll never become true Orientals. You struggle in vain, you could never endure eternal and immobile contemplation, you will never be true gurus. Despite your most straining efforts, and despite the drug, the blood of American pioneers and the people of old Europe still flows in your veins. You were born with ants in your pants, gentlemen. . . . Are you going to Goa together?"

"Two of us are stopping at Benares."

"How long have you been together?"

"Six weeks."

So, once more, the basic instability of the hippie community. For a while I had believed that, finally, in these four pensive hermits, cradled by the winds of the Himalayas and welded by the forces of nature, I had found a solid, homogeneous, durable group. But no. They would separate like all the other groups, as quickly and for reasons as superficial as the ones that brought them together in the first place. There is no coherence behind the comings together and fallings apart of the hippie groups—it is chance. They go, they come like spring winds, the groups clump together and then fall apart like clouds; they share their solitudes with each other for a while, that's all. There are no "hippie communities" in the proper sense of the term, only temporary bivouacs raised in a flash and changed, as some pilgrims leave and new ones arrive, in a twinkling. At bottom, every hippie is alone. He and his fellow-travelers (literally) are only free electrons with no profound affinities, linked together for the moment by the pipe or by the bed. No true friends, no true lovers. Close relationships imply that each partner cultivate or seek something in common—even something quite ordinary—but which attracts, and then endures. The hippies cultivate nothing, nor do they seek anything really; nothing to nourish the mind, nothing to warm the soul, nothing that will still be there tomorrow. The visions in their mind's eye are, in essence, fleeting and incommunicable. If at least the hippies were truly persecuted, that suffering might weld them together. But the "straight" world is just an irritant really, nothing serious, and indeed they could hardly exist without it. Perhaps their drug helps them penetrate into the nature of stones, but it seems, apparently, to blind them to the nature of men.

Tragedy and Defeat

As one might expect, endless distresses fester in this life of drugs and squalor. Out of the many stories I was told throughout my travels in Nepal, Afghanistan, and India, here are just a few:

An American evangelist who has lived in Kabul for twenty years told me that the hippies there—or the "great unwashed" as the locals call them—kill themselves with startling regularity. Urgent middle-of-the-night calls to help a hippie who has swallowed an overdose of something are a commonplace. One hippie cut his throat with a razor during a trip that turned bad.

From consulate to consulate, from embassy to embassy, from hospital to hospital I heard the same chilling story. One nineteen-year-old boy, an asthmatic whose condition was exacerbated by hashish, suffocated during an attack while surrounded by fellow hippies—all of them stoned—none of whom gave him the least help, or even called a doctor. The great virtue of marijuana, as the hippies see it, is precisely that it plunges them into that total indifference to the external world and its problems. An indifference, alas, that quickly turns into an extreme dryness of the emotions. An American told me that, stoned, he watched the fires and horror of the Watts riot in Los Angeles with the same sense of floating awe for the spectacle that he felt at the fountains of Versailles. During a similar riot in Chicago, while houses burned, the word spread among the hippies to get stoned, the better to enjoy the beauty of it all. The hippies commune while Chicago burns —little Neros in bud.

In the hospitals, where there are not enough beds for the natives, hippies are not admitted except in very grave cases. I was told of numerous cases of pneumonia, of chronic bronchitis, of hepatitis; the liver inflammation sometimes triggered off by LSD is invariably fatal. One hippie, who finally died of this liver condition, went berserk and attacked nine nurses and doctors. There are no psychiatric hospitals in the happy kingdom of Nepal, because madness is not recognized there as madness. A deranged individual is either possessed by spirits, or in an advanced state of religious exaltation, and is respected in proportion to the extent of his deviation from the norm. The normal hospitals, then, do not accept the mentally ill. So these hippies under the "bad trip" cloud just wander. I saw at least half a dozen confused girls in this state going through the temples. Since from time immemorial Nepal has had its home-grown equivalents to the traditional "village idiot," no one is shocked. One of these hippie girls wandered nude; another was wearing a man's shirt. One young American clad only in a loincloth set out to climb the icy peaks of the Himalayas, while a Canadian spent his time painting wild, whirling pictures. But in all justice, here it must be said that perhaps this was a case of supergenius rather than madness.

The ambassador from France to Nepal—indeed, M. Français is his name—told me the story of a young French girl who roamed through Katmandu in rags with neither power to speak nor control of her sphincters. He sent someone from the consulate to fetch her. She was an animal crawling on all fours, who urinated on the embassy carpet. The girl is in a hospital now, for life. Another French girl strolled naked through a pagoda, but in this case it might have been the suggestive sculptures that turned her head rather than drugs. The sculptures include a man with a huge penis to whom two women render homage; three males rutting with a young virgin who won't be that way much longer; and a Hercules coupling with a mare. The ambassador had the girl looked for, gave her some clothes belonging to his wife, and put her on the plane for Paris. At the New Delhi stopover, she threw off these "petit bourgeois" clothes and tried to escape.

They are still talking in Katmandu about the English girl who lived in a hut with some twenty bearded, hairy and virile Sikhs. She alone gave nights of easeful delight to all these warriors, worshipers of Rama, who was himself a great lover of women. The Sikhs had no sense that they were taking advantage of a sick girl. They believed that she was a reincarnation of Sita, the woman whom the god Rama had delivered from captivity among the apes and who had come back to grace their beds in the form of a blonde hippie. But this demi-goddess was causing an uproar among the Western community, which finally intervened and sent Sita's reincarnation back home to her parents. Then there was the case of the young girl under LSD who cut herself to feel the magic intensity of the redness of her blood. Her blood whispered under her door all night long, and in the morning she was dead.

Apparently women drug-takers tend to fall part physically and mentally considerably more quickly than their male counterparts. First of all, for a girl to engage in so risky an enterprise as hitchhiking along the hashish trail, where neither daily hygiene is available, nor sexual security, she would have to be a kind of female daredevil, or brainless altogether, or simply devoid of either decency or coquettry. The fragile beauty of a woman does not support hardship well, nor circles under the eyes, nor skin without attention, nor sleepless nights. The girls also slide more easily than the boys into the permanent proselytism for drugs that rings through all manifestations of hippie culture. To show they are involved, liberated, they indulge with even more incontinence than their companions. And since their more delicate organism endures the rigors less hardily, they go to pot (forgive the pun) more quickly. I have been speaking of girls who are basically alone. The girls who are protected by a lover keep a better hold on their health and their looks. But in general, the boys seem to enjoy the sight of stoned girls; the girls become—at first—funnier, more devil-may-care, and also more easy, even lascivious. So the males let their playmates destroy themselves while they watch with an indifference and an irresponsibility that is quite stunning. They offer many smiles around the circle, or oranges, or hashish . . . but let one of their girls lose her footing on the slippery drug path, and she has nothing more to offer them; she is left to go her way alone.

To round off these tales of tragedy among hippie girls, I want to tell one story that I heard while I stood on the banks of an Indian river and watched the body of a pretty girl, laid out on a funeral pyre surrounded by a circle of mourners, go up in flames. It was the sad end of a girl of sixteen, from a well-to-do family, who met a hippie boy on the Pont des Arts in Paris and was drawn by him on to the hashish trail. In her white dress and golden slippers, she announced one day to her father that she was going to spend her school vacation in Geneva. Her father, a wealthy industrialist, asking for no further details, gave her a generous check. In Geneva, the young girl—whose nationality I prefer not to reveal in order not to further identify her—met two long-haired boys who taught her about love, took her on the big leap into a strange, boundless world without limits, initiated her into marijuana and amphetamines, and then took off with her for the East. They had no money and the girl paid all expenses until they reached Turkey, when they were left with not one cent between the three of them. They tried to beg then but competition was too fierce in Istanbul, so the pretty girl turned to prostitution to support the three of them. That is the hippie law: whoever brings in money, shares it with his "family."

They fared well enough through Lebanon, a rich country where prostitution pays well. But then, when they ventured across Syria, Iraq, and the immense expanse of Iran, business fell off because people had less to spend on such luxuries. But as if to compensate for the missing money, she picked up instead a venereal disease which—as prescribed by hippie law—she shared at once with her companions. On the interminable trip across Pakistan, business got worse and worse because people kept getting poorer and poorer, and her disease caused sexual intercourse to become more and more painful, so she started doubling her drug doses. When finally they arrived in India, there was nothing left of her but a rag of flesh covered by rags of cloth. One of her two companions showed me some photos. The white dress of the first picture had been sold to an Arab old-clothes-man, and the golden slippers exchanged for an old washed-out sari. In the second photo, she walked barefoot, and the pretty, round, rosy cheeks of Geneva had become emaciated, discolored, and covered with dusty sores. Her dilated pupils, rimmed by red eyelids, obscured all the once-blue iris. Her lover told me:

> She hurt all the time. Pains in her belly from her infection. She probably didn't even know that she had gotten a bad case of syphilis along with everything else. To ease her pain, she took more and more drugs—in India she made the jump to opium—and to pay for the habit she kept going out on the streets, but no one wanted her any more she looked so bad.

The young man spoke with a even voice, but he seemed sincerely moved while he watched the burning pyre devour a being who had been floating for so long in the half-mists of stupefaction.

In India, they had been arrested for stealing food. As they had entered India without visas, they claimed to have lost all their papers. They were put on a sort of reservation near Bombay where "irregular" hippies were detained for a while in all their squalor, destitution, and drugs. And the girl died there, just because her last resources had been exhausted. Her two companions, up to that point indolence incarnate, finally bestirred themselves to find the necessary sum to fill the last sacred obligation that a hippie who treads Indian soil owes to his dead. They worked hard for several days as stevedores to pay for the wood for the funeral pyre. And while her body was being consumed, they and several other hippies there for the ceremony chanted "Hare Rana, Hare Krishna. . . ." At the end, I watched them sprinkle her ashes into the Ganges, as the rite demands.

That's all that was left of a lovely girl, a cherished doll for sixteen years, when her mother and father could at last retrace her steps and put together the pieces of her story. A simple story of a fall that was no less tragic because it was stupid. It recalls irresistibly the old French ballad of the brother and sister with "her white robe and golden girdle" who run away—hiding from their parents—to dance on the Pont du Nord and drown. With this difference: our children of today travel on their thumbs, not on boats; they drown, not in rivers, but in drugs. And the moral of the story, as true today as when the old tale was written, is "This is the fate of headstrong children."

Embassies Up Against the Wall

When an embassy receptionist sees a long-haired youth with distraught face and haggard eyes arrive at her doors—and such youths arrive every day at the Western embassies and consulates in the East —she knows right away that he is very sick, or has lost his passport, or that the flower-child with whom he shared his bit of floor the night before has run off with his wallet.

I interviewed a number of Western diplomats, all of whom were stunned by the enormity of the problem, distressed by the violence of its impact, and basically didn't know what to do. The United States ambassador at Kabul, Robert Neumann, said:

> I do not object in principle to the hippies retiring from the world. I have been a teacher, and I know that the quest for your own identity can be

difficult. But I do not think this can be achieved by drugs. The best thing for all these hippies who live amongst rats in conditions that would fell the strongest, would be to go back home. But I simply cannot persuade them to go, and I have no authority to make them. Only the governments could do something [that is, both the government of the hippie's home country, and also the host government] and they apparently don't want to bother. The saddest thing is that the hippies are withdrawing from the world at the very moment when there is so much work to do for the still-impoverished people of the world. (*New York Times*, November 16, 1969.)

The French diplomats have also been shaken by their inability to help these young castaways. One of them told me:

They come to our embassy to ask for money when they are absolutely at the end of their ropes. First, no budgetary provision has been made for them. If we did put aside money for them, the word would pass in two days, and we'd have a mob here; and they wouldn't just buy food with the money either. Some of them, who, in desperate straits, were offered shelter in the embassy, stole curtains, art objects, or stealthily examined other people's letters to see if there was any money in them.

Our Western embassies—and that of France especially—do everything they can to repatriate young souls lost on the hashish trail. Every embassy gets six or seven long-distance phone calls a week from parents desperate to find their offspring. All the embassies have set up special teams, staffed by people who blend easily into the hippie scene, who haunt the hippie bars and hotels to get a line on the runaways. They make discreet enquiries here and there, show photos, elicit confidences, gather news from the grapevine. A new profession has been created: runaway-searcher. A hippie can be found while in residence in one of the larger cities, but it is impossible to locate one who is on the road.

In many cases, the finding of a runaway does not resolve the problem. They often refuse to go home, and even in the case of a minor, the embassies have no coercive powers on foreign soil. But even supposing that an adolescent does agree to be repatriated, the way isn't yet clear: the ambassador has to telegraph the foreign minister in his own country; he has to find and inform the parents; the parents have to scrape enough money together to pay for an airplane ticket from halfway around the world; and by the time the ticket comes, the hippie has changed his mind and disappeared again! This time, since he knows

he is being looked for, he takes pains to hide so that he knows he can't
be found. "This has happened to me four times in the last month," the
French ambassador, M. Français, told me,

> and I can't hold the hippies in the embassy while we wait for the plane
> ticket; it's not a prison. And besides, they tend to be very careless of
> embassy property. And when they finally set foot on that Katmandu-to-
> Paris plane, even that's not the end of it. Half the time they slip away at
> the first stop, in New Delhi. We don't have the money to pay for a guard,
> and even if we did, would his authority be recognized by the countries in
> which the plane stops? And what right do we have anyway to keep someone
> from leaving a plane if he wants to? What's more, we are reluctant to call
> in foreign police; that can get very unpleasant. So we're back where we
> started from.

The British embassy has developed a plan to put a brake on these hippie
mood-changes; as soon as a hippie has agreed to be repatriated, the
embassy advances the ticket money to him, but the Foreign Office holds
on to his passport until the debt has been repaid. The countries that have
no embassy in a country on the hashish trail as, for example, Belgium has
no embassy in Nepal, find it even more difficult to help their children in
distress. A Swiss woman, who has been with the Red Cross for twenty
years, and is known and admired among the local people for her dedica-
tion, told me about a young Belgian girl who, tripping on LSD, danced
the light fantastic in the streets of Katmandu completely nude. The
Nepalese authorities, who do not recognize that irrational behavior is a
sickness, threw her into a woman's prison. She became violent, tearing
the clothes they had given her, and throwing bricks at her jailers, until
they chained her. When she was finally released, she fluctuated between
states of exaltation and apathy, collected crowds in the city, danced nude
under the erotic statues of the temples, and was arrested again. My Swiss
friend telegraphed to the parents, "Brigitte very ill," and the parents
replied, "Do everything necessary, we will pay." And pay they did, for
they had to hire a husky male nurse to accompany the girl all the way to
Brussels. Had it not been for the Swiss woman, Brigitte's life would have
ended in some Himalayan dungeon.

    This story received confirmation from an unexpected quarter: the
heroine herself, whose name is Brigitte Axel, wrote a book about her
adventures. The details of the book, entitled *H* (*H* for "hippie" and

for "hashish") corresponded point for point with the story my Swiss friend had told. Brigitte, brought up with all the privileges that personal attractiveness and high social position could bestow, had "let it all hang out" one drugged summer on a beach in Crete, and then she set out on the hashish trail—Turkey, Iran, Afghanistan, India, Nepal. Almost every page of the book told the same story as this one:

A long-haired American [or Frenchman or whatever] pulls up in a little used car. I get in. A., who is plucking a guitar, rises up on the back seat. We set out for X. We find a room together [or a tent], all smoky, where we lay down our sleeping bags and smoke shit [hashish]. During the night I hear a girl moan, B. must be making love with her. C. and D. are on a bad trip; they've dropped too much acid, and beg us not to let them die during the night. I go to sit with them. The next day, we look around the place. There is plenty of sh--. I meet E. He's got lovely eyes, we like each other, and we stay together three nights. Somebody sells something from our pack to get a few dollars. We make parties, we dance, I make cookies, I smoke sh--, my friend F. shoots up [with heroin]. Suddenly he tells me he's leaving for Goa. My girlfriend N., who I met in Istanbul, shows up all of a sudden in braids that she's painted all different colors. She makes herself at home in our tent, and she's got loads of shit, we pass joints around to all our friends. Then I leave for Kabul. On the highway, an Italian comes rolling up in a little Fiat and picks me up. In the back seat, a girl is stretched out tripping on mescaline. There's a guy picking a guitar. We go on to Y. . . .

And so it goes . . . little grains of life, all the same, ad infinitum. Rarely a mildly telling insight, never a bit of questioning.

Didier's girlfriend is Swedish. I call her "the madwoman of Chaillot." You can't tell how old she is, she's dressed in rags, she uncovers her genitals or her breasts without really realizing it. She has attacks of malaria often. She takes opium. She will talk and talk wildly about a whole flashing world, all disconnected like she is. She's traveled with Didier, for a year, always by train; they really look so awful, cars on the road won't pick them up.

Then, exhausted by this concentration on one single topic, Brigitte picks up her dot-dot-dash style again:

Sylvie, in love with an English boy, disappears from my life. I take up, as friends, with two Japanese, Kaso and Kasi. They have set up housekeeping in a strategic corner of the tent. . . . We smoke shit.

Brigitte's straightforward narrative tells us that the great Katmandu crisis was precipitated by her third LSD trip. Someone, a stranger, had given her a pill and she threw it into her mouth without even knowing the strength of the dose. Either it was very strong or she had become very sensitive to it, because this third trip of hers sent her into a "chain trip": she hallucinated almost without let-up for a month, without another drop of the drug.

The embassies and the consulates are hard-pressed to grapple with these whirlwinds that swirl around them. "We aren't equipped to handle the hippies," is the diplomats' constant refrain. "We are dealing with a phenomenon for which none of our traditional modes of action have prepared us. We have neither the resources, nor the authority, nor training about drugs." Also, it must be realized that travel to the ends of the earth for practically nothing has become easier and easier, which certainly spurs these children into flight. Some controls should be placed on cut-rate air traffic, like the charter flights on obsolete planes, or low-priced student tourism on airlines so dubious that half the time the airplane falls apart before the scheduled return flight. And a whole new batch of derelicts are thrust out onto the bosom of a strange country whose language they do not know, nor one person who could help them. These young people lose their equilibrium, the ones who aren't basically sound turn to drugs, get into trouble of various kinds, and sometimes kill themselves.

Every young person who plays at being emancipated leans toward hippiedom.

All the hippies dream of setting out along the hashish trail.

At the end of that road, they find a bare room for vacant souls. . . .

The same room and the same soul they could find for a dollar in a Bowery flophouse.

6

Here, There, and Everywhere

The Canadian Scene

The hippie phenomenon made its way through Montreal and Toronto with dizzying speed. The journal *Médecine de France* (December, 1969) estimated more than 20,000 flower-children in Canada, which is a lot for a cold country, since it takes a burning faith indeed to wander barefoot in a glacial climate. Their center of operations is Yorkville, a Toronto neighborhood well furnished now with wild and startling boutiques and deafening discotheques. Their local newspaper is called "Satyrday"—very clever. I noticed in Yorkville that the police roamed the neighborhood constantly, always in pairs, on motorcycles, in squad cars, and on horseback, with their paddy wagons never too far away. That's because the Canadian hippies, in many of whose veins runs Latin blood, cause considerably more trouble than the more phlegmatic Anglo-Saxon hippies.

I stopped near a club called "The Cop." Ragamuffin boys were squirting water pistols at the legs of fifteen-year-old girls. I threaded my way through a group of older youths, whose topics of conversation were, as always, sex, drugs, and dealing. These offspring of well-to-do parents, whose families would be quite willing to keep them in school until twenty-five, have no particular social purpose; unlike their American counterparts, many of whom who feel responsible for political action against the Vietnam war and for civil liberties, there's nothing much to fight for, which forces them to fall back on silliness: the right to sit on the sidewalks, to take drugs, to close their streets to traffic. They kill time organizing sit-ins, love-ins, sleep-ins, smoke-ins, invade-ins, and even starve-ins, in the course of which they sit on the pavement, make love, sleep, smoke marijuana, invade City Hall, or go on hunger strikes. Many hippies wind up in police stations where they are held for twenty-four hours, after which they return to their amusements in the streets. Some of the older and harder affiliates of the movement join extremist groups like the Québec Liberation Front or pro-Chinese terrorist groups which try to turn the naturally rebellious impulses of these youths to political account.

Their most celebrated guru is David de Poe, a political activist and twenty-seven-year-old eternal student, who was expelled from the University of Toronto. He is paid $600 a year to lead the "Company of Young Canadians," a youth organization sponsored by the Canadian government. It is he, with full flowing beard and long locks sleeking out from under a black sombrero like snakes slithering from a ditch, who directed the historic campaign to close a Yorkville street to traffic. One Saturday evening in August, some 100 flower-children started a fire in a Yorkville trash can and danced around it like voodoo sorcerers. At three in the morning, six of them were arrested, including David de Poe. In his room, he has hung pictures of the hairy Ginsberg and that hippie-Buddha Mao Tse-tung. It goes without saying that the Canadian press—anyway, its straight representatives—is scandalized at the spectacle of Her Majesty's government subsidizing such a fomenter of disorder, such an enemy of hearth and home.

Another luminary in the Yorkville sky, who is perhaps more Grand Guignol than guru, is Pops Gilgour. This seventy-year-old hippie wears a pair of striped red pants that he claims to have stolen from a sleeping policeman, a Boy Scout shirt, and a yellow slicker that could stop traffic. He wears a chain hanging with little bells, bottle openers, can openers, voodoo charms and a dog tail. He carries the spokes of an old umbrella in his right hand, and in his left the lower parts of a life-size plastic mannikin wearing nylon stockings and black panties. He lives in a hut that has taken on the air of a psychedelic bazaar. Pops sometimes finds himself sharing a paddy wagon with harder-shelled demonstrators, and was recently tried in court with a group of sidewalk-sitters. At the age of seventy, Pops has finally acquired the renown to which he had aspired in vain his life long.

But all glory is shadowed. His son has declared, "It isn't good for children to see their grandfather carry on this spectacle and shame our name in the streets of Yorkville. I won't have anything more to do with him." Pops has his parental problems too, but the other way around from the other hippies.

In Canada, during 1962, there were 24 indictments for dealing in marijuana. In 1968, there were 2000. I visited the rooms of several of the drug-takers, which were not much better than the hell-holes I saw in the Near East. I remember a garret in Quebec City—a magnificent French town dominated by the St. Lawrence River—occupied by four kids from fifteen to eighteen. A nauseating odor composed of the bitter fumes of marijuana, the musky smell of unwashed bodies, and the stench of garbage and animal excrement decaying in a corner filled the room. Two dogs, a cat and a white rat slept in the middle of the room. Bob, a freckled redhead, told me that the cat, the white rat, and two of his friends had all gotten stoned together. He was proud of his experiment in creating universal love: thanks to the mescaline, he had succeeded in reconciling the cat and the rat, who went off together on a trip to paradise. Bob, fifteen years old, with the face of an angel, had left his parents because "he had had their fighting up to here." He brought out a packet of grass and rolled a joint that he passed to another hippie, a deserter from the U.S. Army, who ran to hide under the bed every time anyone knocked at the door.

Other Bobs sell pot and amphetamines—five capsules for a dollar —to each other, but they don't trust anyone over twenty. As for LSD, its ravages have made themselves felt in the august halls of old universities. According to Dr. Morton Schuman of Toronto, 10 percent of the students of a certain university have experimented with LSD, and 5 percent of these could not continue their studies. One Liberal deputy of the Canadian Parliament, Patrick McGeer, revealed that some hundred students of the University of British Columbia have experimented with acid. A doctor at the psychiatric hospital in Hamilton, Ontario, reports that the acid-trippers come to him "dazed, terrified, and suffering from visual hallucinations" (*L'Action de Quebec,* May 13, 1967). Little colonies of initiates have set up, as in the United States, little chapels where they claim their right to use LSD as a religious sacrament. The marijuana smokers are, of course, a hundred times more numerous than the "acid droppers," so it is no surprise to learn that the Minister of Education, Leslie Peterson, has declared that the drug situation among students is the most disturbing problem that his ministry has ever had to face.

In May, 1969, an officer in the Ministry of Health of the large and beautiful port city of Montreal "judged it his duty to draw the attention of his superiors to the grave facts that he had himself witnessed." He had discovered that 13 percent of the young people between eight and seventeen years old that he had dealt with were regular sniffers of model airplane glue. Extending his investigation to the city as a whole, he was "horrified" to find that the "sniffers" inhaled all possible household solvents as well as insecticides and lighter fluid. They would do their sniffing in a plastic bag so as not to lose any of the fumes.

The runaway problem is as acute in Canada as in the United States. When I was in Toronto, I learned that during 1967 alone, 1650 young runaway girls had been found by the police, not to mention the hundreds of girls who were not found. And how many flights had never been reported to the authorities for fear of scandal? In Canada, more girls between fifteen and eighteen years old leave home than boys. My source of information, a chief of police, told me also that the number of thefts, breakings-of-the-law, assaults, and rapes in the single hippie village of Yorkville is greater than in the entire rest of Ontario. But the saddest thing, he said, is what happens to these girls who, by and large, have barely emerged from childhood. "These are goodhearted young girls from honorable homes who, in general, come to Yorkville healthy and idealistic. But their hippie guides take them in hand and, in no time they are ruined."

The Canadian winter is a terrible ordeal for the flower-children. The glacial winds force the apostles for the wandering life to dive into their coffee shops to stand pressed up against the walls all huddled together. The owners announce angrily that they can't stay all day without ordering something, so they stroll from a café to a store, from a store to a gallery, and from a gallery back to their café, trying to keep from freezing to death. The long, terrible white Canadian winter requires heavy overcoats, gloves and furred boots. But as the newcomer hippies sold all these articles from their previous lives for a few dollars at the beginning of spring, and as the places where they sleep are hardly heated at all, they catch pneumonia. I have seen them spend the nights in automatic laundries, in the vestibules of apartment buildings, and in the lobby of a provincial legislature. But, despite the efforts of the "Diggers," who distribute food and hot soup to the starvelings of Queen's Park, as well as information about places to sleep, Yorkville becomes depopulated in winter. Smoke-ins and other carryings-on are impractical when your feet are freezing in the snow. So some go back home, whereas others trek to Victoria, the "in" Riviera of the Canadian Pacific Coast, where they have set up a second colony on the temperate island of Vancouver. The flower-children have learned that it is hard to war against a consumer society in a climate where only urbanized and well-equipped people can survive; that is, people who consume a great deal.

Hippies in Britain

In Europe, Great Britain was the first country to be invaded, in the spring of 1965, by the whirlpool of hippieism and drugs. This movement did not spring up spontaneously: it was propelled by a boisterous assemblage at the Royal Albert Hall where American gurus like Allen Ginsberg and Lawrence Ferlinghetti spoke exaltedly of the joys of psychedelia. The participants, some 5000 strong, were asked to come with a flower. "For us, this was the beginning of the Year One, a marvelous and mystic thing," says one Haynes, who prides himself on not having one friend that doesn't smoke marijuana.

We are now in the Year Five of British hippieism, and 100,000 young English people are estimated to have gone the drug route. Their most illustrious guru is Aldous Huxley who—an apt closing of the circle —played an important role in the psychedelic revolution in the United States. His books, along with those of Leary and Watts, have become the hippies' bibles. How could one resist the temptation to expand one's consciousness when it is formulated with lyricism like this:

One brilliant May morning, [he begins], I swallowed four decigrams of mescaline and sat down to see what would happen. A half-hour later, I had a sense of being bathed in a dancing aureole of golden lights. Then sumptuous red draperies appeared before me, swelling and undulating from centers of dazzling energy whose patterns changed continually. Then I saw blue spheres which took on an intense solidity and ascended without a sound. . . . My books became a ruby, lapis lazuli, emerald, and topaz so intense that they seemed on the point of leaving the shelves of my library. . . . A little afterwards, a cluster of yellow tritomes in full flower exploded into my visual field, so passionately alive that they seemed ready to speak. Looking at a bouquet of cream-colored roses and violet iris, I saw what Adam saw on the morning of creation: the miracle, rising from moment to moment, of creation in its nudity. . . . Then the experience, a vividly colored, plastic experience, became mystical and profoundly religious. I understood now what the Hindu vision of beatitude must have been, the felicity of the

interior light, the illuminating Dharma of Buddha. *(The Doors of Perception.)*

Thanks to certain drugs, Huxley avows, one can relive the illuminations of the great mystics of history: in the West, Saint John of the
Cross, Saint Marguerite-Marie Alacoque, Father de Foucault; Shri
Aurobindo, Ramakrishna, Sivanandra for the East. And the great English writer concludes:

> The experience of mescaline is that which the theologians call gratuitous
> grace; not necessarily a salvation, but useful in its power, which one must
> accept with gratitude.

No one can deny that Aldous Huxley is a great master of words,
but whether his dithyrambic flights on hallucinogenic supra-visions
correspond to reality remains to be seen. Professor Zaehner, in his
Mysticism, Sacred or Profane, says that Huxley was carried away by his
own lyricism, and that he did not truly experience all that he claimed
to. Professor Zaehner also took mescaline, and the visions that he
reported—noted as they occurred by reliable witnesses—are much
more of this world. Michel Lancelot, the author of *Je veux regarder
Dieu en face* [*I Want to See God Face to Face*], has also experimented
with LSD under the care of guides. The accounts he gives of his
hallucinations—even though he himself claims a mystic illumination
for the hippie movement—are disenchanting.

Other magi of hallucination like Leary, Watts, etc., have added
their voices to the chorus, as well as the small-time charlatans who
always march in the furrows plowed by the great men. Such a one is
Henry Moore, originally from Oklahoma, who now plies his vocation
in Great Britain as Leary's representative and the local high priest of
LSD. "Thanks to acid," he had declared, "the hippies have discovered
that there is a satisfying answer to *all* the questions the world poses."
This sentence, as pretentious as it is ignorant, is a fair barometer of the
speaker's degree of irresponsibility. He is presently the editor-in-chief
of *International Times,* the English hippie journal. One can imagine
the number of young people he has coaxed into the madhouse, not to
mention the grave. The newspaper, with an average print run of 50,000
copies per issue, specializes in the usual: "police brutality," exaltation

of drugs, and sexual exhibitionism. One issue, which was seized by the police, explained in exhaustive detail the workings of a mechanical penis. The founder of the newspaper, John Hopkins, called Hoppy, charged with possession of marijuana, runs a psychedelic discotheque called UFO—"unidentified flying objects."

Henry Moore turns the young people on, not only to drugs, but to revolt against their parents:

> You have to burn the bridges between you and those bastards [that is, all the rest of us]. Don't buy anything from them. Don't hang out with them. . . . If you can't convert your parents, forget them. . . . Remember that your father thinks the police are right and you are wrong. And your mother would like to think you have no genitals. They won't help you when you're arrested, they'll say you asked for it. But that's exactly what you did ask for: to be arrested.

In London, Hyde Park is the center for the hippies' rambles. Girls and boys stroll nude along the paths during smoke-ins, to give them an added touch of spice. But the most famous event, on the Isle of Wight, which Bob Dylan and other great trans-Atlantic stars lent their luster to, was an event indeed, kicked off with the spectacle of a very beautiful couple making love in front of 500,000 people.

Drug incidents crop up all the time in England, though the press only draws attention to matters that involve the stars. For example, Brian Jones, one of the Rolling Stones, drowned while he was stoned in his luxurious swimming pool. He had already been sentenced in 1966 to nine months in prison for some drug affair. Marianne Faithful, Mick Jagger's long-time girlfriend, was in a drug coma for three days. And the great Mick himself, the demonic leader of the Rolling Stones, was sentenced to three months in prison for possession of benzedrine, a dangerous amphetamine, and Keith Richards got a year for turning his apartment into a smokery. In less than five years, the number of drug arrests had multiplied by sixty.

In 1967, with the hope of braking the surge, Parliament passed the "Dangerous Drugs Act," permitting the rigidly controlled prescription of heroin to addicts, but otherwise banning all other drugs. They might as well not have bothered. Not only did heroin addiction continue to rise, but amphetamine use became so widespread that the drugs were blocked from sale in drugstores.

Drug lobbying groups seem to be abundantly provided with money. The mail organization, a group called Soma, with headquarters in the United States and a London branch, has taken entire pages of advertising against the "immoral" law against marijuana. These ads have been signed by the Beatles, members of Parliament, professors, and even doctors. Each year, Soma representatives organize hundreds of teach-ins defending the legalization of marijuana, along with radio and television debates on the same subject. Soma organized as well the first mass demonstration in favor of this legislation.

Since this orgy of pro-drug publicity has had its fatal side effects —madness, suicides, deaths—the same groups have set up rescue centers for young people who had OD'd ("OD" for "overdose"), so that regular hospitals would not be flooded with such a wave of victims that the public would be aroused and provoke the authorities into disturbing investigations. Soma has also created a sub-agency, "Release," which provides twenty-four-hour-a-day legal assistance. A sumptuous young lady named Caroline Coone with golden hair and amethyst eyes is the guiding star of this agency. Widely distributed flyers invite hippies in distress to call her at 228–77–53, whether their troubles be with the police or with their own health. A charming voice replies with the necessary emergency advice. At the beginning, Caroline made her headquarters in a tiny maid's room; now she works from a private house not far from Nottinghall Gate complete with several telephone lines, secretaries, switchboard operators, and the services of some thirty lawyers who have volunteered their services to the hippies. Caroline finds them work, gives advice on abortions, the Pill, and freakouts—drug trips that turn bad. The hippies have cooking facilities on the third floor of the building, and there is always a cup of hot tea ready for them. This whole organization is well-oiled by the contributions of rich benefactors. George Harrison, the ex-Beatle, sent Caroline $12,000.

But all of these efforts, well-meaning though they may be, don't prevent one string of tragedies after another. One mother told me of her ordeal—a story that is not very different from thousands of others:

> My son was killed by drugs. He was big and husky, six feet tall, but in high school he began to take up with a drug dealer, and started cutting classes. Soon the police started arresting him, we would stand his bail, they would let him go, arrest him again, and on and on it went until he became

permanently classified as a drug user. He was seventeen. He left our house —how could we stop him?—and things went from bad to worse. But in his very darkest times he would come back to me for aid and comfort. We would spend an evening making plans for changing his life and then, without saying a word, he would take off again the next day, for months. His splendid constitution deteriorated, he became emaciated, vacant-eyed, dirty. A doctor who thought he was being clever prescribed large doses of heroin for him, in exchange for a substantial nest egg in fees. Within a month he was practically dead. He took hospital cures three times, but in the end he died, since there was no place for him to go for long term re-education. The fault lies not with our children, but with their pop idols, brazen "heads," whom the press glorifies as if they were gods.

A thousand mothers like this woman are powerless against the "pop" hero image beamed out by television. And since 1954, the number of drug users has continued to increase by 50 percent per year. The Minister of the Interior proposed a very hard law—passed by the House of Commons in March, 1970—to replace the half-measures of the past: any person convicted of trafficking in any drug, including marijuana, was subject to a 14-year prison term and unlimited fines; the illegal possession of heroin could lead to seven years in prison, and that of marijuana, five years; physicians who prescribed excessive doses of heroin could receive up to fourteen years in prison.

Will the severity of these measures block the growth of the cancer? No one can be sure yet. But you can be sure that the British Labour government could never have passed measures so contrary to its traditional liberality were the danger not grave indeed.

Swedish Hippies

Next after England, the hippie style made its appearance on the Scandinavian peninsula and particularly in Sweden. In Stockholm the hippies, their once blue eyes now eaten up by mournful pupils, congregate around the central railroad station, and sit on the sidewalks at the foot of a nearby church not far from grass-covered graves. These are the blond Vikings—in the ninth century warriors and plunderers, drug-besodden and stagnant in the twentieth.

Strange "recipes," which grant an, alas, temporary euphoria— temporary since they simply aggravate the deficiencies they are supposed to ease—run from hand to hand in the schools, and very few adults know anything about them. Professor Cronholm, director of the university psychiatric service at Stockholm's Karolinska Hospital, revealed some of these recipes—very simple, but so dangerous that they have been kept from the press—behind closed doors. The professor emphasized the prodigies of imagination deployed by the adolescents in creating drugs so unpredictably out of the most extraordinary and casual substances. One suggestion, for example, is to evaporate paregoric and inject it into the veins. Abnormal, incredible, but true. Regular cocktails of old-fashioned alcohol have been replaced by an explosive mixture made from preludin (an appetite suppressant) and paregoric on an LSD base (Stockholm Drug Conference, June, 1969). And, while for a long time marijuana was hardly used in Sweden—whether because it was too hard to come by, or because the kids preferred to use their creative imaginations—it has begun now to make its inexorable way through the schools.

Whereas heroin has been the great ravisher in the United States and England, young people in Sweden and Japan mostly curdle their souls with the amphetamine stimulants. The danger is so great that, in March, 1969, Sweden asked the United Nations to include, along with the other drugs outlawed by the Convention of 1961, a series of stimulants. It succeeded in having six of these drugs, including the amphetamines, placed under controls as rigorous as those for narcotics. Dr. Bror Rexed, director of the Swedish Board of Health, revealed that 10,000 young people were known to have given themselves intravenous injections of these products in doses several hundred times stronger than levels prescribed for therapeutic use. "The massive doses and the way in which they are taken," he added, "produce effects as grave as any we have ever seen, including with heroin. Several thousand of our young people are on the way to destroying themselves intellectually, socially, and physically."

In the Netherlands: The Provos

In Holland, the hippie movement is grafted on to that of the "provos"—a shortened form of the word "provocateur." And, in truth, they belong less to the flower-child school than to the Hell's Angels type. These provos have lost ground today, but several years ago they were strong enough to sow terror and chaos wherever they passed. They would distribute the recipes for Molotov cocktails; they threatened to pour LSD into Amsterdam's water reservoirs; they organized public smoke-ins, raped young girls, kidnapped minors, hid deserters. They placed themselves against all and everyone, with no other aim than to provoke the established society and make trouble. One of their leaders, Luud Schimmelpenninck, was elected to the Municipal Council of Amsterdam in February, 1966. This thirty-year-old provo arranged to have bicycles, painted white, put at the disposition of everyone. This share-the-wealth initiative provoked much discussion, but very few bicycles, since they vanished in record time underneath the second coat of nonwhite paint that any freeloader might take the trouble to apply.

The city authorities abandoned an old unused movie theater to the provos where they could unleash their instincts behind closed doors —with the hope that they would keep their instincts there, and not spill them out on the streets. They used their new headquarters for gambling and free love. They also bought an old river barge which they transformed into a combined gambling den, smokery, and brothel, until the day that a rival group of hippies set fire to it. This latter group of hippies, called "Central Station" after their main headquarters in Amsterdam's major railway station, also have their games: rioting and general provocation, which earned them beatings by sailors, who also cut their hair off.

It was in an Amsterdam hotel room that John Lennon, the former Beatle, and his wife, Japanese actress-writer-sculptress Yoko Ono, held a week's love-in for the edification of the press, assuming, on order, all the positions of the Kama Sutra for picture taking. The point was not, however, to provide a systematic photographic study of comparative skin/hair systems—reddish and frizzy against black and smooth. The performance was, it seems, a protest against the war in Vietnam.

The provos infiltrate hippie love-ins and, to liven things up, they turn them into riots. In one of them, all the sidewalk parking meters were torn out, display windows broken, cars set afire, and stores pillaged. The chief of police was relieved of his duties for not being able to contain them—a coup for the provos—and their next target was the mayor, whom they managed to unseat in the next election. That is why the municipal council, in fear and trembling, went so far as to subsidize two hippie groups, "Fantasio" and "Paradiso," whose members graciously offer "ecstasy cigarettes." The sophisticated provos preach "permanent revolution" in two newspapers, *Paper Tiger* and *Provo*. Their guru, Poel Van Duyn, author of the book *The White Menace*, studies Trotsky, no doubt with the intention of raising a new Red Army. If Trotsky could rise from the grave he would be startled indeed to see these new "proletarian" troops wearing little bells, smoking hash, and making love for all to see on the barricades of the world revolution....

German Hippies

In Germany, the Bohemian quarter of Munich, on the grand Leopoldstrasse, is the place where the hippies, called "gammlers," dream their strange dreams. Some of them put their pennies into a sort of German automat called the "Picnic," while others do not hesitate to dissolve one drug or another into their beer mugs—a dangerous mixture of alcohol and drugs that makes the gammlers become violent. They beg in a very aggressive way among the straight, who will give them twenty pfennigs rather than cause a scene. They frequent a clutch of squalid bars, more squalid than anything in England. The ones who have no money for drinking gather in a place called the PN Club, an old barn falling into ruin where amateur rock bands screech out their noises of hell. Joints of marijuana cost 80 cents there, and a capsule of LSD goes for $2.

The gammlers travel a great deal. They are true wandering hippies, setting off for anywhere with a sleeping bag and a pair of shoes, which they don only when absolutely necessary. They can often be found in Hamburg, where drugs are easier than in Frankfurt or Stuttgart. Sailors come from the Orient in general, and Communist China in particular, bringing drugs into the port. The gammlers are even less preoccupied with ideology than the Anglo-Saxon hippies, who worry less about it than the French and Canadians. All the Germans that I met on the hashish trail truly have no other interest in life than drugs and vagabondage. Faithful, however, to the German traditions of thoroughness, they bury themselves in the hundred-volume treatise on drugs that exists in their imagination, and studiously experiment with each paragraph. A sociologist at the University of Munich, Hans Gruner, sees them as the descendants of the mendicant, itinerant monks of the Middle Ages.

The Hippies of France

All the different drug routes meet and cross paths in France: the drug traffic from the Orient to the West; a stage along the hitchhiking highway from America to India; the route of kif which extends from the Scandinavian countries to the sun of the Riviera and North Africa; the D.T.'s throughway that leads from the sky to the cemetery . . . which is to say that hippieism in France is no less cosmopolitan than in Afghanistan or Nepal. Several sections of Paris have been invaded by the movement—the Latin Quarter, Saint-Germain-des-Prés, Montmartre, and others—as well as Cannes and Nice on the Côte d'Azur.

French hippies have not yet reached the point of sitting down en masse on the sidewalk, making love in public, or taking drugs under the noses of the police as in the United States or England. But that will come. For everything—from automatic laundromats to long hair, from exotic drugstores to exotic drugs—comes to France, some five to ten years after the Anglo-Saxon countries. So France can expect within a fairly short time to be edified by the spectacle of coupling couples and demonstrations against this or that. . . . There was a foretaste in November, 1967, on that famous "psychedelic" night at the Palais des Sports in Paris, where the odor of cannabis penetrated the air while, for the audience's delight, a "sexydelic" follies unrolled on the stage.

The most freaked-out creator of freaky happenings "à la française" is Jean-Jacques Lebel, who organized a marathon of "monstrous happenings." "It's total war," he declared during a nude bacchanal in Paris in May, 1965, in which a young blonde girl crouched nude on the hood of a car, her face covered with a death's-head mask, while a young sculptor, obviously in the grip of inspiration, smeared her with noodles. A professor from the Sorbonne was there to study the conceptual interdependence between noodles and sex. The students shouldered their way in to touch . . . the noodles. The blonde girl seized handfuls from her belly and pounded her aggressors with them while they cried, "Here, to me, here." Total war had become macaroni mayhem.

This far-out happening was overtaken, so to speak, by another one in Nice in which a group of longhairs, called the "Panic Group," crucified a living chicken. They had woven a rug from chicken feathers dressed with blood and tomato pulps for maximum effectiveness. This happening ended with a film of childbirth run backward. The wailing baby returned, head first, into the sweet, warm receptacle from whence he came, with a white-coated doctor pushing him back in with all his strength; the next sequence showed the mother walking out of the clinic with her belly huge once again.

Clearly the French hippies are, after all, the masters of the "French style."

Buying drugs at retail in France is often a rather complicated procedure: the would-be purchaser whispers his request into the ear of a hippie-type, who slips it into another long-haired ear, and so on along the chain until the drug is returned to the consumer by the same route . . . that is, unless by ill chance one falls upon a narcotics detective disguised as a hippie. In France, a one-gram ball of hashish costs 20 to 40 cents. A joint of marijuana is 50 to 60 cents, while a capsule of LSD —available in a wide range of colors—goes for $6. In private apartments in Paris or on the Riviera, cocktail parties have been replaced by "hash parties." A group of close friends gathers, each person bringing another close friend, for a "hash-in." "With it" party-givers not only do not hesitate now to circulate a hash pipe at their gatherings, they season plates of rice and pastries with the drug, which produces a much more rapid "take-off." But, ever since Commissioner Carrère came on the scene, your flying-high party-goer is much more likely to be swooped right into jail.

If a person has a hippie look, the chances are that he will be stopped on the street by a shady-looking character who will whisper, "You want some shit?" And he'll flash before you, nestled secretively in the crease of his palm, a brown pasty substance that has very much the look, and even a bit of the smell, of that item. "You want some shit?" is a very French way of bypassing the middleman to get cannabis direct to the consumer.

As for the wholesale trade, it is controlled in part by Levantines (Syrians, Lebanese, Turks, etc.), which is why hashish of Afghan and Pakistani origin—the best—can be found in a fair number of Oriental cabarets in the Latin Quarter. The North Africans are also active in the trade. Certain Arab bistros along Pigalle, in Barbès, and Nanterre supply kif, and these bistros have become the main source of supply in Nanterre for the students from the nearby university. There is also a hashish "made in France," an extract from the hemp cultivated in the

South. In the past year, Commissioner Carrère has had 943 clandestine plants uprooted.

Opium is smuggled into France from Cambodia, India, Turkey, and also Communist China. With a richness of imagination equal to that deployed by nature in the proliferation of species, history has added one more strain to her long roll call of apostasies: the Chinese Communists, who claim to emancipate men through the potion of truth that they bring, in fact sell them the powder of illusion to stupefy. . . .

Heroin is distilled in underground laboratories in Marseilles from a morphine base that is smuggled in from Iran; Iran produces its morphine from the opium that comes from the Asian countries. French heroin is pure and white as innocence, and all the more dangerous for that. Until the drug epidemic began to make itself felt among the French citizenry, the Marseilles distilleries functioned peacefully at full capacity. The business is dominated mostly by Corsicans, who ship the immaculate powder out through the northern ports—Le Havre, Anvers —or through Spain, to the United States, because the Americans pay well and in cash. New York's Narcotics Bureau has confirmed that 80 percent of the white heroin entering the United States on the East Coast was refined in France. The brown heroin, less purified, comes from Latin America—an area that does not employ the same quality controls as France. The Corsicans employ one to two hundred South American delivery agents who travel by air and sea so that, if they are picked up, Marseilles is not pinpointed as the point of origin.

The increase in drug traffic has provoked a counter-reaction in France. In August, 1969, Commissioner Carrère increased the number of narcotics police from 50 to 200. Their director, Commissioner Carrère, whose ambition is as much to prevent the evil from spreading as it is to cut out the already existing infection, is a tireless and brilliant lecturer who crisscrosses France to illuminate the drug problem for audiences of policemen, administrators, and customs officials, as well as for members of the teaching profession, sociologists, and representatives from the medical world. To combat the Hydra-headed monster, this doughty officer has installed himself in a tiny room in Paris which he has transformed into a small museum on drugs well worth the attention of a visitor.

During one operation in 1969 along the Mediterranean cost from

Menton to Montpellier, the police arrested 11 dealers and seized 50 kilos of heroin in one day. At Fréjus, seven young pushers were hauled into court, and customs officers seized 100 kilos of heroin at Menton just as it was being transferred from the Italian car that had carried it over the border into a waiting auto with French plates. The driver of the French car got away, but not before running over a customs officer in his haste. At Besançon, six different drug deals were uncovered in less than a year, and an Algerian drug trafficker was arrested in Marseilles, etc.

American hippies abroad play an important part in the nonprofessional drug traffic. At Bayonne, three Americans were each sentenced to two months in prison and a $10,000 fine for drug smuggling. They were picked up in Biarritz where their pretty little flower-studded mini-car was found to carry a heavy load of hashish, some medicines so toxic that their sale is forbidden in French pharmacies, and some 20 brand-new water pipes, or hookahs. In Paris, a pair of American students were arrested carrying five kilos of "chira." They had recently come back from Pakistan where they had bought a great deal of cannabis for a very low price, to sell in France for transportation money back home at ten times more than what they paid for it. Thus, a goodly number of American hippies, whom one could not consider professional drug traffickers, coolly calculate their vacation budgets on profits drawn from the sale of death.

The rising drug curve in France can be graphically illustrated by the progression of arrests and seizures of contraband. In all of 1965, there were 107 drug arrests in France. In 1969 there were 1200 people arrested (994 users and 206 dealers), eleven times more than five years ago. 86 percent of those arrested were younger than 34, 17 percent younger than 19.

The bulletin of the Paris Police Prefecture announced in February, 1968, that, from 1958 on, the quantities of drugs seized could be calculated in grams whereas in 1969, quantities had mounted to 180 *kilos* of cannabis, 613 kilos of opium, 107 kilos of pure heroin, and 219 kilos of the morphine base. As one kilo of morphine base is equivalent to one kilo of pure heroin, and as one kilo of pure heroin is worth in France, on the average, at the time of manufacture, $4000, these 326 kilos of combined heroin/morphine represent more than a million dollars. As heroin is sold at retail mixed with twenty times its own weight of lactose, these 326 kilos of pure heroin would have gone on the market as more than 7000 kilos of commerical heroin. And as this is sold in the United States at $20,000 the kilo, this seized drug had a potential market value of $134,400,000. You could build a steel mill for this.

Not since the twenties have drugs been seized in quantities above —startling for the period—50 kilos (of opium). Now, in 1969, twelve times more opium than that has been seized and, over and above that, a quantity of heroin sufficient to intoxicate 26,000 people for a year, since a heroin addict absorbs, on average, 15 grams of pure heroin a year.

In the 1930s, the drug-users were mostly adults of the esthetic/intellectual milieus who mostly indulged in morphine and cocaine. And there were also the old colonials who had become accustomed to opium in Indochina. During their long ship voyages home, which could last several months, they "kicked the habit" by the famous "two bottles" technique. One bottle was filled with opium, the other with cognac. Every day they were administered a lesser quantity of opium and a greater quantity of alcohol. By the time they reached the shores of the motherland, their drug addiction had indeed been conquered, to be replaced by a raging alcoholism.

There had been no known drug addicts in France since 1948, affirms Professor Deniker, director of the neuropsychiatric services at Sainte-Anne's Hospital, until its brutal revival in the last few years. Commissioner Carrère thinks that the beatniks were the original contaminating agents. Their early rock parties degenerated into hash or LSD parties, to the point that these substances had to be entered on the list of banned drugs. The wave of drug use has, above all, swept over the young people, as illustrated by the fact that 60 percent of the cannabis seized has been found in the possession of students.

One painful story succeeds another. In the high school at Apt, seven boys were discovered to be smoking marijuana daily. In the Grenoble high school, five students were caught with drugs. At Enghien, at Compiègne, high school kids fell prey to strange kinds of malaise, inquiries were made, and cannabis was found in all their classrooms. At Nîmes, a group of high school kids organized "hash smokers" at one of their teacher's houses. He was sentenced to jail, his wife was charged too, and twenty-one of the students were prosecuted. And I could go on and on for pages.

Most unfortunately, large numbers of these young people escalate into heroin. Some students were caught at Saint-Germain-des-Prés, others in Belleville, selling the white powder. Some doctors have made some dramatic revelations, though often not for publication. A psychiatrist, Dr. Claude Olievenstein, charged that some fifty boys at one high school regularly give themselves heroin injections. A schoolteacher's son, sixteen years old, was found in a state of total delirium; he had begun with marijuana "to be like everyone else," and had escalated into the drugs that kill.

According to Dr. Pierre Bensoussan, it is not rare, incredible though it may sound, to find drug-takers as young as fifteen. Professor Deniker at Sainte-Anne's has noted that the increase in adolescent suicide has paralleled the increase in drug use. "In the United States there are little drug addicts as young as eight to twelve years old." In reporting this fact, the French radio commentator seemed to take comfort from the fact that in France there is no known heroin addiction . . . among children younger than fifteen! Truly, in the kingdom of the blind, the one-eyed are kings. . . .

The French public has finally been forced through several dramatic incidents into awareness of this strange epidemic. A seventeen-year-old girl died in the Bandol casino after her boyfriend had given her a heroin injection of three times the normal dose. This strange "friend" had let her die alone on the seat of a casino toilet. This brute, whose long hair had drained out all his intelligence, was admired by the sub-men of his species and by several sixteen-year-old virgins over whom he had gained influence, more through his syringe than through his penis, preparing his infected mixture with water from the toilets. He propagated his vice among young girls in order to possess them, among boys to dispossess them (of their "bread").

And then the drama of La Ciotat: One Jean-Claude Lamoureux, to be "with it"—"with" his intellectually cretinous little world—sniffed up pure heroin. He died immediately from a lightninglike pulmonary edema. In one single sniff he had inhaled three grams, whereas a confirmed heroin addict will normally not take in more than 15 grams of the pure drug over a whole year. The bells tolled over Christmas, 1969, for six adolescents killed by drugs in the preceding months; and they tolled as well for all of those who will never be known, who have departed incognito into the blue death.

Robert Boulin, the Minister of Public Health, has also expressed grave fears about the situation. He has given three examples of typical drug-provoked upheavals among the juvenile population of France:

1. A young boy, expelled from his high school at sixteen, went to Paris. He began to smoke marijuana, then escalated to LSD, then to heroin. Today he is eighteen, and in a chronic state of delirium. He threw himself out a window, and will be infirm for the rest of his life. His liver is permanently damaged, and his case is irreparable.

2. For those who believe that one try—just out of curiosity—won't hurt, M. Boulin cites the case of a medical student, twenty-four years old, who took only one dose of LSD. His trip was a "bummer," and he has tried to kill himself six times in the last six months.

3. A young girl, twenty-one, who tripped on combinations of hashish and amphetamines, became a prostitute in order to support her habit. Incapable, finally, of walking alone down the street, she had to be hospitalized, and she lies there today in a sort of "zombie" sleep.

One psychiatric hospital, Villejuif, counted twelve admissions in 1967 for drug-related reasons; in 1969, two years later, there were almost a hundred. The director of the Villejuif psychiatric service estimates that there are 20,000 drug-takers in France who are receiving serious medical treatment, and of these, some 8000 are already hospitalized. These figures should be multiplied by twenty, he says, for the great bulk of drug-induced mental illness never becomes known to us.

Three thousand addicts have been committed to hospitals for heroin addiction alone, not to mention all the patients on other drugs: opium, the hallucinogens, the amphetamines, hashish. There is every reason to believe that the number rises much higher than the above estimates. Dr. Pierre Bensoussan declared in *Le Monde* (July 1, 1969):

The official figures are absurd, bearing no relation to reality, because the means placed at the disposition of our drug services are scandalously insufficient. No matter what the ability of our personnel, they can't deal with every case. Our hospitals, clinics and dispensaries are hardly in a better position to know the real extent of it, because the only cases they see are those that are so grave or acute that the individual is *forced* in. Many drug-takers, because of the illegal nature of their indulgences, have a tendency to flee from any official institution as if it were the plague, even if they are promised that they will not be exposed. Distrustful by temperament, they "take care of each other," with catastrophic consequences, or else they don't take care of each other at all, convinced that their behavior has nothing pathological about it.

The police have a different clientele than the physicians. However, the two professions agree in saying that the number of drug-takers in France has doubled between 1968 and 1969. Professor Delay, a member of the Faculty of Medicine and of the Académie Française, has declared that the most stunning thing about the situation is not so much the number of drug-users, but the dizzying fashion in which this number has mounted in recent years, and the fact that the contagion has spread to the youngest sectors of the population to the point that, among last-year high school and university students, it has amounted to a virtual psychic epidemic.

Denying the fairy tale of "innocent" marijuana, Professor Deniker declares that the hemp plant, under all its different pseudonyms, can precipitate psychoses and lead to incurable mental difficulties.

LSD, at last, has begun to inspire fear, and French youngsters take less and less of it. However, certain incidents—the arrest of two boys on Saint-Germain-des-Prés carrying 6000 doses of acid, and the seizure in 1969 of 3518 LSD capsules, as well as the private LSD "parties" that go on in Paris, prove that the danger still exists. One Frenchman—a man who had been to these private parties—told me that hallucinogenic trips, even when not directed toward sex particularly, set up strong attachments between fellow users sitting side by side, much as the sexual act attaches man to woman.

Michel Lancelot, in his book *Je veux regarder Dieu en face* [*I Want to See God Face to Face*], reports several characteristic cases of bad trips in France.

First case: A young woman of twenty-seven took a capsule of 200 micrograms. She went into an hysterical crisis accompanied by bouts of nausea. Her anxiety state persisted for several weeks despite sedatives.

Second case: A girl, twenty-three, took a mild dose to experience lovemaking under LSD. She had terrifying visions, and thought she was going to die. She tried to throw herself out the window, and her friends had to hold her back by force.

Third case: A student of twenty took one dose of 250 micrograms, and was thrown into a state of acute depersonalization plus hallucinations that persisted after the "trip" was over. He had to be hospitalized. Three months after this single ingestion of the drug, he was still under medical surveillance.

Fourth case: A student took LSD without the assistance of a guide, or knowledge of the proper dose. That trip turned so sour that he could no longer reason, he tried to run away, and suffered seizures of violence. His fourth trip was the killer. He had to be hospitalized, and six months later he was no better.

The younger schoolchildren, who haven't "grown up" yet to the big-time drugs, take whatever comes to hand, from ether and white glue to mixtures based on corydrane or shaving lotions like aquavelva, in complete unconsciousness of danger. Some of them inject beer or whisky into their veins. All these poisonous concoctions are laid out for them in publications—veritable manuals, behind their innocent covers, on how to poison yourself— that can be picked up on any newsstand. There are detailed recipes on how to cook up various drugs out of ingredients that can be found everywhere.

We can understand the cry from the heart of Joseph Comiti, the Secretary of State for Youth: "Although I favor the abolition of capital punishment in general, the one group to whom I think it should apply are the traffickers in drugs."

And all these young drug-takers pretend to be "liberated"! Liberated from what? Unless it is liberation from the basic sense of self-preservation that is common to and indispensable to all animals. Look how the cat sniffs at her saucer of milk for a long time before she starts to lap it. Every animal senses that the earth abounds in substances that are poisonous to him, and his instinct keeps him away from them. No insect rests on the hemp flowers that exude the cannabis substance. These drugs are nothing more than poisons at greater or lesser concentration. On the other hand, every poison can be a health-giving medicine at infinitesimal doses, but only a doctor can prescribe them them after long years of study, and only a pharmacologist armed with high precision balances can prepare them. Alas, our adolescents, who have not yet, at any rate, decided to savor the delights of cyanide or arsenic, offer up their veins to the first vicious criminal marching in the street with his syringe and his poison in his dirty pocket, letting him pollute their blood, the most precious substance in the body. These young people clearly possess a sense that the cat lacks: the sense for liberation.

Italian Hippies

In March, 1970, the world was shocked by a huge scandal in the land of *la dolce vita*. Some forty hippies, who lived in an abandoned house in Turin, had taken up devil worship and practiced sexual orgies and macabre bacchanals in a setting of skeletons and skulls that had been disturbed from their rest in a nearby cemetery. A number of tombs had been profaned and pillaged of their objects of value. Thus, this Risorgimento of the avant garde has carried us far back indeed, to the Witches' Sabbaths of the Middle Ages.

The cannabis plant will grow anywhere in Italy. Useless, therefore, to smuggle in hashish. It is there. On the other hand, the smuggling trade in opium and its derivatives is so brisk as to be practically an industry in itself. The smokeries parade under the names of "cultural circles," "recreation associations," "cinema clubs," "academies of avant-garde music." One of these groups, sporting the inoffensive, even wholesome, name of the New Sports Club, settled in a barge on the healthful banks of the Tiber, nestles a smokery frequently by . . . two thousand students from some twenty secondary schools in Rome. A high-powered publicity campaign sponsored by certain "drug vampires" had attracted these young people, whose parents were nothing but pleased by all the fresh air, etc., their little ones would be exposed to through the "sports club." But, instead of hockey sticks, the kids played with sticks of hashish. Inquiries were finally made, and in March, 1970, the police rounded up a hundred boys and girls, and learned of six other such "sports clubs" in Rome. The public feeling ran high, and the Minister of Public Instruction declared:

> We shall act with the greatest firmness. We are consulting with school
> principals, directors, and parents of students to establish ways of exercising

stricter control over absences. We must at any cost protect our youth, and the whole country, from this scourge.

In the country of bel canto, musicians—who carry drugs hidden in their instruments—have played an important role in drug distribution. In September, 1969, the police arrested a Norwegian guitarist who had hidden two and a half kilos of hashish in his instrument; his accomplice was a Dutch composer.

The drug traffic in Palermo and Naples is kept pretty much within the capable hands of the Mafia—one Napolitan was arrested carrying six hundred million lire worth of heroin—whereas drug dealing in Milan is the province of the young. According to the head of the Juvenile Court, each young person arrested was carrying, on the average, a hundred grams of heroin, hashish or marijuana. For 90 percent of these young, most of whom do not work, 100 grams of drugs represents a capital that they would otherwise never have access to, even though they are actually only small time go-betweens to whom the large-scale dealers give "goods" on consignment, with no payments made until the drugs have been sold to the consumer. These small retailers, in their turn, make sales on credit. In this way the dealers, risking a small loss today, try to create a kind of hippie "atmosphere" and a sense of being at ease with drugs that will repay itself many times over tomorrow.

The director of the Toxic Products Center at the University of Rome estimates that 30 percent of the city's students have experimented with marijuana or LSD. After certain "sit-ins," the narcotics police found numerous butt ends from marijuana cigarettes among the debris; they had been distributed free by the students.

Also in Milan, drugs have become the most "politicized." They hold the same position of honor in the leftist movements that was once claimed by free love and atheism. One leftist publication is called *The Red Drug*. Narcotics are distributed along with political propaganda, mostly Maoist, in the state-run universities, in the Catholic universities, and in the "now" nighttime places. The supervisor of the Milan traffic is a Dutch former provo whom the French Sûreté expelled from France after the upheavals of May, 1968. There are many couriers who transport Chinese opium by way of Albania. At Ancona, a port on the

Adriatic, a hundred kilos of opium worth hundreds of millions of lira was intercepted. The best Turkish opium, which contains 12 percent morphine, comes in through Trieste by way of Yugoslavia.

In 1969, in Milan, two Spanish students were arrested along with a young Italian electrician, and later a girl—a flower-seller, who squandered the mite she made selling roses and violets in front of La Scala on drugs—was picked up too. All of them belonged to extremist movements. In Turin, one February evening in 1968, a young German girl performer fainted in a night club. A doctor there recognized the symptoms of drug overdose, and the police arrested the young man who accompanied her, who gave them the name of his supplier: a hippie painter. A raid on the rooms of this latter gentleman led the police to an arsenal stashed in his rooms and, in his car, a complete apparatus for the preparation of heroin. Interpol was notified, and found that this same person had run down a Turk in Istanbul. Meanwhile, in Marseille, the French intelligence organization the Deuxième Bureau identified him as the accomplice of two Arab painters who worked for the Moroccan Liberation Front.

An Englishman named Crew, who lived in a Naples pension and frequented groups connected with worldwide extremist movements, had daily contact with one Philippe Libori, the head of the Maoist movement that operated out of Naples. Crew traveled around in a Volkswagen fitted out with what any well-equipped drug dealer needs: paper envelopes filled with money, precision micro-balances, and several hectograms of drugs. One of his colleagues disposed of the merchandise in a place called the Blue Grotto, frequented by sailors in the American Sixth Fleet. According to the Sûreté, Crew had ties with Daniel Cohn-Bendit, the firebrand of the events of May, 1968, in France, and he, Crew, had distributed anarchist literature at the Sorbonne in May, 1968. "Men like Crew are multiplying rapidly throughout our country," declared *The Red Drug* (December, 1969).

Helene Einaudi, the daughter of Giulio Einaudi, a pro-Communist publisher, and niece of an ex-president of Italy, was sentenced to twenty days in prison. Her apartment had been turned into a "progressive" smokery in which, after discussions of the Maoist creed and Pop art, *la belle* Helene and her guests rolled joints of hashish.

On Rome's Avenue Aurelia one lovely morning, a pretty girl stripped herself nude and threw her clothes away with abandon, saying that the saints had ordered her to atone for her sins by humiliating herself through this penitential strip tease. A persistent odor of grass emanated from that silky peach and well-cared for skin. Her name was Marina Dugovitch, but she was called "The Redhead." And indeed, any passerby could attest that she was indeed a redhead from top to toe, which was only fitting considering that she had belonged to the red clan of Ché Guevara, and had served as a courier between its Italian branches.

Hippies in Switzerland

Even the healthy, rich and happy land of Switzerland has its taints of the infection. At Montreux, eleven young longhairs were sent to prison for organizing hash parties in the twelve-room villa of a rich Swiss who owned several cars, including a Ferrari, while declaring a monthly income of $240 on his income tax. "To our knowledge, there are a dozen apartments in Geneva where drug indulgers meet regularly," the journalist Rolf Zwicky wrote in *Vigilance* (September, 1969). I myself stumbled unexpectedly upon some hippies, in an out-of-the-way ski resort in the Alps, who had found a sheltered retreat in the basement of a big apartment house. To keep the curious away, they had had the wit to tack a sign on the door bearing a skull and crossbones and the legend "high voltage."

The Swiss press speaks now of "the growth of the scourge," "the urgent problem," etc., indicating that the drug problem there is already serious.

To conclude this chapter on hippies and drugs in the West, I can do no better than to give the floor to the most eminent English criminologist, director of the Criminal Division of the Council of Europe, Professor Bishop. He declared, at the Congress of the World Health Organization in Stockholm in 1969:

In five years, drugs will have become a crucial problem for European youth. It will not do for us to console ourselves that this situation is limited for the moment to the Anglo-Saxon and Scandinavian countries; we must recognize that these groups are spreading the word everywhere, and that it is high time to protect ourselves against catastrophe.

7

Hippies and the Sexual Revolution

The four cardinal points of the hippie philosophy are Oriental mysticism, indolence, love, and sensuality, and in this chapter we discuss the latter two phenomena.

When the hippies are not criticizing bourgeois materialism, they spend their time denouncing bourgeois sexual hypocrisy. "Many adults who have preached virginity before marriage and fidelity after it have practiced neither," said one hippie during an interview published in the *New York Times Magazine* on July 27, 1967. "And many who have practiced these have done so out of fear rather than love." Another hippie declared to the interviewer,

> Bourgeois morality creates egotistical, greedy bloodsuckers who have no other purpose than to hoard up the altruistic energies of the being beloved for himself alone. They practice a form of biological capitalism.

One flower-girl said, in the same article, that virginity as a value is also hypocrisy. "What's the big deal when a girl hoards a bit of skin just so she can exchange it for a gold ring or a ranch house in the suburbs?"

And there are graver things to be said. According to the hippies, the sexual morality of our puritan society is monstrously against nature. It leads to the enslavement of the senses, to physiological debility, to a kind of shrinking of life. It creates repressions, guilt feelings, and inferiority complexes that engender grave neuroses. Humanity is sick, very sick, perverse, deceitful, aggressive, and cruel because the "establishment" forces man to permanently constrain his most natural sexual impulses. From whence brother against brother, violence, and wars.

A young American, dressed Indian-fashion, who had been orating on a street corner in Greenwich Village, said to me, "Until several years ago, in the State of Connecticut, sexual orgasm was only legal if it happened between a man and woman who were married, who had their relations face to face, and who used no contraceptives. Yes, all these details were explicit in the law. And if the husband rolled over on his side or put on a condom, his wife could call in the law. . . ."

"And why is there a double standard?" threw out a girl in a mini-skirt. "Why is it that things allowed to boys are supposed to be forbidden to girls? That Victorian interpretation of the Bible that makes it a mortal sin for a woman to disobey God's commandments, while for a man it's fine, is just ridiculous now in 1970 when women are taking their places beside men in so many other ways."

An urchin from Paris that I met along the hashish trail said:

In the days before the Pill, the bourgeois made a virtue out of necessity. Virginity had to be mandatory before marriage to keep girls from dropping kids right and left. But now that a girl doesn't have to worry about getting pregnant, why should the straights care if a girl makes it? You'd have to be nuts or nasty to try these days to keep a girl from playing the violin between her thighs, or changing the bow, as often as she wants to.

The *New York Times*, which published the interview, noted another factor that has precipitated common premarital relations:

A physical factor in this new equation, in addition to the Pill, is that the average age for the onset of menstruation is 12, whereas a hundred years ago it was 17; while our female forebears—who usually married young—had only a year or two between menstruation and marriage, a girl today may have, because of the length and expense of education, more than a decade.

That's why premarital liaisons continue to grow in number. And a study made at West Virginia University, published in *Look* (1967), provides other reasons as well:

A West Virginia University journalist, reporting on sex as a fact of life on campus, found students agreeing on reasons for premarital intercourse. The reasons: physical desire; to show adults you are going to do exactly what you want to do regardless of what they think; to release tension.

Still more and more student governments are demanding that their schools issue a policy on when and why the student health services will prescribe the Pill. Students at the University of California, Berkeley, voted 4 to 1 in favor of campus clinics distributing the Pill to unmarried students 18 and over.

The hippies claim their right to the total sexual liberation that the "straights" have either denied them through narrow-mindedness, or exploited through prostitution and the "pleasure industry." We can all agree that sex is not merchandise. It is as inalienable as the brain or the heart. Sex is neither good nor bad. IT IS. It is a condition of life. To deny sex is to deny life. From whence the cry wrenched from the guts of a young Canadian, Léandre Bergeron, who felt himself to be a walking corpse from the sexual frustrations society had forced on him:

> After twenty years of this aberration, we say, No! this isn't working, I've been had, this isn't possible, stop, stop the music. You're mutilated, atrophied on one side, hypertrophied on the other, twisted, humpbacked, cracked. You crave to turn yourself inside out, to leave your skin, your bones, your polluted blood, you feel that you've been captured, caged, they've civilized us, put us in a box, channeled us, oriented us, so that the life down at the bottom of us can only be heard as a faint moan. Life has been caught in a trap. . . .
>
> What have they done to us? And for whom? And in the name of what? I came into the world like an animal, pure, ready to live, ready to stretch my limbs in the world, to cry a little, to eat, to caress my mother first, then little girls, then big girls . . . to love a woman, to lose myself in her, to take life from her as I take life from the air, then to die. But no. That's not the way things are. My soul was found to be filthy, my soul was crushed from the ancestral sin, I was criminal, I was descended from the ones who ate the apple, who know good from evil. And right away, they imprisoned my penis and my anus. Sex and excrement in the same bag. They taught me that I was divided into two parts, the high and the low, the good and the evil, a part above the waist and that disgusting part below . . . I learned that my little organ belonged to my father, to the tribe, to the others, that it was nationalized, that I couldn't reintegrate it until I had signed a contract with the Church/State. . . . The words have covered the walls of the prison of my being like wallpaper. They have dammed the rivers of my being with words, and forced my currents into great, useless basins.

These imprecations against the "iron noose" of society eloquently summarize the hippie platform in the realm of love. But what is the real situation? When the libido emblazons itself on the skies, when the Pill is distributed in girls' schools, when every American schoolboy and schoolgirl has his own checkbook and car, when adolescents take off for weekends or for long vacations without saying where they are going or with whom—in brief, in 1970, this revolt rings false, it isn't working, we're being had, stop! Stop the music of manufactured, hypertrophied, boxed in, oriented protest. The revolution has been caught in a trap. . . .

We may well have leave to doubt that anyone has ever dictated the cut of Léandre Bergeron's hair, his smiles, his clothes, his gestures, his thoughts, his moods. In trying to make us believe it's so, Léandre Bergeron—without even being aware of it—deforms the truth at least as much as the hypocrites he attacks. His liberal family, his friends, his university, his progressive television, have glorified, in all registers, the exactly opposite standards: judge for yourself, develop your personality, refuse standardization, protest anything you don't like. Léandre reminds me of that politician on television who cried that the opposition was trying to seal his lips, while opening his lips so wide that you could see his tonsils.

Lawrence Schiller, in his book *The Killers of Sharon Tate,* made some pertinent comments on this point:

> These days children reach a certain maturity much earlier than in the past. Kids in high school now learn things that, in an earlier generation, were not taught until university. Sexuality has invaded advertising and the general press. Schoolchildren can read *Playboy.* The songs that play everywhere on the radio today would have been banned twenty years ago, and the people who made and distributed these records would have gotten into trouble with the law. If circumstances permit, sexual life begins much earlier. If Booth Tarkington had written his book *Seventeen* today, he would have had to call it *Twelve,* if not *Eleven.*

It is interesting, as an example, to consider the confession that Susan Atkins, one of the girls in Charles Mason's hippie community, made to Lawrence Schiller. She had left school at eighteen. Here, summarized, is what this ex-high-school girl had to say about her "sexual prison" to the first reporter she saw:

I believe that my father wanted to sleep with me, especially after my mother died [I must add here that this was pure supposition on her part, for nothing in her father's behavior was reprehensible in any legal sense. This was, perhaps, even a repressed desire of Susan's, as we shall see farther on] . . . I was the only girl on the block. I was very developed, very attractive. I don't think my father realized that I had guessed what he wanted. But it was pretty uncomfortable all the way around. More for him than for me since, to tell the truth, I wanted to sleep with him. Yes. . . . All little girls want to sleep with their father, and all fathers want to sleep with their little girls. The same thing is true for little boys and their mothers. It's natural, but people refuse to recognize it. . . . I was successful with boys because they figured they could have me easily. . . . From the age of sixteen on, my family thought I was a whore. That wasn't true, but I could see that they would think that because I was going out with boys all the time.

Let us note that, according to Susan, her family considered her a whore, but that she didn't let that stop her from running after the boys at the high school.

Then Susan described a high-school dance where there were "big glasses of booze" and where she got drunk for the first time. She went on:

We went out with a bunch of guys and girls, driving around in an old heap. One evening a boy got me drunk and I wanted to try the thing everyone had told me was so disgusting. It was good . . . I had been anxious like crazy to turn eighteen—since earlier than that, it's not legal—to leave school and my family. But a long time before that I had already started going out with men, not just boys. I went into bars, got drunk, let dirty old men take me to hotels and do whatever they wanted with me. . . . By the end of the school year, I had no more reputation to lose. Besides, who cared? I went on thinking of myself as a good girl. I got engaged to Robert, but left him to clear off with Al, a very sexy guy who'd been arrested lots of times. Because of him, I got in trouble for car stealing and carrying illegal weapons, but they let me out on probation. I wrote to Robert and persuaded him that I would marry him. He bought me an engagement ring and everything. I let him make love with me once, and then I dropped him. . . . I got a job as a topless go-go girl that I kept for eight months, and I began dropping acid and marijuana. When I left my topless job, I was living with three or four guys. One of these guys wanted to marry me, but all I had to do was look at him and I saw my father. And then I'd laugh just thinking about it. I cut out again because, once I'd gotten a man to fall in love with me I didn't want him anymore, that's the way it was.

Susan went back to San Francisco and moved into a Haight Ashbury pad with a clutch of boys and girls who banged LDS and grass and each other. That's when Charles Manson came on the scene; a bearded, very brown, little man carrying a guitar, whose voice and songs were an enchantment. They hardly said four words to each other. The next day he took her to a hotel room, told her to undress, and looked at her nude body in a mirror for a very long time. She obeyed. She was nineteen then. She became his slave from their first relations, and never broke her vows of obedience even though he slept with her no more than three or four times in two years. But that's another story, which we shall come back to.

So this is the "sexual prison" that has entrapped the post-war generation. In fact, for several years now young boys and girls in the big cities have led all too free sexual lives. And it can hardly be said that they have chosen in an adult way. When someone explains that this is based on suppressed sexual complexes, they reply, "What are they?" Some of them seem to be quite jaded already when it comes to sexual adventure. Sexual liberation is not what they are after. They have it. No, the "sexual prison" idea is just one more gun in their arsenal of systematic, permanent, hysterical accusations against our society. That makes a hit. It goes over well. It gives you style. It gives you political brownie points. So let's believe that we're sexual prisoners, even though it's not true.

It's Léandre Bergeron, not "society," who "dams the river of being with words." For by blocking that river with a prison that exists nowhere but in his diatribes, he keeps himself from reflecting calmly on his own course. And he won't let himself see that the river branches out into other streams besides that of carnal pleasure: there are the streams of the mind, work, adventure, solidarity, tenderness, studies, sport, art, etc., etc., and that is what makes the man. Certainly the first stream, that of pleasure, is a thing of beauty and ought to be let flow freely—along with all the others. But Léandre, like all the hippies, has nothing to do with the others. In the end, his inflated rhetoric obscures more human horizons than it illuminates.

The hippies, in their passionate denunciations of a moral code that is no longer observed—a code that has certainly never weighed on their own lives—remind me of that kind of "inertia of indignation" that has often struck me on the left. Leftist groups love nothing more than to issue calls to arms for causes that have already been won. And—the strangest thing of all—the long-dead enemies that the left continues to hold up to scorn are enemies that the left itself has defeated. But they prefer to leave old accounts artifically open rather than acknowledge their own victory and go on to something else. This morbid concentration on old issues stems from the fact that these blots on man's record once invested the movement with a prestige that cannot be renewed on other registers. So they blow on the embers of old crimes to preserve the savor of their denunciations. I know some men of the left who would rather die than admit that the great issues of 1870 are dead in 1970, who would gladly give five years of their lives if a new tribunal could unjustly convict a new Dreyfus. Our valiant hippies who set off to wrest a sexual liberty that no one is keeping from them belong to the same line.

The hippies' closed doors may really be wide open, but we must in all fairness admit that they have proved to be genuine trailblazers in one sense: they have, on the other side of those doors, done some things that most audacious free spirits of the past would never have dared to do. Earlier seekers after the garden of delights have hardly pushed through the gates. It has been left to the hippies to carry the exploration of sensuality much further. They have struck new paths, and it is into these trails that we will follow them. Hold on tight.

Tantric Love

For a hippie, to live is above all to love, which means that the more profoundly he explores all the aspects of love—romantic, sensual, mystic, carnal, hallucinogenic—the higher will he rise on the tree of life. Making love should be an art say the hippie magazines, taking its place in the pantheon of the arts along with architecture, poetry, music, and cooking. And just as the development of any artistic talent requires a period of apprenticeship, of application, and of imagination, the act of the flesh cannot attain its zenith except after serious study and practical exercises. This is the only way that the world becomes exalted. The Hindus understood well that the sexual act is the art of arts and requires an inventive spirit, and they have immortalized it in their monuments that have served as a fount of instruction for the last thousand years.

That is why the hippie press devotes so many articles to the supreme cult of carnal love among the Hindus. To give an idea, I will summarize the long illustrated study by Thad and Rita Ashby, two American writers, that was published in the *Oracle* of November, 1967. Their article is based on three years of research in Mexico; researches, by the way, that were sponsored by the Sandoz pharmaceutical company, the company that made and distributed LDS in the United States until it was declared illegal. The study begins with an expression of regret that

> The yogis lost the integrity of their sensuality when Hindus adopted British moral values. The British condemned the great Tantric Temple of Konarak by calling it "the obscene pagoda."

I visited these temples—the temple of Konarak and the other great temple, of Kajaruajo—myself two years ago, and I did indeed admire these lascivious, fascinating sculptures. All the sexual variations of which man, woman, and the gods are capable have been carved by masters in the double art of loving and of sculpting. There are also parties of three or four, and even relations between man and animal. The prudish Britons of the 19th century must have been shocked indeed. The imagination with which the sculptors have represented the diverse positions of love—the Hindus describe thirty-two—is touching and naive in the temples of Konarak, powerful and suggestive in the temples of Kajaruajo. The expression of ecstasy on the faces, the clenching of the hands, the abandonment of the torso, the passion of the muscles, the eyes fixed on the great beyond of sensuality—all of this spurts out from the rock. And the stone imbues ecstasy with its nobility and its eternity. This fantastic virtuosity provoked the Ashby's to write, "The inventors of new sexual positions were choreographing sex-play." They go on to discuss the effect of Victorian prejudices on India:

> In India, Westerners fight to keep the jungle out of one's garden. The jungle is almost obscene. God's shameless drunken sailor spending his fecundity. The jungle bursts with sexual digestive display—flowerings, rootings, seedings, fruitings—writhings with Life/Death/Rebirth. Nature, which we now confess includes ourselves, in a super sexual whammy.
>
> The 19th-century Puritan sublimated sex (all erotic energy) into culture. The contemporary (Playboy) Puritan discharges energy (tension)

whenever any arises. Allowing sex to grow and blossom like an exotic perfumed bloom takes more time than Game/Time people have. So our (Western Man's) sex life is anxious. We dissolve the ego of Western Civilization during that one moment of body rapture: orgasm. After orgasm: anger. We alleviate our tension, as do addicts, temporarily, by concentrating pleasure very locally, very genitally. The more we do it, the more we perpetuate our sexual hang-ups.

After orgasm, we tend to lose our sense of generating an exchange of energy (synergy), perhaps. Like a circuit grounded, we dissipate our energy —we cannot contain the charge for long—we lose the magnetic moment of fusion.

If sex isn't fully soul-satisfying, we afterwards feel frustrated and then guilty. If Western man "hates himself in the morning," he is not alone; his woman also hates him. She feels used, not for a great religious purpose that subtly explores her multi-dimensions of ultra purple . . . of silken fire —but used as a means of relieving but not releasing his neurotic tension. Today, Watts, Brown, Marcuse, Von Urban, McLuhan and Leary are engaged in a restoration of the integrity of sensuality. Consciously or unconsciously they all use a more-or-less tantric approach. . . .

What, then, is the tantric approach? The unique thing about tantra, as the Ashbys see it, is that it does not believe in metaphorical love. It believes that the true transference from one being to another is only possible through physical engagement.

The word Tantra literally means "touch." Being anxious, our Western orgasm shows a crescendo profile. Starting slowly, it builds rapidly to a fast final brief banging of gongs. Tantrics think the only way to, say, take a kitten or a wild animal such as a human being, is to touch her, stroke her, pet her.

In Maithuna, the man does nothing (no motion) to bring on orgasm. Most often he delays it, at least until the end of the ceremony. Ordinarily the woman sits astride the man facing him upright, her legs not in lotus but wrapped around his waist; the man puts his hands on her back; she hangs her hands over his shoulders. She is always the active partner. In Tantra man becomes receptive, letting her call the tune. Whether or not his erection continues isn't important, in this position, it can't slip out.

Delaying the orgasm needn't apply to women. Women are not as genitally organized. Their orgasms do not dissipate the divine fire but diffuse it—they're more innocent, like children (polymorphously erogenous). Freud. Brown. Watts. Women feel just as sexy dancing or having their hair stroked. Like cats they are more tactilely sensual. A man is encouraged in our Puritan/Playboy culture to concentrate his sensitivity and his feelings in his [genitals]. Maithuna (with Moksha medicine) re-diffuses man's genital energy. The entire body feels lit up in ultra-purple infra-orange haloes of ecstasy. A crown of lights shimmers round the head, and jewels of fire radiate an electric orgasm from the brain.

Supposing you plug one generator into the wall and put another generator beside it—but not plugged in. Now as the plugged-in generator wraps its field around the unplugged-in generator, the unplugged-in genera-tor begins to whine, soon racing along as fast as the one that is plugged on. The analogy to Tantra is that woman is somehow at this stage of history more plugged in (than man) to the biological rhythms of earth/moon/sun. Man needs to be rapt, wrapped in her field—long enough to hear the "divine whine." After an hour or two of this long sweet communion (the actual duration depends on how high you are) you begin to create somehow the feeling of a third presence. This presence is made up of the two separate selves overlapping, melting down and "bleshing." When this bleshing occurs a field is created—it pours out your pores like shoots of light opening out a way "whence the imprisoned splendour escapes." The purpose is to inhibit man's compulsion for rapid motion. Mate on lap, he can't move too violently. Maithuna is a means of prolonging the experience, abolishing Game/Time, entering awareness of eternity. Slowing a man down, elimi-nating his pillaging, looting motions, allows him enough time, enough eternity to experience a woman, really experience her. Man is about, hints McLuhan in *The Future of Sex*, to become a woman.

When at last the field of electro-magnetism is whining-shining around about both of you, you feel her blood flowing in your veins; scratch her back, and feel her fingernails on your own back, look into her eyes, your two eyes together create a third eye, a third presence, whose eyes shine forth another color. If your eyes are blue and hers green you will look into aqua eyes— right? But then yellow eyes appear! Another presence, a new person has come into being! . . . The communion should last at least two hours. If in that time a man surrenders sensitive awareness of the woman, feeling her blood flow, vibrating to her metabolism, breathing her breath—he will know the meaning of *Tat tvam asi.* It is the awareness of unity physically. Felt in blood and bones: we are one.

Using this as a starting point, the hippies have gone several steps further, by multiplying tantric joys through psychedelic sacraments. The hallucinogenic drugs, they contend, are more aphrodisiac than any other chemical (a conclusion disputed by the medical profession which claims that, except for the amphetamines, the hallucinogens diminish the sexual appetite. And indeed, that is precisely the point we shall be making further on). Timothy Leary affirms that the sexual energy aroused by LSD is universal, cosmic, divine. That is why so many hippies are no longer interested in purely genital fornication; the sexuality released by LSD is considerably more diffused than anything they had experienced before. With LSD, according to Leary, you are released from genital specialization, you can soar with marvelous things you never attended to before—the sound of a flower, the vision of music, the harmony of creation. And Maithuna under LSD will deliver your soul from the thrusts of anxiety, from hate and from the commonplace, and you can explore the cosmos in total communion with carnal and divine nature. In tantric voyages on acid, you will copulate with the universe. You become a tree in flower pushing your roots profoundly into Mother Earth. You become an electro-love generator for the earth, a protector and fecundator for all of nature.

Alas, there is a good chance here—and these are not the hippies talking, but the medical profession—that you will end up in a mental hospital, or will father a monster, from the deterioration of the brain cells or the chromosomes caused by LSD. No doubt the Hindus themselves would sometimes utilize some drug or other to enhance their sensations—almost certainly their own domestic hashish, whose erotic virtues have been celebrated since furthest antiquity, along with its pronounced toxic effects. However, the hashish poisons are still considerably less than that of LSD.

To return to the Ashbys' Hindu practices—which in their pure state, at least, are practiced without LSD—the two researchers conclude: couples who practice Maithuna each day say that the mutual sexual surrender soothes their aggressivity. This art banishes jealously, cruelty, vanities, or wounds of the ego, all of which are based on the false premise that we are separate when indeed we are one. The woman is freed from her hatred of herself and from the sense—instilled in her through an act of love that is still very much like the rape the cave man committed on his woman—that she is an inferior being. Freed from the prison of masculine domination, the woman takes the initiative of movement upon herself. The man must understand that the frigidity of woman is a defense against masculine aggressiveness. But if the man is completely relaxed and open to her, it is the woman who will become aggressive and who will pay him extravagant sexual compliments.

Women who practice Tantra regularly begin to look literally like flowers. The sheen of their silken skins glows with Eros. Innocence and vulnerability shines from their great soft warm dilated eyes. The communion usually inspires women with great self-confidence, for Tantra is a form of worship. Every woman is God's bride, Sakti! Sakta! . . .

In fact, Thad and Rita Ashby have hardly improved upon the exotic island utopia "Pala," brought to life by Aldous Huxley. The inhabitants of Pala, "delivered from the puritan proscriptions against the human body," practice tantra Yoga "cool sex." They use the magic mushroom Moksha, a medicine that instills erotic energy, and for hours they transfix one another in Maithuna. The people of Pala are the happiest in the world. . . .

But the Ashbys have made one discovery that should win them the Nobel Prize: group Tantra. They counsel that a group of men and women engage in Tantra together; that is, the couples should take a drug sitting side by side in a circle in the dark, linked by holding hands, while listening to psychedelic music. They have discovered that such a practice will give rise to a group magnetic field considerably more powerful than the individual magnetic field, in accordance with an exponential mathematical formula.

If everyone would practice "cool sex," say the future Nobelists, society would lose its strains. If the military would practice it, we would enter into a great period of peace and artistic creation, like ancient China during its "out of time" period when the emperor sat, meditated, looked toward the south, drugged himself with opium, but did nothing, absolutely nothing, but love women. Millions of Chinese perfected tantric taoism. They became so expert in the skills of sex that, when they were invaded by the Great Mogul Khan, they surrendered immediately. However, the soldiers of Khan were so drawn by the young Chinese girls trained in the tantric arts that, whoosh, the Mongol invasion was totally absorbed in the bosoms of girls with soothing eyes.

It must be said that this is a rather dubious interpretation of history. In fact, the Mongol invasion cost unhappy China tens of millions of dead, and the conquering barbarians were not assimilated until after two generations. Which indicates too long a wait, even in the Maithuna position.

The Ashbys go on:

> The Chinese Empire—while ruled by Emperors who did nothing, who sat
> looking South, took drugs, wrote poetry, and enjoyed sex as a science—
> lasted thousands of years and produced art which can only be called eternal.

This is also fantasy history. God knows that I venerate peace. But
the truth obliges me to say that Chinese art also came to great peaks
during very bellicose, imperial eras. And the most prodigious outpouring of art in human history came during the Italian Renaissance, while
its princes—the Borgias, the Medicis, the Viscontis—warred and intrigued incessantly, indulging in-between-times in hasty, brutal, dominating, and not very tantric orgasms.

The Ashbys go on to play the prophet on the basis, so to speak,
of the thirty-two positions:

> If we (the Americans) withdrew to our shores, and declared a policy of
> neo-isolationism, and everyone went home to turn on and practice divine
> Tantra, we would in six weeks become a different kind of people, a people
> whose weapon is love. If after LSD, the Hell's Angels became the Diggers
> —then with Moksha plus Maithuna, anything is possible.

The hippies have taken Freud's assumption that the arms of war
are phallic symbols, and leaped to the conclusion that "straight" love
is war or, in other terms, weaponry is nothing but a product of the
sexual frsutrations of males in puritan societies, that is, aggressively
dominating because sexually frustrated. Which proves, therefore, the
Ashbys' theorem that "Prolonged piece may be the only way to prolonged peace."

The reader may well be surprised that a "serious" political writer
like Suzanne Labin has adventured onto the tortuous paths of tantric
love. But since, as the two researchers explain, two-hour communal
pleasures can expunge war forever from our planet, and since this would
have incalculable consequences on East-West relations, it is only natural that even anti-Communist writers might lend an attentive ear to
tantra. First because tantra may assuage the political frustrations that
such writers suffer in their unappreciated struggle. Next, because an-
timissile missiles have been declared obsolete as protection for the

West against totalitarian aggression; a psychological counter-war is what is called for now. Just teach the Maithuna position to all young girls in the West, and if the troops from behind the Iron Curtain should adventure one day onto our free soil, then our young experts will just have to practice their Maithuna on the invading soldiers and, quick like a bunny, the invader will be conquered by ecstasy.

Free Love

One obvious consequence of the hippie philosophy—that is, the primacy of personal pleasure over any other value—is the claim for total liberty of sexual experiences, including the right to change partners when the mood hits, the right to homosexual love, a child's right to masturbate, even the right to union with lower animals. All these claims are posed, developed, and justified in the hippie press, sometimes accompanied by hair-raising descriptions. Our riders of the purple sage are spreading the word by setting up "Leagues for Sexual Freedom" in all the large cities of the United States, and inviting everyone to come to meetings. One group has taken the slogan, "Girls of the world, screw. You have nothing to lose but your chains. . . ." Many of the groups confine themselves to declarations of principle, but others pass the line from theory into action. The *Berkeley Gazette*, on April 24, 1967, gave a detailed description of some of the orgies organized by one of these clubs—all you can get for a dollar, drinks included. Once the kids had gotten squiffy—they were mostly very young—they were ripe for servicing the pacifist-nudist warriors. Two young people of sixteen told about the time they went to a club in all innocence, expecting lectures on sexual liberty. They went up a flight of stairs, and ran first into a woman wearing nothing but a blouse that just reached her navel, running around the room pursued by several naked men. The two sixteen-year-olds opened another door and saw a bedroom filled with mattresses strewn with nude bodies of any sex engaging in sexual relations.

In one hippie commune, eight men shared one girl, according to the *National Police-Gazette* (February, 1963). Nonetheless, most of the time, in communes, people live in couples and stay with each other at least for a while. When one person wants to change, he looks for another partner outside the commune, so as not to create painful rivalries within the group. Then there are the communes—not very numerous—that are big on ceremony, where they play at a marriage ceremony each time a member of the commune makes love with a new partner. If you change ten times during a month, you will participate in the complete ceremony ten times.

Other communes, on the contrary, practice the kind of sexual sharing common to certain ancient Persian tribes. Every member belongs to every other, and must carry out the service of love with good grace—as if one were serving tea—at the first request, whether it be in front of other people or in a corner. In this kind of commune, Roman-style orgies are naturally frequent, except that the lyre has been replaced by the banjo.

In still other communes, a kind of "sexual fascism" reigns in which a fuhrer disposes of all the girls and all the young men who live under his care. This was the case with Charles Manson, who had his serf hippies call him Christ, God, or Satan, according to his humor. His behavior was so much like, in a hallucinant sort of way, that of the terrible 12th-century Persian Hasan Ibn-Sabbah, that one might wonder if Manson copied him deliberately. Like Hasan, Charles picked up, in the course of his wanderings, girls and boys between fifteen and twenty years old, and very beautiful of body and face. Both communities drugged themselves with cannabis, but Manson added the explosive element of LSD. As Hasan launched death raids from a fortress hidden in a lost mountain, Charles ordered his own from Death Valley, one of the most deserted areas of the United States. Like Hasan, who was called "the old man of the mountains," Charles was ambitious, fanatic, cruel, vicious, and a false prophet. Both of them made their followers believe that they spoke the word of God. Like Hasan, Charles refined the practice of assassination by knife, and ordered his kids, whom he had first intoxicated with heavy doses of hashish, to go and disembowel people they didn't even know without mercy. Both men practiced political murder, the Manson killers writing "kill the pigs" on the walls with the blood of their victims, and even engraving it with a knife on the chests of their victims. Hasan plunged the Islamic world into terror for decades, from whence comes our word "assassin," though we do not know whether the word derives from "Hasan" or from "hashishin," "eater of hashish." Charles Manson, unfortunate in having to deal with the police of the 20th century, could order only half a dozen murders. But he planned his murders in such a way that blacks would appear to be the criminals, with the hope of sparking off a racial conflagration which his tribe could watch happily from their lair in Death Valley.

As for the sexual mores that reigned in this empire of perversion and blood, Susan Atkins made this confession (which I summarize) to Lawrence Schiller:

Our family was made up of some twenty girls and about a half dozen boys, because Charles knew that, even though he wanted all us girls for himself, you do need some men for heavy work and hard times. Charles chose his own partner every evening according to his mood, and the other girls were available to the other boys. He also offered us to occasional ranchers who would let us stay on their places for a while, or to a passing friend. We met one guy in New Mexico, and Charles told me to sleep with him. This guy got me pregnant. It was Charles who delivered me. That happened in an empty cabin in Death Valley. He had already delivered other girls, by himself. There were two babies being lugged around in our caravan from one camping place to another. One time, the caravan turned over in a ditch and we had to stay there until the police came. When they saw the way we were living, the police gave us summonses for endangering the life of a child.

After the butcheries at the homes of Sharon Tate and the unfortunate La Bianca couple, the police arrested several girls who were implicated in car thefts and killings that they declared they had committed under the satanic enchantments of Manson. And indeed it seems that the enchantment continued, because the young prisoners —from sixteen to twenty-one years old—startled their jailers by parading nude in their cells and dancing in the costume of Eve to music that only they could hear.

Let us recall that, according to the hippie philosophy, our society has been made aggressive, cruel, and bellicose through the imposition of puritan morality, Victorian inhibitions, sexual repressions, and feelings of guilt. Now here we have a community—exceptional, yes—but no less hippie from the soles of their feet to the ends of their long hair, who lived in indolence, scratching their necessaries by thievery and scrounging, who drugged themselves, whose sexuality was pushed to the extreme—there was certainly no repression there—and who, despite this, indulged in acts of horrifying sadism. They struck the legs, the heads, the bellies of their victims with old daggers or kitchen knives. The lovely Sharon Tate, eight months pregnant, asked mercy for her child; which they bestowed with their knives. Then they plunged a napkin in her belly and wrote the word "pigs" on the door in her blood. In the La Bianca house, they took showers and then gorged themselves on the food in the refrigerator while bodies sprawled at their feet . . . one of the girls plunged a kitchen fork into the belly of one of the bodies.

The hippies will cry that the flower-children can certainly not be identified with a few monsters on whom the glare of publicity has fallen. However, we are not, in fact, dealing here with a few isolated cases; scenes of pillage, aggression, and murder have multiplied in California to the point where professional truck drivers hardly dare to stop en route for a bite to eat, and feel terror if their trucks should break down on the highway. For ordinary people now, the word "hippie" has begun to evoke the same images of theft, abduction, rape and cruelty that the word "gypsy" did in the Middle Ages. I in no way hold the overall hippie community responsible for these scabrous ne'er-do-wells. But this is what the hippies do: they apply the crimes and cruelties of some individuals in our "straight" society against the whole society. Above all, the story of the Manson tribe, and of other "liberated" satanic churches, proves the inanity of the hippie thesis that human aggression derives from nothing but the repressions imposed by the established order on the libido and other sources of pleasure.

Let us close this section by affirming that there are indeed hippie communities that hold to the value of fidelity in love. Certainly the lovers cultivate a highly developed, perhaps overblown, eroticism—which distinguishes them from us ordinary folk—but like the rest of us, each one gives himself only to his or her chosen partner. The jealousy that love arouses in the hearts of men and women is, like the sexual drive, a fact of nature that it is useless to deny. I was reading through some transcripts of Senate drug hearings when I came across this declaration from a hippie who was "straight" indeed when it came to love:

I was fooling around with these things [drugs] before Leary, who thinks he is a second Jesus, began to mix himself in. That acidhead hardly has twenty brain cells left that are still in working order. As for me, I drop acid from time to time, but that doesn't stop me from having some straight ideas. Not too long ago I told my wife that if I ever found her in bed with another man, I would kill her. You know what she answered? That that made her happy, because it meant someone loved her. And I'm the same way. I want to be loved by someone, and have someone jealous of me. (*Congressional Record*, November 6, 1967.)

Nudism

The Leagues for Sexual Freedom claim as their birthright the right to nudity. In San Francisco, there's a sex guide for sale that lists nudist meetings, nudist beaches, etc. The hippies have also organized nude-ins. At one of them, at Gregorio Beach, where I went to observe, there were more voyeurs watching from the cliff above than there were nudes on the sand—in all, only eleven boys with all the signs of full-blown manhood, and a girl with breasts hard as bronze. A freezing wind whistled among the demonstrators, so one young man snuggled into three sweaters, but took off his bathing trunks. It was the best accommodation he could make with his faith in nudism.

The hippie press, always in the avant-garde, constantly publishes ads like, "Meet interesting people who like integral social nudism." It is filled with photos of girls proudly displaying their pubic triangles, with no shame. The hippie magazine *Haight Ashbury* came out with a brutal cover showing a nude young man with a low forehead and sensual lips, whose arm rested along the entire length of the nude body of a very lovely girl. She was standing at his side in such a way that the man's hand came just between the girl's thighs; her gaze was wild. . . . A policeman showed me this issue, which had been seized.

The hippie entertainers have brought nudity to the stage. One of the most fanatic performers, Jim Morrison of the rock group The Doors, gave a demonstration of his private parts before 12,000 young people during a concert in Miami. He was arrested on five charges: two charges of indecent exposure, two of profanation, one of public intoxication, and also for the crime of improper conduct consisting of public exposure of his private parts; but he was just the first to practice what he had been preaching!

"Man, I'd like to see a little nakedness around here. Grab your friend and love him. There are no laws. There are no rules." The performance was so bad that the head of the Greater Miami Crime Commission, Circuit Court Judge Arthur E. Huttoe, called the performance, "a conspiracy to corrupt the morals of our youth." (*Fort Lauderdale News,* March 6, 1969.)

Morrison, who had provoked a "sex riot" in Phoenix, considered himself an "erotic politician." If ever he was elected Senator, he would do a striptease in Congress. While waiting, he would give his lessons where he could, and of course, everyone was talking about the show "Oh Calcutta" on Broadway—or not really, as it played in New York's East Village—where six actors and actresses played nude from beginning to end. This lack of variety must have been boring. . . .

In the Classifieds

Once it had been accepted that a person's sexual tastes were no more to be sneered at than his tastes in colors or foods, no hippie was reluctant to announce his wishes in public advertisements. Moreover, the notion of perversity does not exist in the hippie universe, this word forming part of the vocabulary of "imprisoned-alienated-reactionaries." For the hippies, absolute sexual license is no longer a daring theory, as it was for the old anarchists and nihilists. It has entered into behavior, and its manifestations fill pages and pages of advertisements so audacious that even the most "liberal" sensibilities are shocked. But these ads form such an integral part of the hippie canon these days that they cannot really be passed over in silence. So I will give several examples, out of a hundred thousand:

> Tarzan came back from the jungle stronger and handsomer than ever, to make you happy nice girls married or single 18 to 40. I love you all babies! My pad is on Fifth Avenue & Eleventh Street. Phone. . . . (*San Francisco Express Time,* October 16, 1968.)

> Hey Pussycat. Are you in heat? Horny-Siamese is at your disposal for a free. . . .

> Dear Carol I love you. Rob. Negro Male, 32, avail for French culture and your desire. Call anytime . . . no males, only females. (*Berkeley Barb,* November 28, 1967.)

Other ads detail the sexual proclivities of the advertiser:

BUSTY—The woman or girl I desire must have large bosom. Age and race not important. Please call me at any time. (*Sunday Express*, October 16, 1968.)

Male wants to meet woman with shapely derriere to participate in unusual sex inc. phone. . . . (*Berkely Barb*, November 16, 1967.)

Male wants one or two uninhibited girls 18 to 40 with big derrieres for sex who are fond of french and greek cultures, call. . . . (*Berkely Barb*, October 5, 1967.)

We French will be pleased to note that our "culture" is very much in demand among the hippies:

Strong mature male sterile expert French culture pursuit of happiness. Satisfy married-single females. Gentle, discreet, responsible. Phone. . . . (*Berkely Barb*, November 23, 1967.)

Man 36, white, handsome, continental type, would like to meet shapely sophisticated type of woman 18–30 to fulfill their desires. Am an expert on oral stimulation.

Bachelor, 32, white, intelligent and discreet, likes to satisfy girls with deep tongue action all night. Let's make a "French date." I prefer well suntanned girls. Call Jay . . . girls only please. (*San Francisco Express Time.*)

Desire moderately aggressive young black to force feed me his hot wastes, served directly from source. Write HGS. Box. . . . (*San Francisco Express Time.* October 16, 1968.)

Etruscan-lover (29) Ph.D. prestige-job Stanford, desires aware female to share large week-end sex-fun apartment in Rome. Can instruct in best Indo-European techniques. Write now to. . . . (*Berkeley Barb*, September 22, 1967.)

Who'll be first? Well-endowed Caucasian male 30 seeks passionate and unashamed Mexican, Negro, Indian, Oriental & all-right Anglo girls w/fire in their blood for sex & love. Ecstasy assured, foto, fone to dale. . . . (*Los Angeles Free Press*, January 12, 1968.)

One sensitive man notes:

> There is a certain kind of girl who enjoys men but is awkward waking up
> beside a stranger. Good looking, discreet, adaptable young man will per-
> form and disappear. If you are pretty, call. . . . (*Berkeley Barb,* December
> 7, 1967.)

The hippies find their sensual nourishment in these ads. They read
them avidly, and they provide the most fruitful source of income for
the publication. They are also the most revealing of the human soul,
of the pig that sleeps within all of us. There is a rich pasture here for
psychologists and psychoanalysts. If Freud came back to life and saw
what were once the most secret parts of the libido displayed on these
pages like meat in a butcher shop, would his amazement know any
bounds? What has happened, he would say, to my famous repressions?
There would be no more need to lay his patients on a couch while they
endlessly detail their dreams, straining to extract the demons huddled
inside us like periwinkles deep inside their shells. The hippies have no
more hidden demons. Just put a few ads in the *Berkeley Barb* or the
Los Angeles Free Press expressing your wildest desires in the most
explicit terms, and your cravings will be answered. The libido has
passed from the unconscious to the public market place. Satan himself
buys and sells on the market. For example, this is one ad I picked up:

> Anton Szandor Lavey of the Satanic Church is looking for sinful secretaries,
> lustful schoolteachers, naughty nurses, wanton waitresses, bored house-
> wives, etc., to satisfy his diabolical appetite. Must be reasonably attractive,
> 21 to 35.

Until now, only God was allowed publicly to proselytize for his
cause, while Satan was relegated to the underground, his only access
to souls through shadow and intrigue. But now he too has come out
into the light and, like his adversary, he calls followers to his cause with
banners unfurled.

Seduced and Abandoned

This flotilla of ads with neither reticence nor decency does include
moments of poignancy: cries from people who are alone, either because

they have been abandoned, or because they have never been wanted. Here are a few:

> [From a man] Help! I'm dying inside. Somebody please help keep me from dying. Help me find life in the nothings around me, in my body gone dead. Make love to me letters. Sing stone hard words through my blind staring eyes. Anyone. Please, Help. Write. Now. Pfc. John H. Young (*Berkeley Barb*, October 5, 1967.)

> [From a woman] Desperate mature woman—urgently needs to contact persons knowing where she can buy something that will stimulate a strong desire for love and sex relations. No LSD, pot or heroin. Reply Mrs. E.M.G. . . . (*Berkeley Barb*, September 22, 1967.)

> [From another woman] Want to meet a man who is real easy going, humble and affectionate. Also who strongly believes that "grass" should be legal and enjoys himself. Husband is divorcing me for another. I am very dependent type person and would like to marry someone of my type and have a lot of sex and enjoy a lazy happy life. Believe in New Testament and that All Creation shall be saved and be high forever. I'm 28, overweight but look pretty good in nice mumu's and fancy lounging gowns. I'm 5'5", long hair and poor. Very lonesome for the right man. If possible would like to live in foreign country where "grass" is legal. Give full description. Write to A. B., POB. . . . (*Los Angeles Free Press*, May 2, 1967.)

One can feel abandoned, and still hold on to a sense of humor:

> Mature male would like to trade divorced 45 yr. old turkey, who thought I was stupid, oversexed and nuts, for TWO 22½ yr old swingin' females who might think me intelligent, understanding and kind—Object—to get sandwiched into the act somewhere. Tired of being left out. Have home near the beach. POB. . . . (*Los Angeles Free Press*, May 2, 1967.)

Homosexuality

Although homosexuality is practiced by few hippies, all admit it as one of the inalienable rights of sexual liberty. They believe that the compartmentalization of people into masculine or feminine is an artificial category set up by language, whereas every human being contains male and female hormones and it is, therefore, perfectly natural to satisfy ambivalent tendencies. In this sense, then, homosexuality is so much a part of the hippie social revolution, that "gay" ads fill whole columns in the hippie press:

> Become a true homosexual. Moral duty of every person to be homosexual. Human heterosex is categorically immoral & evil. $100 for any valid disproof. K. Mars. . . . (*Berkeley Barb.*)

> Homosexual Revolution destroys Christian theology. God is only heterosexual. A. S. Lavey is not of Satan. Become Homo-Anti-Christs. Overthrow Heterosex and God. End. Het. Spellman's War. K. Mars. . . . (*Berkeley Barb*, November 23, 1967)

> Gay males for fun (sing pref) by 27 yr old, 6'1" attr. blondish guy, dig 1) hairy chests, 2) trim bods, 3) tans, 4) butch and presentable (no nells), 5) groovy week-ends on outings or around my swimming pool, 6) romantic evenings anywhere, from tent to villa. Exchange photos, interests. POB. . . . (*Berkeley Barb*, November 11, 1968).

> Mature 6'2" male grad desires passive males—age 30–45—for periodic liaisons. Well built intellectual types preferred. Box . . . give phone and details. Discretion guaranteed (*Berkeley Barb*, November 9, 1967.)

There are also services for putting men in touch with one another, like the "telephone Club for Men." Their ad specifies:

> The phone club for men only if you are homosexual and tired of the stud canneries. Here at last is a way to do your thing, our sole function is putting you in touch with others of similar interests. Call 9AM to 9PM. . . . (*Berkeley Barb*, November 7, 1968.)

Homosexuals whose special habits have caused them to lose their jobs receive powerful support from three institutions: the Glide Methodist Church, the Glide Foundation, and Glide Trustees. All three groups organize boycotts against firms that have practiced sexual discrimination, and they encourage heterosexual hippies not to buy from them either. They have created a lobby for the rights of homosexuals, and they lead an active campaign against corporations, government agencies, and insurance companies that refuse to hire homosexuals.

There are few ads from lesbians, and they tend not to have the

Rabelaisian enthusiasm of their male counterparts. Against a hundred ads from males, there will be one from a woman, and they are generally of a rather nondescript type:

> Attractive, discreet, young, restless housewife seeks mutual afternoon satisfaction with equally attractive, discreet, young, restless housewife. Please send phone and photo. P.O. Box. . . . (*Los Angeles Free Press*, January 12, 1968.)

> Very pretty girl, 21, seeks attract nonpetite wellrounded non-hung-up (bi?) girl friend. P.O. Box. . . . (*Berkeley Barb*, October 26, 1967.)

It is difficult to understand how such ads could exist in a country where the laws against homosexuality are quite severe. In France, homosexuality is not illegal except for the seduction of a minor, but even so our classified ad sections do not permit such announcements, whereas homosexuality is legally criminal in the United States, whatever the circumstances may be. There is a permanent campaign, supported by a strong lobby in Washington, to have this legislation repealed. It is a strange country that makes laws against behavior, and then ignores them when the laws are broken.

Omnisexuality

The hippies preach omnisexuality with much more enthusiasm than homosexuality. Paradoxically, despite their frenzy for love, the men and the women can hardly be told apart in their look, their behavior, or their clothes. They are neuters: the same long hair, same pants, same beads and psychedelic tattoos, and they carry on the same activities—or rather, the same inactivities. The men demonstrate no typically masculine aggressiveness; they do not compete among themselves for women, they strive neither for intellectual supremacy, nor for the initiative in forming liaisons, nor for the role of director in sexual relations. Quite the contrary, as we have already seen in the case of Maithuna, they often prefer the passive role. This tendency toward passivity probably explains why there are so many ads from men seeking aggressive and dominating women:

Handsome submissive mature male seeks imaginative dominant women, couple, group, teaching exotic unusual for thrills. (*Berkeley Barb*, October 26, 1967.)

French cultured houseboy for mature single or couple. Obedient service, very humble any whims or treatment, non-white, 35, 5'4". (*Berkeley Barb*, October 26, 1967.)

Gentleman, 50, misses discipline by late mother desires occasional thera- peutic spankings of whippings by lady any age, or by directress of rest home, who is thoroughly experienced in need discipline, believes in and likes to administer the same. (*Berkeley Barb*, November 7, 1968.)

Slave needs handsome young (18/28) white master who digs the whole scene including foot worship and demands fanatic military type obedience. Experiences . . . photo helps. No freaks, swishys or over thirties. (*San Francisco Express Times*, October 16, 1968.)

These ads, which abound in the hippie periodicals, accurately express the loss of virility among males who systematically refuse mili- tary service and the fight for life. Like the young decadents at the time of the Pax Romana, the hippies have become softened and feminized. Far be it from me to condemn all efforts for peace; certainly we all pray for an end to the scourge of war. But when this pacifism turns into contempt for any sense of national solidarity, when the instinct to fight for life, innate in each man, just vanishes rather than becoming rechan- neled into the fruitful paths of intellectual or economic competition, man is on the way toward decadence. It is no doubt true that the elimination of certain traditional overaggressive forms of virility can contribute to a positive gentling of life and to concord among peoples, but only if these tendencies do not tip so far over in the other direction that they slide into masochism.

Perhaps at bottom the hippie is a masochist. In effect, he turns his own aggressiveness against himself, first by dropping out of the schooling that will give him access to a fruitful and comfortable life, then by escalating into drugs that empty him intellectually and damage him physically. And even that is not enough. He pays for ads asking to be whipped. These hippies belong—despite their erotic license—to the same line as the old, utterly chaste, flagellant monks. In different ways, they are both masochists.

The flower-girls have also done away with all the secondary female sexual characteristics. They consider coquetry and modesty completely old-fashioned, and take no care for their own charms. When they have money, it is they who will pay for their companion. Far from being humiliated by the loss of those secondary feminine characteristics that have nourished human poetry for millenniums, they are proud of it. They consider it a mark of liberation from antiquated stereotypes of swaggering masculinity and sainted femininity. For them, these archetypes—which developed, they believe, out of the traditional mental rigidities that could not deal with the fact that man's sexual fountain is by nature ambivalent—are false. One hippie declared in the *New York Times Magazine* (July 24, 1967):

> At a time when sexual excitement by way of the media has reached laughable, if not obscene, proportions, these boys and girls in identical tight pants and shoulder-length hair are signaling that the male and female *secondary* sexual characteristics are not that important; their form of address for one another is "Man." At a time when when racial antagonisms erupt on the street, these boys and girls appear relaxedly integrated. The problems of poverty and the ghetto—together with those of leisure—are no problems to the hippies who embrace all three. In their own sections of cities, there is little serious crime and prostitution.

Matters have reached the point where ads come out that don't even specify which sex is being requested.

Merchandising Sex

No hippie newspaper is so crowded by private ads from hippies haunted by sex that it can't fit in a few commercial advertisements placed by businessmen—maybe hippies, maybe not—who, always and everywhere, are ready to pounce on the hippies like a bird of prey might pounce on a squirrel. For example, any number of ads invite young women to partake of the delights of abortion:

> Mutual self help association for women with undesired pregnancies entirely confidential keep calling. . . . (*Berkeley Barb*, November 23, 1967.)

Or again, in a large display ad, there was a headline, "Pregnant? Need Help?" and then a picture of two hands reaching out to one another, and a phone number (*Berkeley Barb*, November 7, 1968).

Other ads propose:

> Zap you're sterile, but our buttons aren't, so for this and over 150 more original and pregnant button titles, write to A Big-Little Store. . . . Free list, sample button to stores (*East Village Other*, August 5, 1967.)

> "Drug Extension" to prolong the sexual act and get the most out of it. One gram per packet, five for $2.25.

> Orgy Butter: Brand new passionate red and subtly sexually scented orgy butter is a glowing body rub, a luxurious lubricant, different and exciting, orgy butter for the warm & caring innovator who knows what a total experience lovemaking can be. . . . (*Open City*, Janaury 4, 1968.)

Then there is the love filter called "Lace" (from its components Lysergic Acid Ethylene), which has been presented to the press. While the Food and Drug Administration had doubts as to its erotic power, the hippies assure us that "Lace" penetrates the skin; just spray a little on the object of your choice, and she will undress as quick as possible and make love.

There are numerous offers, of course, to exchange piano lessons for exercises in sex, or "Classic, folk and jazz guitar in return for warmth and a stimulating personal relationship" (*Open City*, August 11, 1968).

Under the heading "Underground Sex," there are lists, available for so many dollars, of young girls, or sophisticated and discreet couples for "swinging." (*Berkeley Barb*, November 7, 1968.) Alas, the whisper is, in the East Village and Haight Ashbury, that these ads are screens for a new kind of white slavery. Thanks to the mind-deadening drugs, girls fall an easy prey to professional pimps who take on the hippie look and move in, and send the girls out where they are wanted "at bargain rates."

Incest and Infantile Sexuality

The hippies have not ignored, in their list of "freedoms," the supreme taboo: incest. In the *Los Angeles Free Press* of January 12, 1968, this article appeared:

A friend of mine stated that he has had a most beautiful relationship with his sister. . . . She had a hysterectomy in her early forties, he had a vasectomy some years before also. There is no possibility of pregnancy [I am astonished that such a liberated human being would even give a thought to the matter]. and to the provincials that might be horrified at the thought, he says that they both agree that they have more in common than any two strangers who have ever hit a bed and married as a result, plus no jealousy or other entanglements that befall "normal" people. . . .

The hippies also claim the right of children to sexual liberation. One indignant journalist, in the *Oracle*, claimed;

The bourgeois culture accepts that little kids want to play with their penis. It's all right for little kids to masturbate, but somehow after a certain age—say around three—sex isn't supposed to happen, which is a fantasy because it's an anthropological fact that, alone of the creatures on this earth, our species is capable of sexual enjoyment, play and pleasure from the day it's born to the day it dies. That is the one place that evolution has brought us that is different from every other species of animal.

If we recognize this instead of lying about it, instead of building walls around it, there wouldn't be any question but that heaven IS on earth.

A singing group called "The Fugs"—a term that refers both to the stale, stuffy smell of a marijuana-filled room, and to the potheads who sit there and never go out—put out a record which, according to *Time* Magazine, created a furor among the early teen set. It reproduces the sounds of a couple coming to long simultaneous orgasms. And how many other records are nothing more than an invitation to the young to make love under drugs? "Freakout U.S.A.," referring to a drug panic; "Day Tripper," which simulates drug hallucinations; "Lucy in the Sky with Diamonds," whose initials are LSD. All these records and so many others are to the new musical tastes of the very young, and are sold by the millions.

HIP-pocrates, or "Little Things Mean a Lot"

Every week, in the *Berkeley Barb* and other hippie weeklies, a medical column is published under the honorable name of "Hippocrates." A doctor answers questions like these in detail:

Q: Will sexual activities inhibit the physical development of a young child?
A: Not at all.

Q: I should like to know the physical dangers if any for the passive partner in anal intercourse. I enjoy that sexual experience very much.
A: Anal intercourse is not physically harmful when done in moderation. . . . Sodomy (a legal term for anal intercourse) is a felony crime in most states punishable by long prison terms [the tacit conclusion: you may practice it, but in secret].

Q: I do not appear to have a clitoris. Naturally, due to this fact, I do not have much of an orgasm, either. What is a withdrawn clitoris? Is there anything that can be done in such a case? Is this at all common? . . .
R: I understand this woman's anguish. She should consult a gynecologist. . . .

and on and on for three columns in which we learn that the "clitoris is usually described as a miniature penis . . . the sole functions of the clitoris are sexual arousal and gratification . . . clinical research has shown that size does not determine sexuality or the capacity for sexual gratification." The doctor also provides instructions for women on how to reach the heights through masturbation.

Q: [From a young girl] I get no sexual pleasures unless I'm in a swimming pool and the water is very cold. The colder the water is, the most pleasure I get, but out of the water, nothing.
A: Go swimming a lot in cold water.

Many questions have to do with the hallucinogenic drugs. Can a mother take a drug while nursing a child? Is it dangerous for a child of less than seven years to take drugs? My dog (or my cat) is a year old. Is he old enough to take a trip with me on LSD? etc. Have you ever felt, as I do, that the world has gone mad?

Pornography

Certainly every culture in the world has had its pornography, and there are many clandestine sales outlets (which are becoming less and less clandestine) in Europe. But for the hippies, pornography is an integral part of their philosophy, like sadism in the philosophy of the famous Marquis. The hippies say that obscenity serves a basic need in human nature, and that it is hypocritical to pretend otherwise. Certain extremist forces see pornography as a political weapon against the establishment. Obscenity is a way to ride roughshod over the conventional morality, to show self-liberation from all hangups, to scandalize the established order. And these groups encourage their followers, in their meetings, in their books, in their newspapers, to rub society's nose in excrement.

Malay Roy Choudury made an illuminating profession of faith in the newspaper *Guerrilla*—whose name is itself a profession of faith:

> I defend Obscenity. I'd go on defending Obscenity so long as the flagitious bourgeoisie would go on claiming the atavist superiority of their false air. . . . In fact, there is nothing called Obscenity. Obscenity is an artificial concept, made, fabricated. . . .

At one event, described in Brisbane's *Sunday Truth*, a young long-hair recited poems—"a rosary of evocative obscenities"—while crying out and rolling around on the ground. And then there is the ballet in which a nude man stands near the front of the stage, while young girls keep their eyes fixed on him (*Ladies Lines*, September 9, 1967). The poetess Lenore Kandel, a big attraction at hippie gatherings, has written a group of poems, *The Book of Love*, so full of obscenities that the San Francisco police, quite tolerant of this sort of thing by now, seized the copies and banned its sale.

There are innumerable hippie boutiques that specialize in pornographic films and publications. One shop is proud to offer a selection of fifteen thousand titles. So in America the hippies, having obliterated the cravings for success and money, have just substituted an obsessive concentration on sex and obscenity in their place. This obsession is often more ideological than physiological, in the sense that it aims less to satisfy the "feeble flesh" than to shock the straight world. To my knowledge, not one of the ad-takers in quest of a sister soul—excuse my euphemism, I ought to say "of a brother sex"—was a political conservative. There is no doubt that this flourishing of sexual license is closely linked to the political philosophy of the left, and that the goals —or at any rate, the styles—of this philosophy are revolutionary. Eroticism is no longer a luxury of the privileged classes. It has become an arm of subversion, and ads like this appear in the hippie press:

R. H. does free obscene (and tasteful) tattoos. They help you avoid the draft. Replies care of Elliot Mintz. (*Open City*, January 4, 1968.)

This is one tactic recommended by the new left to help keep one from being drafted. Most of the ad-takers pride themselves on being liberals or "radicals," in the American sense of the extreme left. Here are some examples:

Wanted to meet political, radical and sexually liberal couples interested in backpacking, skiing, and/or photography. (*Berkeley Barb*, January 11, 1968.)

Liberal yng Negro man seeks liberal yng couples for 3-some and/or yng liberal chicks to share pleasure. Race no problem. No single men or fakes please. (*Berkeley Barb*, November 7, 1968.)

And this ad, which is a political manifesto in itself:

Motel keeper catering to All-American Swingers. Star-spangled Orgy Every Night Except Monday. Twice on Fri/Sat/ (*Berkeley Barb*, November 23, 1967).

In France or Italy, a young rebel will join the Communist Party. In America, an obscene ad in the Berkeley Barb is their act of revolution. It is a form of social protest. They raise no red flags over the American universities, they "make the scene" with no clothes on. In the New World, drugs and sex have replaced the Hammer and Sickle . . . and the American revolutionaries are content. For it is more agreeable, after all, to satisfy the claims of sex, and easier than to claim the rights of the proletariat.

8

Foreign Relations, or Hippies vs. Straights

If there is a more suitable neighborhood in the world for the hippies than Haight Ashbury—a racially mixed, rather poor, but extremely liberal area that is represented in Congress by a black—it is hard to know where it might be. If the hippies hadn't come to be adopted by it, Mark Harris writes, it could only have been because they were rotten.

They may not be rotten, but they are incurably asocial. They behave like irresponsible tramps toward their neighbors, not like people who really live somewhere with other people. Anywhere the hippies set themselves up, they invade their new neighborhoods with a spirit of vagabondage that generally causes trouble. Their filth attracts rats and spreads disease. They dump their garbage in a pretty park—a park that the local inhabitants have invested with a great deal of affection and care, while fighting to block a highway that is scheduled to tear their park apart. With their shattering music, the hippies deafen their neighbors until late at night, heedless to the possibility that their neighbors may have to get up early for work. In brief, it is not so much for their eccentricities that they can be faulted, as for their egocentricities.

Racial Minorities

The blacks feel especially hostile toward the hippies. They are the genuine "disinherited" of America, and as they see it, aid which should be directed to them is being deflected away by the hippies. The blacks believe that their families' requirements are legitimate, whereas these daddy's boys have voluntarily abandoned abundance to go play at being poor, as if poverty were a game! And it's so unfair, they say, that so many blacks are prey to cruel maladies that they haven't asked for, while these kids take drugs to throw their minds and bodies out of whack just for the fun of it. A projected plan by the Department of Health to set up a medical service in Haight Ashbury was rejected when the black ghetto of Filmore protested vehemently that their own need for such a service was certainly more justified.

The filth in which the hippies live can hardly be equaled any-where. In a *Newsweek* article of October 30, 1967, the writers com-ment, "In the Haight-Ashbury, traditionally a tolerant and multiracial neighborhood, the flower-children's indifference to cleanliness has an-gered many middle-class Negroes themselves." "They have turned a pretty neighborhood into a slum," one black man said. "If a group of hippies moved into my building, I would go somewhere else. I couldn't tolerate their filth."

The blacks and the Puerto Ricans are more antagonistic toward the hippies than other racial minorities, probably because they see them as privileged whites who can break the law, smoke drugs, and sleep in the parks with no interference from the police, while they would have been sent to prison willy-nilly for the same infractions. And this excites their racial hatred. When the blacks and Puerto Ricans have really begun to fight against the scourge of drugs, and are straining to leave their ghettos and gain access at last to the good things of life, it seems a deliberate provocation to them that the children of rich whites are constructing a new ghetto and closing themselves up in it to wallow in their drugs and filth while contemptuously rejecting the cars, houses, comfort, education, everything that the blacks have wanted so much for so long.

This dialogue was reported in the *Washington Post* of October 26, 1967, but I have seen variants of it many times during my strolls through the Village:

MALCOLM Y: The best thing you white brothers can do is get out of our neighborhood and go down on Van Ness to do your begging.

TEDDYBEAR: We love everybody, we love you.

MALCOLM Y: I don't want you to love me. LOVE! I know what I'm going
to do. I'm going to train my people to kill you, and you, and you [points
a finger at each of the whites]."

In Canada

The appearance of protesters who defy all the foundations of
society—work, marriage, property, authority of teachers and parents—
has aroused a wave of protest among the straights in Canada too; or
rather, not the powerful straights, but the people of the middle classes.

The *Toronto Daily Star* published an editorial on August 24, 1967;
protesting the "police brutality" exercised against a group of hippies
trying to block a street against traffic. In fact, these "brutalities" con-
sisted only of dragging these youths off to the police station. An indignant reader wrote in:

> I take exception to your August 24 editorial "No Excuse for Police Brutal-
> ity." Had I been one of the policemen involved in clearing Yorkville of this
> disgusting vermin, the treatment meted out by me, a citizen and a taxpayer,
> would have been 10 times as harsh.
>   The hippies should be washed down the sewer where they belong.
> Every citizen has a duty to society and must contribute to it in many ways.
> One of the most important is to be law-abiding and another is to earn one's
> own living, and not be a parasite. Why should we taxpayers foot the bill
> for 50 to 100 policemen in Yorkville every weekend, when there is so much
> serious crime for them to contend with? By defending the hippies *The Star*
> is contributing to a further breakdown of our society.

Another reader went him one better:

> Your editorial about police brutality in Yorkville is rubbish. These so-called
> hippies, you say, are peaceful people engaged in an act of civil disobedience.
> Acts of civil disobedience, to the extent of resisting law and order are never
> peaceable. . . . If I had acted like these nuts when I was in my teens, I would
> have got a belt in the ear and a boot in the rear-end from the cops. When
> I got home, I would have got a lot more from my father. . . .

Still another Canadian expressed his outrage with even more vigor:

> When is the press going to get off the back of our police department?
> . . . Force is the only language these lame brains understand. If I had my

way, I would march a well-disciplined regiment into Yorkville and move them with fixed bayonets. If these filthy, unwashed, warped examples of our society want to forget education and all the opportunities of our times —let them. If they want to be primitive—let them. Ship them north to a primitive area, where they can live as they please without the limelight of publicity. I wager they would soon return to become normal responsible citizens.

Women have also expressed their shame:

> Our beautiful Yorkville has become a place of prostitution, drug addiction and crime. . . . We have surely fallen to the depths of degradation if Toronto has to have a side-show of filthy nincompoops to attract tourists. When I was in the west, we were looking at a TV program which showed the highlights of each city in Canada—Toronto's was Yorkville. I hung my head in shame when I was berated by the others in the audience for living in such a "Sodom and Gomorrah."

The same imprecations were published in the *Georgia Straight*, on Victoria Island, to protest an editorial in that newspaper (August 11, 1967) that came to the defense of the hippies.

> I think that you, your paper, and every hippie in Vancouver are completely insane. It's a crime to society you can't all exchange places with the poor, legitimately sick people of Riverview Mental Hospital. But then that's an insult to them, as well as if I signed my name I'd insult myself.

The Skinheads

The hippie communities set up in the country have even more difficulty with the local folk than city hippies; rural people, with their ingrown lives, are even less able to cope with hippie aberrations. During the hippie love-in in Topanga Canyon, the sheriff's patrols crisscrossed the area, sniffing the air for marijuana. The local inhabitants were incensed at seeing their lovely country used as a "huge cesspool." The Topanga Chamber of Commerce voted that all the restaurants that served the hippies would be stricken from their membership (*Open City*, September 27, 1967).

In Europe, the hippie communities do not seem to arouse the same violent hostility; perhaps because the hippie communities are still limited in Europe and don't seem to have actually taken over whole areas, as in America. That is why, even though the drug-and-sex cult does annoy the European bourgeois as well as his American counterpart, there have been no actual run-ins with the long-haired boys. The only fracases I know of were between "straights" and other kinds of aberrant groups, like the Provos in Holland.

In England, the hippies' main enemies are another band of adolescents who parade with a menacing air, wearing neat uniforms; their heads are completely shaven to make it completely clear whom they are opposed to. Naturally they are called "skinheads." One of their most famous run-ins with the hippies was in Piccadilly, where 500 long-hairs occupied a sumptuous 18th-century building for almost two weeks. The authorities, like the crowds of rubberneckers, hostile though they were toward this enforced occupation of other people's property, were powerless to dislodge the hippies by gentle persuasion. And then one fine day, a contingent of skinheads, chanting their slogans, poured into the place to "get the hippies out." A battle was joined that the hippies, conditioned to leisure rather than to fighting, lost in short order.

The Hippies' Defenders

But there are also important circles in England who have come to the hippies' defense. First, the great, powerful liberal press, radio and television, who have limned them in a very appealing romantic glow. And the charitable and research organizations have leaned toward their cause with open-hearted sympathy. Their supporters also include a good part of the teaching corps, in America as well as in England. And even some people in government have been friendly. All of these groups take care not to bend so far toward the hippies that they lose their agreeable positions in the "establishment," but they are attracted to them in principle; not only for the beauty of their philosophy, but in order to stay consistent with their own beliefs in tolerance toward all points of view—or, perhaps, consistent with their own subversive theories. The hippies, like any rebel community in the past, have aroused the irremediable hostility of most of the surrounding communities, but unlike any other hostile group in the past, they have also benefited from the understanding, sympathy, and aid of many highly

placed people. Here is an eloquent sample: an extract from a letter by
Toronto assemblyman Willie Brown to the City's Board of Supervisors:

> It appears to me that you are in danger of making a very fundamental
> mistake concerning both your own identity and that of the young people
> who are coming to us. They are not some horde of invading foreigners.
> They are our children, yours and mine, exercising their right to move freely
> in a country which will soon be very much their own.
>
> You, for your part, are not some select group of medieval chieftains
> who can, at will, close up your town and withdraw behind the walls of your
> own closed society . . . whether we like or dislike, agree or disagree with
> the "hip" community is not the issue here. The issue is whether you can
> by fiat declare a minority unwelcome in our community. If you declare
> against these young people today, what minority is going to bear the brunt
> of your discrimination tomorrow? . . .

A noble, generous and vibrant discourse that has made much ink
flow in America, but for all that it is still not devoid of a healthy dose
of demagogy. For, retorted the majority, who up till that speech had
remained silent, this man speaks as if our cities are not already oversup-
plied with problems: problems of housing, of hygiene, of health, of
thievery, of criminality. He speaks as if there were no such thing as the
terrible, the tragic problem of drugs. He speaks as if a community, in
granting that it has a responsibility to make room for diverse groups,
does not have the right to demand that they respect the laws and
customs of the majority. He neglects to specify exactly how old children
should be before they can move at will around a country as big as a
continent. Most people have, until now, believed that a young person
should be under his parents' direction until the age of eighteen. Should
we now, as Brown says so poetically, "open the doors of our cities" to
the children of fifteen, or of twelve, or of ten, who wander the highways
alone? Why not five? And how can the law continue to hold parents
responsible for the delinquent, even criminal, acts of their children,
when the press, the record industry, and even some of society's representatives encourage them to disobedience and to flight?

The masses have traditionally rejected the intellectuals' taste for
license, and, in the matter of the hippies, they have reacted once again
true to form. It has often been said that the masses are basically

conservative—perhaps because they are closer to hardship. Down deep inside the social cauldron, social pressures are more intense, and the worker senses instinctively that liberty and life's pleasures cannot be had without a minimum of order. His after-work pleasures are different from those of the free-wheeling fancy free. He takes no pleasure in gypsy wandering, nor in general mischievousness for the hell of it. For him, pleasure is promenading with his well-fed and well-nourished family in a well-kept park; a limited pleasure perhaps, but it has cost him centuries of labor to reach this simple level, and he knows that there are still millions of his disinherited brothers who aspire with all the depths of their beings to what he has.

Here I take sides for neither one view of the good life nor the other; I note only that it was inevitable that they clash.

9

Politics and the Hippies

When, in an earlier chapter, I briefly traced the different categories of hippies, I left, for this special chapter, the gurus who have assumed political roles and tried to attract groups of flower-children to their respective causes.

I have noticed during my travels that the great majority of hippies show no interest in problems of ideology. Unlike either the New Left or the Old, they are repelled by the idea of discussing theories; which is only to be expected in view of the fact that their drugs have blotted out everything else: ambition, money, sex, and, it goes without saying, politics. The hippies' souls open only to the marvelous: Oriental religions, astrology, the mysteries of hallucination.

This mood of revolution-as-style does not, however, save them from the tender ministrations of organized revolutionaries. Here they are, under the sun, a vast plankton of young beings, credulous and ardent, bound together by the calls of hedonism, of drugs, and of mysticism, floating down a golden current that runs from San Francisco to Goa, and all with their heads turned firmly against the established order. What an incredible catch for anyone who wants to make the effort! But only the nihilistic extreme left could possibly ensnare such rebellious beings into acting as a political force, because they are the only ones trained to fish with invisible nets. And besides, certainly the conservative forces, as well as the classic left—who continue to have faith in work, studies, decency, and law —would not know what to do with a movement that is so contrary to their principles. The hippie philosophy is unquestionably, in its essence, at the opposite pole from Marxism, which sanctifies work, discipline, science, and the State; but it can certainly be exploited by the nihilist branch of the extreme left as an ideal instrument for hacking away at the existing order.

Political Gurus

Let us first mention all the journalists of the hippie press—one of the main groups of politically activist hippie leaders—who attest to their sympathy with the goals, if not the bureaucracy, of the Communist countries from one end of their columns to the other, and their admiration for revolutionary figures bathed in a glow of romanticism like Ho Chi Minh, Ché Guevara, Mao, and Castro. However, Max Sherrer, the editor of the *Berkeley Barb*, a fifty-two-year-old bearded hippie whose newspaper propagandizes for homosexuality, the "acid stamp," and the Vietcong, writes:

> The U.S.S.R. looks considerably less threatening, after abolishing its concentration camps, to residents of the U.S.A., which may be considering setting them up. . . . (*Berkeley Barb*, November 8, 1967)

Mention should be made of the American Cohn-Bendit, Mario Savio, who, during the student strikes in Berkeley, welded together a coalition of normally apolitical hippies and political groups. Then there is Allen Ginsberg, who played a behind-the-scenes role in the Berkeley upheavals and who appears, at public meetings, at the sides of Communist speakers and leaders of "Fair Play for Cuba"; The Canadian hippie, David de Poe, whose wall is adorned with a photo of Mao Tse-Tung; the American Billy Digger, who wants to spread a system of truly communal life throughout the whole world. The "Diggers" borrowed their name from a 17th-century English community that lived communally. Let us also recall the French hippie Jean-Claude Lamoureux, dead from a heroin injection, who had started a small journal called *La Taupe Rouge (The Red Mole* or, figuratively, *The Red Underground)*.

The journal *TransAction*, which is published by Washington University in St. Louis, published a very interesting study on the politicization of hippies. Personal observations of my own corroborate its conclusions:

(a) True hippies, called the skuzzies, are difficult to catch in political nets; for them, their political brothers are false brothers, and boring at that;

(b) On the other hand, the teeny-boppers—young people of less than sixteen years—are easily impressed by these same murky philosophies. They love to sport protest buttons, to wear sloganeering armbands, to demonstrate in the streets;

(c) All the politically active gurus support either the diverse nuances of communism—Maoism, Trotskyism, Castroism—or terrorist groups like the Black Panthers, or one of the numerous Something-or-Other Liberation Fronts, or the movements for "civil rights" or "pacifism."

(d) Even though the aspirations and means of the various political gurus are clearly quite different from one another, there is a common denominator. Though they all stand by the hedonist ethic of the hippies and defend their right to use consciousness changers, the majority of them take no drugs themselves. *TransAction* reports one illuminating dialogue in this regard:

INTERVIEWER: Do you like drugs?
POLITICAL: Yes, if you mean pot and acid.
INTERVIEWER: Do you turn on with any of the local heads?
POLITICAL: Are you out of your mind? I'm currently in . . . [an impressive array of New Left activities]. I guess you know I'm being tailed by the Feds and my phone is tapped. They're looking for any excuse to bust me. If I got within smelling distance of any pot they would bust me *so fast.* Not only to break me, but to attach the addict label to my cause. . . .

This excuse doesn't get far with the real hippies, the skuzzies. They distrust golden-voiced orators who eulogize drugs but don't take them. The teeny-boppers, on the other hand, are excited by this kind of statement which, in their eyes, enhances the importance of their heros. Among these very young hippies, a certain percentage of them will definitely cast their lot with subversive activism, a certain percentage will make the drug scene, and the rest will go back to where they came from.

But the political guru is a strange, singular being, nothing like the classic portrait of the party political activist, for whom the revolution has much more to do with social mores than with the structure of society. It is a new kind of revolution, but he repairs back to ancient techniques: a hodgepodge of prophecies, fetishism, and mysticism. Many political gurus, returning to the spirit of the first centuries of our era, pass themselves off as messiahs or as avatars—that is, as messengers or reincarnations of God. They often adopt the language of one who has seen the mystic light, mixing it with the phraseology of Marx and of the extreme left. It is difficult to tell whether they are sincere or whether it's all playacting, but it doesn't much matter. The important thing is that they are followed, as if they were true gods or apostles, by a crowd of young people with long hair and bare feet who believe sincerely in their annunciations and illuminations. At the present time there are dozens of them, especially along the hashish trail. One such guru is the avatar Mehar Baba, who affirms that he is the earthly incarnation of a Hindu god. He has gathered young people from all over the world to his feet in India, to whom he preaches the renunciation of the world's material goods, the destruction of the industrial society by boycott, a sort of primitive communism, and the esctasies, not only of meditation, but of such collective intoxications as dance and communions. But he has come out against drugs, a stance that many mystico-political gurus have taken. "Nothing keeps you from pursuing a mirage," he has said, "but it will never quench your thirst. It is the same with the hallucinogens, which will never appease your thirst for Truth and Justice."

It is strange, in this century of Cosmic Man, to see the revival of the ancient tradition of messiahs and avatars. But it is even more extraordinary to hear mysticism and astrology flow out of the mouths of these hippie preachers in one breath, and Marxism in the next. An abstract description triggers little in the imagination; to make the picture a little clearer, I shall tell the story of a guru I came upon in San Francisco.

The Tricky Messiah

This messiah lived in a commune of some thirty persons, who shared a two-story house. I was invited to enter a lovely "meditation" room on the ground floor covered with multi-colored carpet, with psychedelic paintings on the walls and Hindu statuettes on the floor. In the kitchen, two teeny-boppers were baking a so-called "macrobiotic" bread—supposed to prolong life—which the community sold in a restaurant they had opened on a neighboring street. This kitchen was also a model of cleanliness. Nothing was out of place. It looked more like the lodgings of a fanatically clean person living alone, rather than the home of a tribe of some thirty persons, including seven children.

The woman, very beautiful, who conducted my tour around the house, told me that they all believed in vegetarianism, in communism, and in reincarnation. She spoke to me of her guru with a profound admiration, calling him "the messiah." "It is our messiah who painted those pictures on the walls. . . ." "It is our messiah who wrote these pamphlets. . . ." She handed them to me and I read, "Brothers, come join the world crusade of the messiah of San Francisco who will bring about the new order of the future on the earth, from this day forward." The messiah's paintings were dreadful, but the good fairy of the house spoke of their creator with such veneration that I asked to meet him. She answered that he would be at the "macrobiotic" restaurant, and gave me a publicity flier. "Here and Now"—the name of the restaurant —assures its prospective patrons that only organically grown vegetarian products are served in the restaurant, and that the enterprise is non-profit, and the employees are not paid. On Sundays, Tuesdays, and Fridays, at 8 P.M., the cosmic messiah Allen presents the initiation to the cosmos and teaches us how the new age can be constructed "here and now." I ran over.

I saw about six hippie-types eating in a working-class kind of room furnished with several rudimentary tables, but no messiah. There were magazines on the tables and on the counter. I took one, a *Black Panther*. There was a caricature of a policeman with a pig's head on each page, whether on his knees before black judges, or with a bayonet in his belly, or with groin exploding from a bullet shot by a ten-year-old. Still no messiah. I nibbled on some stale but "macrobiotic" carrots while think-ing,

> This restaurant claims to make no profit nor to pay its employees, but my vegetarian meal is costing me a good sight more than a meat meal at any "bourgeois" cafeteria. This is a very smart "communist" messiah who, under the pretext of working in a great Cause, finds suckers to toil away for nothing. He's a "nonprofit organization" so he doesn't have to pay any taxes, all the while fleecing the naive tourists who fall under the spell of his rolling sentences.

When I thought he would no longer come, the messiah appeared —and looked nothing at all like I thought he would. His skull and his face were shaved completely clean. The smooth ball that he wore on his shoulders was a striking contrast to the hairy faces of his young followers. The only antiestablishment element in his ensemble was a round-collared scarlet shirt. He had neither the air of a hippie, nor of a prophet, but rather of an escaped convict turned avant-garde banker. For reasons unknown, this guru had tried to assume a "mystic" role that became him very ill.

He sat down at my table. Immediately a cloud of hairy hippies, who follow him like the apostles followed Christ, formed a circle around him. The red-shirted man began to talk, and a new surprise: his voice was subdued, with neither modulation nor warmth. Despite loaded terms like "vital energy," "reincarnation," "horsemen of the Apocalypse," "cosmic mind," "revolution," "world crusade," etc., his matter was as drab as his voice. His dull chant, which lasted about an hour, played round and round the same things:

> San Francisco is the sacred place of our planet where God has set his tabernacle, and the messiah Allen has been sent to this city to spread the Great Plan to the whole world. His signal will come from the Chosen People, including the Black Panthers. . . . The establishment is trying to destroy those who resist the war that capitalism is waging against communism. But the saints of Christ are the forces of world communism. . . .

This was followed by a pseudo-Marxist gobbledygook in which he must have used the words "thesis" and "anthithesis" at least ten times; then I learned that the cosmic messiah could cure cancer and heart disease, that he could make anything burst into flames just like that, and that he could construct weightless vehicles. He invited all Marxists to join the cosmic crusade of the messiah and added:

> Let us thank heaven for the riots and the wars that it sends us which push people out of their burrows into the universal crusade of the messiah to attain to Supreme Being, Karma, and the mental seeds that they have thrown onto the planet Aura. . . .

The young people listened without interrupting him once. At the end, I asked him, "But what messiah are you talking about?"

"Myself," he answered without blinking an eye. "I have come to teach *true* Communism to the earth."

His "politico-cosmogonic" statements were so delirious that I thought he was just a mystic; he was not the political activist that I had thought he was, despite the Black Panther magazines on the tables. I was about to abandon our discourse when I saw a strange glint in his eye. I decided to pursue the conversation, for there was something sly and shifting behind his extinguished voice. I asked him if he was for or against drugs.

"I do not take them myself, but I am in favor of everything that is natural, and drugs are a product of nature."

I asked him then what he felt about riots. He was in favor of upheavals, and gave me a few cosmic justifications. According to him, an overload of malign energy gushed periodically over the earth, and it had to be discharged in bloody upheavals. As the United States had not yet had its revolution, its time for overload and discharge had come, with the inevitable consequences of blood and flames "here and now." This is the cosmic order.

"Wasn't the Civil War and the American revolution against the English colonialists sufficient to discharge the evil humors?"

His only response was to accuse his own country of being responsible for the last two world wars. He seemed at first to have forgotten Hitler. But no. In a loud, clear voice he claimed to all that the one person truly responsible for that butchery was not Hitler, but Roosevelt. . . . Then he announced that he was going to create chapters of his cosmic crusade in the Soviet Union, Communist China, and North Vietnam, and asked me if I would set up a chapter in France. I said I'd think about it.

This political guru, who had no artistic talent, seemed to be gifted with a certain practical savoir-faire that belied his evil eye. But why would this devil play-act at mystic illumination? The key to the enigma came soon enough, after I had leafed through the pamphlets that this Jesus' Mary-Magdalene had given me. One of them was called, "Letter to the Judge of a Court of Appeals from the Cosmic Master Allen, the new Messiah sent on this planet to set down the angular rock." I read:

The people are harassed by laws, a military, and a penal system that don't make sense anymore. The individual is torn every which way by a double standard of morality. If he kills someone on the street during a riot he is condemned to death, but if he kills on the field of battle he wins a medal. . . . The ridiculous marijuana-baited trap that the San Francisco police set for me—what has this to do with the grand task of constructing the kingdom of God on earth? My trial and all the legal silliness that goes with it are, in comparison with the universal mind of the Cosmic Messenger Allen, like the brain of a goat next to Einstein's brain. The Cosmic Messiah knows positively that the Highest Extra-Terrestrial Powers are working for the coming of paradise on earth through the "Messiah martyred by accusations of traffic in drugs. . . ." [Well, well, I said to myself. Very interested, I went on with my reading.] I demand that my trial be postponed. It looks as if my case had to do with the simple fact of possessing and selling marijuana, whereas in fact, forces seeking my downfall made me fall into a trap. I was sent to San Francisco two years ago by the Highest Supreme Being of the Galactic Command, for this is the place where the world crusade of the Messiah must begin. The angels of the Bible speak to me in this moment of paradise, ordering me to establish the New Order. I had not yet transmitted my message to the people, because I had to wait for vibrations congenial to the flowering of a spiritual event of this importance. But when the vibrations turned negative—as the negative vibrations given off by that Michel of the San Francisco Narcotics Division—I interpreted this event as a test: the Spirit of the Universe wants our great Cause to have to strive against adverse spirits. The prophecy for all this can be found in Daniel, Chapter 12: "If I am that which I am, and I follow it, then certainly I cannot be delivered into the hands of men of the law who are so base?" To paraphrase Isaiah 53:5, I was wounded because of their transgressions, I was crushed because the people's iniquities were so great that they had to create a police, judges, military, which have put out traps for the very Person whom the people await as the God-Man.

He dated his revelations, "Revolutionary period of the thousand three hundred thirty-five days of the World Crusade of the Cosmic Messiah."

So now the mystic badge of purity had been lifted to reveal a seamy underside. The messiah had been caught dealing in drugs, and was liable for a fifteen-year prison sentence. He was setting the stage for his defense by trying to establish that he had acted, not out of cupidity, but from his mystic beliefs. That would give his lawyer a basis on which to plead his irresponsibility. This kind of legal charade has become fairly commonplace among gurus who have gotten in trouble with the drug laws. Our cosmic messiah almost certainly takes no drugs himself, but perhaps he was trying to raise money for his political activities, and then was caught. Let us recall that Timothy Leary and *Oracle* had outlined procedures whereby drugs could be made immune from legal action by stating *in advance* that they would be used as part of a religious rite. The cosmic messiah had not taken this precaution, which explains his efforts after-the-fact to establish that his mission was indeed religious, even though he had been forced to await "vibrations congenial to the flowering of a spiritual event of this importance."

So mystic twaddle turned out to be, in fact, a perfectly sensible piece of legal chicanery turned out by a perfect political guru who, while pleading his case, never forgot his political slogans.

Conscientious Objection

The gurus' potential constituencies have no particular socioeconomic bone to pick, so the gurus appeal instead to their souls. And one issue that reaches the souls of children consecrated to love, drugs, and indolence is pacifism. They are encouraged, not to distribute Lenin's diatribes against imperialism as in the old days, but to refuse military service as individuals. The whole hippie press is full of notices like these:

> ATTENTION, ALL DRAFTEES!
> IF YOU'VE BEEN CALLED FOR YOUR PHYSICAL BUT
> YOU DON'T WANT TO GO
> CONTACT US. NOW!
> WE CAN HELP YOU AND YOU CAN HELP US
> STANFORD ANTI-DRAFT UNION. . . .

In Washington, a draft counseling service called "Venice," which has the services of three lawyers, answers any and all questions about how to stay out of the army. Every American city has its draft counselors, whose addresses are published regularly in the hippie press, along with the addresses of similar groups in Canada, Denmark, England, France, Japan, Switzerland, etc.

The clever hippie tactics against the draft are widely discussed in the underground press. *The Progressive* (October, 1967) is proud to note that not one young person from Haight Ashbury has been drafted for the past three years, because they successfully convinced their draft boards that they were either drug addicts, homosexuals, or incurable psychos. The easiest thing, the magazine said, is to have a hysterical fit while you are actually being seen by the review board. Just pace the room and howl—that should do it. What can they do? Other commentators suggest obscene tattoos all over the body, or a declaration that your religion requires you save people's souls through drugs.

The hippie press also fills its pages with provocative photographs. One picture shows a pretty, well-endowed demonstratress carrying a placard saying, "Get out of Vietnam and into something cute" (*Berkeley Barb*, January 27, 1967). Another photo, widely distributed among the underground press, shows a young man testifying before a Congressional committee dressed in a shirt tailored from an American flag, with the stars on one sleeve and the stripes on the other. A policeman removes the man's shirt, since it is against the law to desecrate the flag, only to find the Vietcong flag painted on his skin underneath. This kind of incident moves the hippies more deeply than a hundred columns of "party line" propaganda.

All this happened in 1967, when the apolitical hippies were repelled by the idea of joining demonstrations against the war. But after several years of subtle propaganda, they began to appear in the antiwar crowds in greater and greater numbers until by the time of the "moratoriums" in Autumn, 1969, the hippies dominated the ranks.

Kill the Pigs!

Pacifist though the hippie movement might be, its basic styles and principles are in direct violation of the law, which made it inevitable that the hippies would clash in a war of attrition against the representatives of order. First of all, to say "hippie" is to say "drugs," which is to say "narcotics agents." To say "hippie" is to say "runaways," which means parents and investigators. To say "hippie" is to say "nudity," which means the vice squad, and then there are the dreadful sanitary conditions they live in, ear-shattering music, and the hysterical screaming during bad trips, which forces the neighbors to turn for help to the police. The hippies break the law all day and all night, which means that the law's upholders are around all day and all night, and the hippies resent this interference as an insupportable intrusion into their private lives. These talkings-to, summonses, raids, arrests, chases, aroused more and more vehement protests from the flower-children against what they call "police statism." And from that time on, the enemy to strive against, always and everywhere, became a monster with the head of a pig (probably the pig symbol arose from the piggy-looking gas masks the police wear during street riots).

From this beginning, a whole literature sprang up to whip up hatred against the "pigs." *Open City* (December 28, 1967) declared:

> I think it's time for people to get together—people from the minorities, people from the community, professionals, workers, writers—to get together and find out who they are. . . . The people who are going to unite us are the heat, the police. . . . Do you realize they busted 2,391 kids for pot in the San Fernando Valley alone this year? Yeah! How long can they continue to do that or how long people will continue to tolerate being busted is interesting to debate. . . .

Stokeley Carmichael, bedecked with the pompous title of "Prime Minister" of the Black Panthers, has declared,

> In order to stop police brutality, we've got to kill some white cops. We don't have to stand and yell about it. We just organize and kill some white cops. There's not a right or wrong about killing. It's a matter of who has the power to do so. It's more honorable to kill a honky cop than a Vietnamese (*Washington Star*, October 13, 1968).

But it's not only the Black Panthers, it's the whole hippie press that calls for the extermination of the police. Someone wrote in the *San Francisco Express Time* (October 16, 1968):

> The porks belong to us, we pay for them, they were put there for our use, we own the pigs, we pay their wages, they are for our use, if they don't do as you wish, fire them. The pigs are the strong-arm thugs of the mutants, we must confront the thugs and the mutants. We must be White Panthers!

The poet John Sinclair was named "Minister of Information" of the White Panthers, and the hippie Emmet Grogan, a leader of the

Diggers, also took an important role in the organization. *The Sun*, a hippie journal that specialized in "Rock and roll, drugs, and fucking," wrote that guerrilla warfare ought to include the dynamiting of the CIA's offices, of police vans, and of recruiting offices.

Even while the political gurus whipped up the hippies' hatred toward the police, they had to simultaneously reassure them, since these wandering bird-children were not likely to appreciate the view from behind bars. One *Oracle* journalist declared, "Despite all the police harassment, more and more people are taking drugs and thumbing their noses at them." So the hippies were pushed a step further into commitment. Not only is prison not to be feared, but a deliberate provocation of arrest is a heroic moral act to be proud of. He explains:

> An arrest causes panic and terror among hippies. They ought to armor themselves against this reaction. I've been arrested eight times during the last three years, and each time it was a test for me. I discovered that there is nothing to be frightened of. I play their game, and offer myself to be arrested. It does no harm (October, 1968).

Another strategy has been suggested to the girls:

> Corrupt the pigs by charm. Offer them flowers, kisses, invite them to come to your room, cajole them, and give them drugs. . . .

At hippie demonstrations, pretty girls brandish mannikins of nude women, with sex and breasts well in evidence, and the legend "Control Your Local Police" plastered across the mound of Venus.

The gurus have let their imaginations run riot in the battle against the pigs. They advise their young followers to join the police themselves, or the FBI, or the narcotics bureau, and burrow from within.

> As part of his alternate service (alternate to entering the American Business community) a hippie might elect to do the following:
>
> (1) Enter Police Force (local, state, FBI, Treasury Department, FDA) as *double agent*.
>
> (2) Report back to local community on pending raids, plans of actions, etc.
>
> (3) Keep diary on general inside attitudes, unofficial orders and procedures. Bug station-house locker room, for example.

(4) After 1 to 2 years resign. Have helpful book. Have fun.

HIPPIES! JOIN THE POLICE! SERVE YOURSELF, & SERVE
YOUR COMMUNITY TOO

Or else

Mail your local friend on the narco squad a few joints in an anonymous
envelope; or address it from one cop to another (use typewriter); or get your
friend in Mexico to do so. Then inform his superior by letter or secret
phone call. Variants:

(A) Plant on superior, inform subordinate, (B) Try it on your (1) local
principal; (2) bank president; (3) landlord; (4) army captain; (5) judge; (6)
legislator. Let your slogan be, RESOW THE SEEDS OF SUSPICION.
IT MAY HELP CLEAR THE AIR (*The Others*, January 15, 1967).

Rhythm, Superstition, Sex, and Activism

Aside from the two great themes, conscientious objection and
"police statism," new hippies are persuaded to enroll in the ranks in
a thousand subtle ways, a thousand skillful pluckings on the strings of
their mysticism, of their need to group, and of their credulity.

One of the first moves to turn flower-children into flower-activists
took place under the disguise of the "symbolic funeral" of their movement. The promoters of the funeral said that the hippie movement was
dead, but that it would rise from its own ashes in a new incarnation,
"Rebirth of the Free Man," which would be crowned by a "Declaration of Independence." The ritual took place in October, 1967, with
a long procession all the length of Haight Ashbury behind a hearse. The
coffin was filled with sandals, beads, bells, Indian feathers, locks of long
hair. At the end of the ceremony, the coffin was ritually burned, with
all its contents, with rites of exorcism. The political gurus of the
organization committee proposed that, after a ceremony of phallic
adoration, the newly born "free men" dress in Army uniforms and
parade across the city carrying papier-mâché bombs. In this way, the
ex-fornicators would be risen as antimilitarist activists.

The great hippie assemblages are immense banks of pistils pas-
sively open to whatever pollen may be carried by no matter what
ideologic bee. However, these bees have to guard well against deposit-

ing doctrinal pollen: the corollas will close up again. So, instead, unlike Orpheus, who played his lyre to "soothe the savage breast," the gurus use music to wake up their lambs and turn them into lions.

Thus, one weekend in July, at the Newport Folk Festival, I saw huge numbers of hippies gather with their long hair, their guitars, and their flower-bedecked VW mini-buses. There was something almost Biblical in the tableau of these young primitives, sitting on the flowered grass in a setting of hills, the air quivering with spiritual revelations. When the appointed moment for revelation arrived, after the concert, they turned out to be prosaically political; but as they were wafted down on the wings of melody, they passed muster very well. One hippie sang of his life in prison for an act of civil disobedience. The song that followed told the story of a Vietnamese family burned by American napam. The Reverend Kirkpatrick, the black minister of Resurrection City, went on next with his ballad against racism in the United States; Guthrie pushed his huge hit about setting fire to military records, and the evening ended with five war songs on the theme "kill the pigs." All this was interlarded with pop and with rock, which meant that the flower-children, after five days of this mixture, had acquired reflexes as conditioned as Pavlov's dog. When the rock went on, their hearts opened to the Vietcong flag; when it was pop, they wanted to kill a pig. So, drop by drop, a subtle propaganda has been sown in the minds of these children who would once have been the last to follow the standard of a slogan.

When a Marxist of the old school gets into a verbal duel with a guru of the new school, need we even mention that the heavy rationalism of Karl Marx doesn't have a chance against the emotional pyrotechnics of the hippies? In a debate between a leader of the Socialist Worker's Party, a Marxist group, and Jerry Rubin, a "committed" hippie, Rubin threw his listeners into delirium by playing a Beatle song, then burning his draft card and some dollars, and then introducing a pretty girl as his "bodyguard." Jerry Rubin, one of the rare gurus who had succeeded in creating an organization, called the "Yippies," has well understood that the combination of records, sex, and subversion can be an explosive mixture for young people. In his book *The Prophetic Minority*, he wrote, in the chapter headed "The Meaning of This Revolution,"

We have put all America on the alert. We have mixed young people, music, sex, drugs, revolt, and treason together. What other combination would be as effective? . . . What we need is a new generation of *obnoxious* people, a new generation of bizarre, unbalanced, irrational people, obsessed with sex, angry, irreligious, infantile, and crazy. People who burn their draft cards . . . people who attract young people with music, and hold them with marijuana and LSD . . . people who proudly wave the Vietcong flag . . . people who aren't afraid to say obscenities on television.

"In his book *Do It*, Jerry Rubin is calling on kids to leave their homes and burn down their schools."

This confusion of genres can mobilize adolescents who would completely shun any sort of conscious commitment, as is demonstrated by the following lines:

Only [Bob] Dylan could have called us there. He was our Shakespeare, our Lenin, our St. Jean of the Apocalypse, and he knew it. But he did . . . enunciate one at a time every word of 15 or so incomparable songs, which many of us knew by heart already—songs which contained our Declaration of Independence (*Open City*, December 22, 1967).

And it is this confusion of genres that posters designed for the fiftieth anniversary of the Bolshevik Revolution exploit, in which a hippie couple dances and sings in front of the smiling photos of Mao, Castro, Trotsky, Stalin, Lenin, Karl Marx, and Ho Chi Minh (*The Realist*, New York). All, with the exception of Mao, were bearded and moustached, which created a visual reflex that made all these Communist gods fit easily into the hippie pantheon, not to mention the impression that all these bearded and jovial lads were nothing more than super flower-children.

Most of the time the political gurus play on the superstitious and fetishistic spirit of the hippies, and their press gives a heavy play to palm reading, astrology, and magic. Thus, Allen Ginsberg and a rock group conceived of an elaborate rite on the tomb of Senator Joseph McCarthy, which was reported in the *Village Voice* as follows:

The ceremony began with Ginsberg standing in front of the grave to chant the Dharani spell to remove disasters. Then Ginsberg created the magic circle by walking around the grave chanting the Tibetan spell to banish evil spirits. Next, the 100 participants recited a mantra and offered food, flowers, candy bars, and artifacts to the spirit of McCarthy. And then they recited the mantra which praises marijuana (BOM! BIM! MAHADEV!) and someone planted actual marijuana seeds in the sod. After attempting a conjuration of McCarthy's spirit, they offered an invocation to Greek and Indian bisexual deities, recalling McCarthy's antagonism to homosexuals, and Ginsberg chanted the Prajnaparamita Sutra followed by a round of "My Country, Tis of Thee." Finally . . . the purified and exorcised spirit was sent back to heaven or to the appointed Karma realm by the ceremony of the Greater Hexagram . . . quoted in (*National Review*, March 19, 1968).

In this way, the belled and flowered children, who hadn't been born yet when Senator McCarthy set out against the Communists, had learned that McCarthy belonged at the side of Satan and Hitler in the catalog of the forces of good and of evil.

Pornography is also an excellent jumping-off place for injecting a political tinge into something that is by nature unpolitical. At the bottom of a full page of pictures, drawn from a porno film of lesbians' buttocks, this huge headline appeared:

DON'T BE DEPRIVED OF YOUR CONSTITUTIONAL RIGHT TO SEE THESE CONTROVERSIAL FILMS, THE SUPREME COURT RULED IT UNCONSTITU- TIONAL TO PREVENT THE SHOWING OF THESE FILMS. SEE THEM UNCUT AND UNCENSORED AS THEY WERE MADE (*Berkeley Barb*, October 7, 1968).

The School of Violence

Some hippie gurus, just as some blacks, intend to achieve their goals in peace, while others do not hesitate to call for violence. But easier said than done; the flower-children have little love for effort in general, or for revolutionary upheaval in particular, so their gurus push them to spectacular, although always apolitical, gestures like smoking drugs or sitting on the sidewalk during a sit-in. This blocks traffic, the police try to persuade the hippies to get up, they resist, the police have to carry them away kicking and screaming, the hippie photographers rush to take pictures, and fatten the files on "police brutality."

A teeny-bopper sit-in on Sunset Strip was invaded by activists from the W. E. B. Dubois Club, a Communist group, who quickly turned the gathering into a riot (*Mindszenty Report*, November 15,

1967). Extremist agitators infiltrate all the big hippie demonstrations. Among one group of photos from a "love-in" that degenerated into a riot, a police officer pointed out at least a dozen young followers of the Progressive Labor Party, a Maoist group. Some of the young people are dressed in the style of the Red Guards.

The Reverend Herman, of the Black Muslim mosque, advises hippies who get caught in a black-white confrontation:

> Stay off the streets. Don't expect a black crowd to know you're sympathetic. No one stops to ask you your feeling or opinion when there's a riot. Your skin is your only passport. . . . If you find yourself in the middle of a battle, don't expect to be able to keep from choosing sides. . . . You must go to one side of the street or the other. When you get there, you may have to throw rocks to survive . . . (*Open City*, August 11, 1967).

So obviously the time has come—which the hippie press emphasizes—for the once peaceful hippies to learn the rudiments of street warfare. In Canada, the leaders of the "Student Union for Peace Action" are training sixty hippies in the art of passive resistance to the police, some hippies playing the role of police howling imprecations at their foes who let themselves be hauled away like sacks of potatos. Some photos of these maneuvers were published in the Canadian press. The guru David de Poe even recommended that his followers start wearing heavy shoes to their drug-and-love festivals, abandoning bare feet or sandals, since these festivals had a tendency to degenerate into free-for-alls, and then the cops would march in crushing toes as they came. De Poe further instructed his people not to wear chains around their necks nor errings, for the "pigs" had an extremely painful habit of grabbing hold of these ornaments and pulling. Another guru refined the tactics even further:

> Don't grin at the police, it makes those mad dogs madder. And when you see a television camera as the police grab you, start screaming. It is good on TV (*The Globe and Mail*, August 12, 1967).

Certain hippie tribes, like Charles Manson's family, carried this violence of the extreme left to the point of Satanism. Lawrence Schiller reported in his book, *The Killers of Sharon Tate:*

Manson spoke constantly of unleashing a war between whites and blacks. He said that he and his nomads would set fire to powders that would kill whites, and the blacks would be blamed . . . that they would show off submachines on cars (stolen) . . . and that they would kill all the dirty white pigs. Then he would lead his band down into Death Valley and from there, well hidden, they would tranquilly watch the revolution.

It is clear now why one of the murderers carved the word "war" on the skin of a cadaver; why Charles Manson, after cutting off the ear of Hinman, the musician, wrote "political pig" with his blood on the walls of his house.

Yippies and Freebies

It is not a simple thing to organize beings who thirst for total independence, and the political gurus don't even try except when the action is clearly limited in time, and for goals that are typically hippie. There's no question of their tacking up posters (too tiring), or working in electoral campaigns (too cerebral). Rather, a typical assignment would be to boycott a certain storekeeper, or a certain neighborhood. A whole business district might be thrown into disarray by having them park hundreds of cars in every possible parking space during the rush hours. Then the owners of the parked cars are invited to litter up the shops and buy ten cents' worth of goods with a ten-dollar bill. In this way, the straight storekeepers would have sold nothing that day (*Berkeley Barb*, November 7, 1968).

The most political gurus go even further: "Flower power," they explain, "cannot stop fascist power. Songs will not help change the way things are. Organize." Words fallen on pretty deaf ears of course, but when you are dealing with young educated people who have time on their hands and nothing to do with it, a little jarring can have wide repercussions. During my investigations, however, I met only two groups of hippies organized in any traditional political sense.

First is the yippies, or Youth International Party, who have their fingers in every violent demonstration. Two Yippie activists, Abby Hoffman and Jerry Rubin, were arrested at the 1968 Democratic Convention in Chicago, along with the rest of the famous "Chicago Eight" —which includes Bobby Seale, president of the Black Panthers. The Yippies call themselves revolutionary anarchists. They are the ones who turn most readily to obscenity as an instrument of social protest, following the illustrious example of Aristophanes who had recruited some ruffians to pour liquid manure on some theater sets. These yippies paint their foreheads with their favorite four-letter words, and claim that "after spraying children with napalm, nothing is obscene." Jerry Rubin has just published *In Praise of nothingness*, a sort of metaphysically pretentious yelping against reason, which is described as the vile weapon of the bourgeoisie, while everything that degrades and mutilates reason is sublime, beginning with Jerry Rubin himself.

The other organization has taken the name freebies, or Fraternity of Free Men. The freebies inveigh against the contemplative life, silent protest, and political detachment. They have torn Jesus, Buddha, Krishna, Huxley, Leary, Emerson, Thoreau, Gandhi, Watts and Daumal down from the flower-children pantheon, to replace them with Marx, Lenin, Mao, Ché, Régis Debray, Castro, and—unexpected choice—the avatar Mehar Baba.

Contradictions Between Communism and Hippieism

There are natural affinities between the extreme left and the hippies, perhaps because both groups want to sweep the established order clean away. When Timothy Leary was convicted on a drug charge, Communists like Guy Endore immediately joined the "Committee for the Defense of Timothy Leary" that was created to raise money. Even Moscow itself paid homage to the flower-children in an approving article, signed Yuri Zhukov, which was published in *Pravda* on June 5, 1967. The *Los Angeles Free Press* (July 21, 1967) published the English translation. The hippie gurus were so flattered by this appreciation from unexpected quarters that they asked their readers to send Yuri Zhukov gifts like Beatle records, eyeglasses for tripping with, hashish pipes, etc.—"decadent" objects which no doubt caused their unlucky recipient endless bother in the puritanistic Communist world.

Affinities there may be, but fundamental incompatibilities exist as well, first and foremost from the point of view of personal liberties. Communists of whatever stripe impose a discipline of the State and of the Party. The hippies can tolerate no authority of any kind. The Communists glorify work, and the physical sacrifice required to construct a gigantic industrial infrastructure. The hippies claim the right to indolence, and are contemptuous of any and all industrial civilization, whether capitalist or Communist. The Communists have a rigid morality, the hippies make a life's work of hedonism. The Communists are atheist and materialist, the hippies are believers and spiritualists. The basic gap between the two movements is profound. One of the political hippies wrote:

> There are people on the extreme left who would like to tell us what we can do and what we should think. One becomes a Marxist guru by spending time in bourgeois libraries and filling your head with the scholasticism of Marx and Lenin. The hippies know that the time of the academic guru, whether Communist or bourgeois, has come and gone. The only authority that the young recognize is the authority of their own action in the collective battle against the State. The institutionalist authority that the extreme left, of whatever brand, has taken upon itself, has to be neutralized, including the academic Marxists.

The old-line revolutionary parties have come to the end of the road with the hippies, but the distrust has become mutual—a tone that can be picked up from this excerpt from an article by Susan Sontag:

> The American New Left is correct to be anarchic, because it is out of power. The freaky clothes, rock, drugs and sex are prerevolutionary forms of cultural subversion, and so you can have your grass and your orgy and still be moral and revolutionary as all get-out. But in Cuba, the revolution has come to power, and so it follows that such disintegrative "freedom" is inappropriate . . . (*Ramparts*, April 1969).

So you see, history changes direction and moves back toward the old values, like discipline, militarism, puritanism, work, obedience, that it had completely rejected earlier. In Havana, the police arrested 300 hippies who had come to Cuba with hearts full of love for their bearded brother Fidel, and the flower-children learned with sadness that Cuba too has its "pigs" with nothing better to do than throw hippies in jail.

In the countries where Communism reigns, the rock, drugs, and lasciviousness which the authorities find so repellent still manage to seep into the society through a thousand subterranean paths. The *Komsomolskaya Pravda*, the Soviet young Communist organ, complained that photos of nude women had inundated the underground hand-to-hand clandestine press that circulates in the U.S.S.R. "with the intention of undermining and overturning the Communist system.

Nude women," said the review in the inimitable jargon of the Bolsheviks, "pack a well-hidden ideological impact, and turn the mind away from politics."

When conservatives declare that pornography, which is spreading everywhere today among Western youth, is an insidious weapon being used to undermine society, the left sniggers at them, acting as if they were backward puritans who see witches everywhere. The "liberals" assure us that nudity, eroticism, even homosexuality and pornography, are forms of art or modes of expression in themselves, and have no relationship to social and political forms. But the Communists, expert in the art of moving the masses, skillful alchemists of passion and commitment, know better. They know that extreme carnality is, in effect, a form of insurrection against social constraints. They know that the revolt of the flesh quickly has its effects in the political domain. They know that the search for larger horizons, if only larger horizons for the senses, cannot help but come up against the rigid limits of the regime, and the more restrictive the regime is, the more quickly and more strongly the two forces will clash. And the new left does indeed flatter itself on its skillful encouragement of eroticism and drugs to addle the senses, sapping the juice from the traditional authority of the family, thereby precipitating the downfall of our political system, which is founded on the family.

So Communism is caught in one of those "internal contradictions" that it ascribes only to its adversary. They use every instrument at hand to weaken the fiber of the Western world, even though those instruments may prove destructive to them as well; apparently they count on their superior ability to pull chestnuts from the fire. But those very chestnuts may carry irreducible and dangerous ferments that menace the Communist world even more vitally than freer societies, because it is so much more of an order, so much more rigidly established. So these powers of the extreme left will have to take great care not to replay the eternal fable of the sorcerer's apprentice, and let themselves be overcome by the nihilist forces that it thinks it is using. If it is true that the hippie generation is lost to the open society of the West, the Communists are beginning to fear that it will never find a place in their closed tribe either. In their offensive against the free world, the forces of subversion may find that they have hold of a double-edged sword.

10

A Philosophy of Life

During the preceding chapters, we have often mentioned several elements in the hippie philosophy, but my readers are probably curious to have a surer grasp on the speculations that guide or enlighten the hippies, and this chapter tries to satisfy that curiosity.

ABSOLUTE LOVE

Love is the alpha and the omega of the hippie philosophy. A universal, unconditional, omnipresent, total love. It is through love of all living things that the hippies are vegetarians, following the example of the Buddhists. In certain volcanic islands of Hawaii, where it is difficult to make vegetables grow, the hippies are forced to eat fish, and they have planted placards in the sands of their beaches which read:

> We offered our respects and gratitude to the fish and the Sea Gods daily, and ate them with real love, admiring their extraordinarily beautiful, perfect little bodies (*Oracle*, November 1968).

I would guess that the fish would rather have been less beloved and less eaten.

The *Oracle*, one of the most illustrious hippie publications, prints the legend "Oracle Loves You" in every one of its issues. Try to imagine opening your newspaper every morning and reading, "The *New York Times* loves you. . . ."

In the Miracle Mile, a psychedelic hippie club in Los Angeles, the customer pays a dollar to get in and instead of receiving a ticket stub as proof of payment, his hand is stamped with the word "Love."

The hippies gargle about love from the beginning of the day to the end. The gentlest of them say "I love you" to the passerby who stands gaping at the gorgon's head in front of him; "I love you" to the grocer who squints with suspicion at their rags; "I love you" to the policeman who sniffs the odor of hashish on them. But these tender declarations of an indiscriminate love are made to people on the street by people who are committed to nothing. Indeed, the hearts of the hippies are cold and their lips stay closed when it has to do with the people who touch them closely, and to whom their love matters enormously: their parents. When they were overcome by the lure of *la vie bohème* and its drugged dreams, they left their homes without a backward look, unconcerned by the anguish they would cause, dropping out of sight for years altogether.

Some of them may vanish so cruelly from their homes because they detest the place (which proves that there is room for hate in at least some hippie hearts), but my investigations have shown that the great majority of runaways feel no anger toward, in the language of the straights, their "loved ones." Very often, they love their parents very much. And if a mother and father, consumed with anxiety, would travel from New York to Haight Ashbury to assure themselves that their child is not dead, no doubt the renegade would kiss them, saying, "I love you."

Only that love has no more weight to a hippie than the love that he declares to every passerby. His love for humankind, like his love for his near and dear, is a love of surface and of display, not even a declaration of principle, but a little nothing that the hippie disperses to the wind like apple blossoms, a perfume that he sprays on the people around him and which evaporates as quickly as dew in the sun. For the psychic base of the hippies is, not universal love, but sacred egotism, an egotism shared by all hedonists; his supreme value is the search for his own pleasure in total autonomy, whatever the pain that he may inflict on someone who loves him.

The same applies to that virtue which is a function of love: kindness. The ease, the carelessness with which the hippies make their parents suffer shows that, on this plane also, their philosophy of love is hollow. I say hollow, not vicious. They really want to be good, they love to feel that they are good, but on condition that this does not cost them the least sacrifice. Their acts of kindness, when they dispense them, are light, gauzy, fluttery, like everything they do or think. They might be willing to spend twenty minutes easing someone's pain, but hardly more than that.

Much is made in the hippie press of the genuine kindness displayed by the "loving guide" hippies who spend long nights by the sides of their friend on acid so that, should the trip turn "bad," they can keep him from hurting himself and offer support. I went to see some of these angels of charity to ask if a few of them would be willing to do much-needed volunteer work at a nearby hospital for handicapped children. They acquiesced in a vague sort of way, but never, dear God never, did the hospital ever see one of these "loving guides," in an access of kindness, come guide a paralyzed child in the exercise of his little atrophied muscles.

Clearly, no one is truly good unless he has it in him to sacrifice a little of his own pleasure or comfort to the happiness of another. Not only do the hippies not renounce any desires of their own, they are always ready to encroach upon other people, even those whom they are supposedly supporting most ardently. For example, during the 1968 "summer of love" in San Francisco, they took over any number of buildings, parks, and gifts of food and much social assistance that had been earmarked for blacks.

In a sense the hippies make a toy of love and kindness, a little party favor that goes off to the highest bidder. This illuminates one of their essential characteristics: they manufacture and consume illusion.

Tribal Love

The hippies' creed of love also includes the proposition that love will bind groups of people together into intimate communion. And indeed, one of the principal reproaches addressed to "society" is that it turns all men into prey for each other—or at the very least, the stranger or outsider becomes prey—and families become citadels of egoism where hearts harden against anything outside them.

It is true that the hippies live in tribes. Firstly, their poverty forces them to cram themselves into a room where they can all share the rent and food—a situation that encourages the, at first charming, habit of offering any food or drug around the circle. Secondly, communal life makes access to drugs much easier; everyone passes around information about suppliers and, with their communal generosity, whoever has, shares, so no one ever lacks for this stuff of life. And finally, it is more agreeable to get stoned in company than all alone, and it is also a wise precaution against bad trips. That is the source, and the totality, of the "communion" of which the hippies are so proud: a group of "heads" being stoned at the same time, each with his own ineffable perceptions.

Carnal Love

The hippies have above all striven for absolute love on the physical —that is, erotic—plane. The particular part of their creed that affirms that the body should be entirely free, that experience of every conceivable carnal pleasure, at every possible moment, is a great good, that every imaginable practice should be engaged in either with a partner of the opposite sex, the same sex, or no partner at all, is, as we have already seen in the chapter on sex, applied to the letter.

This hippie tenet has filtered down to the larger society, speeding up the process of sexual emancipation that has been developing in all the free and sophisticated societies of the West. More and more people in the "straight" world have begun to accept the possibility that all physical pleasure is a good. The hippies' contribution to this revolution consists of breaking down certain barriers that were maintained even among the most liberal "straight" circles, that is, the shame attached to public fornication, to homosexuality, and to prostitution. We should note, however, that though this shame may be ignored in their press, it has not been generally eliminated from their actual behavior. Couples make love in public, yes, but only at great "happenings" intended specifically to "put down" the straights, or perhaps when they are stoned. But most hippie communities are still quite far away from systematic and generalized public lovemaking. Some communities even demonstrate what can only be called sexual reserve.

There are still many hangovers in the dark corners of the hippie soul from those old taboos they decry with such vigor. These hangovers have not, however, stopped them from carrying sexual liberation farther, faster than anyone else. This may be the hippies' most profound contribution to a long-term change in our mores. What can be said about this revolution?

First, there are social limits. No matter how "open" one's mind and spirit may be, there is little to say in favor of human kennels where anyone who has sexual desires for anyone else is authorized to satisfy his desire then and there, no matter whether in the office, in a restaurant, or on the sidewalk. No collective life can maintain the least dignity under such conditions. People must restrain themselves, even in love—above all in love.

The human kennel would not only be untenable socially, it would be destructive to health, beauty, and emotion. Constant change of sexual partners makes one vulnerable to serious venereal diseases, which are then passed on to one's next contact; constant lovemaking from morning to night, from night to morning, is physically and mentally debilitating; and excessive sexual exercise becomes just that—exercise —with less ecstasy each time. Perpetual pleasure becomes more and more bloodless. The senses become blunted and cease to enrich the soul, while all the emotions that accompany the sensations lose their charm and their value. Lovemaking becomes, on the contrary, a source of brutalization.

The fanatics of fornication forget that sex is just one of the elements of love which, in its full expansion, also includes tenderness, respect, admiration, trust, devotion, and shared tastes, efforts, and memories.

Certainly, a complete love is fulfilled in sexual pleasure in marriage, but it doesn't begin there and it doesn't end there. Love's true triumph is its triumph over solitude, doubt, and time; it has not truly won unless the presence of the loved one follows you beyond the bed, unless that smiling image floats in the air you breathe and impregnates your vitals, unless it secretly accompanies your steps in the street and your words in life.

This is the substance of the true, of the great love, the love that men have exalted through time, the love that has dominated their art and their literature, the love that is rarely found along the hashish trail. This real, this true love means a strong attachment, a mutual gift from one being to another, a passionate connection of hearts; in other words, a relationship that could not be more opposed to the pointillistic hippie life of flight. Brigitte Axel, in her book *H*, confessed that she was disturbed, almost shamed, by the only true love that she found during her travels. Why? Because she realized that she risked being bound to another human creature for as long as several months.

A complete love also implies that its object has been chosen, selected out from all the possible options. Each being can only store a finite dose of riches in the treasure of the personality. If he strews his desires, his dreams, his gifts, and his needs as chance takes him, his objects are receiving nothing from him but specks of dust and they can return nothing but dust to him. Only the wind loves everything, which is to say that it loves nothing.

In practice, the Absolute Love of the hippies is, alas, nothing more than a beautiful dream. Or perhaps a nightmare. The nightmare of the absolute dissolution of love.

ABSOLUTE LIBERTY

There is more relationship between the hippies' theories of absolute liberty and their acts than there is between their theory of absolute love and their acts. They rigorously respect their companions' freedom of action. Everyone does whatever comes into his head to do when he wants to do it, without accounting to anyone, nor does anyone ever ask for such an accounting.

However, here too, if you sound the hippies' cult of absolute liberty, you can hear several false notes. When I rose one evening in San Francisco from a circle of people chatting around me, and left, saying goodbye to no one, to take off for Katmandu, that was fine; but if I stand up to say that drugs are a poison and work is sustenance I am received very badly. I am peppered with sarcasms and accusations (of which the worst is complicity with the establishment). At least they don't, in the heat of argument, attack me physically as a Maoist would have done. As always, real ideological liberty is the most difficult kind of liberty to grant and, in this area, the hippies show a little of the intolerance of the extreme left.

We have also seen that jealousy is not yet unknown in the hippie world which means that, in a fair number of couples, at least one of the parties will try to keep the other from fornicating with a third. Is this absolute liberty? But on the whole, it is only fair to say that when it comes to personal freedom, hippies practice to an unusual degree what they preach; the demon of intolerance applies only to ideologies and, even there, they are rarely carried to any sort of aggression against the person of another. I am speaking now, however, of hippies in a state of relative equilibrium; not of those who, in a drug delirium, may become violent.

I must add that liberty as understood by the hippies—which means, simply, that you can do what you want, the way you want, when you want—is a liberty of limited value. Throughout history courageous fighters have mobilized for battle in liberty's name, but why? Have they fought for the right to spend the rest of their lives stargazing, or is liberty rather the precondition for any action toward development and growth? It would be just as futile to pride oneself that one is free and then not do anything, as it would be to congratulate oneself on having wrested the right to read anything—and then not have a book on one's shelf. No more than with love, there's no juice to liberty unless there is substance.

It is true that the gurus claim more than freedom of individual conduct. They have developed a whole metaphysic of *absolute* liberty on the social plane, condensed into the slogan "It is forbidden to forbid" that the French protesting students of May, 1968, had taken over from the hippies.

In fact, these great libertarians were as hypocritical as anyone in history who has ever tried to bring people to submission with soft words of "freedom." These youths, scribbling their brave "forbid us not" on the walls of the Sorbonne, were themselves great forbidders. The portrait of Jaurès was violently forbidden a place next to the portraits of Lenin or of Mao; they forbade professors to lecture and forbade their fellow students to take their examinations.

Moreover, it takes a bad faith indeed to argue that *nothing* should be forbidden: what about forbidding child labor, racial discrimination, spoiled food, slavery, torture, infanticide, murder, and a mob of other destructions? Certainly, "Thou shalt nots" that protect unjust privileges should be done away with, but clear heads have worked for centuries to destroy these constrictions. We haven't needed the hippies and the demonstrators to tell us that each generation owes it to itself to enlarge its field of liberty to the maximum degree consonant with basic morality. But it is one thing to roll back the limits, and quite another to eliminate them altogether. The first goal—to widen the field of action—is possible and fruitful, and all progress is nourished on it. The second—to dissolve all limits to liberty—is rubbish.

But the longhairs intoxicate themselves on liberty with a sincerity that forces one's sympathy. And it is indeed this frantic pursuit of liberty that makes the hippies so inconstant, and so imponderable. I have mentioned above that the hippies flee the elaborated forms of love that imply attachments, and in general, they flee from any profound emotion or commitment, precisely because they fear the bonds of attachment. I believe that this incapacity to sustain any tie—tenuous though it might be—around either the soul or the body, this need for the freedom of birds that is so visceral that they have the courage to pay the price of utter destitution, is the real "sign of the hippie"— much more so than their hollow religion of love. Personally, I would prefer to call the hippies, rather than "flower-children," by the more appropriate name of "bird-children."

But there are limits, whether they like it or not. It would be too much work, for their ethereal humors, to reflect on the diverse kinds of limits there are, so let us do it for them.

First, there are the *inevitable* biological limits, such as the need to eat, drink, sleep, learn to walk, to speak, to read and write, to protect ourselves from danger, to produce food, shelter, and the coverings our bodies require. And all these things demand constant effort and sustained discipline. To curse this kind of limitation makes no more sense than to rebel against the fact that man is mortal.

Next, there are the limits *necessary* for living in groups with one another: taking care of our injured, burying the dead, dealing honestly, sharing burdens, driving on the right, raising children, sheltering old people, protecting the weak, fighting against natural calamities, etc. (The essential limitations of work and law will be discussed later.) To refuse this kind of limitation is to forbid all human society.

And finally, there are *useful* and *voluntary* limits and constraints. Men who have turned their minds to the mysteries of creation, whether in the sciences, letters, the arts, the crafts, philosophy, know that the creator must silence the siren songs of a thousand interior temptresses, place his mind on alert, circumscribe his gaze, whip up his reasoning processes, discipline the imagination, fix the attention, blank out the memory—all very laborious things. The flash of ideas or of new forms probably demands a sufficient concentration of certain chemicals in the brain, and a certain intellectual asceticism is indispensible to maintain this concentration. Whoever has experienced it knows its marvelous fertility. To exclude this kind of constraint from life is to leave the human being in a state of pure animality.

Certainly there are abusive social constraints that have no other function that to maintain either intolerable supremacies of one group over another, or absurd prejudices. True libertarians have struggled against this kind of constraint throughout all of history, and in these combats, the left has incontestably been the liberating instrument. But as soon as the extreme left began to glorify the idea that there should be no limits, it fell into the ditch that has been the downfall of so many reformers: the means gleam with such luster that the ends are forgotten.

It happens too often, alas, that the instrument forged for some other purpose becomes an idol in itself. The revolutionaries aspire to a positive reform, they engage in battle, the struggle becomes heroic, they symbolize the struggle in a slogan, the slogan inflames the masses, and they inflate it into a sword and cross that have no relationship to its original meaning; and one, two, three, the catchphrase, henceforth emptied of all real content, becomes an object of worship. The magic of the word has replaced the real meat of the enterprise. The struggle begins with, "Down with all unjust repression." Then it becomes "Down with all repression." First the phrase rolls trippingly off every tongue, then it becomes personified in the leader of the movement. And thus elitism, and then despotism, are born from the dust of a valorous battle. The process is as old as humanity, as sad as failure.

ABSOLUTE INDOLENCE

The hippies abominate any attempt to force them into a mold, but by all odds the most hateful commandment of all is "Thou shalt earn your bread by the sweat of your brow." They batter against the ancestral taboo of work even more vigorously, and more radically, than against traditional sexual mores.

Their writings abound in sonorous, rhythmic, and often amusing phrases that protest against the law of work: a law that has been part of human functioning even longer than the laws of modesty. All their little sallies are embroidered around the central idea that work kills: "Man does better if he doesn't work." "Society needs your smile, not your muscles." "Every time you do a movement on an assembly line, you blaspheme against nature." "Jobs cause cancer." Work that is ordinarily considered worthwhile, even noble, like scholarship, science, engineering, is not spared: "Truth doesn't live under a microscope." "Studying is unhealthy, it tires the eyes and addles the brain." "Don't tire your mind by seeking, take drugs and you will find." The ancestral and universal ethic of work well done is derided: "Why should a chair stand up straight? Better to have it tipped, so you can lie down." No slash is strong enough against the factory, the store, the office, the construction yard, the school, the university, the places of sweat and unhappiness where men and women make up frivolities for each other's benefit, or stuff their heads with silliness, instead of intoxicating themselves on air, on sun, and on hallucinogens.

From time to time, these slashing curses against work are worked up into a theoretical essay, like this one from *Oracle* (November, 1967):

> We're coming out of an era in the womb of man, of total society in a womb condition of being really taken care of. The baby is inside of his mother. Finding itself in the universe where he doesn't have to invent the oxygen or any of the 98 chemical elements, they're just waiting, he doesn't have to invent the mathematical elements by which hair actually grows, beautiful things. But we're gradually beginning to come out of the vanity as we come out of this, out of the womb, sort of group womb, into the new relationship with the universe. Our real guidance is going to be this metaphysical with fantastic respect for that truth itself which you find, and you've got to find. Once you've found the true inter-relationships you've got to go with them.

Most hippies have broken off all relations with watch-time. They wake up when they wake up, sleep when they sleep, nibble at food when they are not smoking up, and vice versa. The distinctions between day and night, between weekdays and holidays, have no meaning to them, every day ought to be Sunday. They don't recognize their own birthdays, or anyone else's. The months carry no name, the days no date, there is nothing to distinguish one moment from another.

This is no pose or a wish to shock; it is a profound state of soul, and of physical disposition. Their absolute laziness is, no doubt, partly due to their drugs. Also, the wish to do nothing is innate in all of us, and much of our early training is planned specifically to suppress this tendency. But once the habit of work, which was so laboriously taught us, has been lost for a few years, an individual will tumble into an irreversible inertia.

Anyone who is really honest with himself will acknowledge that instinct does not push man to work (as thirst pushes him to drink), but that even so a solid dose of work will always be one of the givens of life. The idea that man can exist without ever having to work again, which has been expressed a thousand times throughout the hippie press, is, alas, puerile, like most of the flower-children's ideas. How could a supposedly grown person write that human beings should henceforth have nothing to do but let themselves drift, their legs crossed in the lotus position, on the waves of society's great uterus where "they" will take care of them. What "they?" The only answer is, "us," that is, human society itself (for lack of extra-human helpers like Snow White's dwarfs or Wells's Martians), and around we go in a vicious circle.

Or perhaps *Oracle* thinks that this "they" is our technology (which *Oracle* has only the greatest contempt for). Alas, this technology is still far from capable of this! Yet, the editors of *Oracle* have visited India many times. They have seen for themselves that the interior visions, the *dolce far niente* underneath the golden sun and the chants of "Hare Krishna" don't turn the water into canals to irrigate the land, nor do they grow rice. Even in the United States, a letter doesn't get from here to there by machine—as the hippies should know, the Post Office Department being one of their main sources of employment. It is true that in the hippie world, you don't have to write to affirm friendship—just get into bed. Nor do you have to wash, cut your hair, nor even get dressed. But you do still have to eat. And what "they" will till the soil, sow the seeds, harvest the crops, transport, pack, and distribute the food? The fetus, in the human uterus, has a very specific "they" to serve him: the father who works, and the mother who feeds him through her body and prepares him to face the world. In the social uterus, the "they" is everyone, and if the hippies won't pull their own weight, then everyone else has to work twice as much.

Despite all our science, and the possibility that all superfluous work will eventually be eliminated, society will still require at least five hours' work a day from each able-bodied adult—even if, the way things are going, everyone will stay in school until thirty, and everyone will retire at fifty. And if we as a society decided to produce less consumer's goods, if all humanity decided to follow *Oracle* into bucolic joys, where there was nothing to do but eat, get dressed, find a place to live, keep warm, take drugs, and listen to records, abandoning the printed word, all technology and all machines—ah, well, this pastoral idyll would require . . . twelve hours work a day! Yes, twelve hours a day, tilling, sowing, harvesting, etc., all by hand. Twelve hours a day instead of the five-hour day that is just around the corner, the life of an animal instead of a life that gives you access to airplanes that will fly you to play shepherd in Katmandu, and that provides the automatic presses for running off *Oracle*. In other words, technology, if used properly, can give you freedom; denial of technology will bind you down.

Even supposing that there could be a real utopia, complete with robots, to serve all our needs, that doesn't mean that man is necessarily going to live in total idleness for the rest of eternity. He will always have to invent, manufacture, and program his slaves, and when he forgets this, he will have forgotten to act as a human being, and his slaves—designed precisely to carry out these functions that man has let atrophy—will stop too. Whatever may happen, we may clearly not move toward that "planetary uterine state" of which *Oracle* dreams, without working now to accumulate that very knowledge for which *Oracle* has such contempt. For the moment, that "uterine state" can benefit no one but a few privileged parasites—the hippies. So now we understand who the hippies' "they" is: first, of course, mother and dad, who knock themselves out with work; then the rest of "straight" society, whose own lives are being kept harder longer for being obliged to subsidize these doctrinaire ne'er-do-wells.

On the other hand, however, the hippies are quite right to protest excessive, unpleasant, or boring work. An excellent first step, if they had only gone further and devised creative innovations. The protests of the socialists and the syndicalists against painful or brutalizing labor has filled libraries well before the hippies, and these protests have borne fruit; more and more workers are steadily being freed from onerous jobs, thanks to a combination of a sense of justice and a technology advanced enough to support translation of this sense of justice into action.

Moreover, there have been thinkers in the past, like Paul La-fargue, to affirm, in the face of the ancestral curse of sweat, the right of workers to idleness. And how serious these ideas are, how fecund, compared to the hippies' utopias. Lafargue argues that work is not a value *in itself,* the way people were taught in the earnest 19th century. It can only enlarge man if, first, it serves a great and human objective and if, after that, it is entered into freely, and the workload is reasonable and conscientiously executed. Lafargue adds that leisure can be as noble as work if it is also lived intelligently. Then it is a delicious bath in which man repairs his forces, cultivates his sensibilities, tastes of nature, and draws upon the very inspirations that lead him to work. Humanity imagines when it is at leisure, and builds when it is at work. Lafargue shows that executives are serfs until they acknowledge their own rights to this fruitful indolence, and can make it flower. But Lafargue is not speaking of the absolute and permanent, hollow and narcissistic laziness of the hippies. He deals, rather, with the golden link of repose which is enlaced harmoniously with the bronze link of work to make the great chain of Prometheus.

Moreover, the theater of our times renews itself and deepens its repertory with a powerful rhythm every year, which means that more themes and more horizons are endlessly being opened to the enterpris-ing spirit, more searching and more creation. There is still a kind of struggling that debases man, but how many other struggles raise him high! And we all know, all around us, a crowd of people in every profession whose work impassions them and literally makes them flower. Two thirds of so-called "professional" people are in this cate-gory, along with a good third of the farmers, craftsmen, and skilled workers. For anyone whose efforts can be translated before their very eyes into a blooming of creativity, or of knowledge, or of the public good, this effort is the very salt of life.

Not only is absolute indolence inconceivable so long as humanity really functions as humanity, it is equally as destructive to the development of the individual human being. For, to the degree that the senses, the muscles, and the brain become permanently relaxed, pleasure itself fades, joy dims, and the individual sinks into a sort of languor that is much closer to death than to life. A complete organism must know how to savor the perfume of lilacs while he rests, and then turn his mind to the structure of their stamens.

Absolute Destitution

It has often been said, and rightly, that the hippie has contempt for his papa's money, but he cashes his papa's checks. He vomits up the materialism of the establishment, but it is this very establishment that keeps him from sleeping naked in the street. He has nothing but sarcasm for the charity that is only "conscience money" as far as the hippies are concerned, but he runs quickly enough to their hospitals and psychiatric centers when things go poorly for him. He sneers at the "science" of the rationalists who look for Truth under a microscope, but his basic sources of satisfaction are the product of their work: LSD, records, cars, the plane for Katmandu. And where do his protest buttons come from and his "liberated" press, if not from sophisticated printing presses? The same presses, in fact, that give him access to the latest work of Timothy Leary proclaiming that our civilization of machines is nonsense.

An Australian hippie journalist, with whom I discussed these thoughts in a café in Kabul, answered that his hippie brothers could not help but avail themselves of the manufactures of the establishment since, until now, through the fault of Galileo, the world has been dominated by the urge to manufacture, to control materials; however, he believed it was possible that a more poetic civilization could well have developed a sophisticated electronics technology.

"Nobody knows what would have happened if Cleopatra's nose had been longer," I answered, "but it is certain enough that the chemistry of LSD, electronics, and the jet plane could not have been developed if everyone has spent the past three hundred and fifty years since Galileo fooling around in the Himalayas and being stoned. Besides, aren't you doing just what the establishment does, except when you're smoking or fornicating? Look what you do to get out the next issue of your firebrand newspaper. It's just like an editor of a regular "establishment" paper: recruiting talent, bitterly bargaining down the price of paper, fiddling around with the news, improvising sensationalism, looking for the most profitable sales outlets, even going so far as to pay your bills to the telephone company, the epitome of corporate capitalism, whose existence is entirely dependent on the millions of miles of telephone cables laid down by the straights."

When it comes, however, to the use of money, the hippies incarnate an incontestably new phenomenon. They do need a minimum to live, and it is this minimum that we have seen them eke out from daddy's exchequer, from pilfering, from begging, or from charity. This minimum poses a grave problem to the hippies, for its only source is the Established Order, and it makes the hippies parasites on this order. That said, the fact that the minimum in question is so extremely minimum—much lower than even the thriftiest "straight" person could possibly manage—is a significant sign of authentic revolution in Western mores. All my investigations show that the street hippie lives on a budget somewhere between $25 and $75 per month, or let's say, to set a mean, $50 a month, twelve times less than the salary of an average American worker.

Certainly, in exchange for their renunciation of the material, they amuse themselves with whatever pleases them: multicolored gewgaws, psychedelic records, drugs. And they feel free as the bird in a tree, discharged from all obligation to work or to study. Their poverty is then the fruit, not of a cruel destiny, but *of their deliberate choice.* It doesn't block them from achieving their goals, it opens the doors for them to satisfy their dreams. Moreover, it is an enchanted poverty, a joyful sharing of youth, companionship, love, "trips," and *dolce far niente.* However, in terms of the material comforts of life, the hippies are much more deprived than the traditional "artist in the garret" or other devil-may-care who may, in an earlier time, have chosen to live *la vie bohème.* Compared to present-day hippie indigence, those earlier bohemians lived in positive comfort. They at least were never reduced to digging into garbage cans for food, or stealing blankets to keep from freezing to death. They had a bed in a room, and soap and water. The fact that the hippies have accepted a considerably more ascetic discomfort proves that they have truly made a great leap away from material values. The contempt that they affirm for money is a contempt that they really live, and sometimes in a dramatic way. No doubt their physical poverty is more a matter of indifference rather than a sort of religious renunciation, and this indifference is reinforced by their drugs which skim all importance from the *things* of life. Be that as it may, we must still deal with the fact that the hippies, as a group, have access to a world of abundance, and they choose total deprivation; in other words, in relation to money they put their philosophy fully into practice. They differ on this point from certain new left protesters who vigorously declare the required metaphysic of contempt for money, and just as vigorously do whatever they can to make it.

One cannot help but be touched by the fortitude and disinterestedness with which the hippies accept this radical renunciation of all riches, but its uselessness is, alas, only too evident. First, this renunciation does not deliver them from material cares, for there still remains that irreducible minimum below which one simply cannot survive, and we have already seen how the hippies gallop around scratching for that little morsel.

But the hippies who design the fascinating psychedelic posters, who compose the bewitching melodies, who assemble strange jewelry, who test, describe, and debate the beyond of consciousness, these are not the naked starving hordes who roam the hashish trail, these are artists who stay at home, who keep enough fire in their chimneys to keep their fingers warm and supple, enough calories in their stomachs to keep their senses from being deadened, enough reading in their heads to keep their brains from atrophying. This fact contradicts the utopians who, for centuries, have believed that deprivation was more of a spur to wisdom of genius than comfort.

This indispensable minimum of comfort and of culture, set well above the minimum vital to life, is precisely that minimum below which the traditional bohemian artist never descended. To refuse that is just a foolhardy denial of the human condition. To go below the minimum is not admirable and fruitful disinterestedness; it is absurd and sterile extravagance. . . .

The hippies say that only impure societies have produced material goods. That is true. But purity does not come from abandoning all comfort; that is just to go back where we started from, with all the naked baseness, cruelty, and depravity of which man is capable. We have to hold on to our ease, and purify society from there. It is certainly a long and difficult task, but the only one that makes sense.

But in fact, there is another reason beside the messianic for the hippies' life of total renunciation. Their anathemas against industrial civilization are nothing but ideological ornament. Their real motivation is physiological; it's just that a person can't really do anything when drugs are his life.

Return to Nature

The hippies who curse industry, money, and the material civilization and look for some objective correlative to their interior paradise have no other choice, obviously, than to glorify the return to nature. Nonetheless, as we have seen, the great majority of hippies practice it hardly at all, prefering to circle around the psychedelic discotheques in the large cities like butterflies circling a light. But their gurus continually exhort them to leave the cities. "My first message," Timothy Leary wrote, "is, flee the concrete and go toward the fields." Nature, according to the hippie philosophy, is the only exterior paradise that can offer food for pleasure worthy of the interior drug paradise. It is also the only setting that appears to fit the perfect lovers of indolence. Alas, this idea, or rather this hope, is also an illusion, as we shall see.

The nature that sings a siren song to many harassed citizens, not just hippies, is not the natural, untouched nature of Spinoza, it is a nature molded and improved by man through long, painful effort, an effort that has cost him a good deal more backbreaking work than his industrial society ever did. Without hundreds of years of clearing land, drainage, irrigation, tilling, construction of roads and tunnels, planting, dams—without these tons of sweat and these billions of bowed spines, these beautiful grasslands would be crawling with thorns and insects, this lovely undergrowth would be overrun with brambles and impene-

trable vines, these clear ponds would be gummy with toads and infested
with marsh fever, these temples of rock would be aswarm with ferocious
beasts and snakes. Yes, nature furnishes us with the means to live, but
in the raw state, without charm, and invested with mortal risk. It is
man's job to distinguish that which is beneficial to us from that which
will do us harm, and to make the beneficial pleasing, even poetic.
Nothing ever has, or ever will, do the work. Man could not comfortably
live his life on two percent of the earth's raw land. If all humanity,
seized by "naturism" and by dreams of lotus land, went to the land,
they would soon enough be showering blessings on the New York
subway.

Nature's grandeur has been the source for a kind of inspiration
that neither industry nor art could evoke, but you still need industry
and art, which is to say the work of man, to take pleasure from it. Those
Himalayan ranges that the hippies flock to are sublime, but almost no
one has ever gazed from their precipices, or hung from their peaks,
listened to the murmur of their streams, inhaled the perfume of their
flowers. No one can go adventuring in these lofty, lunar solitudes,
knapsack on his back and stick in hand, as in the Alps. There are
neither roads, nor inns, nor shelter. You have to hire Nepalese guides
and porters to lug tons of provisions on their backs: food for ten persons
for a month, sleeping bags and tents, shovels, picks and rope, medicines, etc. Only rich mountain climbers can afford to fill their lungs
with the Himalayan air, and their eyes with the Himalayan vistas—a
sight that is indeed hallucinogenic. The hippies (and I too) have to
admire the mountains from so far off that they look like nothing so
much as beautiful postcards. And as I stood looking at the Himalayas,
I was suddenly moved to bless the herculean labors of my Western
people who have carved roads through the mountains of my home, so
that I have been able to gaze from their precipices, to hang by my
hands from their peaks, to listen to the murmur of their streams, and
inhale the perfume of the Alpine flowers.

So we come back once again to vanity, to the inanity of searching
for a happiness—even a happiness in nature—that is separate from the
rest of civilization. We have seen that "Thou shalt flee the cities" is
the least observed hippie commandment. For every ten hippies who
will leave Katmandu to come and contemplate the Himalayas, there are

a hundred who cram themselves into their smoky city holes-in-the-wall. In reality, this invocation of nature is just another weapon in the arsenal of modern protest movements—and not just of the hippies.

Any group that questions our industrial civilization brings up the clear mountain brooks. But I don't understand. I don't understand how running Alpine brooks can be set in opposition to the Golden Gate. For me, the two are equally as exalting, though in different registers; they appeal to different, but not at all contradictory, levels in me— levels that complement rather than contradict each other. The dispute between the respective merits of nature and industry seems to me as puerile as the question that people always put to children: "Who do you love better, papa or mama?" A question to which there is only one answer: "I love them both the same." I love to roll along in a smooth, powerful automobile and, at the end of the trip, stretch out in the shade of a gentle, powerful tree. The glory of nature goes very well with the glory of man.

Neither the heroic plunge into deprivation, nor the lyric flight into nature, brings one any nearer to happiness than the traditional formula, which is basically: Take your tools in hand when it is time to work, and take your sweetheart in hand when it is time to enjoy.

The Communal Life

What can you do if you love company but not society, if you love indolence but not hunger? You can go away with some companions to set up a community on the land. Many hippies have taken this road, following after so many other idealists in the past who have striven against the Law of Bronze—Victor Considerant's term for the ensemble of the rules that hold the social order together. The temptation is great. No more quarreling against the capitalists who try to make us covet goods. We will all go off toward the green valley and begin again at the beginning, ourselves alone, and we will love it. At the beginning, they delight in devising elaborate constitutions that will make all relationships just, harmonious, and fraternal. People will get married in twos, or in fours, or by taking turns, or all together. We will smoke marijuana and drop acid as we like. We will sing the day long, and dance all night. We will forget books, and our parents' irritating letters.

We will whip up extravagant clothes, or won't wear any. We will plant a row of marijuana between each row of carrots. And of course, everything will belong to everybody.

Some fifty of these hippie communities, or "communes" as they are called, have been set up along the sunny coasts of California and Florida. Some of them, turning away from the divine sun, have moved into suburban houses, or sometimes into shanties in the middle of nowhere. The communes range from the relatively well off to the impoverished, and their statutes concerning love go from the not-really-so-free to the more-than-free. But so far, all these communes have foundered on the same rocks that have for centuries destroyed all other such communal "returns to the land."

The homesteaders have all discovered, in effect, a series of astonishing facts: that in the ordinary way of things, if a spermatozoa meets a ripe ovum, there will be a child; that children, out of who knows what deviltry, give their parents pleasure, and they begin to want to keep them jealously for themselves; that fingers, as if bewitched by an evil charm, stiffen on the guitar after fifteen days without food. That soil doesn't turn into food unless the land is tilled and planted. That even then, the land doesn't give up its fruits until it is harvested with great effort and sunburned, peeling skin. That the community's wastes observe the law of gravity and don't fly away, while, if they are left to rot in place, disease spreads. In brief, given this little cluster of phenomena, Gene Carlson, the founder of a commune on Bridge Mountain called "OM Foundation" (from the Indian mantra), promulgated the following Tables of the Law for all hippie tribes:

> A community has to have some sense of order until the people in it have reached a sense of communication in themselves that becomes awareness of order. . . . For example, if someone leaves their mess for someone else to clean up, they need rule or law until they become their own keeper. Then you can not only be a good example to yourself (the I AM) but go a little further to be the WE ARE. Which means to pick up after those who are less fortunate. . . . By "less fortunate," I mean those that have found themselves to be God in thought but not in activity. . . . If somebody's been sitting around the house for days on end without doing anything, like dishes or anything, you're truly not loving by letting them fall into that stagnation. . . . We have two Coordination Ceremonies a week. We gather, we form

a circle, we hold hands, we come to peace, and then we talk. . . . We have lists in the house of what has to be done every day, like mopping floors, emptying garbage, a list of repairs that need to be done in cabins and stuff. . . . Each cabin takes a turn at running the whole thing, each day; in other words, it alternates. This way it makes them responsible to be a leader and when it's not their day, it makes them responsible to be a good follower. It's a real good balance there. . . . Generally we were raised in a world where survival was strictly for self, for self-gain, for self-survival. It was man alone, challenging . . . always opposing each other to survive. Now the the pendulum is coming to a point where the only way we will survive is when everybody is doing for each other. We'll all be feeding each other only to find out that someone will be feeding us. . . .

This is truly a touching text in the immensity of its candor. These people have chosen anarchy because they feel oppressed by arbitrary disciplines, and they reinvent exactly the same disciplines as soon as they have to build a society! And these old/new disciplines exist in their most raw, most naked form: the life of a barracks, with duties assigned by the officer in charge. At least within families, the loving mother takes care of all that.

The situation described by Gene Carlson is not exceptional. In all hippie communities without exception the same litany is chanted. No one wants to do the daily drudgery that must be done for the collectivity to survive. And as the leader has no real authority, he calls meetings: meetings to appoint the money-collectors; meetings to discuss a kitchen that has become "digusting"; meetings about the "chaotic state" of the rooms; meetings to set meal times ("the hippies eat all day long, so by meal time, there's nothing left"); meetings against "people getting up in the middle of the night to put on records." And since there is a new problem every day, every day there is another meeting. The hippie communities are forced to spend half their time in boring confabulations to work out the simplest actions; actions which, in the straight world, are organized automatically, harmoniously, because, since childhood, each person has been trained to function in society.

Other communities have been forced to enact "restrictive immigration" laws just like the most reactionary countries. Each group closes itself, barricades itself against the intrusion of newcomers in order to maintain a standard of well-being for the "proprietors," defined as those who were first to occupy the land (one can hardly imagine a more feudal concept!). Each group turns in on itself like all families, forming economic, egoist, jealous units, except that these families have twenty or thirty members rather than the regular four to six. Other communities that have been faced with the problem of overpopulation have chosen an all-powerful leader to select which of his brothers would be cruelly expelled without recourse. The too-drugged, the too-lazy, the too-wild, the too-asocial, and those whose heads had flown into permanent paradise were all shown the door. The laws of the straight world would never have permitted such arbitrary decisions.

No doubt the OM Foundation would have gone on to regulate the disposition of children in case the parents should separate, and to arrange for the allocation of goods if a member should leave the community. In order to facilitate the internal exchange of goods, it would have created an establishment, called "Psychebank," which would have issued little slips of paper covered with designs and numbers; the community would have named special gurus, to be garbed in black robes, who would arbitrate conflicts between neighbors; and, to enforce the sentences, several strong husky hippies would walk up and down the paths, keeping an eye on things, swinging a stick. . . .

Happily for the hippies' faith, the OM Foundation broke up before having had a chance to reproduce the *integrality* of the establishment.

Later on, in St. Louis, I met a hippie who had slammed the door on one of these communities. He confessed that after his sad experience, he had discovered that a family—where people love each other and fight one another in a small, stable, intimate circle, under the wing of infinite maternal kindness—wasn't such a bad thing as the basic cell of society's life; in any case, it was infinitely preferable to spinning through trumpets, committees, "orders of the day," and the tyrannies of a collective that was constantly being torn apart by the desertions of older members and the arrivals of raw recruits with no emotional ties to anyone else there.

"Well, yes," I said, paraphrasing Churchill on democracy, "the straight family is the worst possible way to live, until you compare it to any other."

ABSOLUTE PLEASURE

There are still more absolutes on the hippie ideological menu, but the one we deal with now, absolute pleasure, occupies a central place, a quasi-divine shrine in the hippie rites, the shrine toward which all the other hippie dreams—their dreams on the senses and the spirit, on man and nature, on this earth and on the beyond—converge. The belief that man can attain a state of "absolute pleasure" by enlarging his consciousness with drugs has been so thoroughly picked over in print—whether by hippies or not—in such a systematic fashion that it has become something close to part of an official "doctrine." Which means that, as is appropriate for doctrines, we should discuss it in depth, but the broad scale of this book does not permit us to dwell long on a particular theme. This discussion, therefore, is being reserved for a later work which will deal entirely with drugs and the expansion of consciousness, while, in this volume, I will touch lightly on a few aspects of the matter so as not to leave a void precisely at this crucial point.

I believe that the complex of hippie ideas on pleasure can be summarized in the three following propositions, in their order of importance:

(1) The rationalist education taught in school, the pursuit of efficiency in life, and "morality," dry up and betray man's capacities to feel powerful sensations by virtue of what might be called his "animal splendor."

(2) These latent sensations, which go beyond, in large part, the normal register of sensations, are capable of forging a "field of consciousness" in man, and thus a "field of pleasure," that is infinitely enlarged and wondrous.

(3) Certain drugs can painlessly break the straitjacket that surrounds this sunken treasure and bring it into full light so that it may completely bloom: this is the "miracle of chemistry."

In sum, the miracle of chemistry delivers our "interior paradise" from the walls of reason, and brings it into an intensity of communion with the "exterior paradise" of "direct" nature that the individual has never known before. Let us rapidly examine these three propositions.

Animal Splendor

The first proposition, according to which the cement roads of reason imprison and dry up the pure fountains of the senses, is nothing new. Throughout time, many men have felt that there is a divorce, even a conflict, between these two styles of living: the feeling-spontaneous-poetic type, and the thinking-careful-scientific type. Doctor Faust is one painful expression of this divorce when, at the dusk of his life, he suddenly discovers that the laboratory where he spent his days is surrounded by fields of flowers that he never rolled in. And there have been not a few philosophers who have believed that the first, so-called "natural" way of life is superior to the second, "artificial" way. A proposition with which the mass of people will agree, since the mind, whose functions they practice with difficulty, is dethroned in favor of instinct, a gift with which they are all endowed.

It seems to me that this ancient debate is a confusion of principles. It is true enough that man cannot make love and integral calculus at the same time. This does not, however, mean that calculus in the morning will cause a deterioration of his taste for love in the evening. Experience, rather, shows the opposite. In general, those individuals whose minds are truly both well-furnished and supple, savor the pleasures of the flesh with more intensity and more fineness of sensation than illiterates. For pleasure in the truest sense is not simply a function of raw sensation; it comes from a confluence between the stream of messages being issued directly from the senses and the stream of interpretations issuing from the brain. Natural colors cannot give us pleasure until we have integrated them into a picture painted by our minds. This vivid, trembling blue field of the sea, linked by the horizon to the serene and tender blue dome of the sky, would be nothing but a mass of water underneath a mass of air for someone who had never rolled the idea of infinity in his head. In sum, the confusion lies in the fact that distinctions have not been made between the primary sensation and the elaborating emotion; the raw sensation is nothing but the raw material. A physical sensation serves no purpose if one is not moved.

Primitive man—or for that matter, many people in our own time—feels perhaps as much raw sensation as the cultivated man, but through his lack of capacity for intellectual elaboration, his emotions are surely less profound and less rich. A clear, objective look at the myriads of poets, artists, and musicians produced by our rationalist civilization offers no jot of corroboration to the idea that our civilization has extinguished the faculties of feeling and of taking pleasure.

Certain apologists for drug "ecstasies," like Aldous Huxley, do understand the generally unrecognized tight coupling between mental richness and sensorial richness if an experience is to be emotionally rich. Also, they are much less insistent than the run-of-the-mill hippie that the processes of reason are the killers of the senses. They even affirm that in their "interior paradises," they experience only the beauties that they can understand, those beauties that arouse the mind, since the mind must go along with them on their trip.

The Sixth Sense

The essential thing for this latter, more intellectual school, is the second of the three propositions mentioned earlier: man is capable of knowing totally unprecedented sensations, as fundamentally different from those that normal consciousness knows as sight, for example, would be for a blind person. These are the famous ineffable, prodigious, inexpressible sensations, transcendant and corporeal at the same time, cosmic and intimate, that the hippies, led by Timothy Leary and Aldous Huxley, sing of. Under the effect of the hallucinogens, colors become sounds and sounds become colors, the naked existence of things bursts out before your eyes, the past and the present become one and time stops, one's own self, or God, comes to seem like a clear grassland, the cells of the one you love become intertwined with your own, each drop of water from a faucet unleashes a myriad of echos in each branch in the forest of your nerves.

I will discuss these assertions in detail in a separate book. For the moment I am content to say that these phenomena have been considerably embellished by the lyricism of writers of talent, but that numerous scientific experimenters have been disappointed. And besides that, we are actually dealing here with a *confusion* of the habitual senses, and

. not with a whole register of new, heretofore unknown senses. The hypothesis that such senses exist is as gratuitous as a hypothesis that we could free ourselves from our biology and live without oxygen.

In all objectivity, we must acknowledge that nothing, in the present state of our knowledge, makes this hypothesis inconceivable. We know that certain chemicals can make the frontiers of our sensations elastic, but so can certain kinds of training. The painter sees colors with more nuance and brio than most mortals, housebreakers have an incredible sense of feel for locks, a dancer's muscles are immediately responsive, the blind are much more sensitive to the nuances of sound than the sighted. But this elasticity does not remove us from our normal biological universe, it *extends* it. And so much the worse for the hippies' theories; the senses are enriched, not by turning one's back on education, but by intensifying it.

The Miracle of Chemistry

We arrive now at the third proposition. The hippies will say that, as long as our sensual universe is extended—even if it can't actually be mutated—that is what counts. Indeed, the important thing is to make this enlargement available to all—not through a long and painful education process that is accessible only to a few, but through the "miracle of chemistry."

So far, this "miracle" has not always proved to operate as the hippies claim. I have met or read many reliable witnesses who have roamed the universe of drugs to its furthest limits, and who affirm that the flamboyant writers have largely exaggerated the joys drugs can bring. People have told me that they felt certain strange and fascinating sensations, along with other atrocious and repulsive ones, but that the forms, the colors, the movements, the fabulous sounds are always fugitive, disjointed, imponderable, as in a dream, with no metaphysical context.

There have been any number of people, perfectly lucid, who have experienced the range of their sensations just as powerfully intensified, who have felt a communion with nature that is just as mysterious from waking on a mountainside to a vividly colored dawn, or stretched out on the gentle sands of a beach in Tahiti, or drifting in silence under the vault of stars. Can a drug offer us more richness than this? Or might we not have leave to doubt that a drug can offer us even as much.

Let us take, for example, a phenomenon that is related to chemical ecstasy—the interior illuminations of the Eastern holy men who fix on their navels for days together seeing the cosmos there. They say that they experience states of soul that are indescribable and ineffable, and we have no reason to suspect their sincerity. However, they say more than that; they claim to meditate, to ponder on the essence of things, more profoundly and more luminously than Lavoisier, Einstein, or Copernicus, and they further claim that they have grasped it. Don't we have a right to expect them to share their discoveries with us? . . . since thought, unlike sensation, is articulated and transmitted through language. But no tangible intellectual fruit has ever blossomed out of these meditations, which is why students of this phenomenon have ended up doubting it. They have come to believe that the Hindu holy men unconsciously fall into a sort of gentle catalepsy, peopled with mirages, in which thought—rather than becoming universalized—is simply replaced by a kind of vapor. Perhaps the hippies' "super-sensation" is at bottom a similar kind of process. Does prolonged drug use, then, really extend the field of consciousness, or does the consciousness not actually just become empty?

And even if drugs do provoke extraordinary interior visions, I question whether the term "expansion of consciousness" is correct, or whether the word "displacement" would not be more apt. Not only do the hallucinatory visions not deepen the intuitions that are available to normal consciousness, but drugs nibble away at the normal mind's capacities. This would indicate, then, that we might expect, not a synthesis of the feeling man with the thinking man, but a new antagonism between the two. The mind will be sucked dry and betrayed by the sensations. This atrophy of the mind and will does not occur, however, no matter how intensely a person feels something, as long as that feeling is spontaneous, not a drug-induced response. Spontaneous, clear-headed feeling is a genuine enlargement of the being, since it causes a deepening of the perceptive faculties, and does not keep the individual from returning to creative and socially useful activity.

We must, however, recognize that, in principle, no one can say that it is impossible to genuinely enlarge the field of consciousness through chemicals, and I myself would not object to government-sponsored research projects designed to discover whether such substances exist, as long as we did not have to pay the price of atrophy of the reason and the will. Who would refuse to see the world as on the day of its creation? . . . provided that he did not risk losing himself in a life of damnation.

However, a simple analysis of probabilities shows that we can hardly expect such a miracle the first time around. We are still almost completely in the dark when it comes to the physiological mechanisms of sensation, though we do know that our nervous system is one of the most complex and subtle structures in the animal kingdom. We can provoke strange chains of associations and extraordinary sensations, good and bad, by chemically altering a few of the myriads of relationships between the molecules, neurons, synapses, and plasma that form the interior cosmos of our body. But there is very little chance that we will fall on just the right combination of equilibria to enrich our sensations without compromising the healthy functioning of that cosmos. Surely centuries of laboratory experiments will be needed to arrive at a solution of this biological problem, if solution there be.

The hippies naively pretend that they are "returning to Adam," whereas they are, in reality, revolting against Adam in the sense that, for the first time, the human body itself, and not just the social order, is being put into question. They are not only recovering creation, they are correcting it. This is by a long way the most audacious of man's ambitions, much more of a true revolution than changing economic systems. Perhaps, once human beings have worked out truly viable, just, and effective economic and social systems—a goal that will still loom out of reach, I would guess, for at least the next few centuries—then perhaps we might be wise to turn our efforts toward the biological perfecting of the species. But then these investigations will be carried out, not by children or demagogues, but by adults, which is to say, people armed with science and with patience.

Meanwhile, while waiting for a new rose to grow in the garden of our chemistry, let us learn to see the one that is already there in this morning of our loves.

ABSOLUTE ANTIRATIONALISM

If there is one single facet of the hippies' life that should have come clear during the course of this study, it is that the hippies are the enemies of reason, which links hippieism to the majority of the current movements of protest, and which fundamentally distinguishes it from the classic left whose revolt was developed in a scientific, materialistic, even atheistic context.

The hippies, even though their spirit of protest and language of emancipation make them the legitimate children of the left, have carried antirationalism much further than the new left, up to a point of the most disordered mysticism. The hippies love to believe, without or against the evidence of their senses, in anything at all, provided that it is transcendant, inexplicable, and decorative. They believe in astrology, metempsychosis, reincarnation, Zen, Tao, Buddhism, Krishna, Rama, in magic, in occultism, in anything that can be imagined but cannot be proved. As their master Aldous Huxley has written in *The Doors of Perception*, "Throughout centuries and in every country, men have given more spiritual significance to what they've seen with closed eyes than with their eyes open." An excellent definition of the hippie culture: the culture of closed eyes.

Their eyes do open, however, from time to time, particularly upon objects as faraway, mysterious, and lovely as the stars. Astrology plays a very important role in the hippie culture. The journal *Avatar* has published a full-color, double-page spread of the zodiacal skies. All the names printed on the journal's masthead are accompanied by astrological signs, "What sign are you?" is one question that the hippies ask each other constantly. The hippie communes are inaugurated on auspicious dates which will put them under the influence of Gemini or Capricorn. *Avatar* (Number 78, 1967) explains that

Astrology is a language of symbols, like Jupiter and Saturn, Aries and Taurus, in comparison to psychiatry which uses words, words like insecurity, paranoia, and schizophrenia. They are both tools that man has created to understand more about himself, but psychiatry is only a baby to Astrology, one has just been born and the other is being re-born.

Some hippies had convinced themselves that flying saucers illumined with the signs of the zodiac would appear during the great Grand Canyon "be-in." *Oracle* has stated that when a hippie plants a vegetable, he accomplishes a sacred sexual union between his body, the seed, and Mother Earth. The hippies need, no doubt, something as exalting as the idea of copulation to inspire them to plant their cabbages. The Hare Krishna Mahamantra, the Hindu chant that Allen Ginsberg has introduced into all the hippie rites—a chant of which the flower-children understand not one word, and which in any case makes no literal sense—calls on the infinite spirits to preserve our planet in spite of its lowly finitude. Allen Ginsberg has written, "that a nation which prefers terrestrial communications through metallic wires, to the inter-stellar communication of the Hare Krishna Mahamantra, does not merit the respect of its young people." The tarot, coffee grounds, clairvoyance, telepathy, nothing is missing. One hippie tribe's supreme goal is to arrive at the degree of "omniscient dematerialization" achieved by a Zen monk who could zing an arrow to its bullseye in the dark. The leader of this tribe, whom I met in Paris, assured me, while trying with all his might to enroll me in his lists, that he had seen it.

"How could you see it, since it was dark?" I asked mischieviously, but got no reply.

I hope that my hairy young friends marvel at these mystic tales without really believing them, in the same way that children marvel at fairy tales. In fact, the mystic search preoccupies the gurus above all. It is still too cerebral for the run-of-the-mill Anglo-Saxon hippie. He fights nothing, including the rationalist tradition, so much as he simply ignores it, just like everything else. His familiarity with the traditions of the American Indian and of the Hindu fakirs is minimal, except for the kind of thing he has seen in the movies. His favorite model of the spiritual life is captured in a pretty song that I heard from some hippies in Toronto:

> To know yourself
> You don't need to concentrate
> Don't look into your mind
> It doesn't know the facts
> Become empty
> And let yourself take in, take in.

Wild Romanticism

I cannot conclude this section without commenting on the hippies' antecedents: the literary antirationalists, from the 19th-century romantics to the surrealists. The majority of these romantics—to use the word in a very broad sense—have all dabbled to varying degrees in magic mysticism, which has helped restore its respectability. They did not go so far as the hippies; though they attacked the rationalist traditions of the 18th century, they still remained within them, if for no other reason than their drive to win prestige in the literary game. They kept their heads sufficiently to respect the tacit convention that their incursions into the supernatural, sorcery, and spiritualism were reserved for the life of the imagination, to poetry, to the role, in sum, of pretty fairy tales for adults. They have never proposed these tales as guides to everyday life, and they still hold that science, which they admire, fulfills a necessary and beneficial function. Victor Hugo consulted books of the occult in the privacy of his study, but he restrained himself from talking about it at the Académie Française.

André Breton breached the first crack in this convention when he published his *Nadja*. In his private life, with which I am very familiar, he continued to act like a "straight" person, accepting all the disciplines that art imposes and that the hippies reject, and even intensifying them on the moral plane. However, the magical deliriums of *Nadja* aspired to much more than the poetic illustration of a "mad love." Breton saw this love as the vehicle of the marvelous, of the surreal in the real. *Nadja* was a decisive influence in the rush of modern antirationalism toward wholehearted nonsense. Surrealism gave respectability to today's hippie fairytale spinners, and it inspired them with the flattering illusion that they were the messengers of a truth higher than the truth available to science.

In fact, the "supernatural" forces that are so much more potent than the slow but sure conquests of sciences are most often vulgar frauds. As Koestler said in *The Lotus and the Robot*, "There is no more true mysticism in India today than there are real cowboys in Texas."

We can leave the heritage of Nostradamus and Cagliostro to the hippies without anxiety. As long as *they* are the ones in charge of it, nothing much can happen.

Absolute Nihilism

A revolutionary is by definition a sleeping nihilist. The only way he knows to move the world is through violent condemnation of it— and perhaps he finds protection here against his own secret doubt. As he rarely has genuine alternatives for society, he exalts the act of destruction above all. The hippies have taken this route as far as it will go, at least on the speculative plane. They have arrived at an absolute nihilism—considerably more radical than that of Saint-Just—whose principle spokesmen today are Marguerite Duras in France and Jerry Rubin in the United States.

For them, present society ought literally to be razed down to the bare ground. The people would be allowed to live, but without houses, without clothes, without tools, without cities, without plumbing, without schools, without art, without knowledge, and without traditions of creation. We would have to begin all over again, strictly à la Adam and Eve. We would, however, be permitted two things that Adam and Eve had to do without: Beatle records and LSD. But before this society in which "everything is false" can be razed, the groundwork has to be laid: ridicule it, provoke it, shock it with eccentricities, with obscenities, make it doubt its own values, lose its faith in itself, and despair. At that point, a simple coup de grâce will make it shrivel up and die.

Need we say that this kind of provocation is cultivated as an end in itself. Praise to those who can hit society where it hurts! The Speech Movement, founded by one Artman, a disciple of Timothy Leary, obliges its followers to sprinkle all their discourses with the most excremental words, at a minimum of three words per minute. Jerry Rubin's Yippies chose a pig, a real pig, as President of the United States and administered the oath of office to him while he urinated on the national flag.

Traditional music, with its chords and harmonies, is, as everyone knows, fascist, and the geniuses of today compose only "aleatory" music; that is, one object is clanged together at random with any other object that may be at hand. In Chicago, I paid two dollars to attend a musical "happening" that proceeded as follows: a girl, who was "wigged out" on drugs, sat on the ground with her skirt pulled up, in front of an amplifier, scraping a violin with an iron rod, while the amplifier gave off fits and spurts of sound at random. Another peculiar person smote a piano with his fists and his hairy feet, while six radios played, at full volume, six different programs at once. The composer —yes, you have read rightly, "composer"—leaned against the microphone, frantically striking red and blue balloons against one another, until one or the other would break, an event he would punctuate by a strident jungle cry.

In September, 1966, London was the site for the first international symposium of "artistic destruction." It lasted five days, during which forty hairy "artist vandals" from ten countries assembled to display and discuss their works. The participants included the Irishman Alexander Trochi who expressed his conception of the universe by creashing an iron bar with all his might at everything around him—dishes, garbage cans, etc. Trochi had founded "Project Sigma" for the "invisible insurrection of a million angry spirits." Then there was the overwhelming hair and beard which covered the face of, one assumed, William Burroughs—that was all you could see—the "genius" author of the classic *Naked Lunch*, in which the hero no longer knew which orifice he was supposed to eat with, and which orifice to fornicate with; Ralph, who had become famous in New York for furiously destroying any piano that crossed his path, considering that instrument the nadir of bourgeois degeneracy; the flashing Parisian painter Lebel who had nude women sit down on ripe tomatoes (to create an impression of . . .), after which he would cover them with spaghetti; a Japanese from the Zero Dimension group who had made it a rule of his life not to let five minutes pass without seeing or doing something revolting; representatives from movements of "regenerative vandalism," like the Provos of Amsterdam and the Spanish nihilist group Zaj, who discussed their most notable creations: destruction of church organs, setting fire to typewriters (car burnings had become too debasing, unworthy of the name of art), slashing paintings in museums, bloody orgies like the ones in Vienna.

These "orgies of blood," by the way, are a kind of mass figurative self-flagellation. They cut out the entrails of a lamb and of a chicken and splatter the clothes and faces of everyone nearby with blood. The Viennese master of vandal art, Nitsch, was dressed all in black, including his shirt, his pants, his mustache, and his temper. He cried out, with tremors of fury in his voice, "Any cretin of a medical student can get hold of all the bodies he wants to learn useless things. But I, an artist, I can't have even one to draw upon in my art." When at one point the tone of the discussion had become academic, even parliamentary, the two delegates from New York cried out: "You don't understand how great we do things in New York!" And Ortiz seized the hatchet that he carries with him everywhere and, in two blows, broke a chair standing in front of the door to the auditorium, while his companion set fire to a motorbike. While this was going on, an Englishman was patiently building towers of books to set them on fire.

But the constant burning and destruction became commonplace after a while, and everyone began to champ at the bit. Artistic vigor fell into the doldrums until, thanks to Otto Mühl's "Happening Salad," a new spirit filled the air. Mühl buried a nude girl under a pile of tomatoes, salad greens, fresh eggs, squeezed melons, grated carrots, and then moistened the whole with milk and beer. He sang and danced around his masterpiece like a cannibal around a missionary cooking in the pot and then, at the peak of the climax, he tore his clothes off and threw himself nude into the sticky reddish mixture, which was understood to symbolize the marriage of animal and vegetable, kissing the young beauty, holding her in his arms, and licking milk, beer, and tomato sauce from all over her body. The girl reappeared nude and radiant. "It's just so great!" she moaned.

At the peak point, Lebel exploded in self-contentment: "It's a waste of time and words," he declared, "to ask if 'happenings' are art. They are more than art. I don't waste time any more writing criticism. I let these happenings happen to me. These nihilist-vandal artists, by rejecting taboos and making the psychic drama of each of us a collective experience, open the door of perception."

Obviously, next to a happening, the contortions of a tom-tom beater are simply mannered academism. To emerge from there and then come across the words of Allen Ginsberg, is like reading a sermon:

> With the orgy an acceptable community sacrament, one that brings all people closer together, certainly one might seduce the Birch Society to partake in naked orgy and the police with their wives together with Leroi Jones the brilliant angry poet.

Statements to shock the "straights," obviously, like these comments by Leroi Jones:

> America's political need is orgies in the parks, on Boston Common and in Public Gardens with naked bacchantes in our national forests.

until, of course, the day when the schools shall all be put to the torch, a specific objective announced by certain gurus. Once this wholesome enterprise has been accomplished, there will be nothing left to do but gather the children together from here and there

> to give them a new kind of teaching, oriented only toward the disciplines of pleasure and the exploration of their own interior paradise, under the tutelage of teachers who, first, would be dropouts who had left school no later than twelve, next Zen and Tibetan monks, swamis and yogas, and finally specialists in pop.

These things are patently said, not out of conviction, but for their own sakes, so that people can beat their hands in applause when they succeed in annoying a pillar of the establishment. The people who say these things don't believe in them seriously, and do not imagine that anyone will take them seriously. And that's where they make their mistake. Their audience includes all too many credulous, gullible young people, and here and there now, one runs into youths who, their heads turned by these expressions of a flamboyant nihilism, put them into practice by attacking passersby at random, setting fire to stores, raping their teachers, and indulging in various wickednesses. And those who don't go to that extreme, do follow their prophets far enough to accept the desert of ignorance as the Promised Land. They abandon school, books, and everything that has some whiff of culture in order to set off, with a few of their long-haired fellows, along the hashish trail.

So this absolute nihilism has a practical purpose: to lay down the suggestion in all quarters that our Western civilization is an absolute degradation.

The apostles of absolute nihilism deceive themselves, however, when they think they have reached the outer limits of excess. There is still another step that goes even further than destruction: to inflict suffering. The end of the end is not just taking our houses away from us, our clothes, our food, our arts, our knowledge, in order to exult in the void with Marguerite Duras; the real end would be to torture us before stripping us of everything. This is that extreme branch of nihilism called Satanism, which is advocated by a few, and which was put into practice by Charles Manson and his little band.

The roots of Satanism go far back into the history of extremist ideas. One of satanism's most notable exemplars was the Marquis de Sade. Recall that poem by Baudelaire, "Abel and Cain," which ends with the victory of the murderer:

> Race of Cain mounts to the sky
> While God lies on the ground.

However, in earlier days, this adoration of evil remained purely metaphysical or nostalgic. The Marquis de Sade never disemboweled little boys. And, again, it is Baudelaire who wrote, "O Satan, take pity on my long misery!" The hippie "ultimists" who have revived these old currents, giving them their own characteristic touch, end up by believing that the mission of their dark genius is to physically kill all the people—pardon me, all the pigs—who aren't with them, which is to say, you and me. The hippies have come a long way from their beginnings in long hair and daisies to this climax of devastation and blood. Were their origins really as simple and innocent as they seemed? Probably yes, in the beginning. Certainly it would be simplistic to try to make Aldous Huxley and the children with long hair responsible for Charles Manson and his killers. It's just that in the light of Charles Manson, the paradise of Aldous Huxley comes to seem more and more artificial—terribly artificial. Even without the demons, and even granting that there are blossoms that can be gathered en route, the hippie trail leads, at best, to Nowhere.

Is that place really more plesant after all than Somewhere?

11

Quo Vadis, Hippie?

The most natural action for an ordinary man is to destroy himself by himself, through some excess in food, drink, or opinion. It is reason that is rare. And it is prudence that I want to honor. Terrassier, my friend, we must throw some cold water on all those fools there.—Alain

The Antecedents

The first question to ask in the face of this sudden explosion of extravagants—a word to take in its precise sense of people who "divagate" in "extra" paths—is where do they come from, historically speaking? Of what evolution are they the products?

I unearthed much more than I had expected rather early on, and I got very excited. I believed that I had found the source of the torrents that sweep over us now in an ancient current, but right away I detected another. I discovered that drugs of all kinds, except, of course, for LSD, have been known through all antiquity and employed on a large scale by all peoples except in Europe, where they played a minor role (perhaps Europe owes her prodigious history to this abstinence?). I discovered also that numerous schools of thought in the past had elevated pleasure into a supreme objective. The Greeks' word for this was "hedonism." Other Greeks and Romans, called "solipsists," proposed that each being is specific, irreducible to a common schema, and that therefore his own self-realization should properly be his ultimate goal. Two illustrious philosophers (whose names rhyme)— Rousseau in France, and Thoreau in the United States—represented the school of rejection of technology and the return to nature. Fourier and his school founded numerous "phalansterian" pastoral communities across the world, and immediately after World War I, the German Wandervögel ("migrant bird") movement carried runaway children, burning with independence and careless of their personal comfort, into lilting vagabondage across Europe, reminiscent of the troubadours of the Middle Ages.

When it comes to "systems," philosophic or social, hippie culture has its numerous precursors here too. We have seen how extensively the hippies draw upon models from mysticism, mythology, and Buddhist and Hindu folklore. Was not Buddha himself, who, 2500 years ago, abandoned his prince's house and his familial attachments to wander barefoot with his hair blowing in the wind in search of the interior truth, the first great runaway? But he did not take drugs. He spent fourteen years in arduous meditation before attaining the state of "consciousness expansion" that he called Nirvana. Now the hippies, children of a scientific society, think they can reach Nirvana with no effort, though with more risks, through chemistry. But like the hippies, Buddha preached universal love for all living things, including animals, and even untouchables, going so far as to live with them. He mistrusted books and reason, cultivating the interior paradise of man and striving for a direct communion with the exterior paradise of the cosmos. Later on, the Tantrics, as we have seen, added the sensual and social touches, the spices of sex and revolt.

The Oriental philosophy was transmitted to Americans through the English, who translated the famous Tibetan Book of the Dead, which won many Western admirers to its lamaic beliefs. Let us not forget that the psychedelic movement began in England among literary people—for example, Aldous Huxley, the psychiatrist Humphry Osmond, who coined the term "psychedelia" (expansion of the soul), and Gerald Herd, who adapted numerous Hindu ritual chants—who had fallen under the spell of India and the East. All these forces were to influence Alan Watts, the ideological father, fifteen years ago, of the hippie movement in San Francisco.

Among the Greeks, the illustrious Diogenes was not, as we have believed, an isolated eccentric. He gave birth to a whole school called the "cynics," whose members lived like animals, "with untouched hair and beard," making love in public, being shockingly obscene, mocking the conventions and the prejudices of respectable society (if they had thought of it, they would surely have willingly adopted the adjective "straight"). They denounced all governments as oppressors, and useless at that. The word "cynic," which has, over the centuries, taken on a veneer of sophistication, derived originally from the Greek word for dog. Diogenes, son of a counterfeiter, took care of his personal needs in public, like a dog. He searched, like the hippies, for proofs that "society" is a parody of true humanity, and that its rules are so many intolerable hypocrisies. Diogenes lived in a cart that he moved around at will. However, he did not take drugs and he did appreciate from time to time an exercise in logic.

The sociologist Will Herberg has found traces of a Christian sect that lived during the second and third centuries A.D. in North Africa. Its members believed that a Christian should live in the purity of before the fall, in Adam's innocence and indolence in the earthly paradise. So they were called "Adamites." They advocated a gentle anarchism, the sharing of goods and women, vegetarianism, nudity, and an absolute sexual liberty, similar to that rejoiced in in the Garden of Eden. They either had no knowledge or refused the knowledge of Good and Evil. They rejected—at least in theory—all the restrictive laws imposed by the so-called "legitimate" societies, whom they accused of narrowness of spirit and dryness of heart. They were pacific, hostile to all authority, to all discipline, and to all rational thought, prefering the phantasmagoria of the spirit and the pleasures of the flesh, which they practiced with a complete license. They are without question the closest group to the hippie genre that history can offer us, even though these Christians have nothing to do with either drugs or Oriental mysticism.

In the Middle Ages, there are plenty of wandering minstrels, knights errant, visionary monks, libertine poets, Satanic magicians, each of whom contribute something to the profile of the quintessential hippie. And there is also the great figure of Saint Francis of Assisi, another "runaway" of mark who abandoned his family and society to go seek the sweetness of living and of loving among the humble ones of the earth and the birds. I have already alluded to the Diggers, an English communist society of the 17th century, and one of the principal ancestors of the hippie movement, as well as to the romantics of the 19th century, who sought pure emotion, divine pleasure, and the cosmic breath outside the social straitjacket and the real. They believed that instinct is superior to reason, and that intuition is more pertinent than experience. They stayed tied, however, to the word and valued their artistic successes, while the hippies mistrust all intellectual creation. The romantics were the true fathers of modern antirationalism, a current that kept growing through the 19th century with the occultism of Villiers de l'Isle Adam, Baudelaire's "Les Fleurs du Mal," the esotericism of Mallarmé, the volcanism of Arthur Rimbaud, the "strangeism" of Guillaume Apollinaire, the dadaism of Tristan Tzara, and the surrealism of André Breton, until its culmination in the "drug-subversion" mixture that dominates hippie culture. I have mentioned only the major figures in the various French schools, but these tumultuous waters flowed through every country, depositing whirlpools of the avant-garde everywhere. The Flappers in New York, the Topos in London, the Wandervögel in Germany, the Zazous in Paris, the Provos in Amsterdam, then the international generation of the Beatniks, all of them drew from this source and enriched it in their turn with a whole spectrum of distinctive bizarreries, in conduct, dress, and ideas.

Where Do We Go From Here?

From the beginning of this book, I have posed the question: May the whole excitement about the hippie movement not simply have been whipped up by journalistic sensationalism? My answer is: No. The walls of American and Canadian police stations, covered from top to bottom with photos of runaway children, are proof enough that this flood is enormous and new; ten years past these very walls bore no more than two or three heads. There is no question, as well, that the drug explosion is an absolutely new phenomenological upheaval of our time. Never before in human history have drugs, heretofore reserved to shadowy fringe groups of adults, penetrated with brazen force into the ranks of the young, especially in the American schools and universities.

In consequence, there is a certain softening already detectable in the fiber of American youth when it comes to will, initiative, patriotism, and love of science and success. Not yet enough to lower the productive capacities of this rich nation, but if it should continue to soak in the hippie-drug culture, like a sunbather soaks in the sun, then the nation will in the end decay, victim of that which Royer Collard has already called "the nihilism of satiety." And the whole West will follow America's decline.

Will things go so far? If we do not react to protect ourselves, there is nothing inherently impossible about it. But the syndrome could also halt of itself; it secretes its own antitoxins, as more and more hippies learn that their drugs, which seem at first like the beckoning figure of Circe, actually mask the head of Medusa. The hippies who have held away from the addictive drugs usually catch themselves again and come back, soul and body more or less crippled, into life. For the movement is running in two directions. There is a strong current of runaways from the straight society toward the hippie world, but there is also an opposing tide. The hippie phenomenon is not yet six years old; it is too early to know which of the two currents will prove the stronger.

In the sphere of mores—less crucial in terms of the actual survival of the West, but equally as significant in setting the path our society will take in the future—the hippie movement has already had undeniable effects. There is nothing surprising in this, since that aspect of our lives called "life style"—something that has not been sufficiently studied by sociologists—has always been swayed by the influence of eccentric minority groups of youth. Today the hippies, tomorrow the elites, and the day after tomorrow the mass of people will no longer dress the same way, will no longer speak to children with the same assurance, will no longer enshrine work in its traditional place of divinity, will allow young girls more liberty, there will be more leeway for adventure. Society will certainly never adopt the whole hippie style but, in the way of cows, it will integrate a few of the new grasses planted by the hippies in the human field into its ball of cud.

But I believe that, though the hippie movement will surely color the development of our civilization, it will turn out to have been really just an episode, not a genuine revolution. The moral framework that undergirds hippieism is in reality marked with the seal of impotence. It can give the illusion of real power, for we are in the habit of believing that any revolt is a step forward. But there are also reactionary revolts, and the hippies' is one of those—despite appearances—because, over and above "society," it zeroes its attack on the only mainspring that has pushed humanity to advance: the spirit of enterprise, which, at bottom, is the source for intuition and reason, order and adventure, audacity and prudence—in brief, everything that gives man a taste for his creations.

Just open the door of a smoke-room in Katmandu, and the messianic theories of the hippie prophets blow away on a current of air; the hippie reality leaps to your eyes in the person of these broken children, and squeezes your heart: they are self-destruction, a symbol of defeat.

At the beginning of the sixties, the extreme revolutionary left made an extreme ideological about-face. The left had traditionally taken up the cudgels in the fight for abundance and reason, but now abundance and reason were flourishing, contrary to plan, in the very heart of the established order. It was no longer possible to accuse society of inefficiency and obscurantism, but as the left wanted to accuse society of something, what better targets than abundance and reason, and so the crusade was launched against the consumer society. By tearing down the goals that it used to profess for itself, the left confessed its historic failure.

The hippies are the children of the marriage between the extreme revolutionary left and neoromanticism. They were born under the secret sign of defeat, and they will always carry a curse. Fearing at bottom that in the end history will reject them as useless beings, they proclaimed themselves useless out of bravado, and threw themselves into the "nihilism of satiety." But this goes profoundly against the current of progress. It is the refuge of people who want to go on living with the spice of revolt, when the real objects of revolt have begun to fade away. That is why the hippies so desperately look for something new. And since they no longer find it in the body politic, they propose to turn their revolution on the body human. I have commented since my introduction: The hippie nestles his revolutionary spirit in the liberation of the senses, because he can no longer engage himself in the liberation of the proletariat. That is, moreover, what gives him that frivolous and artificial air.

Is it so frivolous? One must honestly ask oneself if it is not legitimate, when the most glaring deficiencies of the social structure are eased, to turn attention to the needs of the individual, of his senses and of his soul, his needs as a cultural animal. And indeed there is much to do in this neglected area. Industrial civilization has not left enough room for fantasy, for pleasure, for tranquility, for sensibility. The hippies are not the first to have underlined this fact. But in dramatizing it, they have rendered society the service of forcing our contemporaries to deal with it.

Young rebels are always the first sniffers of the new winds that begin to blow through a century, while the mass of people are far behind. The hippies' value is to have made us see, not that our civilization is rotten—that is to grossly misunderstand it—but that we must rightly begin to realize that a civilization's needs for delight are as profound as its need for efficiency. And also, of course, our civilization is gradually granting to each of us so much leisure that we are going to have to learn how to use it intelligently. It is a great, a captivating task that should begin in the early school years when children should be taught that the sciences are a joyous exercise of the mind, and should be taught to develop their artistic sensibilities, their personalities, and their imaginations. It ought to continue to develop by recognizing that all the elements of life should appeal to the eye and to the heart: the cities, workshops, offices, beaches, love, old age.

This great task will surely take many years, but it will never be accomplished unless reason, far from turning its back, devotes its whole resources to the enterprise. It is curiously true that a little bit of science can be prosaic, dull, with no touch of wonder; but the highest reaches of science carry us right back again to the mysteries of the marvelous. Similarly, a little bit of technology can make our lives harsh and ugly, whereas a great deal of technology, intelligently used, can infuse our collective life with poetry. But hippie nihilism cannot advance us one step into this new growth, if for no other reason than that it carries the young creative people—without whose indispensable ferment such a genuine revolution could never come to pass—away from the center of activity into the nonlife of drugs.

Oh, my happy and sad friends along the hashish trail, I fear not only for our civilization, but for you. You curse us in the name of your dream, while we could share it with you, we could help to make it come true. Then you go to hide in some hole to die. What an atrocious fools' game you are playing! You, who believe yourselves more clearseeing than the straights, have gulped down the dazzling, but hollow, words of other straights, the demagogues of *total* subversion, and you have fallen as their first victims. You could have been the navigators for our time, and instead you are its flotsam, just waiting to disappear altogether. You wander ragged and filthy along the roads that you should have strewn with flowers. You have no emotional ties to another, when you should have taught us love. You live without ideas, when you should have made our ideas live again. There you are without future, without craft—what can I say?—without caring, your pupils dilated and eyes empty, whether or not they turn inward, or toward the outside.

Do you truly believe that you are going to build a culture on that empty gaze?

You are the generation sacrificed to the reign of the false.

Whatever happens, reason must be held to fiercely, even and above all when reason itself is being assailed. And the lines I chose for the epigraph to this chapter remind us that it is reason's lot to be assailed. Its career is painful, but triumphant in the end. For there will always be Alains and Terrassiers to throw cold water on the fools, but the surest cold water is still the shower that reality administers to them.

That is why we must not panic in the face of this nihilist wave, of which the hippies are the unhappy troubadours, breaking at the base of our towers. Our towers will hold if we hold on to ourselves, for this wave, strong though it is today, has neither a center of gravity nor a driving force to push it along very far.

The spirit of enterprise, which was born some 20,000 years ago, and received its baptism 350 years ago at the hands of Galileo, will not disappear from the human scene. It has raised too many powerful, splendid beams. Perhaps it is time to assign that spirit more noble objectives, a more becoming garb, a more gracious step, but it will never be downed to be replaced by the spirit of nothingness.

The conflict between the active and contemplative has endured for centuries. The active principle has always carried the battle because he knows how to contemplate, while the contemplative does not know how to act.

And that is why man will always triumph over anti-man. As Jaurès said, a river keeps faith with its source, by holding to its path toward the sea.

Index

Central Ideas in the Development of American Journalism:

A Narrative History

COMMUNICATION

A series of volumes edited by
Dolf Zillmann and **Jennings Bryant**

Central Ideas in the Development of American Journalism:

A Narrative History

Marvin Olasky
The University of Texas at Austin

LEA LAWRENCE ERLBAUM ASSOCIATES, PUBLISHERS
1991   Hillsdale, New Jersey   Hove and London

Lawrence Erlbaum Associates, Inc., Publishers
365 Broadway
Hillsdale, New Jersey 07642

Library of Congress Cataloging-in-Publication Data
Olasky, Marvin N.
  Central ideas in the development of American journalism : a narrative
history / Marvin Olasky.
    p. cm.
  Includes index.
  ISBN 0-8058-0893-0
  1. Journalism—United States—History. I. Title.
PN4801.04 1991
071′.3—dc20   90-40153
                                                                 CIP

Printed in the United States of Ameica
10 9 8 7 6 5 4 3 2 1

For Peter, David, Daniel, and one to come

Contents

Acknowledgments

This book arose out of 5 years of teaching journalism history at The University of Texas. In lectures I presented both the conventional interpretations and my own, slowly developing contrarian analysis; students who asked hard questions suggested that a wider audience might find my research useful. I thank them for their quiet pressure.

Librarians at The University of Texas, the Library of Congress, and the Newberry Library helped me to find out-of-the-way material, and a grant from the Sarah Scaife Foundation provided additional writing time. The material in Appendix B previously appeared in *American Journalism*. I also thank Jennings Bryant, Robin Marks Weisberg, and others associated with Lawrence Erlbaum; this book shows for a third time their admirable tolerance for decidedly nontrendy ideas.

My children are aspiring journalists who certainly inspired me: Peter (editor of the *Austin Animal-Statesman*), David (editor of an ancient Greek newspaper, *The Ithaca Times*), and Daniel (a crackerjack cub reporter and Civil War general) continued to provide joy and deep satisfaction. My wife Susan is an excellent journalist in her own right; she has a wise head, a gracious heart, and a loveliness that goes beyond narrative. I would not be able to put in a long day of writing if I could not look forward to a family dinner at its close.

Portions of this book appeared as articles in *American Journalism*, *Antithesis*, and *Academic Questions*, and as columns in the *Houston Post*, the *Rocky Mountain News*, and the *Indianapolis Star*. My thanks to their editors.

Introduction

"Public opinion on any subject," Abraham Lincoln once said, "always has a 'central idea' from which all its minor thoughts radiate."[1] This book applies Lincoln's statement not to American public opinion generally but to journalism specifically (which is often at the base of public opinion). Writers and editors have espoused so many different philosophies over the years that American journalism history might seem to be a crazy-quilt, but the thesis of this book is that a broad look at the whole pattern shows three central ideas achieving dominance, sequentially.

The first of these central ideas in journalism—I call them *macrostories* because they overarch the daily bits and pieces of journalistic coverage—could be called the *official story*. Dominant until the 18th century in most of Europe and America, this macrostory was built on the belief that power knows best, and that editors should merely print whatever the king or governor demands. Published news was what state authorities (and, sometimes, their allies in established churches) wanted people to know.

The press continued to be dominated by the official story until growing numbers of journalists, heavily influenced by the ideas of the Protestant Reformation, began to emphasize the *corruption story*. This macrostory, rather than serving as public relations for the state, emphasized the universality of human failings and the tendency for individuals in positions of power to abuse their authority and then attempt to cover up wrongdoing. Journalists from the 17th through 19th centuries who embraced the corruption story invented much of what

1

we associate with modern journalism at its best: A sense of purpose, a willingness to oppose arrogant rulers, and a stress on accuracy and specific detail.

Mid- and late-19th-century editors such as Horace Greeley and Joseph Pulitzer achieved their prominence and influence on the foundations laid down by corruption story journalists. However, they and others scorned the theology on which that macrostory was based; instead of seeing sinful man and demanding personal change, they believed that man is naturally good but is enslaved by oppressive social systems. In this third of journalism's central ideas, the *oppression story,* problems arise not from personal corruption but from external influences, and the role of journalists is to put a spotlight on those influences. The hope is that if man's environment is changed, man himself changes, and poverty, war, and so on, are no more.

This change affected not only story content but reporters' methods. Corruption story journalists tended to have limited personal agendas because they emphasized personal transformation rather than social revolution. Oppression story journalists, who came to dominate the most influential publications early in the 20th century, believed their own work could be the breakthrough to a better world. As the great ends of oppression story journalism—peace, justice, freedom— began to seem attainable, means began to be negotiable.

This book narrates the history of those macrostories in American journalism from its European beginnings in the 16th and 17th century (my starting point is Martin Luther's editorial on the cathedral door in 1517) up through 1917, when the impact of the Russian Revolution began to open up a new phase in journalistic perceptions. Along the way we take a fresh look at Greeley, Pulitzer, and other legends of journalism history, and we also recall long-forgotten figures such as John Stubbes, an English Puritan who in 1579 wrote a pamphlet criticizing Queen Elizabeth. Stubbes was punished by having his right hand "cut off by the blow of a Butcher's knife."[2] A contemporary account tells of his amazing response: "John Stubbes, so soon as his right hand was off, put off his hat with the left, and cryed aloud, God save the Queene."[3] Such bravery deserves to be remembered, and the motivation for such actions understood.

This book is a narrative history rather than a philosophical tome; a previous book of mine, *Prodigal Press,* examined more systematically questions surrounding objectivity and journalistic ethics. I have retained early spellings whenever the meaning is clear. Four appendices provide additional detail; readers who wish to know more about the macrostory concept itself should not overlook Appendix C.

PART I

RISE OF THE CORRUPTION STORY

Chapter 1

Unnatural Acts

In America, we expect journalists to have some independence from government and other leading power centers. We are not surprised to glance at the morning newspaper or television news show and see exposure of wrongdoing. We assume that the press has a responsibility to print bad news as well as good. And yet, that which seems ordinary to us is unusual in the history of the world, and even in much of the world today.

How did the unnatural act of independent journalism come to seem so natural? To begin answering that question, we need to go back, back beyond the start of American journalism, back even before Gutenberg. *Journalism*—information and analysis concerning recent events, published in multiple copies or disseminated beyond the immediate reach of the speaker's voice — is many centuries old. Journalistic products emerged in many lands and in many varieties, but they most often promoted the *official story* of governmental power and wisdom: "If you obey, we will take care of you." (A more modern way of saying the same might be, "Depend on us to establish the proper environment for your life.") Official, state-allied religion often received protection also. Published news was what authorities wanted people to know.

Throughout the many centuries before printing, *official story* publications came and went. One of the better known early journalistic vehicles was the *Acta Diurna*, a handwritten news sheet posted in the Roman Forum and copied by scribes for transmission throughout the empire. *Acta* emphasized governmental decrees but also gained readership by posting gladiatorial results and news of other popular events. Julius Caesar used the *Acta* to attack some of his opponents in the Roman senate—but there could be no criticism of Caesar. (Had there been independent journalism, he might have faced only character assassination on the Ides of March.) Other handwritten publications also emerged during ancient and medieval times, with the goal of passing on news that state or state–church authorities wished leading citizens to know. This was true in Asia and other continents as well as in Europe. Sometimes, ballads and poems that mocked the official news vehicles were passed on orally from person to person, but the official version, with support from the state church, endured from generation to generation.

In Western Europe, kings with support from the Catholic Church were said to rule by divine right, and the *official story* was the only story allowed. Leaders might acknowledge that a different story prevailed in heaven—there, God was sovereign and biblical principles were practiced—but only those who went away to monasteries or nunneries might be able to see God's will being done on earth as in heaven. This dualistic sense of spiritual and temporal realms removed from each other was evident not only in journalism but in artwork and other cultural realms as well. The Bible itself was removed from daily life and available only to the elite who knew Latin; Pope Innocent IV in 1252 forbade translating the Bible into vernacular languages.

The tiny and fairly barbaric part of the world where English was spoken was no exception to the general rule. In 1275 the statute of Westminister I outlawed "tales whereby discord or occasion of discord or slander may grow between the king and his people or the great men of the realm." Anything that could inspire such discord—including the Bible, which stated laws of God under which every man and woman, whether king or commoner, had to live — was banned. After John Wycliffe disobeyed Papal rulings and translated the Bible into English during the late 14th century, English church authorities cracked down, with the synod of Canterbury in 1408 forbidding the translation of Scripture from one language to another. Wycliffe's books were burned in 1410 and 1412. His bones were dug up and burned in 1428.

A technological revolution began around 1450 with the development of movable type in the Mainz workshop of Johann Gutenberg. But technological changes matter little as long as "world views" — clusters of convictions about what's important in life—remain the same. The demand from monasteries and kings or commercial leaders for big, printed, Latin Bibles was growing. Printed volumes met that demand, but the Bibles were usually for show rather than tell. Printing created potential for change and pressure to change from those who saw opportunities, but as long as reading was discouraged by state and church authorities, and as long as independent printers were jailed or killed, there would be little change.

The limited effect of the technological revolution, *by itself,* was indicated by early post-Gutenberg developments in England. Printing began there in 1476 when William Caxton, given royal encouragement and grant of privileges upon good behavior, set up a press in Westminster. Others followed, but were careful to avoid publishing works that might irritate the king or his ministers. Regulations limited the number of printers and apprentices. Royal patents created printing monopolies. It was illegal to import, print, or distribute threatening books, such as English translations of the Bible. In this policy England remained in line with other state–church countries during the early 1500s—but then came the providential sound of a hammer on a door, and the beginning of a theological onslaught (aided by journalistic means) that changed Europe.

Modern journalism began in 1517 as the German prince Frederick the Wise was putting the finishing touches on his life's work of building up Wittenberg's sacred relic collection. Through purchase and trade he was able to claim a "genuine" thorn from Christ's crown, a tooth of St. Jerome, four hairs from the Virgin Mary, seven pieces from the shroud sprinkled with Christ's blood, a wisp of straw from the place where Jesus was born, one piece of gold brought by the Wise Men, a strand of Jesus' beard, one of the nails driven into Christ's hands, one piece of bread eaten at the Last Supper, one twig of Moses' burning bush, and nearly 20,000 holy bones.

Announcements of relic collection highlights were made regularly through proclamations and assorted announcements, the typical journalistic products of the time. Few people could read—most were discouraged from even trying, for reading could lead to theological and political rebellion—but town criers and local priests passed on *official story* messages promoting the goals of governmental authorities and the official, state-allied religion. In 1517 Wittenberg residents were told that all of Frederick's treasures would be displayed on All Saints Day, and that those who viewed them and made appropriate donations could receive papal indulgences allowing for a substantial decrease of time spent in purgatory, either for the viewer/contributor or someone he would designate. Total time saved could equal 1,902,202 years and 270 days.

Quiet criticism of the indulgence system was coming from Professor Martin Luther, who stated that the Bible gave no basis for belief in indulgences and argued that the practice interfered with true contrition and confession. But, despite Luther's lectures, indulgence–buying continued as champion salesman Tetzel offered altruism at bargain prices:

> Listen to the voices of your dear dead relatives and friends, beseeching you and saying, "Pity us, pity us. We are in dire torment from which you can redeem us for a pittance." Do you not wish to? Open your ears. Hear the father saying to his son, the mother to her daughter, "We bore you, nourished you, brought you up, left you our fortunes, and you are so cruel and hard that now you are not willing for so little to set us free. Will you let us lie here in flames? Will you delay our promised glory?" Remember that you are able to release them, for "As soon as the coin in the coffer rings,/ The soul from purgatory springs."[1]

The pitch was strong, but Luther decided to oppose it head-on by making his ideas of protest accessible to all, not just a few. The 95 theses he hammered to

the cathedral door in 1517 were not academic sentences but clear, vivid statements. For example, concerning the plan to obtain money to build St. Peter's,
Luther wrote:

> The revenues of all Christendom are being sucked into this insatiable basilica. . . .
> The pope would do better to appoint one good pastor to a church than to confer
> indulgences upon them all. Why doesn't the pope build the basilica of St. Peter out
> of his own money? He is richer than Croesus. He would do better to sell St. Peter's
> and give the money to the poor folk who are being fleeced by the hawkers of
> indulgences.[2]

Luther then gave printers permission to set the theses in type—and they spread
throughout Europe within a month.

The effect of Luther's theses and his subsequent publications is well known—
but what often is missed is that Luther's primary impact was not as a producer
of treatises, but as a very popular writer of vigorous prose that concerned not
only theological issues but their social and political ramifications. Between 1517
and 1530 Luther's 30 publications probably sold well over 300,000 copies, an
astounding total at a time when illiteracy was rampant and printing still an infant.[3]
Because Luther had such influence through his writing the pressure on him to
mute the truth became enormous, but he said "My conscience is captive to the
Word of God . . . Here I stand, I can do no other."[4]

Luther's lively style and willingness to risk death for the sake of truth-telling
would be enough to make him a model for today's journalists, but it was his
stress on literacy that made independent journalism possible at all. Literacy was
low throughout Europe until the 16th century—perhaps only about 1 out of 100
persons could read. Reading was looked upon as a servile activity; just as
corporate CEOs today have secretaries to do their typing, so the kings of medieval
times remained illiterate and had designated readers. Nor were those of low estate
encouraged to read by state or church authorities. A 16th century French treatise
argued that people should not read on their own, less they become confused;
ordinary folk especially should not read the Bible, because they should learn only
from priests.[5] As one historian has noted, authorities "held it was safer to have
less Scripture reading than more heresy."[6]

Luther and other Reformation leaders, however, emphasized the importance
of Bible reading; Christians were to find out for themselves what God was saying.
Literacy rates soared everywhere the Reformation took root, and remained low
wherever it was fought off. Luther not only praised translation into the vernacular
languages but made a masterful one himself. In preparing his German translation
Luther so understood the need for specific detail to attract readers that when he
wanted to picture the precious stones and coins mentioned in the Bible, he first
examined German court jewels and numismatic collections. Similarly, when
Luther needed to describe Old Testament sacrifices he visited slaughterhouses

and gained information from butchers. He was a vivid reporter as well as a tenacious theologian.

Furthermore, he was a reporter who desired to print not just good news, but bad news also. Luther's Reformed theological understanding led him to write,

> God's favor is so communicated in the form of wrath that it seems farthest when it is at hand. Man must first cry out that there is no health in him. He must be consumed with horror. . . . In this disturbance salvation begins. When a man believes himself to be utterly lost, light breaks. Peace comes in the word of Christ through faith.[7]

Reformation leaders believed that people would seek the good news of mercy only after they became fully aware of the bad news of sin. This was the basis of the *corruption story:* Man needs to be become aware of his own corruption in order to change through God's grace, and writers who help make readers aware of sin are doing them a service.

Luther also made journalism significant by arguing that the path to progress is through change in ideas and beliefs, rather than through forced social revolution or reaction.[8] In Luther's thought the most significant warfare was ideological, not material, so he emphasized dissemination of ideas through publication and opposed attempts to destroy opposing ideas through burning either books or authors. "Heretics," he said, "should be vanquished with books, not with burnings."[9] Luther wanted an exchange of views, not swordthrusts. He described printing as "God's highest and extremest act of grace, whereby the business of the Gospel is driven forward."[10]

Others felt differently about those perceived as heretics. In 1529 Henry VIII of England banned importation of either the writings of Martin Luther or other works, including Bible translations, that supposedly engaged in "reproach, rebuke, or slander of the king."[11] Thomas Hilton was burned in 1530 for selling books by William Tyndale that advocated the supreme authority of Scripture against both state and church. Richard Bayfield, John Teukesbury, and James Bainham were burned in 1531 and 1532, and Tyndale himself was seized in Antwerp in 1536 and killed; his Bible translation was burned in St. Paul's Cathedral. After 1534, as Henry VIII established a national church in England under his headship, those who would not adhere to the latest twist in the *official story* — Sir Thomas More, Bishop Fisher, and others—also suffered execution.[12]

Henry added new antipress legislation almost as often as he added new wives. In 1534 his "Proclamation for Seditious Books" ordered that no one should print any English book without a license from the king's councils or those persons appointed by the king as licensers. His "Proclamation of 1538" left the press with "only one master, the king."[13] The sweeping language of Parliament's regulatory law of 1542–1543 indicates how the official story was to have absolute dominion:

"Nothing shall be taught or maintained contrary to the King's instructions," and nothing shall be published "contrary to the King's instructions or determinations, made or to be made."[14]

Henry VIII's structure of government and society was simple: The state, with its official church, was at the center, giving orders to other social institutions. But in the thought of men such as John Calvin, Scotland's John Knox, and other leaders of the Reformation, the kingdom of God could not be equated with state interests. Instead, the Reformers believed that God reigns everywhere and man can serve God directly in every area of life — government, journalism, education, business, or whatever. Reformed thinkers asserted that there were laws superior to the state or any other institution, and suggested that workers in those various areas did not have to wait for marching orders from the institutional Church, but could instead study the Bible and apply it to their own activities.

The Reformers did not advocate extremist intransigence or easy disobedience of governmental or church authority. John Knox, for instance, appealed for moderation and compromise whenever truly fundamental issues were not at stake. But under such a doctrine, for the first time, journalists could be more than purveyors of public relations. They had their own independent authority and would appeal to biblical principle when officials tried to shackle them.[15] The *corruption story* and the *official story* were heading for the first of their showdowns, and records of Henry's Privy Council, responsible for controlling the press, began to show regular proceedings against writers and speakers for "unfitting worddes" and supposedly seditious libel. During the reign of "Bloody Mary" from 1553 to 1558, the confrontation with those who based their lives on "sola scriptura"—the Bible only—began.[16]

One of the first Protestants to die at the stake was John Hooper, publicly burned at Gloucester on February 9, 1555. He was joined by about 75 men and women who were burned as heretics that year, and many more during the following 2 years. Soon, reports of those killings spread illegally throughout England: Ballads and other publications—one was called *Sacke full of Newes*—attacked the queen and praised the heroism of the martyrs. One notable underground pamphlet, *The Communication betwene my lord Chauncelor and judge Hales,* depicted the tyranny of the state church.[17]

These journalistic critiques readily went from the theological to the political, because the two were intertwined. Mary's marriage to Philip, heir to the Spanish throne, led many to believe that Spain would soon be ruling England in dictatorial fashion. One pamphlet, *A Warnyng for Englande,* gave an account of

the horrible practises of the Kyng of Spayne/ in the Kyngdome of Naples/ and the miseries whereunto that noble Realme is brought./ Whereby all Englishe men may understand the plage that shall light upon them/ if the Kyng of Spayn obteyne the Dominion in Englande.[18]

Coverage of the debate and the burnings showed the typical path of 16th century journalism: From theological debate to theological commentary on current news to sensational coverage.[19]

The 16th century journalist who made the greatest impression on several generations of Englishmen and women originally had no desire to report on current events. John Foxe, born in 1516, was an excellent student. He became a fellow at Oxford, but was converted to the Reformed faith and had to give up his stipend. In 1548 he began writing a scholarly history of Christian martyrdom, but it turned journalistic in 1553 when Mary became queen. Facing death in 1554 Foxe left England and began earning a poor living as a proofreader with a Swiss printer, but he continued to collect historical material about past persecutions and testimony about current ones.

Foxe published two volumes in Latin during the 1550s, but switched to English for his journalistic output, with the goal of telling the martyrs' story in a readable manner. He was able to return to England with the ascension of Elizabeth in 1558 and then spend five more years interviewing, collecting materials, and writing, before publishing the sensational account that became known as *Foxe's Book of Martyrs*. To make sure everything was right, he worked 7 years more before putting out in 1570 an expanded, second edition that contained woodcuts portraying burnings and whippings; later, large-scale editions increased the number of illustrations.[20] Foxe showed no interest in ecclesiastical promotion or governmental work. Until his death in 1587 Foxe kept revising the work, inserting corrections or additions that many people sent him, and avoiding the mere substitution of fables of his own for the official stories of old.[21]

Foxe's writing was vivid. For example, he wrote of how John Hooper, tied to a stake, prayed for a short time. Then the fire was lit, but the green wood was slow to burn. Hooper was shown a box and told it contained his pardon if he would give in: "Away with it!" he cried. As the fire reached Hooper's legs a gust of wind blew it out. A second fire then slowly burned up Hooper's legs, but went out with Hooper's upper body still intact. The fire was rekindled, and soon Hooper was heard to say repeatedly, "Lord Jesus, have mercy upon me; Lord Jesus, have mercy upon me; Lord Jesus, receive my spirit!"[22] Hooper's lips continued to move even when his throat was so scorched that no sound could come from it: Even "when he was black in the mouth, and his tongue swollen, that he could not speak, yet his lips went till they were shrunk to the gums." Finally, one of Hooper's arms fell off, and the other, with "fat, water, and blood" dripping out at the ends of the fingers, stuck to what remained of his chest. At that point Hooper bowed his head forward and died.[23]

Foxe also described the deaths of Hugh Latimer and Nicholas Ridley. Ridley, chained over another of those slow-burning fires, was in agony, but Latimer seemed to be dying with amazing ease — Foxe wrote that he appeared to be bathing his hands and face in the fire. Latimer's last words to his suffering friend were, "Be of good comfort, Master Ridley, [so that] we shall this day light such a candle, by God's grace, in England, as I trust shall never be put out."[24]

Foxe's third famous report concerned the death of Thomas Cranmer, Archbishop of Canterbury and leader of the English Protestants. Imprisoned for months without support of friends, Cranmer received daily ideological hammering from theological adversaries; after watching Ridley die, he wrote out a recantation and apology, in return for pardon. When Cranmer was told later that he allegedly had led so many astray that he would have to burn anyway, his courage returned and he resolved to go out boldly. He wrote in one final statement—a press release of a sort—that his recantation was "written with my hand contrary to the truth which is in my heart, and written for fear of death."[25] He offered a pledge: "As my hand hath offended, writing contrary to my heart, therefore my hand shall first be punished; for when I come to the fire, it shall be first burned." Foxe wrote of how Cranmer made good on that promise; sent to the stake, he placed his right hand firmly in the fire and held it steadily there until it appeared like a coal to observers. Soon, Cranmer's entire body was burned.[26]

Foxe's book became very popular not only because of its combination of theological fervor and grisly detail, but through its use of colorful Bible-based imagery. For example, Foxe's report on the impending death of John Hooper described how light overcame darkness as Hooper was led through London to Newgate prison. Officers had ordered all candles along the way be put out; perhaps,

> being burdened with an evil conscience, they thought darkness to be a most fit season for such a business.: But notwithstanding this device, the people having some foreknowledge of his coming, many of them came forth of their doors with lights, and saluted him; praising God for his constancy in the true doctrine which he had taught them. . . .[27]

Significantly, although Foxe was clearly on the side of the martyrs, he was not just a Protestant propagandist, overlooking the sins of his own side. He openly criticized the greed shown by Protestants under Edward VI, and, having written about executions by Catholics, did not favor executions by Protestants. In a long sermon Foxe delivered on Good Friday, 1570, he asked for mercy on many because Christ himself had been crucified by the church–state authorities of his time.

Foxe's stress on accuracy was maintained by Miles Coverdale, who wrote in 1564 that "it doeth us good to read and heare, not the lying legendes . . . triflying toyes & forged fables of corrupted writers: but such true, holy, . . . epistles & letters, as do set forth unto us ye blessed behavior of gods deare servantes."[28] For a time it appeared that a free press, with careful fact-checking, might arise—but, although Queen Elizabeth's version of *glasnost* allowed direct criticism of her predecessor, Mary, it did not allow objections to her reign or to the domination

of the established, Anglican religion. A proclamation on July 1, 1570, offered a
reward to those who informed against anyone writing or dispersing books in
opposition to the queen or any of her nobles. Other ordinances set increasingly
harsh penalties for unlicensed printing; on political matters, any challenge to the
official story was treason.[29]

The secret tribunal known as the Star Chamber did not hesitate to prosecute
and persecute. William Carter, a Catholic who printed in 1580 a book critical of
the queen, was arrested, tortured, and executed in 1584. More frequently, the
victims of state repression were Puritan rebels, including Hugh Singleton, Robert
Waldegrave, John Stroud, and John Hodgkins. Puritans as an organized journalistic group first went public in 1572 with *An Admonition to Parliament,* a 60-page
attack on state churches. *Admonition* authors John Field and Thomas Wilcocks
spent a year in prison, but other pamphlets soon appeared. Puritan John Stubbes
in 1579 wrote his critical pamphlet, had his right hand cut off, and then raised
his left hand in a salute to the queen.[30]

One of the best-read Puritan products at the end of the 16th century was a
series of pamphlets published in 1588 and 1589 and called the Martin Marprelate
tracts; these tracts humorously satirized and ridiculed the heavy-handed theological treatises put out by defenders of the established church. The tracts, printed
by John Hodgkins on a press that was dismantled repeatedly and moved around
by cart, irritated king and court so much that a massive search for its producers
began. Hodgkins escaped harm until he was unloading his press one day in the
town of Warrington, before curious onlookers. A few small pieces of metal type
fell from one of the boxes. A bystander picked up a letter and showed it to
an official, who understood the significance of the discovery and summoned
constables. Arrested and repeatedly tortured, Hodgkins refused to admit guilt and
implicate others.

The bravery of Hodgkins, like that of Martin Luther, John Hooper, John
Stubbes, and many others, could not not be ignored; persecution of the Puritans,
instead of stamping them out, led to new conversion. When James I became king
of England in 1603 and Puritans presented petitions for religious and press
freedom, he threatened to "harry them out of the land, or else do worse." James,
arguing that he was "above the law by his absolute power," and that "it is
presumptuous and high contempt in a subject to dispute what a king can do, or
say that a king cannot do this or that," advised subjects to "rest in that which is
the king's revealed word in his law."[31] But that is something that Puritan writers,
committed as they were to following God's law whatever the costs, would not
do.

Royal officials made it clear that proponents of the corruption story would be
prosecuted whenever they suggested that all, including the king, were naturally
corrupt, in need of God's grace, and obliged to obey Biblical principles. The Star
Chamber, in a 1606 case *de Libellis Famosis,* stipulated that truth was no defense
against a charge of seditious libel, which was defined as anything that would

reduce public respect for the monarch or his officials. The Star Chamber's powers of inquiry were supplemented in 1613 when James I granted to another government body, the High Commission, power over "books, pamphlets and portraitures offensive to the state."[32]

In the long run, however, James himself undermined the idea of royal authoritarianism by setting up a committee of 54 scholars to prepare a new translation of the Bible. When the committee's work was done, the magnificent "King James" translation had made the Bible more popularly accessible than ever. In Ryken's words,

> Beginning with a conviction that the Bible was where a person encountered God most directly, religion became in significant ways a literary experience. The acts of worship emphasized by the Reformers and Puritans were overwhelmingly literary acts: reading the Bible, meditating on its meaning.[33]

According to a contemporary opponent of the Puritans, those who attended one Puritan service had their Bibles open and looked up verses cited by the preachers. They took notes and, after the sermon, "held arguments also, among themselves, about the meaning of various Scripture texts, all of them, men and women, boys and girls, laborers, workmen and simpletons."[34]

The connection of Reformed faith and literacy became evident throughout England as it had in Europe. But that was not the only way the ideas first developed and popularized by Martin Luther had consequences for journalism. The Puritans also set in motion a movement toward a different social structure. The change began with an emphasis on reading and thinking. Edward Reynolds wrote:

> The people are hereby taught, first, to examine the doctrines of men by the rule and standard of the Word; . . . for though the judgment of interpretation belong principally to the ministers of the Word, yet God has given all believers a judgment of discretion, to try the spirits and to search the Scriptures, whether the things which they hear be so or no.[35]

Church authorities were no longer the central arbiters — they also were under the authority of Scripture and could rightfully be criticized by anyone who could point out in the Bible where they had gone wrong. "Capable is the poorest member in Christ's church, being grown to maturity of years, of information in the faith," Reynolds wrote, for "Are we not all a royal priesthood?"[36] Out of this sense of individual competence grew an idea of the formal church organized as a major activity among others, rather than (along with the state) the center of power. Journalists could have independent authority under God, and not merely serve as public relations appendages to state or state–church.

Other innovative journalistic approaches could grow logically out of the Puritan emphasis on individual salvation. Everyday "human interest" stories and not just official doings would for the first time be considered important, for, as Puritan Richard Greenham wrote:

> Surely if men were careful to reform themselves first, and then their own families, they should see God's manifold blessings in our land and upon church and commonwealth. For of particular persons come families; of families, towns; of towns, provinces; of provinces, whole realms.[37]

Furthermore, the Puritans' style of communication reflected a desire to have ordinary individuals receive information that could help them choose rightly. Puritan William Perkins argued that in expressing ideas, "the plainer, the better."[38] Robert Bolton argued that delivery of truth, rather than "self praise and private ends," was the goal of communication, and John Flavel wrote that "words are but servants to matter. An iron key, fitted to the wards of the lock, is more useful than a golden one that will not open the door to the treasures."[39]

All of this, and more, developed in one century from those ideas put down in words hammered onto the door of the Wittenberg cathedral. Material developments were useful, but beliefs and bravery carried the day and led to a new era.

Chapter 2

Perils of the Puritan Press

While James I was asserting his sovereignty in England, new journalistic forms were emerging in the Reformed strongholds of Amsterdam and Augsburg. The first newspapers—printed information sources on a regular (in these cases, weekly) schedule—were published in those cities in 1607 and 1609.[1] By 1620 Amsterdam, known for its Reformed emphasis on literacy and liberty, was the refuge for emigre printers from France, Italy, England, and other countries. In that year the first newspapers ever printed in English and French came out—in Amsterdam. In 1621 another Amsterdam publisher started exporting his English-language newspapers to England, and the king's agents now had to track down bundles of newspapers, not just destroy printing presses.

The British government, under pressure, tried to co-opt the opposition by allowing licensed publication of a domestic newspaper, *Mercurius Britannicus,* and some political pamphlets during the 1620s. Criticism of governmental foreign policy became a sore point, however, and James struck back at his press opponents, issuing edicts decrying "the great liberty of discourse concerning matters of state."[2] Printer Thomas Archer was imprisoned, but Puritan doctrines won increasing acceptance, particularly in English towns. Opposition to James and his successor, Charles I, increased.

When one Puritan critic, Alexander Leighton, wrote and published a pamphlet in 1630 entitled *An Appeal to Parliament,* Charles and his court were outraged. Leighton insisted that Scripture was above everything, including kings, so that subjects could remain loyal while evaluating their rulers against biblical standards; Leighton said his goal was to correct existing problems "for the honour of the king, the quiet of the people, and the peace of the church." The Star Chamber saw the situation differently, terming Leighton's work "seditious and scandalous." On November 16, 1630, Leighton was whipped at Westminster, and had one of his ears cut off, his nose slit, and one side of his face branded. One week later the mutilation was repeated on the other side.

The penalty did not stop other Puritans. John Bastwick, Henry Burton, and William Prynne were hauled into the Star Chamber in 1637 and charged with seditious libel for writing pamphlets that criticized royal actions. Each man was sentenced to "perpetual imprisonment" without access to writing materials, and loss of ears. The royal authorities, believing they had the populace on their side, proclaimed a public holiday highlighted by the public mutilations. But when the three men were allowed to make public statements (according to the custom of the day) as the officials waited with knives, they were cheered. Prynne was actually arrested and maimed twice; when he was released from prison and allowed to return to London, he was greeted by a crowd of 10,000.

Barbarous attempts to control the press prompted even more determined opposition; as a *Boston Gazette* essayist would note over a century later, the English civil war had as its "original, true and real Cause" suppression of the press, and "had not Prynn lost his Ears, K. Charles would have never lost his Head."[3] The verbal battle of Parliament versus crown, Puritans versus Anglicans, official story versus corruption story, led to war during the 1640s. The changed political environment led to a journalistic surge, as Puritan-dominated Parliament, remembering past oppression, abolished in 1641 the torture-prone Star Chamber. The result, according to a parliamentary committee in 1643, was that many printers "have taken upon them to set up sundry private Printing Presses in corners, and to print, vend, publish and disperse Books, pamphlets and papers. . . ."[4]

Some of these publications were regular newspapers with high standards. Samuel Pecke's weekly, *A Perfect Diurnall,* began with these words: "You may henceforth expect from this relator to be informed only of such things as are of credit. . . ."[5] Pecke did not make up things. Although clearly a Puritan partisan, he truthfully reported Royalist military victories, and twice covered wrongful conduct by Parliamentary soldiers. He also gave opponents space to express their views: When Archbishop Laud was executed for murder, Pecke included a transcript of the Archbishop's speech from the scaffold.

Similarly, when John Dillingham began his newspaper *The Parliament Scout* in 1643, he pledged "to tell the truth" and not to "vapour and say such a one was routed, defeated," when there actually had been no battle.[6] Dillingham wrote of plundering by Cromwell's soldiers, the bravery of some captured Royalists, and the need for better medical treatment of the wounded on both sides. Partisanship and fairness could go together, apparently, as editors believed that God could judge them for lying even if their backers cheered.[7]

By 1644 London, a city with a half-million residents, had a dozen weekly newspapers. This was more journalistic variety on a regular basis than had ever before existed.[8] Some Puritan leaders did not like criticism any more than the king's officials did, but most were committed to the idea of biblical rather than personal authority, and of letting individuals read for themselves.[9] One Puritan leader and friend of John Milton, Samuel Hartlib, reflected general hopes when he predicted in 1641 that "the art of Printing will so spread knowledge that the common people, knowing their own rights and liberties, will not be governed by way of oppression."[10]

Parliament in 1643 did pass a law that restricted sales of pamphlets and newsbooks, but it received little enforcement and much criticism. Puritan pamphleteer William Walwyn noted that licensing might restrict some evil publications but would also "stopt the mouthes of good men, who must either not write at all, or no more than is suitable to the judgments or interests of the Licensers."[11] Another Puritan, Henry Robinson, proposed that theological and political combat should "be fought out upon eaven ground, on equal termes, neither side must expect to have greater liberty of speech, writing, Printing, or whatsoever else, than the other."[12]

The most famous response to the new law was penned by Milton himself. Licensing, he wrote, brought back memories of Bloody Mary, she of "the most unchristian council and the most tyrannous inquisition that ever inquired," and was inconsistent with the "mild, free and human government" that the Puritans said they would provide. Milton's most famous words in his *Areopagetica* were,

> Though all the winds of doctrine were let loose to play upon the earth, so truth be in the field, we do injuriously by licensing and prohibiting to misdoubt her strength. Let her and falsehood grapple; who ever knew truth put to the worse, in a free and open encounter.[13]

Milton had faith in God's invisible hand over journalism; he asked, "For who knows not that truth is strong, next to the Almighty? She needs no policies, nor stratagems, nor licensings to make victorious; those are shifts and the defences that error uses against her power."[14]

The greatest journalistic talent of 17th-century England emerged during this mid-1640s period of relative freedom. The story of Marchamont Nedham typifies the 17th-century journalistic attempt to follow the tightrope walk of John Foxe, John Stubbes, and other 16th-century writers who prayed for reformation without revolution.

Nedham was born in 1620 in a small town near Oxford. He studied Greek, Latin, and history as a child, received a bachelor's degree from Oxford University in 1637, and spent the next 6 years as a schoolteacher, law clerk, and dabbler in medicine. During those 6 years, Nedham underwent a theological and political transformation that led him to side with the Puritans. When King Charles established in 1643 his own weekly newspapers, the *Mercurius Aulicus,* Nedham was hired to help out with a competing newspaper from the Parliamentary side,

Mercurius Britanicus. Within a year Nedham was in charge and doing almost all of the writing for a newspaper that was eight pages long and typographically clean enough to make possible headache-less reading of it three centuries later.

Nedham's writing was sensational and colorful; rather than theorizing or preaching, he provided specific detail about the vices of Royalists. Lord Ratcliffe, for example, was "bathing in luxury, and swimming in the fat of the land, and cramming his Hens and Capons with Almonds and Raisins," and Lord Porter was "that Exchequer of Flesh, which hath a whole Subsidie in his small guts and his panch, and hath bestowed the Sessments, and taxes of the State in sawces."[15] Nedham saw himself turning darkness into light by exposing corruption; when Nedham reviewed his first year as editor, he wrote that

I have by an excellent and powerful Providence led the people through the labyrinths of the enemies Plots . . . I have brought the secrets and sins of the Court abroad, from her Majestie to Mistris Crofts her very maid of honour, and from his Majesty to his very Barbour.[16]

Another time, he listed his successes in investigative journalism and exposure:

1. The King could not keepe an evil Councellour, but I must needs speake of him.
2. The Queene could not bring in Popery, but I must needs tell all the world of it. . . .
4. The Common Prayer could not be quiet, but I was still crying out Idolatry, and will-worship.
5. The Bishops, Deans, and Doctors, could not play at Gleeke, and drinke Sacke after evening Prayer, but I gave in their names. . . .
9. I would never let Aulicus tell a lie to the world, but I blew a Trumpet before it, that all might know it.
10. I undisguised the Declarations, and Protestations, and Masqueries of the Court.[17]

Nedham, although thoroughly partisan, was not a propagandist at this time. His leads summarized factually the "new business of King and Parliament."[18] He desired accuracy and criticized the Royalist newspaper editor, John Birkenhead:

Oh! what Prodigious Service hath he done, he could tell of Battailes and victories, when there was not so much as an Alarme or skirmish, he could change Pistolls into Demi-Cannons, and Carbines into Culverings, and Squadrons and Troopes into Regiments and Brigades, he could rally routed Armies and put them into a better condition when they were beaten then before.[19]

Unlike Birkenhead, Nedham commented on his own side's difficulties:

The King is too nimble for us in horse, and his designers ride, while ours go on foot, and we lacquey beside him, and usually fall short of his Army, and we shall scarce be able to encounter him, unless he please to turn back and fight with us.[20]

Furthermore, he made theological points through laying up specific detail, rather than by preaching: "Prince Rupert abides in Westchester . . . the young man is lately grown so devout, that he cannot keep the Lords day without a Bull baiting, or Beare baiting."[21]

Nedham rarely drew attention to himself, but in one issue he explained that "I took up my pen for disabusing his Majesty, and for disbishoping, and dispoping his good subjects."[22] Exposure was his goal: He wanted to take off the "vailes and disguises which the Scribes and Pharisees at Oxford had put upon a treasonable and popish Cause."[23] He enjoyed his effectiveness: "I have served a Parliament and Reformation hitherto in unmaking and unhooding incendiaries of all sorts . . . Everyone can point out the evill Counsellours now."[24] But, in a question-and-answer note (an early version of "Dear Abby") at the end of each issue of *Mercurius Britanicus,* he regularly cautioned against arrogance: When asked, "What are we to do or expect now in this time when our forces are so considerable?" Nedham answered, "Not to trust nor looke too much upon them, but through them to a Diviner power, lest we suffer as we did before."[25]

In short, Nedham saw his calling as one of truth-telling, rather than promoting allegiance to a certain set of leaders. He worked hard to maintain some distance from those Puritan leaders who began to trust in their own power. In June 1645, Nedham made it clear to his readers that Parliament did not tell him what to write—he had independent authority, under God.[26] Two months later, Nedham disobeyed a licenser's request that he delete a hard-hitting passage, and received only a reprimand.[27]

Yet, as some Puritan leaders gained great power and decided they were above criticism, they backed off from their own principles. In May 1646, Nedham published that era's equivalent of the Pentagon Papers; the official charge noted his publication of "divers passages between the two Houses of Parliament and other scandalous particulars not fit to be tolerated."[28] One writer attacked Nedham's "sullen and dogged wit" and suggested that "his hands and feet be as sacrifices cut off, and hung up, to pay for the Treasons of his tongue."[29] Nedham's limbs were spared, but he was jailed for 12 days and released only on condition that he do no more newspaper editing.

Nedham abided by his "no editing" pledge but continued to write. At a time when both Anglicans and Puritan Presbyterians opposed independent churches, Nedham made himself unpopular with both sides by writing a pamphlet that warned those who would not tolerate independent churches, "Take heed therefore lest while ye raile against new lights ye work despight to the Spirit of God. To Quench it in a mans self is a great sin, [but it is worse] to labour to quench it in others."[30] Nedham attacked "compulsive power" in religion—but compulsion increased as tensions between Parliament and Oliver Cromwell's New Model Army grew.

The Army, with hands and guns and support from those members of Parliament who were disposed to use force rather than reason, increasingly seemed determined to brook no opposition. Parliament empowered a Committee on Examinations to investigate pamphlet publishers and to demolish the presses and imprison press owners found to be part of the opposition. On September 27, 1647, the House of Commons provided stiff fines for publication of nonlicensed publications. In 1648 many pamphleteers were arrested. In 1649 Parliament increased penalties, ordered all news-books to be licensed, required every printer to make a bond of 300 pounds not to print anything offensive to the government, and confined printing to London and the universities at Oxford and Cambridge, with limited exception for two other presses.

Some Puritans criticized this tightening. In January 1649, a "Petition of firm and constant friends to the parliament and Commonwealth" urged the granting of liberty to the press, and pointedly told military leaders that if

> you and your army shall be pleased to look back a little upon affairs you will find you have bin very much strengthened all along by unlicensed printing. . . . The liberty [of the press] . . . appears so essential unto Freedom, as that without it, it's impossible to preserve any nation from being liable to the worst of bondage. For what may not be done to that people who may not speak or write, but at the pleasure of Licensers?[31]

John Owen, Cromwell's religious advisor, recognized that it is better to have 500 errors scattered among individuals than to have one error gain power over all.[32] Nevertheless, the tendency to reduce debate continued.

Nedham saw the dictatorship coming. In October 1647, he published a pamphlet anticipating the purge of Parliament that took place the following year, in which the military ousted and excluded from further influence 231 of its Parliamentary opponents. Nedham noted that "Mr. Cromwell hath them [Parliament] in the Mill, grind they must, seeing that they are at his Beck who holds a Whip and a Bell over their guilty Heads." He then presciently argued that when Cromwell "hath used them long enough under the name of Parliament, then (perhaps) they shall be disbanded severall waies, that the Sword-men may stand for ever."[33] Calling Cromwell "King Cromwell" and "The Grand Segnior," Needham saw dictatorship leading to more bloodshed and noted sardonically, "Tis a godly thing States to reforme by Murther."[34] Reflecting on how good intentions can lead to sad results, Nedham exclaimed, "Good God, what a wild thing is Rebellion."[35]

The dramatic result of Nedham's rethinking of rebellion was that he amazed his former allies by joining the Royalists. Presbyterian minister John Hackluyt, a chaplain in the Parliamentary army who shared Nedham's concern about dictatorship, also switched sides, in the hope that a humbled King Charles might consent to a constitutional monarchy. The suggestion of one historian that Nedham joined the king's side because he "liked excitement and power" seems weak: The king's side was a losing side, and in a little over a year Charles would be executed.[36] To become a Royalist late in 1647 showed either great stupidity or uncommon bravery. Nedham was not dumb, and it appears that he was risking all to try to preserve some liberty in England. From September 1647 through January 1649, Nedham edited *Mercurius Pragmaticus,* a newspaper deeply critical of the new dictatorship emerging.

Nedham's reporting, as usual, contained exciting detail and perceptive analysis. He showed how Cromwell and his associates won a Parliamentary majority through intimidation and created public fear through artfully designed troop movements. He exposed other plans and pretensions, including dissension among the army-Parliamentary forces: Cromwell's "face is now more toward an Aristocracie than Zion, which hath raised a deadly feud betwixt him and the Adjutators, who looke upon him as fallen from grace."[37] In 1648 Nedham also produced several satirical pamphlets, including one entitled *Ding Dong or Sr. Pitifull Parliament on his death-bed,* under the pen name Mercurius Melancholicus. In that pamphlet he wrote, "Sir Pitifull Parliament hath taken griefe, which hath so prevailed over his powers, and mastered his faculties, that he is now become a meere Skelleton . . . harke how he groanes."[38]

As the Puritan reforming zeal turned to revolutionary power lust, Nedham week after week in *Mercuricus Pragmaticus* showed the degradation of the movement: "See how Wealth/ Is made their Heaven! They swell/ With Pride! and live by Blood and Stealth,/ As if there were no Hell."[39] Meanwhile, poverty dominated the countryside, and there "the citizens (like silly sheep)/ Must fast, and be content."[40] Civil war, Nedham feared, was bringing out the worst in men: "Faith and Religion bleeding lie,/ And Liberty grows faint:/ No Gospel, but pure Treachery,/ And Treason make the Saint. . . . Away with Justice, Laws and Fear;/ When Men resolve to rise,/ Brave Souls must scorn all Scruples where/ A Kingdom is the Prize."[41] Might apparently was making right, with preaching secondary: "Militia too, they needs must gain,/ Those pretty carnal Tools:/ For Pauls old Weapons they disdain,/ As fit for none but Fools."[42]

In November 1648, two months before King Charles' execution, with the revolutionary party at its height, Nedham published *A Plea for the King and Kingdome.* He decried the movement "to a Military Government" that would lead to "the utter subversion of our Law . . . and the inslaving of the Kingdome." Nedham was not alone in thinking the forces of Cromwell were going too far: Of the 250 men who remained in Parliament following Pride's Purge of December 1648, only about 60 sat regularly as puppets of the army, and fewer than half of those finally approved of the King's execution.

Many Puritans spoke out vigorously against the coup; many were arrested. William Waller, a Puritan general who split from Cromwell, called the takeover tyrannical and labeled it "treason in the highest degree."[43] But the king was executed; in the words of the newspaper *A Perfect Diurnall,* "The executioner at one blow severed his head from his body. Then when the King's head was cut off, the Executioner held it up and showed it to the spectators."[44] This was the first modern revolutionary execution, with millions more to follow.

Soon after Charles' execution, Nedham went into hiding. Other journalists expressed veiled concern about a move toward dictatorship. Dillingham wrote in February 1649, following Charles' execution, "There's Kings gone, them and Lords in two dayes: how easie it is to pull down." He asked readers to turn to II Samuel, where the daughters of Israel are told to weep over Saul. He mocked utopian plans and economic panaceas.[45] Nedham, however, went further than others. For 2 months during the spring of 1649 he put out an underground edition of *Mercurius Pragmaticus* that featured reporting like this:

> Both King and Bishops thus exil'd/ The Saints not yet content:/ Now with fresh flames of Zeal grow wild,/ And cry, No Parliament . . . The State's grown fat with Orphans Tears,/ Whilst Widows pine and moan;/ And tender Conscience in sev'n years,/ Is turn'd t' a heart of stone.[46]

Nedham concluded that "No Powers are safe, Treason's a Tilt,/ And the mad Sainted-Elves/ Boast when Royal Blood is spilt,/ They'll all be Kings themselves."[47]

Nedham, from various hiding places, also sent out several pamphlets that did not endear him to the new masters of England. Immediately after the revolutionary leaders celebrated victory with a parade and feast on June 7, Nedham published *The Great Feast at the Sheep-shearing of the City and Citizens*. The last page gives a sense of the whole:

> At Grocers Hall, they grocely fed,/ With which their paunches out were spread,/ Whilst thousands starve for want of bread,/ Let's thanke the Parliament./ Neere forty Bucks, these Holy ones/ Devour'd, and left the dogs the bones,/ And Musick grac'd with Tunes and Tones,/ This Bacchanalian Feast:/ And after that, a Banquet came . . . Tyrants feast with joy.[48]

With that publication the search for Nedham intensified; a few days later he was captured, sent to Newgate prison, and almost executed. He escaped in August and was free for 2 weeks, but was captured and sent back to prison, where he spent 3 more months.

It turned out that Nedham was not executed, because Oliver Cromwell had other plans for him. Cromwell, in effect the new king, wanted to merge the official story and the corruption story, the latter restricted so as to chastise the corruption of subjects but not the new rulers. He offered Nedham a deal: Write for me, and live. Nedham gave in, signed an oath of allegiance to the new government in November 1649, and was released to begin work on a 100-page pamphlet that presented "The Equity, Utility, and Necessity, of a Submission to the present Government."[49] Nedham argued at length that the Royalist cause was done for, and that wise men, understanding the "improbability of Success in the new Royall enterprize," should submit in recognition of "Necessity, the Custome of all Nations, and the Peace of our own."[50]

One of Nedham's title chapters—"That the Power of the Sword Is, and Ever Hath been, the Foundation of All Titles to Government"—shows how the official story had come to dominate Nedham's thinking or at least his expression, with Cromwell as king. A person disobeying another who had come into power, whether or not the ascent was lawful, and regardless of "allegiances, oaths, and covenants" formerly entered into, was "peevish, and a man obstinate against the reason and custom of the whole world."[51] Nedham used examples from the then recent Thirty Years War to show how allegiances quickly change under pressure:

> One while, you might have seen the same town under the French, the next under the Spaniard. And upon every new alteration, without scruple, paying a new allegiance and submission, and never so much as blamed for it by the divines of their own or any other nation.[52]

Such is life, Nedham argued.

Nedham's writings thoughout the early 1650s showed that mixture of cynical wisdom and broken spirit. Cromwell's government, with its deeply flawed practice but a base in biblical principles, did not prove to be as terrible as Nedham first had feared. The leaders did not engage in the mass murder that characterized revolutions to come. Still, petty dictatorship emerged; as Puritan Denzil Holles complained, in what would also be a preview of future revolutionary outcomes, "The meanest of men, the basest and vilest of the nation, the lowest of the people, have got the power into their hands . . ."[53] It is sad to see Nedham reporting to such individuals and editing the official public relations weekly for the regime, *Mercurius Politicus*.[54]

And yet, Nedham at times was able to work within the system to keep a slight breeze blowing. The Council of State, as publisher, approved of Nedham's plan to have *Politicus* "written in a jocular way" to attract attention.[55] Nedham produced good coverage of local news along with cautionary reports of persons hanged for treason.[56] But Nedham also kept hope alive in his pamphlet *The Excellencie of a Free State*, which he serialized in *Politicus*. Nedham observed that

> The Interest of Freedom is a Virgin that everyone seeks to deflower; and like a Virgin, it must be kept from any other Form, or else (so great is the Lust of mankinde for dominion) there follows a rape upon the first opportunity.[57]

He wondered whether there was political life after rape, or whether government was merely "an artifice . . . occasioned by necessity."[58]

Eventually the petty aspects of Cromwell's rules, not the major thrusts, turned English public opinion massively against what became associated with all of Puritanism, rather than its revolutionary elements that had achieved power. The "rump Parliament" formed after Pride's Purge passed laws forbidding the celebration of Christmas and attacking traditional pastimes such as dancing, playing at cards or dice, and so on. In 1655 Cromwell divided England and Wales into 12 military districts, each ruled by a major-general with authority to "promote godliness and virtue" by enforcing laws against horseracing, cock-fighting, and so on. No recreation was allowed on the Sabbath; in 1659 a French observer wrote that "the religion of England is preaching and sitting still on Sundays."[59] Popular resentment grew.

As the revolution ran down in the late 1650s Nedham saw that a monarchical restoration was likely: "'Tis neither dishonour nor scandal," he wrote, that "after all other experiments made in vain, where the ends of government cannot otherwise be conserved, to revert upon the old bottom and foundation."[60] It would have been easy for Nedham, following Oliver Crowell's death in 1658, to join others in beginning to grease the slide on which the dead king's son, Charles II, soon would return. But Nedham did not join the plotters—instead, against his own personal interests, he warned Puritans that hopes of a peaceful, constitutional monarchy were foolish, because Charles II would be vindictive and would once again empower "the Episcopacie."[61] In 1660 Nedham again deliberately stuck with a lost cause, this time suggesting that Charles II should be fought because his promises of mercy were unreliable: "Tush! remember that blessed line of Machiavel; he's an oafe that thinks an oath, or any other tender, can tame a prince beyond his pleasure."[62]

Such jabs killed Nedham's chances to remain in English journalism following the monarchical restoration. They almost killed Nedham. In May 1660, a pamphlet entitled *A Rope for Pol. Or a, a Hue and Cry after Marchamont Nedham,* suggested that he deserved death because of the influence his writing had "upon numbers of unconsidering persons, who have a strange presumption that all must needs be true that is in Print."[63] A broadside, *The Downfall of Mercurius,* argued "now the time is coming which no doube/ Will do him justice, vengeance will find him out./ . . . Thus with the times he turned. next time I hope/ Will up the ladder be and down the rope."[64] In April 1660, Nedham fled to Holland.

He was allowed to return 4 months later, but on the condition that he abstain from any further involvement in political journalism.[65] Nedham stayed out of politics for 15 years and concentrated on medicine. From 1676 to 1678 he wrote four political pamphlets in opposition to the Whig leader Shaftesbury and in opposition to the dictatorship of Louis XIV in France. They did not make much of a mark, nor was Nedham's death in 1678, at age 58, much noted.

The legacy of Nedham—his early fervor, his later suspicion, and his deliberate bad timing—*should* be noted, however. Three times—in 1646, 1649, and 1660—he stuck out his neck for what he believed, and three times he came close to having it chopped off or stretched out. Through that experience he became suspicious of all ideologies that promised earthly salvation; many American journalists would later follow in his footsteps.

His dashed hopes were shared by Puritan journalists generally. In May 1662, the new, Royalist-dominated Parliament passed a bill enacting a new, stringent censorship system. No more, said Parliament, would

> evil disposed persons [sell] heretical, schismatical, blasphemous, seditious and treasonable books, pamphlets and papers. . . indangering the peace of these kingdoms, and raising a disaffection to his most excellent Majesty and his government.[66]

The official story was triumphant, not only in journalism but in legal preaching.[67] English newspapers born during the years of civil strife suffered governmental infanticide. Despite early promises to the contrary, Charles II increasingly tried to rule on the French, divine-right model, and his press clippings reflected that: Palace writers had God always in the background, looking on benevolently, but Charles at the center, master of the realm. A tight censorship eliminated regular news coverage unless it helped to propel the official story.

For proponents of the corruption story, life was even harder than it had been before the revolution. For example, in 1663 John Twyn was convicted of sedition for printing a book arguing that citizens should call to account a king whose decrees violated biblical law. After Twyn refused to provide the name of the book's author, his "privy-members" were cut off before his eyes, and he was then beheaded. Twyn's body was cut into four pieces, and each was nailed to a different gate of the city as a warning to other printers or writers.[68]

Chapter 3

A New Planting of the Corruption Story

After the monarchical restoration in England, British officials across the Atlantic also placed restrictions on press freedoms. Royal governors appeared to believe that the Puritan idea of "read for yourself" simply caused too much trouble. In 1671 Governor William Berkeley of Virginia responded to a query concerning the state of religion in the colony by saying that the drawbacks of emphasizing reading and study would outweigh the benefits:

> There are no free schools nor *printing,* and I hope we shall not have these hundred years; for *learning* has brought disobedience, and heresy, and sects into the world, and *printing* has divulged them, and libels against the best government.[1]

Berkeley's successors in Virginia clamped down hard on any displays of independence. Philip Ludwell was heavily fined in 1678 for calling Governor Herbert Jeffreys a lawbreaker. When printing finally was allowed, it was carefully regulated: Printer John Buckner received a reprimand in 1682 merely for printing the colony's laws without official permission; Buckner was forced to post a bond of 100 pounds that would be forfeited were he ever to print anything again. Governor Francis Lord Howard in 1685 issued a proclamation condemning the "over lycentiousnesse of the People in their discourses" and reminding the public that criticism of the royal government was criminal sedition.[2] Other proclamations and incidents—in 1690, 1693, 1699, 1702, and 1704—also sent a message to those who might wish to oppose the official story.

Attempts at independence often received severe punishment. In 1666, one

Maryland critic of the official story received 39 lashes across his back. Protests concerning such treatment occasionally appeared: In 1689 a Maryland group that called itself the Protestant Association protested the colony's laws,

> especially one that against all Sense, Equity, Reason, and Law Punishes all Speeches, Practices, and Attempts relating to his Lordship and Government, that shall be thought Mutinous and Seditious.[3]

The Protestant Association complained that the government had punished "Words and Actions" it disapproved of by "Whipping, Branding, Boreing through the Tongue, Fine, Imprisonment, Banishment, or Death."[4] But for many years Maryland and other colonies did not have the critical mass of residents committed to the Reformation concept that those in various spheres of society had a right to carry on their activities, under God, regardless of royal approval. Royal governors hoped to avoid all criticism.[5]

Only in New England, the center of Reformation thought in the New World, was publication and education emphasized; the Puritans set up a printing press and college in Cambridge, Massachusetts, in 1636, just 6 years after their arrival in a wilderness where mere survival was not assured.[6] New Englanders tried from the colony's founding to restrict royal authority. John Winthrop had the opportunity to gain special favors for Massachusetts from Puritans then dominating Parliament, but he declined because he did not want to accept the idea that Parliament had jurisdiction over the colony; Winthrop wanted the idea of a self-governing commonwealth to be established. The General Court (Massachusetts' legislature) at one point declared—in a statement that Samuel Adams would pick up a century later—"Our allegiance binds us not to the laws of England any longer than while we live in England."[7]

In the 1660s, however, monarchical restoration in England placed new pressures on New England. Well-connected courtiers in London contested the Massachusetts Bay charter that Charles I had given to Puritan leaders in 1629; the courtiers claimed that they had received previous royal grants to the same land. The General Court, desperate to avoid a royal crackdown, forced evangelist and writer John Eliot in 1661 to retract "such expressions as doe too manifestly scandalize" the government of England." Eliot's book *The Christian Commonwealth,* which advocated election of rulers, was ordered "totally suppressed."[8] In October 1662, the General Court passed the first formal censorship act in Massachusetts, imitating the act passed by Parliament under the urging of Charles II.

Pressure on New England writers did not come only from London. The Puritans allowed wide debate concerning biblical interpretation, but would not allow publication of tracts hostile to the fundamentals or essentials of Reformed Christianity. Quakers, with their reliance on "inner light" rather than the Bible only, and their methods of protest that included walking naked inside churches to protest the "nakedness" of the institutions, were not tolerated. But the Puritans did encourage reporting of bad news that tended to be swept under the rug in most other places.

They were lenient in this way because bad news was seen as a message from God. Boston printer Marmaduke Johnson in 1668 published "God's Terrible Voice in the City of London, wherein you have the Narration of the late dreadful Judgment of Pleague and Fire." In 1674, when Benjamin Goad was hanged in Boston for committing bestiality, Samuel Danforth wrote of crime and punishment and offered a "why":

> God's end in inflicting remarkable judgments upon some, is for caution and warning to all others. . . . Behold now the execution of vengeance upon this lewd and wicked youth, whom God hath hanged up before the Sun, and made a sign and example, and instruction and admonishment, to all New England.[9]

Johnson published a short piece entitled, "Cry of Sodom enquired into, upon occasion of the Arraignment and Condemnation of Benjamin Goad, for his prodigious Villany."[10]

"News sermons," first presented in church and frequently published, became an established form of New England communication. The sermons, Harry S. Stout has pointed out, had a "topical range and social influence" and were "so powerful in shaping cultural values, meanings, and a sense of corporate purpose that even television pales in comparison."[11] In Stout's words:

> Unlike modern mass media, the sermon stood alone in local New England contexts as the regular (at least weekly) medium of public communication. As a channel of information, it combined religious, educational, and journalistic functions.[12]

Sermons on royal births and deaths, military defeats or victories, election results and government decisions, and most of all crimes (preferably with punishments) were common.[13] Printers moved naturally from publication of Bible commentaries to publication of theological treatises and sermons to publication of news sermons and pamphlets on current events.[14]

Puritan theology not only allowed but emphasized the reporting of bad news, for the coming of well-deserved calamities was a sign that God still reigned. It was no accident that the best-known Massachusetts minister of the late 17th century, Increase Mather, also became its leading journalist. Mather argued in 1674 that God was not pleased with the sins of pride and envy that were common in New England, and that "a day of trouble is at hand."[15] The long title of one of his published news sermons in 1675 provided, in order, the "why," "what," "where," "when," "how," and "who" of the news:

The Times of Men Are in the Hands of God. Or a Sermon Occasioned by That Awful Providence Which Happened in Boston in New England, The 4th Day of the 3rd

Month 1675 (When Part of a Vessel Was Blown Up in the Harbor, and Nine Men Hurt, and Three Mortally Wounded).[16]

Mather's forecasts of general disaster hit home in June 1675, when a tribe of Wampanoag Indians burned and looted homes in the town of Swansea and killed nine residents. Indian attacks escalated in August 1675, as Wampanoags led by Chief Metacom ("King Philip") were joined by the Narragansetts and Nipmucks in an attack on towns in western Massachusetts and other outlying areas. A ballad contextualized the news: "O New-England, I understand/ with thee God is offended:/ And therefore He doth humble thee,/ till thou thy ways hast mended."[17] In the summer of 1676 Philip's forces were within 10 miles of Boston, but so many had been killed in battle that a final push was beyond their grasp; when Philip was captured and executed, the war was over. The tribes were left devastated, but 1 in every 16 colonists of fighting age was also dead, many women and children had been killed or carried into captivity, and 12 towns were totally destroyed.

For the Puritans, the war was an exceptionally clear example of judgment for their sins, and many ministers/writers went to work on it. Chief among them was Increase Mather, whose *Brief History of the War with the Indians of New-England* was filled with information about who, what, when, and where:

> March 17. This day the Indians fell upon Warwick, and burnt it down to the ground, all but one house. . . .

> May 11. A company of Indians assaulted the Town of Plimouth, burnt eleven Houses and five Barns therein. . . .[18]

Mather then contextualized the news by seeing God's hand not only in the beginning of the war but in its prolongation; reporting on the aftermath of one battle, he wrote, "Had the English immediately pursued the Victory begun, in all likelyhood there had been an end of our troubles: but God saw that neither yet were we fit for deliverance."[19]

Like other Puritan journalists, however, Mather was careful to juxtapose evidence of God's anger with dramatic news of God's mercy. When one house was about to be set on fire by hundreds of Indians who surrounded it, it appeared that

> Men and Women, and Children must have perished, either by unmerciful flames, or more unmerciful hands of wicked Men whose tender Mercies are cruelties, so that all hope that they should be saved was then taken in: but behold in this Jount of Difficulty and Extremity *the Lord is seen.* For in the very nick of opportunity God sent that worthy Major Willard, who with forty and eight men set upon the Indians and caused them to turn their backs . . . however we may be diminished and brought low through Oppression, Affliction, and Sorrow, yet our God will have compassion on us, and this his People shall not utterly perish.[20]

Mather's reportage was a prototype of the cavalry rescues beloved in Western movies, but the emphasis here was on God's grace, not man's heroism. And, Mather reported that when New Englanders recognized their reliance on that grace and pledged covenantal obedience, the war ended.[21]

Emphasizing the importance of accurate reporting, Mather concluded his news account with the words,

> Thus have we in brief, plain, and true story of the war with the Indians in New England, how it began, and how it hath made its progress, and what present hopes there are of a comfortable closure and conclusion of this trouble.[22]

He then appended to the main text of his pamphlet a sermon/editorial on the war, entitled "An Earnest Exhortation to the Inhabitants of New England." In it, Mather explicitly presented the "why" of the war: God's punishment because of sins such as "contention" and "pride."[23] But he also argued that too much guilt, like too much pride, could "run into extreams." Instead of pouring it on, Mather offered hope: God's "design, in bringing the Calamity upon us, is not to destroy us, but to humble us, and reform us, and to do us good in the latter end."[24]

The tradition of news and news analysis followed by hard-hitting but eventually upbeat editorial was beginning. The next step for American journalism came in 1681 when a general meeting of the Massachusetts ministers urged careful coverage of "Illustrious Providences," including

> Divine Judgements, Tempests, Floods, Earth-quakes, Thunders as are unusual, Strange Apparitions, or what ever else shall happen that is Prodigious, Witchcrafts, Diabolical Possessions, Remarkable Judgements upon noted Sinners: eminent Deliverances, and Answers of Prayer.[25]

Here was a definition of news not unlike our own in its emphasis on atypical, "man bites dog" events: "unusual" thunders, "strange" apparitions, and other "prodigious" or "remarkable" happenings—except that the "why" was different, because for the Puritans, all unusual occurrences showed a glimpse of God's usually invisible hand.

The ministers' resolution also provided a method for recording of events that anticipated the relation of correspondents and editors that would follow in later years. First, each minister was to be a correspondent, with the responsibility to "diligently enquire into, and Record such Illustrious Providences as have happened, or from time to time shall happen, in the places whereunto they do belong."[26] Second, to avoid the supplanting of fact by fiction, it would be important to rely on eyewitnesses and make sure "that the Witnesses of such notable Occurrents be likewise set down in Writing."[27] Third, it would be important to find a main writer/editor who "hath Leisure and Ability for the management of Such an undertaking."[28]

That person turned out to be Mather himself—and he proved himself to be right for the job. Mather read widely and well, citing in appropriate places in his *Essay* the work of leading scientists of the day such as Johannes Kepler, Tycho Brahe, and Robert Boyle. He himself wrote reports about comets, magnetism, lightning, thunder, and other natural phenomena, and would not report about an event unless a reliable source made a written, signed statement; after noting one extraordinary occurrence, he noted, "I would not have mentioned this relation, had I not received it from serious, faithfull, and Judicious hands. . . ."[29] Mather and others thought accuracy important because events were their report card signed by God, and they wanted to know where they stood, for better or for worse.[30]

American journalism began, in short, because the Puritans, in historian David Nord's words, were "obsessed with events, with the news. They could see all around them the providence of God. The great movements of celestial and human history were the prime considerations, but little things carried meaning as well."[31] In addition, Puritans set the stage for an honoring of the journalists themselves. The idea that God was acting in the world made journalism significant, for Increase Mather wrote that "it is proper for the Ministers of God to ingage themselves [in recording] the providentiall Dispensations of God."[32] Increase's son Cotton even wrote that

> To *regard* the illustrious displays of that Providence wherewith our Lord Christ governs the world, is a work, than which there is none more needful or useful for a Christian.[33]

By the 1680s, with journalism viewed as significant, and Boston becoming populous and prosperous enough to support a weekly newspaper, only a tense political situation was forestalling the establishment of one. Charles II, pressed by courtiers who wished to get their hands on New England's growing wealth, demanded that Massachusetts "make a *full Submission and entire Resignation* of their Charter to his pleasure." Removal of the charter would mean that freedom of the press and other liberties would not be under local control, but under regulation from London. Boston erupted in protest, and Increase Mather told a Boston town meeting that if Massachusetts acquiesced to royal pressure, "I verily Believe We Shall Sin against the GOD of Heaven." Mather asked the townspeople to say no, be patient, and trust God:

> If we make a *full Submission and entire Resignation* to Pleasure, we shall fall into the *Hands of Men* immediately. But if we do it not, we still keep ourselves in the *Hands of GOD;* we trust ourselves with His Providence: and who knows what GOD may do for us?[34]

For the next 6 years, as Mather's advice was taken in Massachusetts, crown and colony were at loggerheads. In 1684 the Court of Chancery in London vacated the charter, and soon all of New England came under the direct control of a royal governor who hated Puritans, Sir Edmund Andros. In 1687 John Wise and five of his associates received heavy fines for stating that taxes were legitimate only when levied by the Assembly.[35] In 1688 Andros, using power given by Charles' successor James II, ordered Increase Mather's son Cotton arrested for editing and supervising the printing of a pamphlet criticizing the Anglican state church. Cotton escaped imprisonment at that time but remained under threat from royal officials who repeatedly complained that the young writer "and others of his gang" opposed orders that "will not serve their interest (by them called the interest of Jesus Christ.)"[36]

Puritan prospects seemed bleak as Increase Mather headed to London to lobby for restoration of the Massachusetts charter. Even when William and Mary, backed by Parliament, seized power from James and in 1689 removed Andros from control of New England, the issue was still in doubt.[37] Journalistic freedom was under attack as the General Court, trying to show itself "trustworthy," warned in 1689 that those who published materials "tending to the disturbance of peace and subversion of the government" would be treated "with uttermost Severity."[38]

One journalistic friend of the Mathers decided at this difficult time to try publishing a Boston newspaper. Printer and writer Benjamin Harris knew first-hand the dangers of independent journalism. In 1679 he had been jailed for publishing in London an independent newspaper, *Domestick Intelligence;* sentenced to a harsh prison regime, Harris said simply, "I hope God will give me Patience to go through it."[39] After Harris did go through it he continued to print pamphlets that exposed wrong-doing. One of the pamphlets suggested that honest investigators followed in the footsteps of a "God [who] will not be mocked: There's no Dissembling with Heaven, no Masquerading with the All-seeing Eye of divine Vengeance."[40]

We know little about Harris the man; he seemed to stay in the background, content with reporting the good and ill deeds of others.[41] But several of his beliefs seem evident from his pamphlets. He stressed accuracy: One pamphlet reported that, "among the many Examples recited in this book, there are none but what are of approved Verity and well Attested."[42] At the same time, however, he wanted to send a clear message:

> I shall only add my Wishes and Prayers, that past Examples may prove future Warnings; and all that read these signal Instances of God's Judgments, may thereby . . . hold fast the Truth . . . conserve the pure Faith, and walk answerable thereunto in their Conversation, which will bring a Blessing in Life, and Comfort in Death, and Glory to Eternity.[43]

Harris clearly had no desire to be a martyr, and clearly felt that one prison term was enough. When royal officials searched his London printshop in 1686, seized pamphlets considered seditious, and issued a warrant for his arrest, Harris and his family escaped to Boston. There he opened a bookstore-coffeehouse and published *The New England Primer,* a best-selling schoolbook filled with Biblical quotations and moral precepts. But Harris could not stay away from journalism. Hoping that the departure of Andros pointed toward greater freedom, and apparently aided by Cotton Mather, Harris on September 25, 1690, published the first newspaper in America, *Publick Occurrences Both Foreign and Domestick.*[44]

Belief in Providence was evident throughout the four-page newspaper. Harris' expressed purpose for publishing it was in line with his previous writing: "That Memorable Occurrents of Divine Providence may not be neglected or forgotten, as they too often are."[45] Harris' combination of reporting and teaching showed as he reported "a day of Thanksgiving to God" for a good harvest and noted, concerning a tragedy averted, that God "assisted the Endeavours of the People to put out the Fire."[46] When a man committed suicide after his wife died, Harris explained that "The Devil took advantage of the Melancholy which he thereupon fell into."[47]

Such reports were politically safe, but when Harris emphasized God's sovereignty not only over local events but over matters involving international relations as well, controversy followed. Harris' report of mistreatment of prisoners by Mohawk Indians, and his criticism of royal officials for making an alliance with those Indians in order to defeat French forces in Canada, was based on his belief in Providence; Harris wrote,

> If Almighty God will have Canada to be subdu'd without the assistance of those miserable Salvages, in whom we have too much confided, we shall be glad, that there will be no Sacrifice offered up to the Devil, upon this occasion; God alone will have all the glory.[48]

Furthermore, Harris took seriously reports of adultery in the French court. British officials, hoping at that time for peace with France, were refraining from comments that could arouse popular concern about trusting those of low morals; because sexual restraint was not a common court occurrence in Restoration England either, they probably thought such news was a non-story. Harris, however, went ahead and reported that Louis XIV "is in much trouble (and fear) not only with us but also with his Son, who has revolted against him lately, and has great reason if reports be true, that the Father used to lie with the Sons Wife."[49]

Puritans who liked to emphasize God's sovereignty over all human activities were pleased with *Publick Occurrences;* Cotton Mather called it "a very noble, useful and laudable design."[50] The royal governor and his council were not amused, however: 4 days after publication the newspaper was suppressed, and Harris was told that any further issues would give him new prison nightmares. Harris gave in. He stayed in Massachusetts for a time and was given some public printing jobs because of his good behavior, but returned to England in 1695 and was arrested for publishing another short-lived newspaper, *Intelligence Domestick and Foreign.* A changed political climate allowed his release, however, and he was able to publish another newspaper, the *London Post,* from 1699 to 1705.[51]

The squelching of *Publick Occurrences* in 1690, by officials desperate to avoid offending the powers of London, represents a low tide in American journalism. But better news came in 1692, when Increase Mather was able to return from England with a new charter that was almost as good as the old one. The King retained the power to appoint a Governor who could veto legislation, but the people of Massachusetts could elect a legislature that alone had the power of taxation. (This part of the new contract became crucial during the 1760s and 1770s.)

Increase Mather had no time to rest, however, because as he returned to Boston, accusations of witchcraft followed by irregular trial procedures, were dominating the news from Salem. Until 1692 Massachusetts was not known as a center for witch-hunting: Historian Chadwick Hansen has pointed out that, "while Europe hanged and burned literally thousands of witches, executions in New England were few and far between."[52] From 1663 through 1691 trials of witches in New England led to twenty acquittals and only one execution, in large part because witches had to be tried for specific acts seen by two unimpeachable witnesses.[53] But in Salem in 1692, judges who overstepped traditional restraints began accepting what was called *spectral evidence,* and the trouble began.

Spectral evidence was testimony by individuals that they had seen not the accused, but a ghostly likeness or spectre of the accused, engaged in actions such as burning houses, sinking ships, and so on. The leading ministers of Massachusetts, including Increase and Cotton Mather, opposed the acceptance of spectral evidence. They did so not only because proceeding without witnesses of flesh and blood action violated common law practice, but because such action opened the door to abuses and general hysteria. In May 1692, before anyone was executed, Cotton Mather pleaded that the Salem judges not stress spectral evidence, for "It is very certain that the divells have sometimes represented the shapes of persons not only innocent, but also very virtuous."[54]

The Salem magistrates did not listen. Led by or leading local hysteria, they jailed several hundred residents and executed 20 from June through September 1692.[55] Cotton Mather was upset. In 1688 he had taken into his house a child diagnosed as suffering diabolical persecution and had apparently cured her. He offered in 1692 to make his own house a shelter home by taking six or more of those who said they were suffering from witchcraft.[56] But Cotton Mather did not publicly condemn Salem justice. Increase acted differently. He went to work investigating the trials and wrote a pamphlet, *Cases of Conscience,* that exposed the judicial practices of Salem and condemned use of spectral evidence.[57]

The Salem magistrates paid attention to Increase Mather's hard-hitting writing, or at least the public furor it stirred. Increase's insistence that self-incriminating confessions should not be accepted as proof hit home. His stress that only the testimony under oath of two actual witnesses, "as in any other Crime of a Capital nature," was sufficient to convict witches, was accepted.[58] Once Increase's pamphlet appeared, executions in Salem stopped. As Perry Miller concluded, "Increase Mather—and he alone—brought the murders to an end."[59] Cotton Mather's quiet protests had not stopped the hangings, but Increase Mather's bold journalism saved lives.

That was a signal triumph for the preacher-journalist. But the end of the witch trials also brought a signal defeat, one that has provided solid ammunition for centuries to those who hate the Mathers because they hate the Mathers' world view. Massachusetts Governor Phipps, worried about reaction in London to reports of New England justice gone berserk, "commanded" Cotton Mather to prepare a defense of judicial conduct in some of the trials.[60] Cotton Mather complied by rushing out an abysmal quasi-justification, *The Wonders of the Invisible World*. (Weird excerpts of it now find their way into history textbooks as "proof" of Puritan zaniness.)

Cotton Mather apparently realized he was doing a bad job even as he was doing it. He gave his hasty public relations work a clearly reluctant beginning: "I live by Neighbours that force me to produce these undeserved Lines."[61] He added an equally mournful note at the end by reporting that he had completed "the Service imposed upon me." In between, in Cotton Mather's most wildly excessive writing, came a pitiful attempt to semi-legitimize for the public what he had in private termed improper judicial procedure.

Perry Miller has pointed out that, because of Mather's defense of judicial murder, "thousands of Americans are still persuaded that Cotton Mather burned witches at Salem."[62] The truth is far more intriguing: Mather accepted a task he should have refused, completed it while gritting his teeth, and has received three centuries of abuse for that which he grudgingly defended. This is not to defend Mather: He disgraced himself. Had he stayed with what he knew to be true he would have stood alongside his father at this point as a 1690s pioneer of journalistic bravery. Sadly, at age 29, Cotton Mather still aimed to please.

Indirectly, the outcome of the charter and witch trial controversies contributed to two major developments in American journalism.

First, the witch trials showed that local governmental authorities could be deadly wrong. Massachusetts citizens began to show more caution in declaring guilty those arrested under ambiguous circumstances, including writers. In 1695 when Massachusetts charged Quaker pamphleteer Thomas Maule with printing "wicked Lyes and Slanders . . . upon Government" and also impugning the religious establishment, he shrewdly pleaded that a printed book was no more evidence of his guilt than "the spectre evidence is in law sufficient to prove a person accused by such evidence to be a witch."[63] When Maule was acquitted by the jury, press freedom had won its first major trial victory in America.[64] Maule celebrated by publishing in 1697 a pamphlet, *New-England Persecutors Mauled with their own Weapons.*[65]

Second, as a considerable degree of self-rule for Massachusetts was reestablished at the end of the century, leaders could return to Reformation principles and relax the censorship procedures that had stopped Benjamin Harris. Licensing laws remained on the books, but in 1700 Increase Mather published a treatise without a license, as did others. Moreover, even as ministers were complaining of theological laxity, the corruption story was being widely accepted, even by political officials, as the most appropriate narrative framework. That broad acceptance opened the way for publication in 1704 of the *Boston News-Letter,* America's first newspaper to last more than one issue.

The *News-Letter*'s first editor, Boston postmaster John Campbell, had good ties to both the political establishment and to theological leaders. Campbell's writing was duller than that of Benjamin Harris, but he also was ready to print bad news noting that an "awful Providence" was "a Warning to all others to watch against the wiles of our Grand Adversary."[66] Campbell faithfully recorded what Increase Mather had termed "extraordinary judgments," and also reported mercies such as the rapid extinguishing of a fire through "God's good signal Providence."

Like Harris, Campbell hoped through his newspaper to see "a great many Providences now Recorded, that would otherwise be lost."[67] He editorially attacked immorality, profaneness, and counterfeiting.[68] Like many of his predecessors, he stressed accuracy: When Campbell reported a minister's prayer at the hanging of six pirates in Boston in June 1704, he noted that he was quoting the prayer "as near as it could be taken in writing in the great crowd."[69] He made many errors but tried to apologize for even small ones, such as the dropping of a comma in one issue.

The popularity of news ballads and news sermons meant that Campbell could run more short news stories and leave some contextualization to others. For example, Campbell gave large space to a great storm that had created much damage in Europe and to the capture and execution of those six pirates, but did not need to contexualize the events fully; Campbell knew that Cotton Mather's sermon on the pirates, and Increase Mather's on the storm, were being published.[70] (Increase Mather was arguing that "We must be deaf indeed if such loud calls, if such astonishing Providences, do not at all awaken us."[71])

The *News-Letter* went on peacefully for the next decade and a half. It survived financially by mixing *corruption story* coverage with profitable publication of official notices. When a new postmaster, William Brooker, was appointed in 1719, Campbell continued publishing his newspaper and Brooker put out his own weekly, the *Boston Gazette.*[72] Two years later a third newspaper, the *New-England Courant,* edited by James Franklin, joined in. Then came one more aftermath of the witch trials, and the most remembered press dispute in Massachusetts colonial history, one that gave Cotton Mather a chance to make journalistic restitution for his cravenness during the witch trials nearly three decades before.[73]

The new conflict began in 1721 when Dr. Zabdiel Boylston, supported by

Cotton Mather, wanted to fight a smallpox epidemic raging in Boston by making use of the latest scientific innovation, inoculation. Dr. William Douglass, the only Boston physician with university training in medicine, knew for certain from his training that inoculation was dangerous nonsense. He tried to outflank Cotton Mather by appearing holier than him: Douglass charged that Boylston and Mather, instead of relying solely on God to fight disease, were restoring to "the extra groundless *Machinations of Men.*"[74]

Cotton Mather thought this argument was theological and scientific nonsense. By then he had matured enough to keep from buckling under, and also had confidence in his understanding of the medical questions involved. (He had become known as one of the leading scientists of his day and was voted a member of the Royal Society in London.) Mather argued that God often uses human agencies and accomplishments to serve godly ends, and maintained that position when anti-inoculation politicians attacked him sharply. At one point a committee of Boston selectmen told Boylston to stop inoculations, but Boylston refused and Mather stuck to his supportive position, despite taking great abuse from the *News-Letter* and *Courant.*[75]

Those editors sided with officialdom and opposed inoculation; in doing so, they brought up Mather's defense of the Salem witch trials, and argued that he was deluded then and deluded again.[76] Mather this time did not give in. Because the *Boston Gazette* favored inoculation, Mather and his associates had a ready vehicle for their ideas. The debate raged for weeks, until it became clear that inoculation worked. Mather had erred once before in a crucial situation, but this time his journalistic effort saved lives.[77]

PART II

MACROSTORIES IN CONFLICT

Chapter 4

The Establishment of American Press Liberty

By 1730 the last British attempt to reassert licensing control over the feisty Puritans had failed, and Massachusetts journalism was generally peaceful. Editors such as Bartholomew Green, who succeeded John Campbell as owner of the *News-Letter* in 1723, emphasized press responsibility to help readers know "how to order their prayers and praises to the Great God."[1] Local news continued to be reported in reverential context, as in this coverage of a storm:

> The Water flowed over our Wharffs and into our streets to a very surprising height. They say the Tide rose 20 Inches higher than ever was known before . . . The loss and damage sustained is very great. . . . Let us fear the GOD of heaven, who made the sea and the dry land, who commandeth & raiseth the stormy wind, which lifteth up the waves; who ruleth the raging of the sea, and when the waves thereof arise, He stilleth them.[2]

As editor during a relatively quiet time, Green had the luxury to be known not primarily as a combative journalist but as a gentle man. When he died in 1733, an obituary described Green as "a very humble and exemplary Christian" known for "keeping close and diligent to the work of his calling."[3] In that same year, however, New York editor John Peter Zenger was thrust into the vortex of a controversy that would determine whether the press liberty developed in reformed New England could spread through the other colonies.

Zenger's *New York Weekly Journal* was not the first newspaper outside of New England. Many had been starting in a generally north-to-south movement:

the *New York Gazette* in 1724, the *Maryland Gazette* in 1727, and the *South Carolina Gazette* in 1732.[4] The first newspaper outside New England, the *American Weekly Mercury* (Philadelphia, 1719) had even shown a willingness to see God's sovereignty in politics, although at a distance. Editor Andrew Bradford wrote that Massachusetts royal officials were "remarkable for Hypocrisy: And it is the general Opinion, that some of their Rulers are rais'd up and continued as a Scourge in the Hands of the Almighty for the Sins of the People."[5] But no one outside of Boston had dared to criticize officials close at hand.

Zenger, however, put into practice the ideas taught in the Dutch Reformed church at which he played the organ each Sabbath — God's sovereignty, the Bible above all. He took on William Cosby, New York's royal governor, who clearly thought he was above the law. When a farmer's cart slowed down Cosby's coach, the governor had his coachman beat the farmer with a horsewhip and nearly kill him. When Cosby desired some land owned by Indians, he stole their deed and burned it. When Cosby granted new lands to those who applied legally, he demanded and received bribes often amounting to one third of the estates. Cosby made enemies who were willing to fund Zenger's newspaper and provide anonymous articles for it, but it was Zenger whose name was on the newspaper, and it was Zenger who would go to jail.

Zenger first sent a message in the *Journal*'s second issue by differentiating an absolute monarchy from one based on Biblical principles of fixed law and limitations on power. In an absolute monarchy, the article argued, the "Will of the Prince" was over all, and "a Liberty of the Press to complain of Grievances" was impossible.[6] In a limited monarchy, however,

> Laws are known, fixed, and established. They are the streight Rule and sure Guide to direct the King, the Ministers, and other his Subjects: And therefore an Offense against the Laws is such an Offense against the Constitution as ought to receive a proper adequate Punishment.[7]

Law (applying biblical principles) was above the king, not under him, just as the Bible itself was over all human royalty.

Such a belief undermined the official story in another way as well. Marchamont Nedham under pressure concluded that might makes right, but an early essay in the *Journal* pointedly asked, "If we reverence men for their power alone, why do we not reverence the Devil, who has so much more power than men?"[8] The article concluded that respect was due "only to virtuous qualities and useful actions," and that it was therefore "as ridiculous and superstitious to adore great mischievous men as it is to worship a false god or Satan in the stead of God."[9] Subjects had the right to evaluate their king. Obedience was not guaranteed.

The *Journal* prominently featured "Cato's Letters," written in England by John Trenchard and Thomas Gordon. They argued that governmental authority must be limited, and that such limitation was possible only if individuals were free to speak the truth to those in power. Everyone was to be restrained by Biblical principles of conduct: "Power without control appertains to God alone, and no man ought to be trusted with what no man is equal to."[10] Zenger also reprinted sermons emphasizing freedom from the official story's faith in kingly wisdom. One, by Jonathan Dickinson, argued that "Every person in the world has an equal right to judge for themselves, in the affairs of conscience and eternal salvation."[11] Dickinson showed that the lessons of not only royal domination but Cromwellian rule had been learned; he commented, "What dreadful work has been made in the world by using methods of force in matters of opinion and conscience."[12]

New York's royal governor, not wanting to admit that the state's domain was limited, brought a charge of "seditious libel" again Zenger and threw him into jail. Journalists at that time had little defense against such accusations. Journalists who proved that their statements were true might be even worse off. (Under English law truth made the libel worse by making it more likely that the statements would decrease public support for the king and his officials; a common legal expression was "the greater the truth, the greater the libel.") Jurors were only to determine whether the accused actually had printed the objectionable publication. If they agreed that he had, judges decided whether the statements in question were critical and deserved punishment.

The story of Zenger's trial on August 4, 1735, has often been told. The situation certainly was dramatic: Judges in their red robes and white wigs were ready to convict Zenger for his criticism of the royal governor, but the jury included "common People" among whom Zenger's newspaper had "gain'd some credit." A packed courtroom sympathetic to Zenger kept the judges from silencing defense attorney Andrew Hamilton when he turned directly to the jurors and suggested that they disobey English law: Hamilton wanted them to declare Zenger innocent even though he admitted to printing the material in question and was thus under the power of the judges. Hamilton argued that Zenger deserved such support because he had been "exposing and opposing arbitrary power by speaking and writing Truth," and the jurors agreed.[13] They delivered a verdict of "not guilty"; royal officials decided not to provoke a riot; Zenger went free.[14]

The story has often been told, but why it turned out as it did has rarely been understood. According to one leading textbook, *The Press and America,* the trial began because of a class uprising by "wealthy merchants and landowners" and ended with popular embrace of a "right to criticize officials."[15] But *The Press and America,* along with the other major 20th-century texts, does not explain what Zenger's defense of "speaking and writing Truth" meant in the context of his era. The trial records show that "Truth" was equated with the Bible, and Zenger was said to be merely following the lead of the Bible, which attacked corrupt leaders as "blind watchmen" and "greedy dogs that can never have enough." Zenger's defense, essentially, was that if God's authors produced such a critique, so could New York's.[16]

The context of Zenger's defense is clarified further by an essay published in his newspaper, the *New York Journal,* in 1733. The article proposed that true freedom required the subjecting of consciences "to divine authority," because only through the Bible would people know how to use liberty without turning it into license.[17] In historical context, then, the Zenger verdict was not what the texts say it was: a "class uprising" that led to a proclamation of freedom *from* any restraint. Instead, the journalistic desire to be governed by "Truth" in this context was a desire to *accept* a system of internal restraints developed from biblical principles.

In short, Hamilton won the case not by proposing a new revelation, but by placing Zenger in the line of Martin Luther, John Foxe, John Stubbes, March-amont Nedham, Increase Mather, and others. Zenger was one more victim of what Hamilton called "the Flame of Prosecutions upon Informations, set on Foot by the Government, to deprive a People of the Right of Remonstrating (and complaining too), of the arbitrary Attempts of Men in Power."[18] Only the spread of Reformation principles concerning literacy, independent journalism, and the rights of citizens to read for themselves, allowed Hamilton to turn to the jurors and ask them to support the truth-teller, regardless of what royal officials desired.[19]

The verdict meant little legally: A runaway jury had disobeyed established English law and gotten away with it. But as the verdict reverberated through the colonies and through England itself, it encouraged corruption story proponents and discouraged the officials from trying printers for seditious libel; no case of that sort was brought anywhere in America after 1735. The year after the Zenger case, Virginia had its first newspaper—the *Virginia Gazette,* published in Williamsburg. Editor William Parks exposed corruption, including the stealing of sheep by a member of Virginia's House of Burgesses. When Parks was threatened with prosecution, he used the Zenger defense of truth-telling and produced court records showing the accusation was accurate; the case against Parks was dropped. By 1750 there were 14 weekly newspapers published in the British colonies, and the first semiweekly and triweekly newspapers had emerged.

Increasingly, the newspapers were independent of governmental control and free to provide, as *Maryland Gazette* editor Jonas Green promised his readers, not just "a Weekly Account of the most remarkable Occurrences, foreign and domestic," but also an examination of "whatever may conduce to the Promotion of Virtue and Learning, the Suppression of Vice and Immorality, and the Instruction as well as Entertainment of our Readers."[20] Newspapers ran lively debates on many subjects, including politics. The idea that fundamental law came from God, not from the state or from any persons, was opening the door to questioning of many traditions, including even monarchical control. Journalist Elisha Williams argued in 1744 that:

The Powers that be in Great Britain are the Government therein according to its own Constitution:—If then the higher Powers for the Administration rule not according to that Constitution, or if any King thereof shall rule so, as to change the Government from legal to arbitrary . . . no Subjection [is] due to it.[21]

Journalists were the ones who would have "Eyes to see" when rulers went "out of the Line of their Power."[22]

At the same time, the lessons of the failed Puritan Revolution — particularly those concerning the lure and potential abuse of power—were well known to the colonists. Recent college graduate Samuel Adams wrote in 1748,

Neither the wisest constitution nor the wisest laws will secure the liberty and happiness of a people whose manners are universally corrupt. He therefore is the truest friend to the liberty of his country who tries most to promote its virtue.[23]

His conclusion was:

The sum of all is, if we would most truly enjoy this gift of Heaven, let us become a virtuous people: then shall we both deserve and enjoy it. While, on the other hand, if we are universally vicious and debauched in our manners, though the form of our Constitution carries the face of the most exalted freedom, we shall in reality be the most abject slaves.[24]

During the Seven Years (French and Indian) War of 1756 to 1763, colonial newspapers were free to bring charges of graft against those supplying American troops; for example, the *New-York Gazette and Weekly Post-Boy* reported that many of the guns purchased were out of date and practically useless, and joked that beef supplied for soldiers' food was more effective than powder because its odor would drive away the enemy. That such charges, when well-founded, could be made without legal repercussion, showed how firmly independent journalism was established in America. The colonists found themselves surprised, then, after the war, when England began to crack down.

Samuel Adams led the protests in Massachusetts. If transported to our present age of television journalism, Adams would be a washout: he had a sunken chest, a sallow complexion and "wishy-washy gray eyes."[25] Adams' lips twitched and trembled, for he suffered from palsy. His clothes were drab and sometimes sloppy. Besides, Adams was a financial misfit who lived in an old, shabby house, and wrote much but earned little. John Adams put the best complexion on the surface prospects of his cousin when he wrote that "in common appearance he was a plain, simple, decent citizen, of middling stature, dress, and manners."[26]

Looking beyond appearances, however, Adams possessed advantages. His good classical education made ancient times as real to him as his own; references to the political ups and downs of ancient Israel, Greece, and Rome came easily to his pen. He had the ability to write under almost any conditions. Adams typically composed his columns after evening prayers; his wife Elizabeth would go to bed but would sometimes wake in the middle of the night and hear only the sound of her husband's quill pen scratching on and on. But when Adams had to, he could write forceful prose amidst a town meeting.

Adams was also in the right place, at what became the right time. He lived in America's largest port city, and the second largest city in all of the colonies, after Philadelphia. The 20,000 residents of Boston in 1770 may not seem like many now, but at that time they were enough to support six weekly newspapers, including, during the decade before revolutionary warfare broke out, the *Boston Gazette*. The *Gazette* was published every Monday afternoon, and a crowd often awaited its issues hot off the press. Adams had a regular column but never signed his own name to it. Instead, he used a pen name—such as "A Puritan"—that connected him with independent journalism's honorable lineage. Other columnists did the same; for example, Josiah Quincy, Jr. signed his columns, "Marchamont Nedham."

Furthermore, Adams was modest. He did not write about himself, and had no problem with being in the background. Many journalists today make themselves the stars of their stories, but Adams believed that "political literature was to be as selfless as politics itself, designed to promote its cause, not its author."[27] Adams' self-effacement has made life harder for some historians: John Adams wrote that his cousin's personality would "never be accurately known to posterity, as it was never sufficiently known to its own age." (A minister wrote on October 3, 1803, the day after Adams' death, that there had been "an impenetrable secrecy" about him.[28]) But Adams' willingness to have others take the credit worked wonders during his time. He chaired town meetings and led the applause for those who needed bucking up; for example, he pulled John Hancock onto the patriot side and promoted Hancock's career.

And, Adams had a strong belief in the God of the Bible. The Great Awakening had made a permanent theological impression on him. That impression is evident in Adams' writings and actions, in his prayers each morning and in his family Bible reading each evening. He frequently emphasized the importance of "Endeavors to promote the spiritual kingdom of Jesus Christ," and in good or bad times wrote of the need "to submit to the Dispensations of Heaven, Whose Ways are ever gracious, ever just.' "[29] During the struggle of the 1760s and 1770s Adams regularly set aside days of fasting and prayer to "seek the Lord." In 1777, when Adams wrote to a friend about the high points of one celebration, he stressed the sermon delivered that day; the friend wrote back, "An epicure would have said something about the clams, but you turn me to the prophet Isaiah."[30]

Adams, in short, worked within the tradition of Foxe, Mather, and others who called for reformation, not social revolution. John Adams called Samuel the Calvin of his day, and "a Calvinist" to the core.[31] (William Tudor in 1823 called Adams "a strict Calvinist . . . no individual of his day had so much the feelings of the ancient puritans." For Tudor, that meant Adams had "too much sternness and pious bigotry."[32]) Yet, Adams did not merely rely on established procedures; he advanced the practice and significance of American journalism in four ways.

First, observing that "mankind are governed more by their feelings than by reason," Adams emphasized appeals to the whole person, not just to a disembodied intellect.[33] Emotions were to be taken seriously, for the "fears and jealousies of the people are not always groundless: And when they become general, it is not to be presum'd that they are; for the people in general seldom complain, without some good reason.[34] Adams assumed democratically that an issue of importance to the populace is not silly.[35] He argued that ordinary citizens could "distinguish between *realities* and *sounds*'; and by a proper use of that reason which Heaven has given them,' they can judge, as well as their betters, when there is danger of *slavery*."[36]

Second, Adams emphasized investigative reporting more vigorously than any American journalist before him had: He did so because "Publick Liberty will not long survive the Loss of publick Virtue."[37] Adams argued that it was vital to track activities of those:

> who are watching every Opportunity to turn the good or ill Fortune of their Country, and they care not which to their own private Advantage. . . . Such Men there always have been & always will be, till human Nature itself shall be substantially meliorated.[38]

He went on to praise exposure of leaders who "having gained the Confidence of their Country, are sacrilegiously employing their Talents to the Ruin of its Affairs, for their own private Emolument."[39] Adams, however, emphasized restraint in such exposure, as he emphasized restraint in all actions: Only those "capable of doing great Mischief" should be held up "to the publick Eye."[40]

Third, Adams defined more thoroughly than his predecessors the limits of protest. His strong sense of lawfulness is indicated by his reactions to two incidents, the Stamp Act demonstrations of August 1765, and the related attacks on private homes such as that of Thomas Hutchinson, the royal governor. Adams favored the former action because legislative methods and petitions already had failed; the House of Commons would not listen, so the demonstration "was the only Method whereby they could make known their Objections to Measures."[41] He opposed the assault on the Hutchinson home, calling it an action of "a truly *mobbish* Nature."[42] When Adams and his colleagues planned the Boston Tea Party, they made it clear that nothing except tea was to be destroyed; when the patriots dressed as "Indians" accidentally broke a padlock, they later replaced it.[43]

So far was Adams from revolution in the way the term is currently understood that he wrote, in the *Boston Gazette* in 1768, that the security of right and property, is the great end of government. Surely, then, such measures as tend to render right and property precarious, tend to destroy both property and government; for these must stand and fall together.[44]

He opposed dictatorship, whether popular or monarchical:

The Utopian schemes of levelling, and a community of goods, are as visionary and impracticable, as those which vest all property in the Crown, are arbitrary, despotic, and in our government unconstitutional. Now what property can the colonists be conceived to have, if their money may be granted away by others, without their consent?[45]

Some of the patriots did not share Adams' emphasis on restraint, and it is not hard to compile a list of patriots' "mobbish" acts. Yet the principles of the revolutionaries, and most of their practice, emphasized defense of property and freedom of political speech.

Fourth, Adams argued that writers should pay careful attention to the connection between attacks on political rights and attempts to restrict religious rights. In a *Boston Gazette* column that he signed, "A Puritan," Adams described how he was pleased with attention paid to politics but

surpriz'd to find, that so little attention is given to the danger we are in, of the utter loss of those *religious Rights,* the enjoyment of which our good forefathers had more especially in their intention, when they explored and settled this new world.[46]

He saw acquiescence in political slavery as preparation for submission to religious slavery:

I could not help fancying that the Stamp-Act itself was contrived with a design only to inure the people to the habit of contemplating themselves as the slaves of men; and the transition from thence to a subjection to Satan, is mighty easy.[47]

It is astounding that some historians have seen Adams solely as a political plotter; for Adams, the religious base came first. One of his arguments against imposed taxes was that the money could go for establishment of a state "Episcopate in America . . . the revenue raised in America, for ought we can tell, may be constitutionally applied towards the support of prelacy. . ."[48]

Adams favored investigative reporting and appropriate emotional appeal because he wanted readers to know about and *care about* attempts to take away their freedom, political and religious. He opposed destructive revolutionary acts because he saw them as eventually reducing freedom, political and religious— with the results of the English civil war as a case in point. From all these strands

Adams was able to weave an understanding of when journalists, and citizens generally, should be willing to fight.

The understanding came out of the Puritan idea of *covenant* and its political–economic corollary, *contract*. In 1765 Adams had written of himself and his neighbors,

> We are the Descendants of Ancestors remarkable for their Zeal for true Religion & Liberty: When they found it was no longer possible for them to bear any Part in the Support of this glorious Cause in their Native Country England, they transplanted themselves at their own very great Expence, into the Wilds of America. . . .[49]

Their ancestors took those risks in order to establish "the Worship of God, according to their best Judgment, upon the Plan of the new Testament; to maintain it among themselves, and transmit it to their Posterity."[50] Crucially, they did so on the basis of a signed contract: "A Charter was granted them by King Charles the first," Adams noted, and "a successor charter" was granted (through the lobbying of Increase Mather) in 1691.[51]

Adams, in column after column, explained the basis of the contract: The colonists "promised the King to enlarge his Dominion, on their own Charge, provided that They & their Posterity might enjoy such & such Privileges."[52] Adams wrote that the colonists "have performed their Part, & for the King to deprive their Posterity of the Privileges, therein granted, would carry the Face of Injustice in it." Colloquially, a deal's a deal, and London's attempt to tax the colonists was one indication that the deal was being broken, because the charter gave the colonists "an exclusive Right to make Laws for our own internal Government & Taxation."[53]

In emphasizing the breaking of the contract, Adams was not developing new political theology. John Calvin had written that "Every commonwealth rests upon laws and agreements," and had then noted "the mutual obligation of head and members." John Cotton, following that line of argument, had concluded that "the rights of him who dissolves the contract are forfeited."[54] Puritans long had insisted that just as God establishes a covenant with man, so kings have a contract with their subjects (and although God would never break His agreement, kings often did). But Adams took that idea and developed from it a theory of when writers should criticize and when they should refrain from criticism. Once a government had been established along biblical principles, criticism of its departure from those principles was proper—but criticism designed to topple the government in order to establish it on new principles was improper.

To put this another way, Adams in the 1770s approved of a conservative revolution designed to restore previously contracted rights, but not a violent social revolution designed to establish new conditions. This made sense not only as a pragmatic way to avoid bloodshed and chaos, but because of Adams' belief (expressed as early as 1748) that societies in any case represent the strengths and weaknesses of their members. The real need in a contract-based society was individual change (which can lead to social change) and not social revolution.

Other New England writers also argued that London had broken its contract with the colonists. John Lathrop declared in 1774 that a person who "makes an alteration in the established constitution, whether he be a subject or a ruler, is guilty of treason." He asserted that colonists "may and ought, to resist, and even make war against those rulers who leap the bounds prescribed them by the constitution, and attempt to oppress and enslave the subjects. . . ."[55] Lathrop, after referring to writings of Luther, Calvin, Melancthon, and Zwingli, concluded that King and Parliament, by attempting to lord it over colonial assemblies, were overthrowing England's constitution.[56]

During the 1770s patriots outside of New England also expressed such ideas. The single book most quoted by Americans during the founding era was the Book of Deuteronomy, with its emphasis on covenant.[57] The *South-Carolina Gazette* expressed concern that British officials were claiming "the power of breaking all our charters."[58] A columnist in the *Pennsylvania Evening Post* declared that "resisting the *just* and *lawful* power of government" was rebellion but resisting "*unjust* and *usurped* power was not."[59] The *Virginia Gazette* saw British authorities moving to apply "the Rod of Despotism" to "every Colony that moves in Defence of Liberty."[60] In Connecticut, the *Norwich Packet* argued that liberty was like an inheritance, "a sacred deposit which it would be treason against Heaven to betray."[61]

The patriotic journalists sometimes used non-political stories to make their points. The *Boston Evening-Post* reported a hanging: "Saturday last was executed Harry Halbert, pursuant to his sentence, for the murder of the son of Jacob Wollman.—He will never pay any of the taxes unjustly laid on these once happy lands."[62] Rather than raging against the British system generally, they pointed to specific violations of the contract. Massachusetts citizens were supposed to be able to control their own government, with the royal governor having a relatively minor role and not a large bureaucracy—but Josiah Quincy, Jr., in the *Boston Gazette,* showed how "pensioners, stipendiaries, and salary-men" were "hourly multiplying on us."[63] In New Hampshire, the Executive Council was supposed to provide the governor with a broad array of colonists' views; the colony's correspondent complained in the *Boston Evening-Post* that relatives of Governor John Wentworth filled all but one Council seat.[64]

Increasingly, the patriot journalists saw such exposure of corruption as part of their calling. Adams wrote in the *Boston Gazette,* "There is nothing so *fretting* and *vexatious,* nothing so justly TERRIBLE to tyrants, and their tools and abettors, as a FREE PRESS."[65] Isaiah Thomas, editor of *The Massachusetts Spy,* wrote that, without a free press, there would be "padlocks on our lips, fetters on our legs, and only our hands left at liberty to slave for our worse than Egyptian task masters. . . ."[66] But again, the emphasis was on officeholders' betrayal of existing laws, not on revolutionary imposition of new ones: The mission of the

Boston Gazette, its editors declared, was to "strip the serpents of their stings, & consign to disgrace, all those guileful betrayers of their country."[67]

Examination of many of the stories leading up to the revolution shows how steeped in the Bible the patriot journalists were. That is not surprising, because in New England alone during 1776, ministers were "delivering over two thousand discourses a week and publishing them at an unprecedented rate that outnumbered secular pamphlets (from all the colonies) by a ratio of more than four to one."[68] That is also not surprising because, right up to the revolutionary war, ballads concerning bad news were still putting their stories in corruption story context; for example, in 1774, a fire story noted that "There's not a Day goes by, but we behold/ A Truth, that Men need often to be told:/ That this vain World with all it's glit'ring Toys,/ Does but deceive the Mind with empty Joys."[69] It was natural for the *Massachusetts Spy* to comment simply but evocatively, when the Intolerable Acts closed the Port of Boston, "Tell it in Gath, publish it in Ashkelon."[70]

Under extreme pressure, Adams' response to the Intolerable Acts, contained in a resolution passed by Suffolk County, continued to emphasize contract, not revolution. The resolution recommended economic sanctions against the British and proposed the formation of an armed patriot militia, but it also attacked any attempt

> by unthinking persons to commit outrage upon private property; we would heartily recommend to all persons of this community not to engage in riots, routs, or licentious attacks upon the properties of any person whatsoever, as being subversive of all order and government.[71]

Newspapers portrayed the war, once begun, as a defense of order and legitimate government: "We have taken up arms, it is true," the *Virginia Gazette* noted, "but this we have an undoubted right to do, in defence of the British constitution."[72]

Samuel Adams had his counterparts in other colonies: Cornelius Harnett was called "the Samuel Adams of North Carolina" and Charles Thomson was called "the Samuel Adams of Philadelphia."[73] But Adams himself was the best at taking Bible based theories and heightening them journalistically. His printed response to the adoption of the Declaration of Independence shows Adams at his finest, and shows his sense of God's providence."[74] Adams began,

> We have explored the temple of royalty, and found that the idol we have bowed down to has eyes which see not, ears that hear not our prayers, and a heart like the nether millstone. We have this day restored the Sovereign to whom alone men ought to be obedient.[75]

He explained that previous generations:

lopped off, indeed, some of the branches of Popery, but they left the root and stock when they left us under the domination of human systems and decisions, usurping the infallibility which can be attributed to revelation alone. They dethroned one usurper, only to raise up another; they refused allegiance to the Pope, only to place the civil magistrate in the throne of Christ, vested with authority to enact laws and inflict penalties in his kingdom.[76]

Adams followed those statements with his key rhetorical question: "Were the talents and virtues which Heaven has bestowed on men given merely to make them more obedient drudges, to be sacrificed to the follies and ambition of a few. . .?" He responded,

What an affront to the King of the universe to maintain that the happiness of a monster sunk in debauchery . . . is more precious in his sight than that of millions of his suppliant creatures who do justice, love mercy, and walk humbly with their God![77]

He crescendoed with the editorial fervency that moved a generation:

The hand of Heaven appears to have led us on to be, perhaps, humble instruments and means in the great providential dispensation which is completing. We have fled from the political Sodom; let us not look back, lest we perish and become a monument of infamy and derision to the world![78]

Chapter 5

First Surge of the Oppression Story

In the end, the patriots saw their victory as a victory of ideas, disseminated through newspapers. As the editor of the *New York Journal* noted in a letter to Adams, "It was by means of News papers that we receiv'd & spread the Notice of the tyrannical Designs formed against America, and kindled a Spirit that has been sufficient to repel them."[1] British officials had a different perspective: Admiral Howe's secretary Ambrose Serles complained,

> Among other Engines, which have raised the present Commotion next to the indecent Harranges of the Prechers, none has a more extensive or stronger influence than the Newspapers of the respective Colonies.[2]

British leaders were appalled that Samuel Adams' central idea of corruption in leadership had defeated their official story of faith in King.

Yet, had the British better known their own country's history, the shock would have been less. Adams, continuing what John Foxe had begun two centuries ago, was merely showing once again that nations rose and fell primarily because of world views, often communicated through journalistic means. By the 1760s, 250 years had passed since Martin Luther first showed the potential power of journalism. During that time, the uses of sensationalism, investigation, and accurate exposure had become apparent, and principles of reforming but non-revolutionary journalism and contextualized coverage had been established.

Those concepts formed the baseline for journalism in the new republic. Some historians call the last quarter of the 18th century a deistic period, and sentiment of that sort certainly was present and growing among societal elites at Harvard College and elsewhere. Yet, in reporting of both crime and political news, news ballads and newspapers of the 1780s and 1790s continued the corruption story emphasis, with its "good news" conclusion. Coverage of a New Hampshire execution, for example, emphasized the evil that had been done, but concluded "O may that God/ Who gave his only Son,/ Give you his grace, in Heaven a place,/ For Jesus' sake—Amen."[3]

Newspapers, rather than embracing deism, often portrayed it as containing the seeds of its own destruction. In 1782, for example, 6 days after a man had killed his wife and four children and then himself, the *Connecticut Courant* reported the news and then contextualized: The perpetrator had

> rejected all Revelation as imposition, and (as he expresses himself) 'renouncing all the popular Religions of the world, intended to die a proper Deist.' Having discarded all ideas of moral good and evil, he considered himself, and all the human race, as mere machines; and that he had a right to dispose of his own and the lives of his family.[4]

The *Courant* related how the man gave opiates to his family and then went around slaughtering the sleepers with knife and ax—but the incident really began when the man "adopted this new theoretic system which he now put in practice."[5] Ideas had consequences.

The most famous journalistic work of the 1780s was *The Federalist,* a collection of 95 columns published in New York newspapers during 1787 and 1788. The columns, written under the pen name of "Publius" by Alexander Hamilton, James Madison, and John Jay, and designed to convince New York voters to ratify the Constitution, showed a thoroughly biblical view of the effects of sin on political life. Madison argued that "faction"—power-grabbing attempts by groups of citizens "united and actuated by some common impulse of passion, adverse to the rights of other citizens"—was impossible to avoid because it grew out of "the nature of man."[6] Hamilton emphasized the "active and imperious control over human conduct" that "momentary passions and immediate interests" would "invariably" assume.[7]

Other pen-named columnists of the period also argued that the nature of man would lead to attempts at dictatorship, unless careful restraint was maintained. "Brutus" (probably Robert Yates, an Albany lawyer) wrote, "It is a truth confirmed by the unerring experience of ages that every man, and every body of men, invested with power, are ever disposed to increase it"; lust for power was "implanted in human nature."[8] The only way to fight the lust was to divide in order to avoid conquest—to limit and decentralize governmental power and to allow private interests to check each other. As Madison wrote in *Federalist* No. 51,

The policy of supplying, by opposite and rival interests, the defect of better motives, might be traced through the whole system of human affairs, private as well as public. We see it particularly displayed in all the subordinate distributions of power, where the constant aim is to divide and arrange the several offices in such a manner as that each may be a check on the other; that the private interest of every individual may be a sentinel over the public rights. These inventions of prudence cannot be less requisite in the distribution of the supreme power of the state.[9]

The press also had a vital role in this slow but freedom-preserving system of checks and balances. John Adams, after noting that the Constitution stipulated the election of key leaders, asked "How are their characters and conduct to be known to their constituents but by the press? If the press is stopped and the people kept in Ignorance we had much better have the first magistrate and Senators hereditary."[10] In Alexandria, Virginia, the *Gazette* also thought the press was vital in the plan to limit governmental power, for

Here too public men and measures are scrutinized. Should any man or body of men dare to form a system against our interests, by this means it will be unfolded to the great body of the people, and the alarm instantly spread through every part of the continent. In this way only, can we know how far our public servants perform the duties of their respective stations.[11]

Such ideas underlay the First Amendment's insistence that "Congress shall make no law . . . abridging the freedom of speech, or of the press." Cromwellian restrictions on the press following the English Civil War showed how quickly a victorious government might clamp down on those trying to check its power; freedom needed to be maintained. Yet, the freedom was not to be absolute. As John Allen of Connecticut argued,

Because the Constitution guarantees the freedom of the press, am I at liberty to falsely call you a thief, a murderer, an atheist? The freedom of the press was never understood to give the right of publishing falsehoods and slanders, nor of exciting sedition, insurrection, and slaughter with impunity. A man was always answerable for the malicious publication of falsehood.[12]

John Adams put it succinctly: Journalism is to be free "within the bounds of truth."[13] Pennsylvania adopted the Zenger principle of truth as a defense in its libel law, and other states would follow.

The first major test of newly established press freedom in America grew out of the French Revolution. France, after turning aside opportunities for Reformation during the 1500s, never had developed decentralized spheres of authority: king and church together continued to claim all power. France never had developed the mass literacy and movement toward independent journalism that animated English during the 1600s and its American colonies during the 1700s. When the

monarchy fell in 1789 and church power also diminished, journalists untrained
in self-restraint leaped into the enormous vacuum. As historian James Billington
has noted, "In revolutionary France journalism rapidly arrogated to itself the
Church's former role as the propagator of values, models, and symbols for society
at large."[14]

Those French journalistic values were very different from those of Samuel
Adams or the *Federalist* authors. French journalists such as Marat were students
of Jean-Jacques Rousseau, who demanded not a restrained state but a total
state. Rousseau argued that man was essentially good and would, with a proper
education, act virtuously. Education was too important to be trusted to parents
or churches, so it would be up to the state to teach all children to become "social
men by their natures and citizens by their inclinations—they will be one, they will
be good, they will be happy, and their happiness will be that of the Republic."[15]

As Paul Johnson has noted, Rousseau's ideas demanded total submission of
all individuals to the state. The ideal constitution Rousseau drafted for Corsica
required all citizens to swear, "I join myself, body, goods, will and all my
powers, to the Corsican Nation, granting her ownership of me, of myself and all
who depend on me." State-controlled citizens would be happy, because all would
be trained to like their master and to find their personal significance in its grace:
"For being nothing except by [the state], they will be nothing except for it. It will
have all they have and will be all they are." State control of communication was
thus a complement to state control of education, because "those who control a
people's opinions control its actions."

Some of this may sound gruesome, but the goal was to create a new type of
person by creating a new environment. Rousseau argued that "Everything is at
root dependent on politics," because everything can change if only a new social
system is created: "Vices belong less to man, than to man badly governed."
Individuals had no rights when they stood against the "General Will." This was
completely the opposite of the American pattern of a limited government designed
to keep sinful men from gaining any more power than absolutely necessary. It
also ran counter to the American concept of a limiting press, one designed not to
rule but to report on wrongdoing and confront readers with the workings of
Providence.

Ideas had consequences. Cromwell had executed a king and several others;
the French revolutionaries executed 20,000 in 2 years, then turned on themselves.
For a short time after 1789 all French journalists had some freedom. Then only
the few in power did, and opponents risked their lives: In 1793 the French
National Council decreed the death penalty for anyone who was convicted of
writing anything that promoted dissolution of the National Assembly or restoration of the monarchy. (Two journalists were executed, 56 more were arrested or
exiled, 42 journals were suspended, and 11 presses were smashed.) Eventually,
no journalists had freedom, as a military dictator, Napoleon Bonaparte, seized
power.

French journalists, demanding much, helped to create the conditions under which all could be lost. American journalists had grounded themselves in firmly established legal principles, but the French revolutionaries basked in illegality. The American Revolution was a defense of established rights, but the French revolution was an offensive for new entitlements. The American Revolution had fixed goals, but the French Revolution was a star trek—"let's head out there."

Different goals created different reactions. Because the American Revolution was limited, resistance to it was limited. Because the French revolution was unlimited, resistance to it inevitably would grow. That was fine, believed the revolutionaries, because their goal was to break down everything; the current environment was one of *oppression*. Individual change was insufficient, and those who strove for it were selfish, but through total transformation of the oppressive environment mankind could be transformed. Faith that this could occur through governmental action, if vast power were put in the right hands, underlies what I call the *oppression story*. Journalists saw themselves as the transformers; for example, Nicholas Bonneville, editor of *Le Tribun de Peuple,* saw his journal as a "circle of light" whose writers were to be "simultaneously a centre of light and a body of resistance." They were to be "legislators of the universe," preparing a "vast plan of universal regeneration" based on belief in "the Infallibility of the People."[16] But, because the people were to act according to what journalists told them, for Bonneville that pledge essentially meant, "I believe in my own infallibility."

In the United States, a few writers heavily influenced by Rousseauian thought also took that pledge. The leader of the pack was Benjamin Franklin Bache, who had been educated in France while living there with his grandfather Ben Franklin. Bache demanded direct rule by "the people" who were coursing in the streets, and cursed those advocates of separation of power who pointed out the virtues of representative democracy. Typical of Bache's style was his labeling of George Washington as "the man who is the source of all the misfortune of our country."[17] He went on to charge Washington with having "debauched" and "deceived" Americans, and then left as his successor "bald, blind, crippled, toothless Adams."[18]

Adams during his presidency also was regularly defamed by francophile editors such as James Callender, who falsely called Adams a traitor and charged that he had "proved faithful and serviceable to the British interest."[19] Adams was bald, but he could see, walk, and bite back. He opposed plans of Bache and others that "would lead in practice to a hidden despotism, concealed under the party-colored garment of democracy." He attacked those set on "contaminating the country with the foul abomination of the French revolution."[20] Speaker of the House Jonathan Dayton warned of a French-style revolution in America, with assistance from the French navy and French troops invading from the former French territories of Canada and Louisiana. Lawyer Jonathan Hopkinson warned Americans that Bache and his supporters desire "the overthrow of your government and constitution."[21]

Underlying the danger were the ideas; one congressman attacked philosophers who believed in "the perfectability of mankind" and thus became the "pioneers of revolution."[22] Yale University President Timothy Dwight warned of the danger of "the Bible cast into a bonfire . . . our wives and daughters the victims of legal prostitution . . . our sons become the disciples of Voltaire . . ."[23] Some leading journalists were seen as revolutionary moles; Bache, for example, was depicted as a French agent, a "dull-edged, dull-eyed, hagard-looking hireling of France," and Thomas Paine's radicalism and atheism was much decried.[24]

The controversy led to a lowering of self-restraint on both sides. Supreme Court chief justice McKean in 1798 accurately described conditions when he noted "the envenomed scurrility that has raged in pamphlets and newspapers printed in Philadelphia for several years past, insomuch that libeling has become a national crime." He added:

> the contest has been who could call names in the greatest variety of phrases; who could mangle the greatest number of characters, or who could excel in the magnitude of their lies; hence the honor of families has been stained, the highest posts rendered cheap and vile in the sight of the people, and the greatest services and virtue blasted.[25]

How easy it is to tear down, as editor John Dillingham had noted following the Cromwellian takeover in England.

Critics of the press revived the common mid-century distinction between liberty and license—and there was widespread concern that journalists were not using wisely the freedom they had gained. One of Benjamin Franklin's last statements about journalism was a complaint:

> Now many of our printers make no scruple of gratifying the malice of individuals by false accusations of the fairest characters among themselves, augmenting animosity even to the producing of duels, and are, moreover, so indiscreet as to print scurrilous reflections on the government of neighboring states, and even on the conduct of our best national allies, which may be attended with the most pernicious consequences.[26]

Franklin proposed a combination: freedom of the press plus "liberty of the cudgel." Libel laws should be tougher, Franklin suggested, for government officials "at the same time that they secure the person of a citizen from assaults, they would likewise provide for the security of his reputation."[27]

Charles Lee was confident in 1798 that careful lines could be drawn between liberty and license: "The freedom of the press differs from the licentiousness of the press, and the laws which restrain the latter, will always be found to affirm and preserve the former."[28] The Federalists, then the majority party in Congress, searched for the right formula and in 1798 passed the Sedition Act, which stated that "false, scandalous and malicious writing" aimed at the President and other officials was punishable "by a fine not exceeding two thousand dollars, and by imprisonment not exceeding two years."

The furor created by the Sedition Act was surprising in some ways. As Leonard Levy has noted, the act was

> the very epitome of libertarian thought since the time of Zenger's case. The Sedition Act incorporated everything that the libertarians had demanded: a requirement that criminal intent be shown; the power of the jury to decide whether the accused's statement was libelous as a matter of law as well as of fact; and truth as a defense, an innovation not accepted in England until 1843.[29]

But in those charged times the Act was quickly turned into a political weapon not against disloyal revolutionists but against the loyal opposition, the Jeffersonians. The Sedition Act, on the books from July 14, 1798—appropriately, Bastille Day—to its expiration in 1801, led to 14 indictments, 11 trials, and 10 convictions. Four of the five major Republican papers, including the *Boston Independent-Chronicle,* the *New York Argus,* and the *Richmond Examiner* were penalized.

Once some of the less scrupulous Federalists seized the opportunity to prosecute their opponents, the legal situation rapidly deteriorated. For example, Matthew (Spitting) Lyon, a Congressman-editor from Vermont, was jailed for 4 months and fined $1,000 merely for charging John Adams with "unbounded thirst for ridiculous pomp, foolish adulation, and selfish avarice."[30] Lyon was obnoxious—he gained his nickname for spitting in the face of a Congressional opponent during a debate in which words failed him—but opinions of that sort could be fought with scorn rather than suppression. When Lyon's constituents reelected him to the House of Representatives from jail, he became a hero.[31]

Local Federalist politicians overreached even more when a drunkard named Luther Baldwin was arrested while Adams was passing through Newark, New Jersey, on his way from the capital (then in Philadelphia) to his home in Quincy, Massachusetts. One barfly, noting that Adams had already passed by but the cannons for his 16-gun salute still were firing, commented, "There goes the president and they are firing at his ass." Baldwin, drunk, said, "I don't care if they fire through his ass." Arrested for that statement and jailed for several days, Baldwin also emerged a hero.

We might say that the law itself made sense—indeed, was a great leap forward—but its execution was poor. The trouble, however, is that laws of that type always tend to be passed in situations so heated that the execution is likely to be terrible. Armed with examples of abuses, proponents of absolute freedom for journalists went on the offensive. John Nicolas of Virginia denied that journalistic liberty could be distinguished from "licentiousness," or "truth" from "falsehood."[32] George Hay in Philadelphia published *An Essay on the Liberty of the Press* that argued for total freedom for even "false, scandalous, and malicious" comments; Hay's goal was that "A man may say every thing which his passions suggest . . ."[33] Others argued similarly.

The legal debate ended in a draw that lasted for over a century. The extreme views of Nicolas, Hay, and others were not embraced by the courts. The Sedition Act was allowed to expire in 1801; Congress enacted no other Sedition Act until World War I. Instead of either absolute freedom of federal control, the formula for the nineteenth century became that proclaimed by the Massachusetts supreme court in *Commonwealth v. Clap* (1808). The court observed that critiques of government officials or candidates, if true, "are not a libel. For it would be unreasonable to conclude that the publication of truths, which it is in the interests of the people to know, should be an offense against their laws."[34] The court also added sternly, however, that

> For the same reason, the publication of falsehood and calumny against public officers, or candidates for public offices, is an offense most dangerous to the people, and deserves punishment, because the people may be deceived, and reject the best citizens, to their great injury, and it may be to the loss of their liberties.[35]

Truth was a defense against prosecution for libel, but falsehood was no defense. The Zenger jury's faith was now law, and "license" still was excluded.

The political debate also ended in a compromise. Some political fallout was immediate: The Sedition Act helped the Federalists lose the presidential election of 1800. But by 1800, the sails of American supporters of revolutionary ideas were drooping—in large part because potential supporters had seen the consequences of those ideas played out in France. Some of the leading revolutionary journalists left the country (or were pushed out under the Alien Act). Other left this world; Benjamin Franklin Bache died of yellow fever as the Sedition Law was going into effect. But others, witnessing the brutality of the Revolution and its ending in Napoleon's dictatorship, turned away from revolution and the ideas that brought on revolution. On his deathbed, Thomas Paine retracted all the attacks on Christianity he had made in his last book, *The Age of Reason*. He said, "I would give worlds, if I had them, if *The Age of Reason* had never been published. O Lord, help me! Christ, help me! Stay with me! It is hell to be left alone."[36]

Thus ended the first attempt to bring to American journalism the *oppression story* faith that if man's environment were changed through social revolution, man himself would change. But few Americans at that time, trained as they were in biblical ideas of original sin in human nature, were buying such a concept. Instead, the first three decades of the 19th century showed an increasing number of publications that were explicitly Christian in orientation. The total number of newspapers rose from 359 in 1810 to 851 in 1828 and 1,265 in 1834—and, as one contemporary observer noted, "Of all the issues of the press three-fourths are theological, ethical, and devotional."[37] The *New York Christian Advocate* became the largest circulation weekly in the country, with 25,000 subscribers in 1828 and 30,000 in 1830.[38]

With the centralizing attempts of the revolutionaries defeated, the United States was able to continue its decentralized development. As Alexis de Tocqueville observed of early 19th-century America,

> It is in the township, the center of the ordinary business of life, that the desire for esteem [and] the pursuit of substantial interests . . . are concentrated; these passions, so often troublesome elements in society, take on a different character when exercised so close to home and, in a sense, within the family circle. . . . Daily duties performed or rights exercised keep municipal life constantly alive. There is a continual gentle political activity which keeps society on the move without turmoil.[39]

In many European countries, national newspapers emphasized politics above all else; in America, where the central institutions were family, church, and local organization, local newspapers thrived.

In this quiet period for American journalism hundreds of unsung editors went about their business of reporting both sinfulness and special providences. One typical editor, Nathaniel Willis, had at one time been impressed by the journalism of Benjamin Bache. Born in 1780, Willis from 1802 to 1807 edited a vitriolic Maine newspaper, the *Portland Eastern Argus,* and aspired to revolutionize society. During that period he was happy to "spend Sabbaths in roving about the fields and in reading newspapers"; one Sunday, however, he went to hear what he thought would be a political speech by a minister, and was surprised to hear instead a discussion of biblical basics.[40] Willis, "much interested," eventually came to believe "that the Bible is the Word of God—that Christ is the only Saviour, and that it is by grace we are saved, through faith."[41]

Applying that understanding to his occupation, Willis decided that good journalism required analysis of issues and not just partisan political attacks. Local politicians who had backed his Maine newspaper did not care for his new scruples; Willis resigned, moved to Boston, and with co-editor Sidney Morse began putting out the Boston *Recorder*. Willis and Morse announced that they would show theological truth while putting out a concise weekly *news*paper (including "the earliest information of all such events as mankind usually deem important").[42] The *Recorder* also promised accuracy—"Care will be taken to distinguish between rumor and well-authenticated fact"[43]—and promised, if necessary, a salute to government like that offered by John Stubbes:

> When it be necessary to disapprove of public measures, that respect for Government, which lies at the very foundation of civil society, will be cautiously preserved; and in such cases, a tone of regret and sorrow will best comport with the feelings of the Christian patriot.[44]

Coverage of a major Syrian earthquake in 1822, "EARTHQUAKE AT ALEPPO," shows how the *Recorder* combined news and theological contextualization. Its first-person account by missionary Benjamin Barker told how Barker was racing down the stairs of a crumbling house when another shock sent him flying through the air, his fall broken when he landed on a dead body. He saw:

> men and women clinging to the ruined walls of their houses, holding their children
> in their trembling arms; mangled bodies lying under my feet, and piercing cries of
> half buried people assailing my ears; Christians, Jews, and Turks, were imploring
> the Almighty's mercy in their respective tongues, who a minute before did not
> perhaps acknowledge him.[45]

An overall report continued the theme of sudden destruction, with "hundreds of decrepit parents half-buried in the ruins, imploring the succor of their sons," and "distracted mothers frantically lifting heavy stones," looking for their children.[46] But the *Recorder,* describing how the earthquake led many to think about God and the brevity of life, then stressed the "triumphs of divine grace over the obduracy of the human heart, and over the prejudices of the unenlightened mind."[47]

Coverage of politics showed an emphasis on individual responsibility rather than grand societal solutions. *Recorder* essays argued that civil government has strictly limited jurisdiction, and should be turned to only for defense or punishment of crime; family, church, and voluntary association were to take leadership in dealing with social problems.[48] Other newspapers also emphasized the moral questions involved in both personal and governmental actions. The *Lexington Western Monitor,* a Kentucky newspaper, was typical in its summary of one major role of the press: "To strengthen the hands of virtue and to rebuke vice."[49] The *New York American* viewed "the Press as the great instrument of Liberty," as long as there was a "FREE and INDEPENDENT PRESS, FREE from all controls but that of religion and morality, INDEPENDENT of any influence but the good of our country and mankind."[50]

Newspapers like the *Recorder* covered international news in line with their theological concerns. Missionary activities received great coverage, with many publications complaining that the British East India Company—agent for the British government in India—was restricting the activities of missionaries for fear that Christian development would "prove fatal to the British government in India."[51] The *Columbian Phoenix* complained that British leaders thought "the Religion of the Most High God must not be suffered to interfere with the arrangements of the British government."[52]

Sensational stories about India's "Juggernaut festival"—in which people prepared for sacrifice to local gods were "crushed to death by the wheels" of a moving tower while onlookers shouted with joy[53]—led into reports that British agents were collecting a "Juggernaut tax." The *New Hampshire Patriot* complained that British leaders

> take a premium from the poor ignorant Asiatic idolater to indulge him in falling down and worshipping the moulten image, Juggernaut.—By this piece of religious fraud, they raise a handsome revenue to the British government.[54]

Great Britain's peaceful coexistence with human sacrifice, wife burning, and infanticide was attacked by *Niles' Weekly Register,* which reported that two American missionaries were evicted from India because "the revenues of Juggernaut must not be unhinged."[55] A Rhode Island newspaper argued that the British government would sponsor the worship of Beelzebub if the state could make money off of it.[56]

Many editors emphasized scandals in the royal family and argued that British evangelical societies were "mere political engines" organized for "pretendedly pious purposes . . . With England religion is merely a political engine. Of what profession it is, is scarcely thought of, so it pays a tribute in cash or in service or pretences."[57] The *Boston Yankee* called England "this modern Babylon . . . We abhor the deep and abominable depravity of her *state* religion, which is no better than popery."[58] One editor ran this pointed reminder: "What has Britain done for the Protestant cause? Why, she has persecuted a large majority of her own Protestant subjects, dissenting from the dogmas of her national church, with inquisitorial cruelty."[59]

The most articulate journalistic writer on politics and morality during the 1830s was William Leggett of the *New York Evening Post.* Leggett's major political principle was support for "equal rights," by which he meant that law should not discriminate among citizens, benefiting some at the expense of others. He believed it unfair for government to be "offering encouragements and granting privileges" to those with political clout. He set about to expose any governmental redistribution of income, whether through taxes, tariffs, or government aid to individuals, businesses, or labor groups.

Leggett foresaw problems whenever "government assumes the functions which belong alone to an overruling Providence, and affects to become the universal dispenser of good and evil."[60] He did not want government to become:

> the greater regulator of the profits of every species of industry, and reduces men from a dependence on their own exertions, to a dependence on the caprices of their Government.[61]

Leggett complained that some already were beginning to argue "that because our government has been instituted for the benefit of the people, it must therefore have the power to do whatever may seem to conduce to the public good."[62] Yet "under the sanction of such a principle, a government can do any thing on pretense of acting for the public good," and the effect would be erratic,

> not unlike that of weak and vacillating parents over their children, and with about the same degree of impartiality. One child becomes a favourite because he has made a fortune, and another because he has failed in the pursuit of that object; one because of its beauty, and another because of its deformity.[63]

Presciently, Leggett argued that the growth of "this power of regulating—of increasing or diminishing the profits of labour and the value of property of all kinds and degrees, by direct legislation"—would lead to a growth of governmental power and citizen desire to grab some of that power. As Leggett wrote, government was in danger of becoming

> the mere creature of designing politicians, interested speculators, or crack-brained enthusiasts. It will gradually concentrate to itself all the reserved rights of the people; it will become the great arbiter of individual prosperity; and thus, before we know it, we shall become the victims of a new species of despotism, that of a system of laws made by ourselves. It will then remain to be seen whether our chains will be the lighter from having been forged by our own hands.[64]

Once such a system were established, Leggett pointed out, changing it would be difficult:

> One of the greatest supports of an erroneous system of legislation, is the very evil it produces. When it is proposed to remedy the mischief by adopting a new system, every abuse which has been the result of the old one becomes an obstacle to reformations. Every political change, however salutary, must be injurious to the interests of some, and it will be found that those who profit by abuses are always more clamourous for their continuance than those who are only opposing them from motives of justice of patriotism, are for their abandonment.[65]

Yet, if change did not occur, citizens would be left enslaved:

> A government administered on such a system of policy may be called a Government of Equal Rights, but it is in its nature and essence a disguised despotism. It is the capricious dispenser of good and evil, without any restraint, except its own sovereign will. It holds in its hand the distribution of the goods of this world, and is consequently the uncontrolled master of the people.

Leggett died of yellow fever in 1839, at age 38, but other journalists continued to develop similar ideas over the next decade. A common theme was evident on many editorial pages: The world is filled with tyranny; journalists by embracing power have contributed to that pattern; America remains a land in which state governments and local newspapers are their own masters.[66]

Chapter 6

The Great Debates of Journalism

What journalism textbooks call the "penny press era" — the 1830s and 1840s— is the period for which materialist explanations appear to be the strongest. By the 1830s, the traditional newspapers were vulnerable because they were expensive. The typical price was 6¢ per copy, a sum needed to pay for production and distribution, because advertising revenues were small; 6¢ was not small change when the average daily wage for farm laborers was 85¢. A newspaper that sold for 1¢ rather than 6¢ could (in theory) dramatically increase circulation, perhaps sixfold, which would mean that total income from circulation could remain constant, whereas increased advertising rates could pay for the additional costs involved in printing and distributing many more copies.

The change would be feasible only if improvements in production and distribution also came. The necessary technology became available in the 1830s when steam-driven presses, able to produce copies far more quickly than those hand-operated, came on line. The Hoe cylinder press, for example, could produce 4,000 papers per hour. Distribution was improved when newspaper boys, often youth rendered homeless through the family disruption that came with urbanization, were employed to sell single copies of newspapers on the street. All that was needed was an entrepreneur capable of seeing and grasping the new opportunities.

Several tried, but the first to make a success of a "penny newspaper" was printer Benjamin Day, who in 1833 began selling the *New York Sun* in 1833. Day was wise enough to establish a simple and lively style for his newspaper, but to ground it firmly in the same *corruption story* attitude toward the news that had made newspapers such as the *Boston Recorder* successful.[1] He did so primarily by installing as *Sun* editor George W. Wisner, who had worked on traditional Christian newspapers and understood that it is neither accurate nor stimulating to pretend that all is well in the world.

Wisner, like his Puritan predecessors, emphasized sensation, exposure, clarity, accuracy, and specificity. He understood the Mather emphasis on bad news and wrote of how news stories:

> must generally tell of wars and fighting, of deeds of death, and blood, of wounds and heresies, of broken heads, broken hearts, and broken bones, of accidents by fire or flood, a field of possessions ravaged, property purloined, wrongs inflicted. . . . the abundance of news is generally an evidence of astounding misery, and even the disinterested deeds of benevolence and philanthropy which we occasionally hear of owe their existence to the wants or sorrows or sufferings of some of our fellow beings.[2]

Wisner's practice followed his principles: A drunkard hauled into court acknowledged that he "could not see a hole through a ladder."[3] Wisner ran tales of adultery.[4] He told of how a woman was seduced and abandoned.[5]

Wisner believed that specificity was important both to win readers and to make his product morally useful. He listed names of all criminal offenders and saw such posting as an inhibitor of others inclined to vice:

> Much complaint has been made from a certain quarter, and emanating from a particular class of individuals, against the publication of the names of persons who have been arrested by the watch, [but . . .] such publications have a tendency to deter from disorders and crimes, and to diminish the number of criminals."[6]

A typical story shows how Wisner was not afraid to shame offenders:

> Patrick Ludwick was sent up by his wife, who testified that she had supported him for several years in idleness and drunkenness. Abandoning all hopes of a reformation in her husband, she bought him a suit of clothes a fortnight since and told him to go about his business, for she would not live with him any longer. Last night he came home in a state of intoxication, broke into his wife's bedroom, pulled her out of bed, pulled her hair, and stamped on her. She called a watchman and sent him up. Pat exerted all his powers of eloquence in endeavoring to excite his wife's sympathy, but to no purpose. As every sensible woman ought to do who is cursed with a drunken husband, she refused to have anything to do with him hereafter.[7]

The emphasis was still on personal responsibility. Wisner, following the Reformed view that the heavens display the glory of God and the streets show the sinfulness of man, told stories to make his points, and also displayed a sense of humor. He opposed dueling but once accepted a challenge from a seller of quack medicines whom Wisner had criticized. Wisner, given his choice of weapons, said that they would have to be syringes filled with the doctor's own medicine, at five paces. The duel was called off.[8]

After a few years Wisner moved on to Michigan and died shortly thereafter, but others among the new penny papers followed his pattern: They were snappier in tone than some of their predecessors, but had the same willingness to print bad news and demand that people abide by the consequences of their actions. *New York Herald* editor James Gordon Bennett emphasized man's sinfulness, writing in 1836 that "I have seen human depravity to the core—I proclaim each morning on 15,000 sheets of thought and intellect the deep guilt that is encrusting our society."[9] Theologically, Bennett repeatedly told readers that he considered atheism absurd.[10]

The real threat to journalism's long tradition did not come from material change or from Bennett, who was committed to the idea of an independent press, but from the return of the oppression story in the 1840s.[11] Repulsed during the 1790s, it was not a factor in journalism history for the following four decades — yet during that period, much was changing in America theologically, both within Christianity and outside of it. Increasingly, liberal theologians began to proclaim that man was not inherently sinful, and that if man's environment were changed, man himself could become perfect. A host of panaceas, ranging from diet change (meat was out, graham flour was in) to the abolition of private property, became popular as ways of changing mankind.

Many of the proposals for change involved an opposition to property rights, which journalists—aware of how essential privately owned printing presses are to editorial independence — had strongly favored over the years. Unitarian leader William Ellery Channing clearly named one of the assumed villains: "Avarice was the chief obstacle to human progress . . . The only way to eliminate it was to establish a community of property."[12] Channing later moderated his communistic ideas concerning property, but he typified the liberal New Englander's approach to the problem of evil. Evil was created by the way society was organized, not by anything innately evil in man. Change society and evil could be eliminated.

One of the radical attacks on private property was led by Albert Brisbane, who had journeyed to Europe in 1828, at age 18, and eventually become a disciple of Charles Fourier. Fourier, famous in Marxist history as a "utopian socialist," argued that man's natural goodness could be restored if society was reorganized into small units called *phalanxes,* each with 1,620 members. Each phalanx member would be paid from the common product and would live in a common dwelling called a *phalanstery,* with a common dining hall featuring seven meals a day. Bodies might also be in common, because "free love" would be encouraged. The communes would emphasize agriculture, but each member would be free to work when and where he wanted.

For Fourier and Brisbane, this economic vision came from pantheistic theological roots and was designed, in Brisbane's words, to create "a humanity worthy of that Cosmic Soul of which I instinctively felt it to be a part."[13] But Brisbane, desiring success and believing that material change would lead to spiritual transformation, learned to downplay his theology before the public:

> I held that it was not worth while to excite religious antipathies to the idea of an industrial reform. The great point to be gained was the organization of society on a true, practical basis. I saw that when once the material operations and relations of men were properly organized, opinions would modify themselves by the influence of a new life and a higher education.[14]

Brisbane began to develop a following. The going was still slow, however, so he asked one veteran journalist, Park Benjamin, how he could gain a mass audience. Benjamin suggested that Brisbane first work on a talented but somewhat loony editor named Horace Greeley, for Greeley was "just damned fool enough to believe such nonsense."

He was. The collaboration of Brisbane and Greeley gave the *oppression story* its first long lasting presence in American journalism. In 1841, Greeley was a 30-year-old frustrated office seeker just starting up a new penny newspaper, the *New York Tribune*.[15] Greeley was enthralled by the "ennobling tendencies" of Transcendentalism and enamored with the movement's leaders: "Its apostles are mainly among the noblest spirits living."[16] He called himself a mere popularizer of Emerson's transcendentalist teachings, and at the same time a Universalist who believed in salvation for every man and salvation of society by man's efforts.[17] Greeley also wanted people to revere him as a great thinker; as fellow editor E. L. Godkin noted, Greeley castigated office seekers, but he was "as time-serving and ambitious and scheming an old fellow as any of them."[18]

Naturally, Greeley was attracted to Brisbane's proposal of salvation through commune. With a new convert's enthusiasm, Greeley published a magazine edited by Brisbane and entitled *The Future, Devoted to the Cause of Association and a Reorganization of Society*. He then gave Brisbane a front-page column on the *Tribune* that gave the communalist the opportunity to "spread ideas broadcast over the whole country, gaining a great number of adherents."[19] As one Greeley biographer noted, "The *Tribune* threw itself wholeheartedly behind Brisbane, and soon found itself building up news interest, discussion, and circulation at an extraordinary rate as it helped him popularize his cause."[20] And, it is arguable that the penny press began making a worldview difference not because of its existence in and of itself, but because of the ideas of Brisbane and Greeley.

In any event, Greeley threw himself personally into the commune movement, as he attended Fourierist conventions, became president of the American Union of Associationists, and financially backed three phalanxes—the Sylvania Association in Pennsylvania, the North American Phalanx in New Jersey, and Brook Farm in Massachusetts.[21] Greeley received ample stroking; in 1844, for example, when he went to a New York City banquet honoring Fourier's birthday, Greeley was toasted by Brisbane as the man who had

> done for us what we never could have done. He has created the cause on this continent. He has done the work of a century. Well, then, I will give a toast: 'One Continent, One Man!'[22]

Greeley's political activities helped him attract many young, idealistic writers, some of whom—Margaret Fuller, George Ripley, and Charles Dana particularly—had great literary skill. The *Tribune* became *the* place to work; as editor E. L. Godkin would later note, "To get admission to the columns of the Tribune almost gave the young writer a patent of literary nobility."[23] One *Tribune* reporter recalled that the furnishings were poor, but

> Ill-furnished and ill-kept as the Tribune office was in those days, it harbored a moral and intellectual spirit that I met nowhere else during my thirty-five years of journalistic experience. Every member of the force, from reporter to editor, regarded it as a great privilege to be on the Tribune and to write for its columns. . . .[24]

Greeley himself had great journalistic instincts. He demanded from his reporters "vigor, terseness, clearness, and simplicity."[25] He emphasized comprehensive news coverage, and described how an editor should make sure that nothing "of interest to a dozen families occurs, without having the fact daily, though briefly, chronicled." He noted that if an editor can "secure a wide-awake, judicious correspondent in each village and township" and have him send "whatever of moment occurs in his vicinity," readership is assured.[26]

Greeley also insisted on good typography. One anecdote shows how even Greeley's fiercest competitors respected the *Tribune's* superiority in this regard. It seems that Greeley once fired a printer who misread Greeley's notoriously messy handwriting and thought the editor was calling not for an early morning milk train to bring the fruits of farm labors to New York City, but a "swill train." When the editorial was published and an angry delegation of Westchester County farmers assaulted Greeley, he in rage scribbled a note to the composing room foreman ordering that the printer be fired. The foreman knew Greeley's writing and could read the message, but to the average reader only the signature was clear. The fired printer asked to hold onto Greeley's note as a souvenir. He then took it to other newspapers and answered questions about previous employment and reliability by flashing the note. The name of Greeley on it — all else being illegible—was accepted as all the recommendation needed.

All of these factors allowed Greeley the freedom to make his newspaper a proponent of social revolution without unduly alienating otherwise delighted subscribers.[27] And for a while, other leaders of New York journalism gave Greeley a wide berth. In 1846, however, he was challenged to a series of newspaper debates by his former assistant editor on the *Tribune,* Henry Raymond. Raymond, 26, had moved from assisting Greeley on the *Tribune* to assisting James Watson Webb on the *New York Courier and Enquirer,* and Greeley still had high regard for him; Greeley later would write that he had never seen "a cleverer, readier, more generally efficient journalist" than Raymond.[28] But the philosophical differences between the two were sharp: in 1854 journalist James Parton would muse, "Horace Greeley and Henry J. Raymond, the one naturally liberal, the other naturally conservative—the one a Universalist, the other a Presbyterian. . ."[29]

The debates took place because neither Greeley nor Raymond tried to hide their views, and because both thought their readerships would be informed by a debate on basic issues of political economy. The arrangement agreed to was straightforward: The *Tribune* would publish an initial Greeley column defending Associationism, and the *Courier* would then print that column along with a response by Raymond; Greeley would then print Raymond's reply and a reply of his own; the *Courier* would print Greeley's new column and a new response by Raymond; and so on. Each party agreed to publish a total of 12 articles from its own side and 12 from the other.

The format of the debates was clear, but the course of argumentation was anything but direct. Greeley opened the debate series on November 20 by trying to establish a natural rights base for his opposition to private property: he asserted presuppositionally that each member of "the whole Human Family" had an equal right to the earth, and that, therefore, every New York resident had "a perfect right . . . to his equal share of the soil, the woods, the waters, and all the natural products thereof." The problem, however, was that "Civilized Society, as it exists in our day, has divested the larger portion of mankind of the unimpeded, unpurchased enjoyment of their natural rights"; the solution would be "Association," by which all property would be communal rather than private.[30]

Raymond in response did not challenge Greeley's presuppositions but concentrated on drawing out four steps that logically would follow acceptance of Greeley's theory: (a) if equal distribution of all land was right, then the current unequal distribution was wrong; (b) if the wrong was to be righted, then none of the current patterns of property ownership should stand; (c) if land could not be owned rightfully, than the product of that land could not be owned rightfully; (d) because all property originated in land ownership, no one could rightfully own anything at all. Raymond then went on to argue from history that although difficulties did arise out of property ownership, "without it they would be increased a thousand fold . . . Without it civilization would be unknown—the face of the Earth would be a desert, and mankind transformed into savage beasts."[31]

Greeley at this point could have stood his ground and attempted to argue that private property's detriments were greater than its benefits, but he did not think he could prove that case historically; instead, in his second essay he retreated to a better defensive position by writing that he wanted to argue about current reality, not history and theory, and so would stress the importance of property being used for the good of all rather than for individual, assumedly selfish, purposes.[32] Raymond in his second essay accepted the move away from theory and demanded that Greeley lay out the specifics of his program, and explain how communes could attract needed capital without expropriation by force.[33] Greeley responded with details of the Associationist program, and tried to prove his peaceful and moderate intentions by stipulating that those who provided needed capital for the communes could be rewarded by receiving shares of the commune's production.[34]

Raymond, in his third essay, took that detail and held it high as proof of Greeley's inconsistency; Raymond argued that Greeley was in one breath calling the distribution of capital unjust, and in the next indicating a willingness to ratify that unfairness and even modify Associationism to extend it.[35] Greeley responded that his goal was not so much to rectify past abuses as to prevent further ones, so he therefore was willing to recognize capital accumulations as long as future profits would go primarily to those who labored, not merely those who invested.[36] Raymond, in his fourth reply, wrote that Greeley's scheme was unrealistic because, apart from a market system, it was not possible to determine exactly the value of labor or product.[37]

Here the debaters were approaching what is still a key question of economics, although the current phenomenon of Marxist economies abandoning command manufacturing and pricing decisions indicates that the argument is virtually over. In the mid-19th century, however, massive experience with administered pricing in industrial economies was still in the future, and Greeley could assert in his fifth essay that it would not be hard to distribute proceeds to "Capital, Labor and Skill as impartial justice shall dictate."[38] Raymond for his part replied that administered distribution was impossible without tyranny: those who wished to choose freely and make their own economic arrangements "must be overruled, *put down* by the strong hand: or they must be consulted and gratified—and that would simply be a return to the existing social state."[39] Raymond contended that Greeley was unwilling to confront some basic issues of man's nature—including, most particularly, the question of "sin" and its effect on social progress.[40]

By the end of the fifth debate some key issues in political theory and economics had been discussed, but the debates still had not achieved the intellectual intensity that could make them profound rather than persnickety. Both debaters, in fact, were becoming exasperated with each other's penchant for floating like a butterfly rather than stinging like a bee: Raymond complained on December 24 of "the difficulty of conducting an argument with an opponent who recognizes none of the common rules of reasoning, and who repudiates his positions as fast as they become unpleasant." Greeley replied that Raymond's counterpunching was "founded only in the grossest ignorance and misconception of what I have presented."[41]

With the sixth editorial page essays, however, the long-term salience of the debates increased because Raymond's jabs drove Greeley to confront the question of how social progress could occur. Greeley acknowledged at the start, "I know well that an Association of knaves and dastards—of indolent or covetous persons—could not endure without a moral transformation of its members." Then came Greeley's key emphasis on structural rather than personal change as the root of progress; he argued that the structure of Association "strongly tends to correct the faults inimical to its existence,"[42] for people placed in a good environment will undergo a moral transformation. Raymond, in his sixth essay, pounced on Greeley's admission, arguing that "this concession is fatal to the whole theory of Association. It certainly implies that Individual Reform must *precede* Social Reform—that the latter must have its root in the former."[43]

Raymond went on to call Greeley's assertion that Associationism would be self-correcting "a gross absurdity," for "Association is thus expected to make its own indispensable conditions. It is to create its own creator—to produce its own cause—to effect that personal reform in which it must originate."[44] Raymond then stated his position: Only the "personal reform of individual men," through Christianity, can lead to social progress. Raymond argued that reformers should "*commence* their labors by making individual men *Christians*: by seeking their personal, moral transformation. When that is accomplished, all needed Social Reform will either have been effected or rendered inevitable."[45]

Greeley, in his seventh statement, had two replies to Raymond. First, Greeley defended the causal relationship Raymond attacked. Greeley argued that personal change among the best and the brightest would lead to societal transformation, which in turn would lead to change among the masses:

> Give but one hundred of the right men and women as the nucleus of a true Social Organism, and hundreds of inferior or indifferent qualities might be rapidly molded into conformity with them.[46]

Greeley could write this because he saw man as a product of his environment: "I believe there are few of the young and plastic who might not be rendered agreeable and useful members of an Association under the genial influences of Affection, Opportunity, Instruction, and Hope."[47] Greeley's emphasis on plasticity would become increasingly common in the second half of the century as environmental explanations for social problems became more common.

Greeley's arguments also pointed toward future ideologies by putting forward what a half century later would become known as the "Social Gospel": He tried to show that Raymond's demand for Christ first was absurd, because "Association *is* the palpable dictate of Christianity—the body whereof True Religion is the soul."[48] In arguing that Associationism was Christianity-in-practice, a material emphasis that transcended the spiritual, Greeley described slum living conditions and asked,

Can any one doubt what Christianity must dictate with regard to such hovels as these? Can any fail to see that to fill them with Bibles and Tracts, while Bread is scanty, wholesome Air a rarity, and Decency impossible, must be unavailing? 'Christianity,' say you! Alas! many a poor Christian mother within a mile of us is now covering her little ones with rags in the absence of fuel . . .[49]

Greeley's statement jarred Raymond to lay out his full position on January 20, 1847. He first noted partial agreement with Greeley as to the need for action:

The existence of misery, and the necessity of relieving it, are not in controversy, for we have never doubted either. It is only upon the *remedy to be applied,* that the Tribune and ourselves are at variance.[50]

But Raymond argued that Greeley was unnecessarily revolutionary when he insisted that:

to benefit a part, the whole must be changed; that to furnish some with good dwellings, all must abandon their houses and dwell together under a common roof; that the whole fabric of existing institutions, with all its habits of action and of thought, must be swept away, and a new Society takes its place, in which all must be subject to common customs, a common education, common labor, and common modes of life, in all respects. This, its fundamental position, we deny. We deny the necessity, the wisdom, and the possibility of removing existing evil, by such a process.[51]

Raymond, rather than linking philanthropy with upheaval, saw individual and church action as efficacious. He praised "individuals in each ward, poor, pious, humble men and women, who never dreamed of setting themselves up as professional philanthropists," but daily visit the sick and help the poor. He also argued that:

Members of any one of our City Churches do more every year for the practical relief of poverty and suffering, than any Phalanx [the Associationist name for communes] that ever existed. There are in our midst hundreds of female 'sewing societies,' each of which clothes more nakedness, and feeds more hunger, than any 'Association' that was ever formed.[52]

Raymond then portrayed Greeley's ideas as abstractly ineffective:

Hundreds of thousands of dollars have been expended by the Associationists, in propagating their *theories* of benevolence, and in making benevolent experiments, yet where is the practical good they have accomplished? . . . The *Tribune* sneers at practical Christianity . . . Does the taunt come with good grace from a system which theorizes over starvation, but does not feed it; which scorns to give bread and clothing to the hungry and naked, except it can first have the privilege of reconstructing Society?

Now the two debaters were focusing on the basics. Raymond had called Greeley superficial for not getting at what Raymond saw as the root, spiritual causes of material poverty, and now Greeley struck back with his assessment that capitalism, not spiritual decay, was the culprit: "Association proposes a way . . . of reaching the *causes* of the calamities, and absolutely *abolishing* Pauperism, Ignorance, and the resulting Vices."[53] Journalists, Greeley went on, should not merely praise those who mitigated "woes and degradations," but should fight oppression: "*Relieving* Social Evils' is very well; we think eradicating and preventing them still better, and equally feasible if those who have power will adopt the right means, and give them a fair trial."[54]

Raymond's response on February 10, however, continued to insist that views of human nature, and not merely issues of relief versus prevention, were the continental divide separating his position from that of Greeley. Raymond, instead of accepting Greeley's assertion that Associationism was true Christianity, argued that it was anti-Christian. For example, Raymond pointed out Associationism's belief

> that the Husband and Wife, instead of being *one,* as the laws of God have decreed, shall be entirely independent of each other in name and in property, and that each shall have perfect liberty of action and *affection.*[55]

Raymond argued that the near absolute liberty the communes were designed to allow would inevitably feed into anarchy, and that their maintenance would be possible only through totalitarian "Social Science," which would be designed to "control all departments of Social Life."[56]

Increasingly the debates hinged on the view of man that divided the two editors. When Greeley argued on February 17 that all man's problems "have their root in that *isolation of efforts* and antagonism of interests on which our present Social Order is based," Raymond replied by emphasizing individual corruption rather than social oppression as the root of most social ills.[57] Although Greeley believed that "the Passions, feelings, free impulses of Man point out to him the path in which he should walk," Raymond argued that evil feeds on those passions and impulses of man's natural inclination, and that channelling those inclinations into paths of work and family was the only alternative to anarchy and barbarism.[58]

The last three debates showed even more clearly the conflict of two faiths. Greeley's Associationist belief was that human desires are:

> good in themselves. Evil flows only from their repression or subversion. Give them full scope, free play, a perfect and complete development, and universal happiness must be the result . . . create a new form of Society in which this shall be possible

. . . then you will have a perfect Society; then will you have 'the Kingdom of Heaven . . .'[59]

Raymond, however, argued that:

this principle is in the most direct and unmistakable hostility to the uniform inculcations of the Gospel. No injunction of the New Testament is more express, or more constant, than that of *self-denial*; of subjecting the passions, the impulses of the heart to the law of conscience.[60]

Greeley responded, on March 12, with his faith that the *education* intrinsic to commune life was the key to developing individuals who would not need God's grace or biblical restraint: "I do not believe that a rightly-trained, truly-developed human being will any more have "a passion for a dozen different women,' etc., than he will have a passion to commit a dozen murders."[61] Associationism also stressed structuring of the social environment:

Excesses and vices are not an essential part of the passions, but on the contrary depend on external circumstances, which may be removed. All that is necessary is to discover a society in which every bad route for the action of the passions will be closed, and in which the path of virtue will be strewn with flowers. . . . How could the passions lead to crime, when every thing should be arranged to *satisfy them* in the most agreeable manner?[62]

But Greeley would not assent to Raymond's assertion that Associationism was anti-Christian; rather, he made backing of communes a Christian necessity, and argued in his 11th essay that it is

the duty of every Christian, every Philanthropist, every one who admits the essential Brotherhood of the Human Family, to labor earnestly and devotedly for a Social Order, which shall *secure* to every human being within its sphere the full and true development of the nature wherewith God has endowed him, Physical, Intellectual, and Moral.[63]

Raymond, in his 11th response, argued that Greeley was socialist in economics, antinomian in ethics, and overall a person who was trying to create a new god in Greeley's own image: Greeley's thought, Raymond charged,

pretends to be religious, and even claims to be the only true Christianity. But . . . it rejects the plainest doctrines of the Bible, nullifies its most imperative commandments, and substitutes for them its own interpretation of the laws of *nature*. Thus the God in whom it professes faith, becomes, in its definition, simply the 'principle of universal unity.'[64]

Raymond accused Greeley of similarly twisting the concept of the Trinity and the meaning of the words "Kingdom of Heaven."[65] He concluded, concerning Greeley's belief, that:

> Its whole spirit is in the most direct hostility to the doctrines of the Bible. It recognizes no absolute distinction between right and wrong . . . and aims at nothing beyond the 'full and true development of the nature of man.' . . . It is the exact antagonist of Christianity; it starts from opposite fundamental principles and aims at precisely opposite results.[66]

The key question that all reformers and journalists should answer, Raymond insisted, concerned the locus of evil action among humans: did evil come from within, or was it generated by social institutions? Raymond stipulated that,

> Before a cure can be applied or devised, the cause of the evil must be ascertained: and here at the very outset, the theory of Association comes in direct collision with the teachings of Christianity.[67]

The cause, Raymond argued, was "the sinfulness of the heart of Man." The remedy, he argued,

> must reach that cause, or it must prove inefficient. The heart must be changed. The law of Man's nature must cease to be the supreme law of his life. He must learn to subject that law to the higher law of righteousness, revealed in his conscience and in the Word of God. . . . and that subjugation can only be effected by his own personal will, with the supernatural aids furnished in the Christian Scheme.[68]

And thus the lines were clearly drawn. Greeley believed that "the heart of man is not depraved: that his passions do not prompt to wrong doing, and do not therefore by their action, produce evil."[69] Greeley, in his 12th and final essay, reiterated his faith that "social distinctions of master and servant, rich and poor, landlord and landless," are the cause of social problems. He followed Unitarian practice in referring to Jesus as a "divinely-sent messenger and guide" but was unwilling to accept Christ as God's son. He concluded his side of the debate on April 28 with some exasperation:

> I can not see how a man profoundly impressed with the truth and importance of Christ's teaching . . . can fail to realize and aspire to a Social polity radically different from that which has hitherto prevailed.[70]

Raymond's final response reiterated the centrality of "Sin, as an active power, in the human heart," and argued that Associationism at best would deal with superficial problems, but not "the lust, the covetousness, the self-seeking," out of which battles arise.[71] Greeley trusted man's wisdom, but Raymond concluded that

> the principles of all true REFORM come down from Heaven. . . . The CHRISTIAN RELIGION, in its spiritual, life-giving, heart-redeeming principles is the only power that can reform Society: and it can accomplish this work only by first reforming the individuals of whom Society is composed. Without GOD, and the plan of redemption which he has revealed, the World is also without HOPE.[72]

As the debates ended, interest in them was so high that Harper's quickly published all 24 of the articles in a pamphlet of 83 closely printed, double-columned pages, which sold out.

It is hard to evaluate the long term effect of the debates on American society and journalism. But if we keep in mind the statement of Lincoln's that began this book—"Public opinion on any subject always has a 'central idea' from which all its minor thoughts radiate"—the significance of the debates is clear. Raymond and Greeley were really arguing about what the "central idea" for Americans, and American journalists, should be.

The battle was not one of change versus the status quo. Raymond agreed with Greeley that social problems were great—"Far from denying their existence, we insist that they are deeper and more fundamental in their origin."[73] But Raymond saw himself as arguing for "a more thorough and radical remedy than the Tribune supposes"—namely, the change of heart that acceptance of Christianity brings.[74] That concept was common in the Christian journalism that dominated the early 19th-century press. It underlay the *corruption story* and its emphasis on the universality of sin and the need for all individuals, including rulers, to repent and change. Raymond in the debates repeatedly stated this doctrine:

> No truth is more distinctly taught in the Word of God than that of the sinfulness of the human earth: the proclivity of Man's nature to act in violation of the rule of right. . . . It is solely because malice, covetousness, envy, lust, and selfishness in general exist, as active principles, in the heart of man, that their fruits exist in Society. It is solely because the foundation is poisoned, that the streams which flow from it are bitter.[75]

But would that belief remain dominant in American journalism?

Not if Horace Greeley had anything to do with it. He embraced part of that methodology but rejected the theology behind it. Instead of seeing sinful man and a society reflecting that sinfulness, he believed that man was naturally good but was enslaved by oppressive social systems. Greeley in the debates was developing the rationale of the *oppression story* emphasis on problems arising not from internal sin but from external influences. That is why the debates were so grinding: Raymond and Greeley were arguing not only about theology and economics, but about the future of American society and the future of journalistic practice. The tectonic plates were shifting as they spoke. Soon the earthquake would come.

PART III

BREAKTHROUGH OF THE OPPRESSION STORY

Chapter 7

The Irrepressible Conflict in the Press

Just as the Greeley–Raymond debates did not have a clear winner, so the social upheaval of the 1840s did not have a clear, short term outcome. Despite good press clippings from the *Tribune* and some of its allies, the commune movement died during the 1850s. Virtually all of the communes failed and disappeared; the idea of a noble human nature, so attractive in the abstract, showed its weakness in practice. Commune members often neglected their work. "Free love" proved not to be so free, as disputes raged.[1]

Brisbane believed the reason for failure in the 1840s and 1850s was not too much forced community but too little:

> Unless associative life is completely organized, so that all the sentiments and faculties of the soul find their normal development and action therein, it cannot stand. In fact, it will be discovered one of these days that, according to a law which governs the spiritual or passional nature of man, there must either be the complex harmony of a perfect organization, with a high order of spiritual activity, or man must remain in his little isolated, individual state.[2]

Socialism in one community was insufficient. Control over much more terrain was necessary, and Brisbane recommended to his adherents that they begin a long march through the institutions of American society—"years of patient, careful propagation"—so that the result, decades later, would be "complex harmony."[3] The goal became one of building a strong central government, so that the entire nation could be socialized.

Greeley began his own long march by placing in *Tribune* editorial positions many of his commune associates—most notably Charles Dana and George Ripley. They in turn hired others on the left, including Karl Marx as a European correspondent. Greeley himself continued to look for the magic bullet by which the misery descending on needy citizens could be stopped: "full of error and suffering as the world yet is," he wrote, "we cannot afford to reject any idea which proposes to improve the Moral, Intellectual, or Social condition of mankind."[4] Paralleling Marx, he argued that "The whole relation of Employer and Laborer is so full of antagonism, inequality and injustice, that we despair of any reform in it but a very thorough and radical one."[5]

Greeley worked with many New York proto-Marxists, but did not remain faithful to any particular faction for long.[6] At one time he became a believer in "anti-rentism," the idea that charging rent for use of property or land was wrong.[7] That movement never took off, and Greeley moved on to other brief but entangling alliances. His inability to learn from failures was more serious than his absent-mindedness, which was so extreme that he detailed an office boy to keep him informed as to whether he had eaten anything that day. (Once fellow journalists at a restaurant distracted Greeley as he was about to eat and substituted an empty plate for the full one that had awaited him; when Greeley's attention returned to his table he looked down at the empty plate, sighed, and rose to leave.)[8]

In his habits of mind if not in his enjoyment of food, Greeley was the prototype of some elite American journalists of recent times. He also created the mold in that he became ever more ardent for social change as his personal life disintegrated. Horace and Mary Greeley believed that children were without sin, so they kept their son Arthur (Pickie), born in 1844, isolated from playmates or other means by which corruption could enter into him. At age 5 Pickie's hair had never been cut, less that constrict his freedom, and he still wore baby clothes, to give him freedom of movement: Pickie was to be a beautiful combination of intellect and nature, equipped with "choice" thoughts and language. But one day the 5-year-old stood up before a commune meeting and starting complaining that his mother was "so particular, particular, particular, particular." When she reminded him that he had been saved from corruption, he began shrieking at her, "Don't you dare shut me up in a room . . . I want fun." The Greeleys did not change Pickie's regime, but he died shortly after, during a cholera epidemic.

Commune decline and family silliness, combined with sadness, showed Greeley that utopia was not around the corner. But during the 1850s, as Greeley was looking around for a new cause, one presented itself. He would involve himself deeply during the 1850s in the battle over slavery, and would prod that battle toward a culmination in civil war. The Civil War and its aftermath, with the expansion of federal power that resulted, would change the American republic and the American press system by turning both toward an embrace of centralization as savior and a belief that means are less important than ends.

The war, of course, was a long time coming. It's instructive to go back to

William Leggett, who in the 1830s made his position on slavery and its potential abolition very clear. Leggett called slavery "a deplorable evil and a curse" and favored "the speedy and utter annihilation of servitude and chains."[9] Yet, carrying on John Milton's faith in the combat of ideas, Leggett also demanded "the strenuous assertion of the right of free discussion." He wanted liberation to come through a change in minds and hearts, and not by military arms or even by assertion of national political power: "We disclaim any constitutional right to legislate on the subject."[10]

Leggett had faith that Americans, both north and south, eventually would answer "no" to a series of rhetorical questions he posed:

> Have their ears become so accustomed to the clank of the poor bondman's fetters that it no longer grates upon them as a discordant sound? . . . Can the husband be torn from his wife, and the child from its parent, and sold like cattle at the shambles, and yet free, intelligent men, whose own rights are founded on the declaration of the unalienable freedom and equality of all mankind, stand up in the face of heaven and their fellow men, and assert without a blush that there is no evil in servitude?[11]

Leggett opposed revolutionary violence, but he praised anti-slavery civil disobedience and noted that, pragmatically, suppression does not work in America for long:

> The first great impulse which the abolition cause received in this city was, we are persuaded, the attempt to suppress it by the means of mobs; . . . and we do hope that, in view of the pernicious consequences which have flowed from violent measures hitherto, a course more consistent with the meekness of Christianity, and with the sacred rights of free discussion, will be pursued henceforth.[12]

Leggett died before his faith that free discussion would lead to an anti-slavery outcome could be severely tried. Some 1,000 miles away, however, another journalist put Leggett's optimism into practice under far more difficult conditions. Elijah Lovejoy, born in Maine in 1802, completed his theological training in 1833 at Princeton Theological Seminary (then a stronghold of Calvinist thought) and moved to St. Louis in 1834. There he was ordained as a minister and began editing a Christian newspaper, the *St. Louis Observer*. When he saw a slave, Francis J. McIntosh, burned at the stake, he became an abolitionist and began encountering massive opposition.

Lovejoy stayed in St. Louis as long as he could, but when a pro-slavery mob wrecked his press in July 1836, Lovejoy moved to the free state of Illinois and established the *Alton Observer*.[13] Freedom from slavery did not guarantee freedom of the press, however. Three times, Lovejoy saw his printing presses smashed and thrown into the Mississippi River by pro-slavery men; he did not fight back. Lovejoy became pastor of a Presbyterian church and moderator of the Alton

Presbytery, but he also ordered a new press. When it arrived at the Godfrey & Gilman warehouse, Lovejoy and 20 of his armed supporters stood guard over it until it could be installed at the *Alton Observer*.

A pro-slavery mob formed on the night of November 7, 1837. Its participants, most of them drunk, began hurling rocks at the warehouse windows. The defenders threw back earthenware pots they had found in the warehouse. Soon, gunshots began coming from both sides. When the mob put up a ladder at the building and one of its members began climbing to the roof with a smoking pot of pitch in order to set fire to the building, Lovejoy and a friend rushed out to overturn the ladder. One mob gunman fired his double barreled shotgun at Lovejoy. Five bullets hit him, and he died.

Lovejoy's associates then laid down their weapons and were allowed to leave; the mob broke the press into pieces and dumped the broken parts into the river. Lovejoy was buried on November 9—his 35th birthday—and after the Civil War Alton citizens erected a monument to him. It stands to this day on a hill overlooking the Mississippi, with a plaque introducing Lovejoy as "Minister of the Gospel, Moderator of Alton Presbytery," and explaining in Lovejoy's own words what befell him: "If the laws of my country fail to protect me I appeal to God, and with Him I cheerfully rest my cause—I can die at my post but I cannot desert it."[14]

A few years later and 300 miles to the east, another editor faced similar persecution. Cassius Clay of Lexington, Kentucky, saw slavery as a sevenfold evil: "morally, economically, physically, intellectually, socially, religiously, politically."[15] But he saw the need for long term change that the south could embrace, and advocated emancipation over a generation's time. To that end, in 1845 (at age 35) Clay began publishing the *True American,* "a paper devoted to gradual and constitutional emancipation."[16] With the words "God and Liberty" as his newspaper's motto, Clay advocated a constitutional convention designed to state "that every female slave, born after a certain day and year, should be free at the age of twenty-one". Clay argued that over time this plan "would gradually, and at last, make our state truly free."[17]

The moderate program began to pick up support, and also furious opposition. Clay soon had the joy of printing letters to the editor such as this one: "C.M. Clay: You are meaner than the autocrats of hell . . . The hemp is ready for your neck. Your life cannot be spared. Plenty thirst for your blood—are determined to have it . . ."[18] But Clay kept at it, arguing that the elimination of slavery would help the south to prosper economically, spiritually, and socially. In one article he commented on a rise of divorce in the south and urged southern women to:

> Put away your slaves . . . If you want to drink, go to the pump or to the spring and get it; if to bathe, prepare your own bath, or plunge into the running stream; make your own beds, sweep your own rooms, and wash your own clothes; throw away corsets and nature herself will form your bustles. Then you will have full chests,

glossy hair, rosy complexions, smooth velvet skins, muscular, rounded limbs, graceful tournures, elasticity of person, eyes of alternate fire and most melting languor; generous hearts, sweet tempers, good husbands, long lives of honeymoons, and—*no divorces.*[19]

Clay, expecting attempts to destroy his press, made a fort out of his three story red brick newspaper office, and with six loyal friends prepared for siege. Familiar with the story of Lovejoy's death, they lined the outside doors and window shutters of the building with sheet iron to prevent burning. Clay purchased two small brass cannons at Cincinnati, loaded them to the muzzle with bullets, slugs, and nails, and placed them breast high on a table at the entrance. His friends stockpiled muskets and Mexican lances. Those measures forestalled the attack for a time, but Clay came down with typhoid fever and eventually had to give up and watch as his press was packed up by slaveholders and shipped out of town.

That was the last time he was helpless. In 1847 Clay resumed his anti-slavery writing and speaking, had to fight numerous duels, and survived. (He had a lifetime record of about 107 wins and no losses, compared to Muhammed Ali's 32 and 4 as a pro.)[20] The original Cassius Clay could also talk a good fight. Once, facing a hostile crowd, Clay held up a Bible and said, "To those who respect God's word, I appeal to this book." Then he held up a copy of the U.S. Constitution and said, "To those who respect our fundamental law, I appeal to this document." Then he took out two pistols and his Bowie knife and said, "To those who recognize only force . . ."

Clay, although ready to defend himself, believed that nothing good would come from aggression. He demanded free speech in the hope of convincing his neighbors but did not want to war on them. He stressed the power of personal transformation through God's grace, which would lead to societal reformation. "We recommend less haughtiness and indifference on the part of the rich towards the poor, and less invidiousness toward the rich on the part of the poor," he wrote. "Let true Christianity prevail, and earth will become the foreshadowing of Heaven."[21] And Clay, unlike Lovejoy, managed to survive many assassination attempts. He was knifed and beaten by clubs; once, gushing blood from a lung wound, he even lost consciousness and dramatically gave as his last words, "I died in the defense of the liberties of the people"—but he did not die. He kept speaking out against slavery in the 1840s and helped to form the Republican Party in the 1850s.[22]

By then, the lines were drawn, and it may have been too late for anti-slavery plans that would not end in violence. Any possibility for a peaceful resolution disappeared when anti-slavery journalism moved from corruption story grounds of sadly dealing with sinful man, to an oppression story vision of eradicating slavery as the first step toward social revolution and class warfare. The role of the press in making the conflict irrepressible should not be overstated—and yet, if we examine the four alternative ways of fighting slavery that existed at one time, and then see which one was seized on by some leading journalists, that press role does loom large.

There will be some oversimplification in summarizing in a few paragraphs the options that have been dissected in thousands of books over a century, but baldly describing the lay of the land in this fashion might show the editorial choices that were open. The first of the anti-slavery approaches that editors could call for would be the personal one. Slaveholders could free their slaves, as did Washington and Jefferson on their deaths. Also on the personal level, opponents of slavery could reason with slaveholders, and ministers could preach against it. Editors, for their part, could cover separation of slave families, brutality against slaves, and so on. If all failed, those opposed to slavery could put money alongside their words by buying slaves and then freeing them.

A second alternative was collective but nongovernmental. The first half of the 19th century, as Alexis de Tocqueville observed, was the golden age of associations in America, and anti-slavery individuals frequently came together in the search for a way out. They formed societies to support colonies for ex-slaves in Africa or in the west. Some joined to purchase and then free slaves. Some set up schools for slaves. Some wanted to boycott southern economic products, and others wanted to fund southern industries that would not employ slaves. Thoreau hoped to convince many that nonviolent action, such as non-payment of taxes, could create pressure for change, but he found few supporters.

A third alternative, once tensions had grown to the point of war, could have been Washington's temporary acceptance of secession, followed by a trade embargo that some thought might kill the rebellion. Unlikely as this seems, Greeley embraced the idea in 1851 and stated that the south should secede; he argued that southerners would realize after a couple of independent years that they needed the north's industry, and would then beg for readmission. At that point, Greeley argued, the north would be in a position to make demands, one of which would be the elimination of slavery.[23] Greeley intensified his calls in 1854 as he argued that the north should laugh at

> the too susceptible nerves of our too excitable Southern brethren. Instead of bolting the door in alarm, and calling for help to guard it, in case the South should hereafter threaten to walk out of the Union, we would hold it politely open and suggest to the departing the policy of minding his eye and buttoning his coat well under his chin preparatory to facing the rough weather outside . . .[24]

But Greeley, even though he saw materialism as dominant, was too savvy a journalist to argue for long that change would come that easily. And so he arrived at the fourth alternative, violence: the north eradicating slavery by using its superior numbers and industrial capacity to eradicate part of the south. Greeley thought that a little blood would go a long way, for he believed that only a few wealthy southerners, along with a handful of politicians along for the ride, were truly pro-slavery. Greeley did not travel in the south until after the war, and he employed correspondents who were better preachers against slavery than reporters of actual sentiment. Even in 1860, Greeley's correspondent in Memphis was writing that "an insignificant clique" favored secession, but "the masses are heart and soul for the union," so the north should not be concerned with "threats, or predictions of disunion."[25]

In the early 1840s Greeley's commune enthusiasm led the *Tribune* into expectation of utopia around the corner; Greeley's hopes for rapid social progress during the late 1850s again led him to provide considerable space for unreliable accounts that supported his dreams. For example, a letter from Alabama argued that people in that state were "divided into two classes—the rich and the poor," and that the poor would readily unite with northern workers to "create a new system of Truth, Equality, Justice."[26] Karl Marx, peering across the Atlantic with a dialectic telescope, helped to convince Greeley's assistant Charles Dana that slavery had weakened the south so much that it would be unable to mount a war effort; the north could push hard without losing much blood.[27]

With social revolution so near and slavery the only large obstacle, Greeley became a proponent of terrorist means to gain anti-slavery objectives. As one historian noted concerning *Tribune* correspondents in Kansas during the mid-1850s, "the crew Greeley assembled went forth with hatred in their hearts. . . ."[28] The *Tribune's* coverage of the battle between northerners and southerners in Kansas was predictably propagandistic, with northerners always depicted as peace loving citizens brought to conflict by southern terror. The *Tribune* wanted fighters and weapons shipped to Kansas immediately, to preserve the peace.[29] Correspondent James Redpath wrote that because there would be no peace as long as slavery existed, he would "fight and kill for the sake of peace."[30]

Greeley's response to the events of May 24, 1856, indicates his hardline position. That night in Kansas, John Brown and seven other men invaded the homes of several farming families—the Doyles, the Wilkinsons, and the Harrises. These families had done no one any harm. They did not own slaves. They were simply from the south. They were also trusting: When William Doyle opened his door in response to a request for directions, John Brown's men grabbed him and took him 200 yards from the cabin. John Brown then placed a revolver against Doyle's forehead and pulled the trigger, killing him instantly. Doyle's 22-year-old son William was then stabbed in the face, slashed over the head, and shot in the side. His 20-year-old son Drury had his fingers and arms cut off and his head cut open; then he was stabbed in the chest. A third son, 14-year-old John, also would have been executed, but the mother, Mahala Doyle, clutched him and screamed, "Not him; Oh God, not him." John Brown let him live.[31]

Brown and his followers—four of them were Brown's sons—then moved on to the Wilkinson home, took the man away from his wife and small children, and cut his throat. They then went to the Harris cabin, occupied that night not only by James Harris and his family but by three other men who had stopped by; one had come to buy a cow. The door was unlocked, because the region until then had been safe. Harris and two of the men turned out to be northerners and were allowed to live; the southerner was murdered by the river with sabers. One blow severed his left hand, raised in self-defense; others split open his skull, and he fell into the river. The murderers washed their swords and walked away as the cold water carried away part of the dead man's brain.

The goal of the massacre was terrorism, pure and simple: Kill those who sided with a hated system, focus attention on what became known as "bleeding Kansas," and raise tensions so high that warfare capable of destroying the hated system would become more likely. Terrorists need press publicity, preferably somewhat sympathetic—and John Brown and associates got it. The *Tribune* called Brown's terrorism a self-defense strike needed to disrupt the southern horde of Kansas settlers.[32] Greeley advocated shipment of more arms to Kansas and dispatched a military expert to advise John Brown.[33]

Greeley used events in Kansas to further Republican candidate John Fremont's hopes in the election of 1856; historian Jeter Isely has concluded that "Reading Greeley's journal at this late date gives the impression that his staff had no concern for accuracy with regard to Kansas of 1856."[34] Reporter W. A. Phillips sent frequent articles, and the *Tribune* itself sponsored mass meetings of protest and the establishment within each northern city of "Kansas committees" to send aid. The *Tribune* publicized books, pamphlets, and plays on Kansas, and even serialized a novel telling of how Kansas southerners were "ruffians, half-tipsy, with hair unkempt and beards like cotton-cards, squirting tobacco-juice in every direction, and interlarding their conversation with oaths and curses" aimed at defenseless folk. One of the poor sufferers was the heroine, gentle Alice, who took to her sickbed in fright and remained sorrowful until she had a vision of Fremont's election and Kansas' freedom, at which "the thin lips of Alice quivered tremulously. It was her last smile on earth."[35]

Greeley went at it again following John Brown's raid on Harper's Ferry. During the month following the raid the *Tribune* ran 26 columns and 15 editorials on Brown.[36] The *Tribune* correspondent was consistently pro-Brown and anti-southern; he generalized about the south, "Everything shows how far this region is behind the age."[37] But he was also sarcastic about particular southerners, such as prosecutor Charles Harding, whose "face is a vindictive as well as a degraded one," and who "has a way of expressing profound contempt by ejecting saliva aloft, and catching it on his chin, which he practices with great success."[38]

Greeley displayed extreme arrogance during this crisis, and knew exactly what he was doing: In a letter to his associate editor, James S. Pike, Greeley wrote that he was in the "position of the rich old fellow, who, having built a church entirely out of his own means, addressed his townsmen thus: 'I've built you a meeting-house,/ And bought you a bell;/ Now go to meeting/ Or go to hell!' "[39] Isely commented, "Greeley believed that John Brown's raid . . . would bring thousands into his church. The *Tribune* featured Brown as a saint sprung from the Book of Revelation to herald the coming of universal freedom."[40]

The *Tribune* had feisty competition. Bennett's *New York Herald* had long made fun of Greeley's support for "all the *isms* and *ultras* of the day," including "Fourierism, atheism, community of property socialism—every species of wild and extravagant thought and doctrine."[41] Abolitionism, Bennett wrote, merely was the latest cause of "the clique of enthusiasts, fanatics, Fourierists, and infidels of all descriptions who are engaged in [the *Tribune's*] activities."[42] Bennett called John Brown "a notorious Kansas shrieker—one whose hands had more than once been dipped in human blood."[43] Bennett also called Greeley a member of "an anti-slavery oligarchy" that was attempting to establish a new "inquisition."[44]

The *Herald,* however, had little influence on those who saw American chattel slavery (correctly, I believe) as a central moral problem, and not just an economic one. More influential among some of those who founded the Republican Party was the newspaper built by Greeley's debating adversary of 1846 and 1847, Henry Raymond. That newspaper, begun in 1851 and known as *The New York Times,* opposed slavery fervently, but not without an eye to the difficulty of altering an imbedded institution. Raymond, unlike Greeley, did not see anti-slavery agitation as a step toward class warfare, and did not sanguinely look to blood as the answer to social problems; therefore, he was not taken in by those who said that the outbreak of civil war would lead to a southern social revolution that could then spread north. *Times* reporting from Kansas and Harper's Ferry bemoaned the provocations and appealed for calm.

The most fascinating New York newspaper in the months directly preceding the civil war was probably the *New York World,* a daily newspaper begun in 1860 in an attempt to revive Christian journalism. After Abraham Lincoln was elected in 1860, the *World* proposed that anti-slavery newspapers

> forbear to indulge in that acerbity of tone which, while it has never done any good, has occasioned much of the unfortunate asperity which exists among our Southern brethren. Let the exultation of approaching victory be tempered with manly generosity, and the whole tone, bearing and language of the party be of a character to confirm [hopes for] a moderate, a conciliatory, a conservative, a truly national and constitutional administration.[45]

There can still be peace, the *World* insisted, "if the press and orators of all parties will drop the vituperative style in which they are wont to indulge, and practice a reasonable courtesy and magnanimity."

World news coverage stressed accuracy at a time when propaganda seemed more and more ascendant. "The news from Kansas is uncertain and contradictory," the *World* noted in November, 1860:

> Nothing illustrates the evils of excessive partisanship more than the impossibility of getting trustworthy accounts of important events occurring far from the great

centers. Here is a matter, of which it is extremely important that all parties should know the truth, yet it is impossible to arrive at the truth. The determination of partisan newspapers, and of their correspondents, to throw all the blame upon the other side, leads to distortion, misrepresentation, and even positive mendacity.[46]

The *World,* for its part, criticized many northerners for attempting to excommunicate the south, and criticized southern slaveholders for engaging in

the separation of families, the taking of the parent from the child and the child from the parent, ignoring the marriage tie, withholding even that amount of education which would enable the colored man to read God's oracles—when the South would defend all this as being within the aegis of the quiet of the gospel, the South are doing wrong to the gospel, and perverting it.[47]

The *World* quoted Matthew 5:9—"Blessed are the peacemakers, for they shall be called the children of God"—and asked Christians of both sides "to humble themselves, and confess before God that they have disparaged our common Lord and Redeemer."[48] It favorably covered proposals for gradual emancipation— children of slaves would be freed—and publicized suggestions to smooth the way by payments from the North: "That would test the northern conscience, and put us right under a reformed constitution."[49]

The tendencies of the *World* found some support in the South. In Texas, Governor Sam Houston published his last hope:

Providence has ever guarded the people of these United States. He sustained the hope of our struggling fathers until they gained the liberty that we now enjoy. He gave them the wisdom and the prudence through which our government was formed. For eighty-four years that Same Providence has shielded us, amid danger from without and dissention from within. He has encircled us with His protecting Arm and has preserved our liberties intact. Let us in the hour of Prayer, implore Him to shield us still in the time of peril, that we may be preserved a United people . . ."[50]

By 1860, however, such fairmindedness had little chance to be accepted, for the tensions were too great; Houston, for example, was denounced as a "Texas Brutus."[51]

Columns in the *World* tended to go deeper. One analysis of the divided nation showed how each leading "journalistic fire-brand" thought his own views superior to "written constitutions" and decided to "erect his own judgment or his own happiness, into a tribunal."[52] With extremism rampant, many northern newspapers "vilif[ied] southern states, institutions, and men," and southerners in turn

reacted to vituperation . . . From studying methods of emancipation, they turned to the consideration of schemes for the perpetuation and extension of the happy patriarchal institution . . . masters, alarmed for the safety of their families, clamored for more stringent laws whereby to circumscribe and oppress the slave.[53]

The Greeleyite revolutionary position had not "ameliorated the condition of the servile masses of the South" and held out no "hope than that of insurrection and bloodshed," the column argued. It ended with a plea that journalists "stay the streams of section reviling."[54]

Greeley was the chief culprit, according to the *World*.[55] Southerners who read his work saw him as representing northern hatred of the south—in the words of the *Raleigh Register,* Greeley was "the vilest, the dirtiest, the most mangy hog in the Abolition pen."[56] Other newspapers moving toward the *oppression story*—including the *New York Post, Chicago Tribune,* and *Hartford Courant*—followed Greeley's lead.[57] And the *Tribune* itself, becoming during the 1850s America's first semi-national newspaper, had no readership in the south, but distributed a weekly edition of 200,000 copies from Maine to Minnesota. That was 10% of free state votes, and often the most articulate 10%; as historian James Ford Rhodes recollected years later, *Tribune* readers "were of the thorough kind . . . questions were discussed in their family circles and with their neighbors, and, as differences arose, the *Tribune,* always at hand, was consulted and re-read."[58]

How great was the *Tribune's* influence? According to one press-watcher, "every man, and woman too, of education, culture, and moral feeling" was praising the *Tribune;* it had a grip on "the affections of all the best people."[59] The *Tribune,* in short, "was more than a metropolitan journal, it was a sectional oracle."[60] The *Tribune* prophesied that America was faced with an either/or decision:

It may be that a new era of religion—of Justice and Brotherhood between man and man—is commencing; or it may be that this is only a fresh spasm, to be followed by a more palpable moral lifelessness. Which shall it be?[61]

The *Tribune* may have pushed hundreds of thousands of northerners to push hard for the new era.

The *Tribune,* of course, was not responsible for the Civil War. Journalism was one compelling force among many, and the *Tribune* was one newspaper among many. But if the *Tribune* and its followers had seen the south as a culture and not as the potential arena for class struggle between slave owners and a combined poor White/Black coalition, it seems likely that a wiser course could have been followed. And if the *Tribune* and other newspapers had not glorified in death a man, John Brown, who represented the deepest fears of the south, many southerners might not have believed that the North would soon be sending other Browns to achieve what he tried to start.[62]

Many southern journalists also were irresponsible. One *World* column, "THE

SOUTHERN FRANKENSTEIN," criticized those who had urged on forces that were now out of control:

> The South has, in plain terms, been dragooned into its present rebellious attitude by the unscrupulous and persistent mendacity of its politicians and journals, abetted by some of those at the North. There are indications that some of the southern 'leaders' would be glad, if it were in their power, to allay the storm which they have aided in raising. They begin to discover that the consummation of their plans promises at the best no better thing that absolute hopeless bankruptcy. . . . The sagacious among these suicidal agitators would, doubtless, be glad to annul the share they have had in bringing about the present deplorable disaster. But it is too late.[63]

By the end of 1860 it *was* too late. Bandwagon headlines rolled through southern front pages: "Georgia Moving!" "Ten Thousand Cheers for Florida!" "Alabama All Right—Convention Called."[64] Those who wished to wait were called traitors. In the rapture of the moment, even those few newspapers that had counted the costs of war realistically jumped on the bandwagon. In January 1860, the *Richmond Dispatch* had stated forcefully,

> It is impossible to exaggerate the horrors and sufferings which for years would follow a dissolution of the Union. . . . It would be war from the start, war to the knife and knife to the hilt. The widely extended border between the North and South would be a line of fire and blood. Every accessible bay and inlet of every river would be entered, and, ever and anon, large masses of men hurled upon the capitols and important points of Southern States. But the horrors of ordinary warfare would be far transcended by the barbarities of this cruel strife.[65]

But in January 1861, the *Dispatch* strongly called for secession, and did not mention the costs.[66]

It was too late. Had the south not replied to fanaticism with rage of its own, another course might have been possible. By 1860, however, the alternative courses were being abandoned, and the *oppression story* was about to claim its first few hundred thousand victims. A Georgia newspaper reported that "The tone of the Northern press . . . should convince all southern men that the hour for dissolution is come. . . ."[67] The *Albany [Georgia] Patriot* cited a Greeley report and argued, "We might as well sing Psalms over the dead carcass of a buzzard, as to appeal to the Union for *rights* and *justice*."[68] One month later, the *Patriot* reported that "Insult upon insult has been heaped upon the South, and we are daily informed that these wrongs and aggressions are to be repeated. . . . For our part we would prefer to strike the blow this very hour than to wait for the morrow."[69]

It was too late. In a letter to Stephen A. Douglas, Mississippi lawyer S. S. Fairfield complained that the state's newspapers were "generally in the hands of young and inexperienced men."[70] Fairfield described how Mississippi agendas were set:

When a scheme is put on foot the [Jackson] *Mississippian* roars and all the little county papers yelp, the cross road and bar room politicians take it up and so it goes, and if any one opposes them they raise the cry of abolitionist and traitor.[71]

A thoughtful North Carolina editor complained, "Madness seems to rule the hour, and fearful forebodings cloud the prospect."[72] The *New York Herald* feared a long war and ran a headline, "Blood! Blood! Blood!—Who Will Be Responsible?"[73] But the *New York Tribune,* confident in February 1861, that the radical upheaval to come could eliminate oppression, added to its masthead the words, "NO COMPROMISE!/ NO CONCESSIONS TO TRAITORS!"[74] Soon, the cannons were roaring.

Once war began, the *Tribune* plunged ahead with plans to celebrate a quick victory, on the materialist theory that the nonindustrialized south could not possibly fight a war. In theory, the northern army could crush its numerically inferior opponents, the northern navy could blockade the Confederate coast, and the "laws of trade" would kill the south.[75] Day after day Greeley ran the same paragraph on the editorial page: "The Nation's War Cry. Forward to Richmond! Forward to Richmond! The Rebel Congress must not be allowed to meet there on the twentieth of July! By that date the place must be held by the National Army!"[76]

Under pressure, the poorly trained Union army advanced and was routed at Manassas. The *Herald* said it was Greeley's fault. Greeley was in shock: The material superiority of the north had not led to early victory. The south fought on, and many of the radical journalists who had predicted northern victory without bloodshed were angry with President Abraham Lincoln for his early attempts to win the war with as little bloodshed as possible. Journalists during the first year of the war called him a "political coward," "timid and ignorant," "pitiable," "too slow," and "shattered, dazed, utterly foolish."[77] Southern newspapers called their opponent a drunkard, but northern newspapers were often more creative in their labeling of Lincoln as "an awful, woeful ass," the "craftiest and most dishonest politician that ever disgraced an office in America," a "half-witted usurper," a "mole-eyed monster with a soul of leather," "unmentionably diseased," and the "woodenhead at Washington."[78]

Lincoln put up with it as best he could, and even laughed at Greeley's frequent nastiness: "I do not suppose I have any right to complain," Lincoln said, for "Uncle Horace . . . is with us at least four days out of seven."[79] In any event, the war ground on. Occasionally, it was brought home to some northern editors; in July 1863, a mob advanced on the *Tribune* building yelling "Down with the *Tribune.*" The mob destroyed the furniture on the first floor and started a fire with the goal of destroying the building, but 100 policemen arrived with orders to "Hit their temples, strike hard, take no prisoners." Twenty-two men were killed. Many more were seriously wounded.

Hundreds of thousands more died during the civil war, but eventually material did triumph. By 1865, the southern opposition to centralization was demolished, and the road to rapidly increased governmental power was open. The first step was to do away with the defeated opposition leaders; journalists who already had waded in blood reported that "all the interests of humanity demand that Davis, Lee & Company, shall be tried, found guilty, and hanged by the neck until they are dead."[80] The next step was to reconstruct first the south, and then the entire nation, on an economic plan that expropriated large holdings in land, still the primary basis of wealth. Abraham Lincoln did not favor such radical plans, but his assassination removed the enemy of both maddened southerners and ambitious northern radicals. And Andrew Johnson, at first, did not seem likely to present much of a barrier.

Nevertheless, during the quarter century after the Civil War, progress did not come as quickly as Greeleyite journalists had hoped. First, Andrew Johnson and several other conservative political leaders stood in the way; then, a certain realism concerning the limits of federal power sank in for a time. The next chapter examines the obstacles, beginning with Johnson, who saved southern leaders from hanging trees, and in turn saw much of the journalistic wrath turned on himself.

Chapter 8

Obstacles to Power

In one sense, it is surprising that President Andrew Johnson was treated so poorly in the press; his rise contained the stuff of which memorable human interest stories are made. Orphaned and penniless at the age of 4, Johnson became an unschooled tailor who was taught by his wife to read and write. Hard work and good business sense enabled him to make a success of his small shop. Johnson read and thought about politics and government. He paid a man to read to him throughout the day while he plied his needle. Johnson's opponents would often decry his lack of formal education, but the tailor's desire to study and learn began a lifetime pattern of self-education: After Johnson was elected senator from Tennessee, he was one of the leading visitors to and borrowers of books from the Library of Congress.

Johnson's problem as president, however, was that during those years of sewing and listening he developed a fixed set of political principles, at the center of which was opposition to governmental and economic centralization. He worried about states becoming "mere satellites of an inferior character, revolving around the great central power" of Washington."[1] He opposed "concentration of power in the hands of the few."[2] He opposed government economic activities such as railroad grants, predicting that they would result in "nothing but a series of endless corrupting legislation."[3] Consequently, Johnson was called callow and callous by Horace Greeley and other journalists who saw the federal government as hero in an upcoming saga of forced social restructuring.

Underlying the battle of Greeley versus Johnson during the 3 years following the Civil War were Greeley's hopes for a final victory that would make up for the failed hopes of the 1840s and 1850s. The war won by the north at immense cost must be followed by the winning of the peace, he wrote.[4] That peace, he hoped, could end not just the antagonism of master and slave, but also that of capitalist and worker. The federal government could move from restructuring the south to restructuring the entire country. Socialism in one commune had not worked, but perhaps a shake-up of the entire country would.

Some writers have seen the Radical Republican program of the late 1860s merely as an attempt to punish the south for seceding and to ensure enfranchisement of Blacks. But Senator Thad Stevens, the leading radical politician, argued for federal confiscation of all southern landholdings larger than 200 acres; historian Gregg Singer has observed that,

> The radical element of the [Republican] party was determined to carry out a reconstruction policy in the South as a prelude to the reconstruction they intended to bring about in the nation as a whole. The southern states were to be used as social science laboratories . . . as a kind of pilot study for reconstructing the whole nation. . . .[5]

Andrew Johnson was certainly aware of the danger: From the first, he spoke of his responsibility to defend the Constitution against radical attempts to establish dictatorship. His message to Congress in December 1865, called the federal government "a limited government" that must remain limited if the Constitution is to endure, for "the destruction of the one is the destruction of the other." The gauntlet was hurled down.

In February 1866, the Radical Republicans passed a bill (to widespread journalistic applause) that gave the federal government total power in the southern states, with federal agents to act as judge and jury. Johnson vetoed it. He argued that it represented

> an absorption and assumption of power by the General Government which, if acquiesced in, must sap and destroy our federative system of limited powers, and break down the barriers which preserve the rights of the States. It is another step, or rather stride, to centralization and the concentration of all legislative power in the National Government.[6]

He pointed out that punishments for arrested southerners would not be defined by law but imposed by court martial, and that there would be no appeal from those decisions, not even to the U.S. Supreme Court. Furthermore, he believed that presidential appointment of those august Federal agents gave himself or other presidents too much power, power "as in time of peace certainly ought never to be entrusted to any one man."[7] Leading journalists called Johnson a traitor, weakling, coward, bribed drunkard, and murderer: The *Milwaukee Sentinel* ludicrously charged that "Johnson was privy to Lincoln's assassination."[8]

Johnson also disapproved of the welfare parts of the bill's segment concerning aid to Blacks: "A system for the support of indigent persons . . . was never contemplated by the authors of the Constitution."[9] Johnson was not a person who lacked compassion for the ex-slaves: He told a delegation of Black leaders that he wished their goal of full political, social, and economic equality "could be done in the twinkling of an eye, but it is not in the nature of things, and I do not assume or pretend to be wiser than Providence."[10] Johnson preferred charitable initiatives to federal programs, and personally sent $1,000 to support a school to educate Black children in Charleston. Fundamentally, however, Johnson argued that Black labor power was essential in the south; economic laws of supply and demand would lead to Black economic advancement that would then give ex-slaves the power to demand full political rights.

Following his veto, Johnson warned a crowd assembled on the White House lawn that the Radical Republicans wished "to concentrate all power in the hands of a few."[11] He argued that some radicals hoped to lead the United States toward a repeat of the French Revolution.[12] Johnson dared his opponents to do their worst: They "may talk about beheading," he said, "but when I am beheaded, I want the American people to be the witness."[13] He insisted that Blacks would not be able to gain and maintain voting rights merely through new use of federal bayonets: That would just create a White backlash that could delay *permanent* enfranchisement for decades. Such statements were treated with scorn in much of the press, which provided the radicals in Congress with fresh ammunition every day: Virtually every afternoon the Clerk of the House would read to the assembled members an anti-Johnson newspaper clipping, and the radicals would cheer.[14]

Johnson did not give in. In August 1866, he continued to argue that the radicals had "usurped powers which, if permitted, would result in despotism or monarchy itself."[15] Johnson decided to take his case to the country. Before the speaking tour, Senator Doolittle of Wisconsin warned Johnson not to "allow the excitement of the moment to draw from you any *extemporaneous speeches*. You are followed by the reporters of a hundred presses who do nothing but misrepresent."[16] Doolittle was right, as historian George Milton has related:

> Johnson swayed those who heard him. Time after time he faced a hostile crowd and converted it into a friendly one. But while he was convincing a hundred thousand, the Radical correspondents, in reporting his speeches, so distorted and misrepresented them that they turned three million against him.[17]

Greeley's *New York Tribune*, instead of printing the substance of Johnson's remarks, portrayed Johnson as a moron who was good only for "gritting his teeth, and accompanying his words with violent gesticulation."[18]

Johnson, in his speeches, repeatedly answered the accusations against him and tried to explain the world view underlying his policies. In New York City on

August 29, 1866, in Utica on August 31, and in Buffalo on September 3, he talked about the nature of treason, the wonder of God's mercy, and the threat of dictatorship. Just as journalists who emphasized man's corruption and God's grace had done, he applied the Bible to political events, telling St. Louis residents that "The Saviour of man came on earth and found the human race condemned and sentenced under the law, but when they repented and believed, he said let them live."[19] In Cincinnati he proclaimed, "If I have pardoned traitors I have only obeyed the injunction of scripture—to forgive the repentant. . . . Hang eight millions of people! Who ever heard of such a thing? Yet because I refuse to do this, I am called a traitor."[20] He told the crowds that because God had been merciful to them, they should be merciful to other offenders. He typically concluded with his desire to have 36 states in the Union, and not to end up with 25, due to the exclusion of the South.

Radical partisans ridiculed Johnson's concerns. Journalist David Ross Locke had his humorous persona, "Petroleum V. Nasby," give mocking reports of Johnson's supposedly drunken progress:

> He wuz fightin traitors on all sides. . . . all he wanted now wuz to heal the wounds uv the nashen . . . he mite hev been Dicktater, but woodent; and ended with a poetickal cotashun which I coodent ketch. . . . He asked em, ef he was Judis Iskariot who wuz the Saviour? . . . The crowd hollered 'Grant! Grant!' and the President thanked em for the demonstration. It showed him that the people wuz with him in his efforts to close his eyes on a Union uv 36 States and a flag uv 36 stars onto it.[21]

The *Cleveland Leader* called Johnson's speech in that city "the most disgraceful ever delivered by any president of the United States."[22] Greeley's *Tribune* called Johnson's trip "the stumping tour of an irritated demagogue," and Lowell in the *North American Review* labeled it "an indecent orgy."[23]

Testimony during Johnson's impeachment trial would show that one frequent charge against Johnson—that he was a drunkard—was a vicious untruth; the only drunkard during the trip was General Grant, who accompanied Johnson but in Cleveland was put aboard a boat to Detroit so that his condition would not be revealed.[24] The *New York Tribune* and Joseph Medill's *Chicago Tribune* were particularly biased.[25] *The Independent* gave Johnson "lascivious" eyes, "the face of a demagogue" and "the heart of a traitor."[26] The magazine argued that Johnson was a "trickster . . . touched with insanity, corrupted with lust, stimulated with drink."[27]

Month after month the drumbeat went on: "We have demanded and shall continue to demand that this Aaron Burr, this Benedict Arnold, this Andrew Johnson shall be put out of the way of injuring the government which he first disgraced, then betrayed, and would willingly destroy."[28] The roughness of some of Johnson's extemporaneous sentences allowed other put-downs: Greeley snorted in one editorial that Johnson's "verbs never agree with their nominatives, or their hearers or anything else."[29] George Milton has correctly described press coverage of Johnson's speaking in this way:

> The type of thing that the Radical press had to say about this President of the United States shows to what low estate journalism had fallen. Editorially and in their news columns, such papers as Joseph Medill's *Chicago Tribune* and Horace Greeley's *New York Tribune* gave vent to vituperation which a decent man would be asked to apply to a convict.[30]

Johnson had convicted himself in the eyes of many reporters and editors when he refused to support radical demands for governmental centralization and social revolution in the South. There were some limits on Johnson-bashing: A St. Louis reporter was fired after he filed a largely imaginary account of a Johnson speech.[31] But as long as a journalist provided the minimum of fact and contextualized it in a way that heaped ridicule on the President, he was not only safe but often applauded.

In 1867, the situation of the moderates deteriorated further. Thad Stevens was so confident that he began to proclaim openly his revolutionary intentions: When he pushed forward a bill to divide the south into military districts, with commanders having arbitrary power for an indefinite period of time, he argued baldly that "every government is a despotism," and that his bill was crucial because it "would assure the ascendancy of the Union [Republican] party."[32] The radical willingness to use violence had not stopped with John Brown's terrorism and the resultant war: *The Independent,* which earlier had demanded the execution of southern leaders, screamed in September, 1867, "The People [capital P] are waiting anxiously for the impeachment of the President," and if Johnson tried to stop the process, "let him be tried by a court martial, and shot by twelve soldiers in a hollow square."[33]

Many newspapers, serving as organs of a dominant party and perhaps propelling that party toward greater extremism, had their greatest power ever. Those radical newspapers, of course, did not have monopoly power at that time, because moderate newspapers existed in most cities. But the influence of the radical press was great, and newspaper vituperation certainly contributed to Johnson's impeachment by the House of Representatives on February 24, 1868.

Greeley and Medill were exultant following the impeachment, as the House began presenting its evidence for the Senate trial. Johnson did not give up. One Sunday after church Johnson read a Bible passage to an attendant:

> Behold, here I am: Witness against me before the Lord . . . whose ox have I taken? or whose ass have I taken? or whom have I defrauded? whom have I oppressed' or of whose hand have I received any bribe to blind mine eyes therewith? and I will restore it to you.[34]

But truth was a porous defense against a furious Greeley, who charged that any senator who sided with Johnson was dishonest.[35] Magazines such as *The Nation* and newspapers such as the *Washington Chronicle* and the *Philadelphia Press* also fought their opponents not with open argument, but by wholesaling words such as "corrupt," "scoundrel," "fraudulent," and "dishonorable."[36]

A two thirds vote of the Senate was needed to convict Johnson, and the pressure on Republican senators to fall in line was enormous. In the end, when one more Senate vote was needed to convict Johnson, his future came down to a decision by a Kansas printer-turned-politician, Edmund G. Ross. Ross' background—anti-slavery immigrant to Kansas in 1856 and leader of radical forces there—led Greeley to believe that he would vote to convict. Yet, Ross had replied to demands that he prejudge Johnson by writing, "I have taken an oath to do impartial justice according to the Constitution and laws, and trust that I shall have the courage to vote according to the dictates of my judgment. . . ."[37]

Ross displayed that courage and refused to convict Johnson. A Kansas newspaper editorialized that Ross had

> sold himself, and betrayed his constituents; stultified his own record . . . and to the utmost of his poor ability signed the death warrant of his country's liberty. This act was done deliberately, because the traitor, like Benedict Arnold, loved money better than he did principle, friends, honor and his country, all combined. Poor, pitiful, shriveled wretch, with a soul so small that a little pelf would outweigh all things else that dignify or ennoble mankind.[38]

Greeley attacked Ross with particular viciousness, calling him "the greatest criminal of the age . . . a miserable poltroon and traitor."[39]

After Johnson's close escape, Greeley kept up his attacks. For the 1868 election he backed U.S. Grant, who had joined the radicals. Greeley told *Tribune* readers that a Grant triumph would mean great prosperity, but a victory for Democratic candidate Horatio Seymour would begin "the first phase of the counter-revolution . . . Anarchy and strife, terrorism and assassination, will pervade that section where the fires of Rebellion still smolder."[40] Thomas Nast's cartooning in *Harper's Weekly* was so effective that Grant afterward said he owed his election to "the sword of Sheridan and the pencil of Thomas Nast."[41] Meanwhile, Grant received adulatory coverage from the *New York Tribune* and other newspapers; the *Philadelphia Enquirer* was typical in its depiction of him as "the possessor of those analytical powers which enable men to judge character with close and correct appreciation."[42]

In 1869, with Johnson returning to Tennessee and Grant's analytical powers in the saddle, there was no check on the Washington radical forces and their campaign contributors. One observer, George W. Julian, wrote, "I have never seen such lobbying before as we have had in the last few weeks and such crookedness and complicity among members."[43] Another, James W. Grimes, complained that "the war has corrupted everybody and everything."[44] What Leggett had feared was coming true: The federal government now had such power that citizens were becoming "mere puppets of legislative cobbling and tinkering." Those business leaders who had backed the Radical Republican power grab called in their markers, and the *New York Herald* was able to observe that "All our railroad legislation is procured by corrupt practices and is formed in the interest of jobbery."[45]

The corruption of many Radical Republican state governments in the South during Reconstruction is legendary. With radical newspapers—42 in Georgia alone—supported by government revenues, the press often tried to cover up scandals. Newspapers received contracts for public printing at high rates and then received more money than even those contracts allowed. In South Carolina, for example, the *Charleston Republican* was supposed to receive $24,538 but received $60,982 instead; the *Columbia Daily Record,* after contracting at unusually high rates that would have yielded $17,174, was paid $59,988. Bribes and payoffs were so common that one South Carolina senator, C. P. Leslie, was able to produce a classic line in their defense: "The State has no right to be a State until she can afford to take care of her statesmen."[46] The most famous episode of the day came when the Speaker of the South Carolina House of Representatives lost a $1,000 bet on a horse and, 3 days later was voted a gratuity to cover his loss, in tribute to "the dignity and ability with which he has presided."[47]

Ironically, with all this press concern for the character of President Johnson and certain senators, scandals involving Radical Republican leaders at first were downplayed. When radical leader Schuyler Colfax, accused of receiving a bribe, took 10 days to produce a weak defense—he talked about a $1,000 bill arriving unsolicited in the mail—most radical newspapers rushed to his defense. The *Boston Advertiser* was typical when it called the charge "all fuss and parade."[48] Cartoonist Nast, scourge of Tweed Ring politicians and other nonradical miscreants, was told by a friend, "The whole subject offers a rich theme for your pencil, but I doubt the wisdom of availing yourself of it."[49] Nast did not.

Eventually, however, some editors became cranky about covering up ever more scandals. Leading Republican editors such as Greeley, Horace White (who had assumed editorship of the *Chicago Tribune*), and Samuel Bowles of the *Springfield Republican,* joined with moderates such as Murat Halstead of the *Cincinnati Daily Commercial* and Henry Watterson of the *Louisville Courier-Journal,* in a search for an alternative to Grant. At a confused "Liberal Republican" convention in 1872, Greeley fulfilled part of his lifelong ambition by snatching the nomination from Charles Francis Adams, son and grandson of presidents. However, Greeley missed the great prize as he was smashed by Grant's popularity; given the *Tribune's* earlier boosting of Grant, in one sense the Greeley defeat was a story of Frankenstein's monster turning on Frankenstein.

Greeley, heartbroken, died 3 weeks after his electoral defeat. At the funeral, liberal minister Henry Ward Beecher was upbeat: "Today, between the two oceans, there is hardly an intelligent man or child that does not feel the influence of Horace Greeley."[50] But Greeley had a different summing-up. As he was dying, perhaps speaking wildly, he said, "My life has been a fevered march," and he

> had been tempted by the glittering bait of the Presidency. . . . And now, having done wrong to millions while intending only good to hundreds, I pray God that he may quickly take me from a world where all I have done seems to have turned to evil, and wherein each hour has long been and henceforth must be one of agony, remorse, and shame.[51]

In one of his last statements Greeley wrote:

> I stand naked before my God, the most utterly, hopelessly wretched and undone of all who ever lived. I have done more harm and wrong than any man who ever saw the light of day. And yet I take God to witness that I have never intended to injure or harm anyone. But this is no excuse.[52]

Senator Ross of Kansas, who in Greeley's words deserved "everlasting infamy" for refusing to convict Andrew Johnson, had a happier ending, after much suffering. In the short run Ross *was* infamous: He was burned in effigy many times, and a justice of the Supreme Court of Kansas suggested that he commit suicide. At a mass meeting in Lawrence led by a man named Hugh Cameron, Ross was warned not to return to Kansas; when he did so, a local tough invaded his print shop and beat Ross so thoroughly that the ex-senator never completely recovered his health. Years later, however, Grover Cleveland appointed Ross governor of the Territory of New Mexico, and one day Ross was amazed to see Hugh Cameron. Cameron had walked all the way from Kansas to New Mexico to apologize for his leadership of that mass meeting.

During Grant's second term, public opinion turned against the Radical Republicans. In the 1876 election, Democratic candidate Samuel Tilden gained 250,000 more votes than the Republican candidate, Rutherford Hayes, and piled up safe majorities in all the states he needed to win the Electoral College except for three (Florida, South Carolina, and Louisiana) where he had narrower leads. Only some Electoral College chicanery allowed Hayes to assume office—but on condition that the radical program for the south be abandoned.

Johnson's predictions of a southern White backlash proved accurate, and southern Blacks were left free but still in chains for several generations. Their erstwhile allies in the northern press moved on to other concerns; the *New York Tribune* justified its malign neglect by declaring that "after ample opportunity to develop their own latent capacities" the ex-slaves had proven that "as a race they are idle, ignorant, and vicious."[53] A prediction of *The Nation* proved accurate for several generations: "The negro will disappear from the field of national politics. Henceforth the nation, as a nation, will have nothing more to do with him."[54]

The end of reconstruction in the South also signalled the complete failure of attempts to reconstruct economically the north. With the Christian ideas of the early 19th century largely abandoned, but no ideology yet dominant enough to take its place, some reporters in large cities embraced a total cynicism; others, seeing death and destruction occurring apparently at random, embraced a Social Darwinist faith in natural determinism. The chief spokesman of the latter was Yale professor William Graham Sumner, who believed that blind evolutionary forces had created man, and argued that all life is a struggle against the forces of nature, with some surviving and other proving inadequate.[55] Tooth-and-claw was the way the world worked and the way any society had to work:

> Nothing but might has ever made right. . . . If a thing has been done and is established by force (that is no force can reverse it), it is right in the only sense we can know and rights will follow from it which are not vitiated at all by the forces in it.[56]

Reporters who applied that thinking often became ruthless in their invasion of privacy to get a story. For example, the *New York Tribune,* which maintained its materialism following Greeley's death and shifted easily toward Sumner's views, treated suicide as a helpful self-selection of the unfit and cheered for the stronger side in international conflicts, regardless of justification.[57]

Small town newspapers, however, often showed a less strained quality of mercy. Typical news reports showed crime as affecting not only the criminal and his victims, but family members of all involved; one poignant story told of an old outlaw who resisted arrest and was killed, along with his 10-year-old grandson.[58] Concern for family also was evident in a story of a man unable or unwilling to support his wife and two small children, who were housed temporarily in the city hospital: "Mrs. Dongan is hardly thirty, but her sorrows and heartaches have changed her features so that she appears to be fifty years old. Her children are aged 8 and 4."[59] An article headlined "A WIFE BEATER ARRESTED" told how a man

> had tanked up on mean whiskey and went home and lit into his wife, who was dreaming on her pillow. The woman was badly bruised up, and the husband will get his reward in the county court.[60]

When small-town newspaper editors assembled at press association conventions, they frequently spoke about the obligations they felt in protecting "the sacredness of home and private affairs."[61] These beliefs influenced reporting methodology as well as results. For example, a Dallas reporter was interviewing a woman who had abandoned her husband to run away with another man. The new man proved to be a bum. The woman was thinking of returning to her husband. The husband was coming to talk with her. The story of the interview continued as follows:

> Just at this point of the conversation the door of the room in which Mrs. Finnegan and the reporter were in opened and a clean shaved gentleman, neatly dressed, and who looked to be about 30 years old, entered. He glanced from the reporter to Mrs. Finnegan and stretching out his hand appealingly, said, "Jennie."

> The reporter, recognizing in the gentleman by his actions Mrs. Finnegan's husband and feeling the weight of his presence, retired from the room into another where he thought to wait for an interview with Finnegan, but owing to the fact that the husband and wife in their excitement raised their voices so that almost every word they spoke could be heard by the reporter, he left the house not caring to be a listener to their conversation.[62]

Some regional newspapers during this period showed an impressive willingness to take stands against expansion of centralized government power, and to stick to that policy even when it hurt. For example, in 1886 and 1887 West Texas faced an enormous drought, and Congress passed a bill appropriating $10,000 for the distribution of seeds to farmers in that area. When President Grover Cleveland vetoed the bill, arguing that it was wrong "to indulge a benevolent and charitable sentiment through the appropriation of public funds for that purpose," the *Dallas News* supported the veto, even though the appropriation would have benefited some of its own readers.[63]

The *Dallas News* did not stop there, however. It noted that Cleveland's message "recalled Congress more strictly to constitutional lines of thought" and served an additional purpose: The message "advertised in a special manner to the whole country the deplorable fact of the suffering," and proposed private and church philanthropy.[64] The *News* established a relief fund, and so did some newspapers from other states; for example, the *Louisville Courier-Journal* announced plans for raising and forwarding aid to West Texas, and editorialized that

> We believe Kentucky alone will send $10,000 in seed or in money. She will do it because those men are bone of our bone, and to justify the President's confidence that the people will do what is right."[65]

Reporters emphasized the words of Clara Barton, president of the American Red Cross, after she toured the troubled areas: "The counties which have suffered from drought need help, without doubt, but not help from Congress." Private sources could do the job, she added, and she was right. Contributions arrived from all over Texas; the people of Kentucky and other states responded also. West

Texas eventually received not $10,000 of Federal funding, but over $100,000 in private aid.

The editorial power of other regional leaders, such as the *Kansas City Star,* was also in line with the well-known passage from Edmund Burke:

> To be attached to the subdivision, to love the little platoon we belong to in society, is the first principle (the germ as it were) of public affections. It is the first link in the series by which we proceed toward a love to our country, and to mankind.[66]

Star editor William Rockhill Nelson made a success of the newspaper by emphasizing community news and encouraging self-help. He publicized and praised those who grew better corn or cattle, or baked better cakes. Improvements in local butter-making were not seen as of secondary importance to national political developments.[67]

Nelson, like Horace Greeley a generation earlier, promised readers rapid coverage of local events:

> news will be furnished of fires before the smoke has cleared; murders, before the body of the victim is cold in death; and weddings, before the happy bride can collect her senses or the groom put on his traveling duster. The Evening *Star* proposes in brief to give all the news with lightning-like rapidity and deadly precision.[68]

But Nelson differed from Greeley by emphasizing personal rather than societal change; Nelson, uninterested in the *oppression story,* emphasized examination of the ethical conduct (or corruption) of individuals. At a time when the James gang was praised by some for its vaunted (and exaggerated) policy of income redistribution, the *Star* offered a large reward for the arrest of Jesse James and others, and editorialized that

> Few perhaps realize how much damage Missouri has sustained from the exploits of the James and Younger gang. The failure to bring justice on any of those desperadoes has produced a general impression throughout the country that the majority of Missourians are in sympathy with lawlessness and violence.[69]

The *Star* also fought for restrictions on governmental power and on governmental provision of monopolies to favored groups. Eight Kansas City aldermen in 1882 were under the thumb of the Corrigan street-railway monopoly and its mule-drawn cars; the *Star* termed them the "Shameless Eight" and, in a 2-year battle, stopped the franchise monopoly. Nelson wrote,

> If I owned the Metropolitan Street Railway, I would run it just as I try to run the *Star.* I wouldn't ask for a franchise. I would simply furnish such good service that the people would always be scared to death for fear I would go out of business.[70]

The *Star* constantly emphasized individual initiative, not government action. Nelson urged backyard vegetable gardens, conducted an experiment on a trial acre to show that good profits could be realized from intense cultivation of a small tract of land, and distributed free pamphlets giving the results of the experiment. Seeing alcoholism as destructive of character and not wanting to be compromised in his fight against it, Nelson gave up $50,000 in whiskey advertising. He saw the little platoons of the small town that Kansas City still was a crucial force in avoiding the problems beginning to plague eastern and midwestern urban areas: "The fact that local politics in large cities is generally corrupt is no reason why Kansas City should consider gang rule an essential part of its metropolitan government."[71]

This type of *local* emphasis, and interest in rooting out corruption rather than declaiming about oppression, was a serious obstacle to fulfillment of the old, Greeleyite dreams during the last quarter of the century. This became particularly evident as the debate about income inequality and social reform that had led to the commune movement of the 1840s and 1850s broke out anew during the 1880s and 1890s. Emphasis on limiting governmental power could be found not only on the pages of newspapers in Kansas City and Texas but in the columns of the *New York Times,* edited by the successors of Henry Raymond (who had died in 1869, 3 years before Greeley).

The *Times* became known for publicizing and editorially backing the conclusions of New York's most famous social worker of the 1880s, Josephine Shaw Lowell, when she warned that even temporary governmental relief of the poor "has the tendency to become regular and permanent . . . when it has once been accepted, the barrier is broken down. . . ."[72] She argued that guaranteed income "tends to break down character," and added that "it is the greatest wrong that can be done to him to undermine the character of a poor man."[73] Intrinsic in the writing of both Mrs. Lowell and the *Times* was the belief that man is naturally corrupt, and that changes in material are second in importance to changes in worldview.[74]

That understanding was increasingly opposed during the last two decades of the century by some popular journalists who saw natural goodness ruined by an oppressive environment. Edward Bellamy was only one of hundreds who emerged from newspaper work to write "social problem" novels such as *Dr. Heidenhoff's Process* (1879), which enthusiastically forecast modern 'shock' treatments for neurosis. Bellamy hit it big nearly a decade later with *Looking Backward, 2000–1887.* In that novel, a man through a curious mishap found himself alive, without having aged, 100 years in the future. The world was radically transformed, with peace and abundance for all—and the secret was merely "cooperation." Folks could get all they wanted from cooperative stores. Folks also attained oneness with the universe. Freedom was nonexistent—people were members of an industrial army—but this minor flaw was largely ignored.

Hundreds of newspapers serialized and distributed the writings of Bellamy,

Henry George, and other radicals.[75] The set speeches of *Looking Backward* and its follow-up tract, *Equality,* were learned by a generation of future social reformers:

> How can men be free who must ask the right to labor and to live from their fellow-men and seek their bread from the hands of others? How else can any government guarantee liberty to men save by providing them a means of labor and of life coupled with independence; and how could that be done unless the government conducted the economic system upon which employment and maintenance depend?[76]

Underlying this appealing doctrine was a view of man's nature completely opposite to that imbedded within corruption-story journalism:

> Soon was fully revealed what the divines and philosophers of the old world never would have believed, that human nature in its essential qualities is good, not bad, that men by their natural intention and structure are generous, not selfish, pitiful, not cruel, sympathetic, not arrogant . . .[77]

In short, men were "godlike . . . images of God indeed."[78]

In the early 1890s some newspapers and magazines also began giving favorable publicity to the work of early "Christian socialists" such as Professor Richard Ely. Ely founded the American Economic Association "to strive to find out the underlying principles of industrial society";[79] his goal was to apply principles enunciated by Brisbane and Greeley to all of American society, and he demanded that all unite behind the "coercive philanthropy . . . of governments, either local, state, or national."[80] Journalists fulsomely praised the gospel of salvation-through-government that was promoted by books such as William H. Fremantle's *The World as the Subject of Redemption.*[81] Government alone, Fremantle asserted, "can embrace all the wants of its members and afford them the universal instruction and elevation which they need."[82]

Much of the new doctrine was cloaked within older theological robes. Fremantle, for example, praised the worship of governmental power as a mere furtherance of Christian worship of God: "When we think of it [the Nation] as becoming, as it must do more and more, the object of mental regard, of admiration, of love, even of worship (for in it preeminently God dwells) we shall recognize to the fullest extent its religious character and functions."[83] He saw the Nation as the new Church, and as such obligated to take on the church's traditional functions of charity:

> We find the Nation alone fully organized, sovereign, independent, universal, capable of giving full expression to the Christian principle. We ought, therefore, to regard the Nation as the Church, its rulers as ministers of Christ, its whole body as a Christian brotherhood, its public assemblies as amongst the highest modes of

universal Christian fellowship, its dealing with material interests as Sacraments, its progressive development, especially in raising the weak, as the fullest service rendered on earth to God, the nearest thing as yet within our reach to the kingdom of heaven.[84]

It is hard to know how much of this many journalists absorbed and *believed*— but, as the next chapter shows, the notions of Bellamy, Ely, Fremantle, and others began to receive wide press support in the late 1890s and early 1900s. It was easier to attribute problems to social maladjustment than to innate sinfulness; if personality was a social product, individuals were not responsible for their vices. Crime reporting began to change as journalists began to attribute "anti-social action" to the stress of social factors beyond an individual's control. Editorial pages began calling for new governmental action as that action was seen not merely as a way of dividing up spoils but as a means to achieve a cooperative commonwealth, in which men and women could become godlike. Not just at populist meetings and granger halls, but in newspaper offices as well,

thoughts and theories sprouted like weeds after a May shower. . . . They discussed income tax and single tax; they talked of government ownership and the abolition of private property; fiat money, and the unity of labor, . . . and a thousand conflicting theories.[85]

To summarize: During the 30 years after the civil war the *oppression* story, although not apparent on most newspaper front pages, was putting down deep roots. Greeleyite ideas were slowly triumphing over those of Raymond; Greeleyite beliefs in man's natural goodness, and their typical political manifestation in an attack on individual property and a call for federal power, were becoming marketable commodities. Ideologies contending that the problem was not individual corruption but systemic oppression were becoming more acceptable, but they still needed the right press packaging.

Chapter 9

Of Muckrakers and Presidents

The first developer of better press packaging for the rising *oppression story* was Joseph Pulitzer, a native of Hungary whose own rag-to-riches tale began when he tried to join the Austrian army in 1864 and was rejected due to "weak eyes" and an "unpromising physique." In America, however, a Union Army decimated by 3 years of warfare was desperate for soldiers and wary of relying on a draft that was provoking riots in northern cities. The north sent recruiters to comb Europe and sign up anyone who could hold a bayonet, weak eyes or not. Pulitzer enlisted, ended up spending a year in the cavalry cleaning up after mules, and came out at war's end never having fought Confederates but ready to turn the tables on those who had taken advantage of his poor knowledge of English to make him the frequent butt of practical jokes.[1]

For Pulitzer, journalism became a weapon to avenge himself on his oppressors. In the late 1860s he became a superb reporter in St. Louis, working 18 hours a day and learning to hit the bullseye with dart-like English sentences. He also saved his money, studied the financial aspects of newspapers, and during the 1870s was able to buy first a small, German-language newspaper, the *Westliche Post,* and then (using his profits) a virtually bankrupt English-language newspaper. When he merged that cheap newspaper with another in similar distress, he suddenly had a publication with an Associated Press franchise and a name that would become mighty in journalism, the *St. Louis Post-Dispatch.*

The *Post-Dispatch* built circulation, and profits for Pulitzer, by slamming into individuals who found it hard to hit back; Pulitzer found a market for gossip and salacious stories.[2] The *Post-Dispatch* particularly liked going after ministers—

not just ministers engaged in scandalous conduct, but any who inadvertently provided opportunities for assault. When one sick reverend, on doctor's orders taking medicine with an alcoholic base, inadvertently breathed into the face of a woman who sat down next to him on a streetcar, she moved to another seat. The incident would have been forgotten immediately, except that a Pulitzer reporter who happened to be at the scene wrote a story that appeared under the following decked headline:

ROCK AND RYE. Rev. Dr. Geo. A. Lofton Goes Upon a Saintly Spree/ He is Said to Have Been Intoxicated and Grossly Insulted a Lady/ A Terrible Clerical Scandal Involving the Pastor of the Third Baptist Church.[3]

This story proved typical of local coverage that often came under attack but was enormously successful at building circulation.

In coverage of national politics, Pulitzer was a liberal Democrat who learned the usefulness of character assassination by studying the Radical Republican press of the 1860s and 1870s. For example, the *Post-Dispatch* used headlines such as "GRABBER GARFIELD" to attack in 1880 Republican presidential nominee James Garfield. The murkier the charges were, the more the *Post-Dispatch* shouted that they were "so clear, so well founded . . . so thoroughly convincing, that there is nothing left but to believe them."[4] Even one of Pulitzer's sympathetic biographers has noted that "a strain of irresponsibility was evident in Pulitzer's developing style of journalism."[5] Increasingly, the *Post-Dispatch* showed little concern for accuracy. Once, when it misidentified a young man who supposedly had urged adultery upon a chorus girl, the *Post-Dispatch* corrected itself but at the same time made fun of the man who was irate because he had been defamed.[6]

Pulitzer used his St. Louis profits to buy the *New York World* in 1883. He bullseyed the new immigrant market (one he understood well from personal experience) by combining easy-to-read, gripping stories (good for learning English) with economic envy.[7] Pulitzer's first edition of the *World*, on May 11, 1883, hit the pavement running with its front-page stories about a Wall Street plunger, a Pittsburgh hanging, a riot in Haiti, and a wronged servant girl. Typical *World* headlines were like a dragon's fire: "DEATH RIDES THE BLAST," "SCREAMING FOR MERCY," "BAPTIZED IN BLOOD," "A MOTHER'S AWFUL CRIME," "A BRIDE BUT NOT A WIFE," and "VICTIMS OF HIS PASSION." Readers who paid a penny in response to such appeals would encounter, on inside pages, Pulitzer's political agenda: tax large incomes, tax corporations, tax inheritances, redistribute income.

In the early 1890s, Pulitzer stopped short of calling for outright socialism, Bellamy-style; yet, the *World's* constant juxtaposition of current horror with future social salvation transmitted the message of hope through science and material progress, evenly distributed by benign government agents. Features such as "Experimenting with an Electric Needle and an Ape's Brain" showed that scientific transformation of man's thought patterns was just around the corner, and stories such as "Science Can Wash Your Heart" suggested that immortality was possible. In the meantime, however, monstrous crime and terrible scandal rode mankind. In one sense Pulitzer was merely imitating the methodology of the Puritan press two centuries before: emphasize bad news so that the need for the good news becomes even greater. But the message was totally changed: Instead of pointing readers toward man's corruption and God's grace, the *World* portrayed itself as the battler against systemic oppression, and proposed running over anyone (including business owners in American, Spaniards in Cuba, and Boers in South Africa) who stood in the way of "progress."[8]

The *World's* circulation soared to 60,000 in 1884, 250,000 in 1886, and 1 million during the Spanish–American War of 1898. For journalists yearning to transform society and have fun and profit, the *World* became the New York workplace of choice, much as the *Tribune* was a generation before. The *World's* full-time force numbered 1,300 in the mid-1890s, and the growing arrogance of what had become a major institution soon was apparent: Pulitzer argued that "The World should be more powerful than the President," because the President came from partisan politics and was elected to a 4-year term, while the World "goes on year after year and is absolutely free to tell the truth."[9] By 1900, Pulitzer was spending most of his time on his yacht, with 75 employees trained to cater to his whims. As one biographer put it, "The yacht represented the logical end toward which the eccentric despot, so concerned with democracy, had been working for decades. It gave him *complete control*. It was an absolute monarchy."[10]

Pulitzer began the process of framing the *oppression story* for twentieth century popular consumption, but it was William Randolph Hearst who took Pulitzer's insights, spread them across the nation, and in doing so enabled proponents of the rising macrostory to go on the attack once more. As one reporter described his excitement upon going to work for Hearst,

> At last I was to be the kind of journalist I had dreamed of being. I was to enlighten and uplift humanity. Unequaled newspaper enterprise, combined with a far-reaching philanthropy, was to reform . . . the whole United States. The printing press, too often used for selfish ends, had become a mighty engine for good in the world, and I was to be a part of the directing force. Proudly I was to march under the banner of William R. Hearst, helping to guide civilization's forward strides. The banner was a yellow one, to be sure, but yellow probably only the better to attract that part of humanity which otherwise might remain indifferent to Mr. Hearst's principles. Glaring headlines of various hues, and an occasional scandal would easily be excused, I thought, if they hastened the millennium.[11]

Hearst's union of rhetorical violence and centralizing vision was in turn picked up by a group of early 20th-century magazine writers who became known as "muckrakers" and heavily influenced practice for decades to come.

Hearst, unlike Greeley or Pulitzer, was born—in 1863—with a silver spoon in his mouth and bars of silver to stack; George Hearst was owner of rich mines and a California seat in the U.S. senate. George Hearst paid for young Willie to meander through Harvard, work for a short time on Pulitzer's *World,* and decide that the pleasure of journalistic power was greater than anything life as a playboy could offer. George Hearst had won a failing newspaper, the *San Francisco Examiner,* in a poker game; when Willie begged for it, his father handed it over.

Young Hearst loved newspapering. He would examine newspaper proofs by standing above them and turning pages with his toes while manifesting curious emotional reactions. One young editor, James Coleman, recorded his first experience with this curious procedure:

> My eyes strained wide and I tried vainly to keep from swallowing my bubble gum when Hearst suddenly spread the proofs on the floor, and began a sort of tap dance around and between them. . . . The cadence of it speeded up with his reactions of disturbance and slowed down to a strolling rhythm when he approved. Between dances, he scribbled illegible corrections on the margins and finally gave the proofs back to me.[12]

Hearst made the *Examiner* profitable by adopting Pulitzer's combination of sensationalism and exposure of oppression. In 1895 he purchased the *New York Journal* and soon became famous for sending dozens of reporters to the scenes of crimes on bicycles or in carriages pulled by fire and cavalry horses; Hearst himself could be seen "leaping wild-eyed and long-legged into a carriage, to be whisked like a field marshall to the scene of battle."[13]

Hearst ordered his editors to "make a great and continuous noise to attract readers; denounce crooked wealth and promise better conditions for the poor to keep readers. INCREASE CIRCULATION." As one historian has noted, the "yellow journalism" pioneered by Pulitzer and Hearst was characterized not only by big headlines and exciting stories, but by "ostentatious sympathy with the underdog. . . .' "[14] Hearst's capital-S Sympathy was his first step toward making readers think he cared about them; calls for socialism came next. Hearst wrote in one signed editorial that socialistic management was the key to advancement, for

> Combination and organization are necessary steps in industrial progress. We are advancing toward a complete organization in which the government will stand at the head and be the trust of trusts. It is ridiculous to attempt to stop this development.[15]

By 1904 Hearst was explicitly arguing that "the greatest need of this republic today is an aggressive and well organized radical party."[16] Liberal Herbert Croly compared Hearst to Robespierre, writing that Hearst's ambition was to bring about a "socialistic millennium."[17] Hearst evidently believed that the press had the power to "so exert the forces of publicity that public opinion" would compel such an outcome.[18] His editorial writers worked hard to press issues into a class struggle mold; one of the *Journal's* classic editorials portrayed

the horse after a hard day's work grazing in a swampy meadow. He has done his duty and is getting what he can in return. On the Horse's flank you see a leech sucking blood. The leech is the trust. The horse is the labor union.[19]

The *New York Journal* ran big cartoons showing Mark Hanna, McKinley's campaign manager, as a fat bully dressed in clothes filled with dollar signs, with McKinley a puppet on his lap. Hearst's viciousness seemed unlimited; as one observer noted, Hanna was depicted as "an amalgam of all sins. He was foulness compact . . . He sent poor sailors, forced on his ships by bestial labor masters, out to sea on the wintry lakes cold and starving, unpaid and mutinous."[20] Hearst's discretionary coverage screamed that he favored the poor; such posturing was worth millions of dollars to him. Hearst sold enough newspapers to make Louis Wiley, business manager of the *Times,* cry out that crusading should be considered "a commercial trade."[21]

Day after day, Hearst's newspapers in San Francisco, New York, and then across the country, provided an artful combination of sensation and hope. On the one hand, the present was tragedy, with headlines such as "He murdered his friends" or "He ran amuck with a hatchet."[22] A woman already in jail for beating a man senseless with a beer bottle, stabbed her jailer with a hat-pin; a maidservant poisoned her mistress' soup.[23] In New York, a boy shot and killed his father, who was beating his mother; another woman told "How She Horsewhipped Husband," and an 11-year-old drank a bottle of acid because she did "not want to live."[24] On the other hand, the future would be much better. Someday, wealth now used for "barbaric" displays of wealth could be used to fight "distress and misery."[25] Science (actually, pseudo-science) would help: the *San Francisco Examiner* reported that one professor had produced "solidified air" and another had found out that what a woman eats determines the gender of her baby.[26]

Hearst made an idol out of circulation, but he also tried making one out of himself. He began instructing his reporters and editors to praise him at every possibility. He posed as a benefactor of the poor, sending pale children on jaunts to the beach. A reporter sent to cover one expedition, however, later wrote that she was given only one container of ice cream to be dealt out on a Coney Island trip:

When at last I placed a dab on each saucer, a little fellow in ragged knickerbockers got up and declared that the Journal was a fake and I thought there was going to be a riot. I took away the ice-cream from a deaf and dumb kid who couldn't holler and gave it to the malcontent. Then I had to write my story beginning: "Thousands of children, pale-faced but happy, danced merrily down Coney Island's beaches yesterday and were soon sporting in the sun-lit waves shouting, 'God bless Mr. Hearst.' "[27]

Once, when Hearst ordered all his reporters to mention his newspapers' "comic supplements" in their stories whenever possible, one reporter filed this report from a disaster scene,

> I was the first to reach the injured and dying. "God bless Mr. Hearst," a little child cried as I stooped to lave her brow. Then she smiled and died. I spread one of our comic supplements over the pale, still face.[28]

Some Hearstian efforts were serious, not ludicrous. When Governor Goebel of Kentucky was assassinated early in 1901, the *Journal* printed a quatrain by reporter Ambrose Bierce: "The bullet that pierced Goebel's breast/ Can not be found in all the West;/ Good reason, it is speeding here/ To stretch McKinley on his bier."[29] Soon afterward the *Journal* editorialized that "if bad institutions and bad men can be got rid of only by killing, then the killing must be done." When the anarchist Czolgosz assassinated President McKinley later that year, the killer was said to have been arrested with a copy of the *Journal* in his coat pocket.[30] Hearst was hanged in effigy, circulation for a time dropped, and President Theodore Roosevelt said that Czolgosz had probably been led to his crime by "reckless utterances of those who, on the stump and in the public press, appeal to dark and evil spirits."[31] But Hearst bounced back, changing the name of his New York morning edition to the *American*.

Hearst showed through such conduct that he was the prototypical solipsistic journalist of the 20th century, moving around real individuals as if they were make-believe characters.[32] Some opposed him: Congressman John A. Sullivan called Hearst the Nero of American politics for his attempts to incite class conflict, and others labeled Hearst a socialist and hung his picture with red flags underneath it.[33] For a time, Hearst was able to convince some voters to accept their role in his dreams. He used his newspaper clout to win election to Congress by a big margin, and wrote after the landslide:

> We have won a splendid victory. We are allying ourselves with the workingman, the real Americans. This is just the beginning of our political actions. Our social aspirations have a greater chance than ever to be realized.[34]

Hearst was on his way. But the movement he represented was, with its newspaper base, a big city phenomenon. The key question was whether his emphasis on oppression would spread around the country. As it turned out, it did, at least in part through the influence of national magazines such as *Munsey's, McClure's, Cosmopolitan, Everybody's,* and *The Arena,* which provided an outlet for freelancing radicals, particularly in the years 1903 through 1906. *Munsey's* for a time was the most popular, with popular fiction and reportage covering ownership of popular utilities and similar subjects attracting a circulation of 700,000 monthly.[35] *The Arena* was less popular but more consistent in promoting socialist ideas, as it pushed its 100,000 readers to "agitate, educate, organize, and move forward, casting aside timidity and insisting that the Republic shall no longer lag behind in the march of progress."[36]

The hopes of the radicals, although diverse in some aspects, tended often to parallel those of Horace Greeley two generations before. For example, Upton Sinclair, at first a believer in communalism, invested profits from his book *The Jungle* in a New Jersey commune, "Home Colony"; it failed, but Sinclair thought it a good try, an "industrial Republic in the making."[37] After seeing what went into some cans of meat Sinclair espoused another of Greeley's favorite causes, vegetarianism, and also argued that meat eating had no place in an agricultural system managed on principles of efficiency and nutrition.[38] Sinclair for a time had new causes every year, but eventually, like Greeley, became an apologist for terrorism—in this case, that of Lenin rather than John Brown.[39] Like Greeley, Sinclair also confused holiness and hatred, eventually declaring that Jesus had been an anarchist and agitator whose vision of violent upheaval was covered up by church institutions.[40]

Sinclair was one of the first major journalists to explicitly adopt socialism; others moved in that direction more slowly as they abandoned youthful Christian allegiances and sought a new faith. Ray Stannard Baker, after reading Bellamy's *Looking Backward* and Henry George's *Progress and Poverty*, was among those who became annoyed at the idea that God, not journalists, brought salvation; as Baker wrote in his memoirs, "I was temperamentally impatient. I wanted explanations promptly. I wanted to know what *I* should do to help save the world."[41] When Baker's father suggested other ways to save the world, Baker responded, "I'm on my way up. If my strength and grit hold out I'm going to make my influence felt before I get through with it."[42] In 1899, after 2 years of New York journalism, Baker wrote to his father that "The longer I am in my present work, the greater seem the responsibilities and opportunities of high grade journalism."[43] Five years later, he was still writing that he had "a mission to perform," and felt successful: "I think we have struck the right Grail."[44]

The most famous of the radicals, Lincoln Steffens, wrote that he began his quest as a student at the University of California during the 1880s, where professors "could not agree upon what was knowledge, nor upon what was good and what evil, nor why."[45] To find out about good and evil, Steffens wrote that he had to become a journalist. He certainly saw evil—"graft and corruption" were everywhere—but he did not see them as coming from within. Once, discussing the Biblical fall within the garden of Eden, he said the culprit was not Adam, or Eve, or even the snake: "It was, it is, the apple." Good people were corrupted by a bad environment—and the goal of journalists, Steffens believed, was to change the environment by working to eliminate capitalism, which he saw as the 20th-century equivalent of the apple.

Steffens and other leading muckrakers generally shared two biographical elements. First, most came from elite colleges: Burton Hendrick came from Yale, Baker from the University of Michigan, Will Irwin from Stanford, David Graham Phillips from DePauw and Princeton, George Kibbee Turner from Williams College, Lincoln Steffens from the University of California at Berkeley, Ida Tarbell from The Sorbonne.[46] Second, many had experience with the newspapers of Pulitzer, Hearst, or both. Charles Edward Russell, for example, served as city editor of Pulitzer's *New York World,* managing editor of Hearst's *New York Journal,* and publisher of Hearst's Chicago entry, the *American;* he left those posts to freelance and become a Socialist Party politician. Lincoln Steffens, David Graham Phillips, and others had Pulitzer/Hearst reporting experience.[47]

Such apprenticeships often were vital in the development of writing styles that could both appeal to magazine readers and proselytize them for causes of the left. The sense of mission also tended to grow during years of training; many Pulitzer and Hearst alumni felt that their mission was

> to set forth some new and wonderful truth of world-wide importance, in a manner to make the nations of the earth sit up and take notice—to cause the heart of humanity to throb and thrill, from Greenland to the Ganges—a message in words that would enthuse and enthrall, gleam and glitter, dazzle and delight.[48]

Liveliness often tended to slide into viciousness, however, as it had in coverage of Andrew Johnson. Apparently, when journalists believe or argue that poverty and war can be ended if only certain steps are taken, those who refuse to step lively are commonly depicted as villains; as French revolutionary writers showed during the Reign of Terror, the furor is doubled when the journalists have keen personal ambition.

In America's 20th century, William Randolph Hearst was the first journalistic leader to assault regularly those who stood in his path. When Hearst could not get the Democratic presidential nomination in 1904, he called Judge Alton Parker, the party's nominee, a "living, breathing cockroach from under the sink," and labeled the party's chairman "a plague spot in the community spreading vileness."[49] At one time, Hearst's New York newspaper had 2,000 names on its S-List (persons to be mentioned only with scorn), and a reporter had to be assigned to read copy just to make sure mistakes of honesty were not made. Through all this, Hearst retained the support of leading journalists of the left; Charles Russell praised him, and Upton Sinclair declared in his book *The Industrial Republic* that a bright socialist future would not be far off if Hearst became president.[50] Steffens wrote a sympathetic profile of Hearst and explained that the publisher "was driving toward his unannounced purpose to establish some measure of democracy, with patient but ruthless—force."[51]

Members of the media elite who learned from Pulitzer or Hearst also tended to follow them in their virulence. For example, when the U.S. Senate in 1906 debated the Pure Food and Drug Act, Senator Joseph W. Bailey of Texas spoke in opposition, saying:

> I believe that the man who would sell to the women and children of this country articles of food calculated to impair their health is a public enemy, and ought to be sent to prison. No senator here is more earnestly in favor of legislation against adulterated food and drink as I am. . . . But I insist that such legislation belongs to the states and not to the general government. When something happens not exactly in accord with public sentiment, the people rush to Congress until it will happen after a while that Congress will have so much to do that it will do nothing well.[52]

But David Graham Phillips ridiculed that statement, saying that Bailey opposed good food and was participating in the "treason of the Senate." Within Phillips' understanding, anyone opposing federal legislation in a good cause was corrupt and uncaring.

The term *muckraking,* which came to describe journalistic behavior during this century's first decade, grew out of President Theodore Roosevelt's response to the early articles in Phillips' series. Before the series Roosevelt already was a media critic: After meeting Steffens and publisher S. S. McClure in October 1905, Roosevelt told McClure

> It is an unfortunate thing to encourage people to believe that all crimes are connected with business, and that the crime of graft is the only crime. I wish very much that you could have articles showing up the hideous iniquity of which mobs are guilty, the wrongs of violence by the poor as well as the wrongs of corruption by the rich . . . [showing] that you stand as much against anarchic violence and crimes of brutality as against corruption and crimes of greed. . . .[53]

When the series began Theodore Roosevelt in 1906 could have let the attacks on certain senators slide by; he had been personally friendly to several of the magazine writers and needed their help in passing his own reform package. But Roosevelt was a fighter, and he had long been critical of Hearst on both ethical and ideological grounds. (Hearst, for his part, had called Roosevelt one who "has sold himself to the devil and will live up to the bargain."[54]) Roosevelt complained that

> the man who in a yellow newspaper or in a yellow magazine makes a ferocious attack on good men or even attacks on bad men with exaggeration or for things they

have not done, is a potent enemy of those of us who are really striving in good faith to expose bad men and drive them from power.[55]

In 1906, the president felt, it was time to oppose those magazine writers who peddled Hearst's politics and defamatory tendencies on slick pages rather than newsprint.

Roosevelt let fly in a speech full of such memorable critiques of journalistic practice that it deserves quoting at length. He said:

> In Bunyan's *Pilgrim's Progress* you may recall the description of the Man with the Muck-rake, the man who could look no way but downward, with the muck-rake in his hand; who was offered a celestial crown for his muck-rake, but who would neither look up nor regard the crown he was offered, but continued to rake to himself the filth of the floor.

> In *Pilgrim's Progress* the Man with the Muck-rake is set forth as the example of him whose vision is fixed on carnal instead of on spiritual things. Yet he also typifies the man who in this life consistently refuses to see aught that is lofty, and fixes his eyes with solemn intentness only on that which is vile and debasing. Now, it is very necessary that we should not flinch from seeing what is vile and debasing. There is filth on the floor, and it must be scraped up with the muck-rake; and there are times and places where this service is the most needed of all the services that can be performed. But the man who never does anything else, who never thinks or speaks or writes, save of his feats with the muck-rake, speedily becomes, not a help to society, not an incitement to good, but one of the most potent forces for evil.

Roosevelt argued, much as Marchamont Nedham and other Puritans had, that exposure of wrongdoing was vital, but that writers must remember

> that the attack is of use only if it is absolutely truthful. The liar is no whit better than the thief, and if his mendacity takes the form of slander, he may be worse than most thieves. It puts a premium upon knavery untruthfully to attack an honest man, or even with hysterical exaggeration to assail a bad man with untruth. An epidemic of indiscriminate assault upon character does not good, but very great harm. The soul of every scoundrel is gladdened whenever an honest man is assailed, or even when a scoundrel is untruthfully assailed.

Roosevelt concluded that:

> The effort to make financial or political profit out of the destruction of character can only result in public calamity. Gross and reckless assaults on character, whether on the stump or in newspaper, magazine, or book, create a morbid and vicious public sentiment, and at the same time act as a profound deterrent to able men of normal sensitiveness and tend to prevent them from entering the public service at any price.

Hundreds of favorable responses to Roosevelt's speech indicate that his concern about press bullying was widely shared. Protests about the media elite's ideological agenda were common:

> Socialism—that's where these leaders of the magazines and newspapers are headed for. The Sentimentalist who looks to find there the Kingdom of Brotherly Love upon Earth, the honest man, hysterical with anger at the crimes of high finance, the brave fool spoiling for a fight, the good citizen who says to himself, 'that the evil is so great the whole must be swept away—' all alike are following the lead of the statesmen of the yellow press towards the ruinous experiment of straight-out socialism.[56]

Such complaints, although addressed to a modern ideological development, had an old-fashioned ring to them. After all, Andrew Bradford, editor in Philadelphia of the *American Weekly Mercury* two centuries before, had opposed "that unwarrantable License which some People of much fire, but little judgment have taken of endeavouring to subvert the Fundamental Points of Religion or Morality."[57]

A downward curve for the political prospects of William Randolph Hearst may be dated from the time of Roosevelt's speech, although other factors contributed to the failure of the publisher's ambitions.[58] For a while, Hearst retained the support of journalists on the left, but as he lost elections and the sensationalism of his newspapers seemed a bit embarrassing, radicals edged away from him. Hearst in turn lost his patience with them, and by the 1920s and 1930s was stoutly opposing governmental control of the economy. (Perhaps because of Hearst's "treason" to the left after 1920, he is often regarded by journalism historians as a bad guy, and Pulitzer—who left money to found a journalism school at Columbia and to hand out prizes—is given a white hat.[59])

Although the muckrakers abandoned their one-time standard bearer, they did not drop their flag. The media elite's opposition to Roosevelt was particularly intense in that the president was himself at times a writer-reformer; it is especially hard for those who see themselves as altruists to be depicted as malefactors by one of their own. A few lesser known reporters wrote confessional statements backing up Roosevelt's charges; one Hearst veteran acknowledged himself to be "a veritable Hessian of the press, even a hired assassin of character, striking from the dark, or from behind the mask of journalistic zeal for public welfare . . ."[60] But the leaders soldiered on, unrepentant.

Upton Sinclair claimed to speak for those journalistic leaders—"I know, more or less intimately, nearly every man who at present is raking muck in America"— in issuing a strong reply to Roosevelt's accusations.[61] Sinclair wrote of how all the leading muckrakers shared a belief:

> that the history of humanity up to the present time represents a series of failures. Races emerge from barbarism. They are joyous and proud and strong; they struggle

and conquer, they toil and achieve. . . . But all the time there is a worm within the
bud, which gnaws at it; and just when the flower seems most perfect, its petals fall,
and it is scattered and trampled into the dust.[62]

The worm for Sinclair was private property, and he wrote of how he and the
other leading muckrakers had realized that to kill it, they needed to lead "a revolt
against capitalism."[63] The problem, however, was that people were forgetful, so
it was up to journalists to be no less than "the faculty of recollection in the
growing social mind." The muckraker, Sinclair wrote, "represents the effort of
the race to profit by experience, and to do otherwise than repeat infinitely the
blunders which have proved fatal in the past." The muckraker "as forerunner of
a revolution," Sinclair concluded, "will be recognized in the future as a benefactor
of his race."[64]

Those reporters who had little thought of being benefactors—they had a job
to do and a paycheck to get—might scowl at such notions. And yet, with all the
cynicism that journalists love to show, the streak of pride would grudgingly show
itself: one reporter reminisced of how, for a time, he had been

battling for the people, and making tyrants quail, in a truly heroic journalistic style.
I was forging shafts of ripping, tearing words that would demolish the fort of the
robber chiefs who were taking unlawful tribute from the public. I called the gas
company 'the Gorgon-headed monopoly,' 'the banded infamy,' and 'a greeder
gorger from the public purse.' I felt myself as heroic as those who had led the
crusades of old. I was a lieutenant of a modern Godfrey or a Richard the Lion-
hearted in a holy war. Pen and typewriter, mightier than sword and cannon, were
my weapons. In the press was concentrated the strength of an army, and this I
directed.[65]

Top college students who enjoyed writing began gravitating more and more
toward journalism; Walter Lippmann, for example, went from Harvard to an
internship with Lincoln Steffens, and also became a protege of Charles Edward
Russell.

Steffens and Russell, in turn, set the standard for "the right stuff" in leading-
edge journalism much as had Horace Greeley two generations before; they trained
a generation of young journalists to see not only poverty and corruption as the
responsibility of capitalism, but all war as the result of capitalist desires to find
"a dumping ground abroad for a surplus domestic product . . . for all times, and
in all places, and under all conditions, Capitalism is War."[66] When the young
journalists came to editorial power during the 1930s, some would argue as did
their elders that the solution to all problems was socialism, which could be
achieved only through raising inter-class hostility. (And, because the oppression
was go great and the final victory so crucial, smearing some individuals along
the way would not matter.)

Few journalists early in the century matched Steffens and Russell in clarity of political theology. Some, such as Ray Stannard Baker, merely found themselves attracted to the Socialist Party's "high & unselfish ideals," with its "community spirit of service" that offered "brotherhood nearer than anything I know to the real church . . . I must join something."[67] Still, the trend was clear, and many of the media elite were ready to adopt a Marxist perspective as long as it was given a spiritual gloss. For example, David Graham Phillips, whose attacks on the Senate justified Roosevelt's famous response, also wrote novels in which heroines compared Karl Marx to Jesus Christ, not unfavorably:

They were both labor leaders—labor agitators. The first proclaimed the brotherhood of man. But he regarded this world as hopeless and called on the weary and heavy-laden masses to look to the next world for the righting of their wrongs. Then— eighteen centuries after—came the second Jew—and he said 'No! not in the hereafter, but in the here. Here and now, my brothers. Let us make this world a heaven. Let us redeem ourselves and destroy this devil of ignorance who is holding us in this hell!'[68]

The passage concluded, "It was three hundred years before the first Jew began to triumph. It won't be so long before there are monuments to Marx in clean and beautiful and free cities all over the earth."[69]

Most elite journalists in the years before World War I were content to locate social problems in the environment rather than in man himself. Will Irwin, for example, wrote of his desire to change "an American habit of mind"; he was upset because when Americans "find any institution going wrong, we think first of individual dishonesty." Irwin's goal was to teach readers "to attribute the unfair working of social forces to faults in the system of things."[70] Even "moderates" such as William Allen White argued that capitalism was a product of "diabolical self-interest" and that journalists should be "preparing the ground for a nationalization of industries that may pass from control to ownership—from industrial bonds to government bonds and then to the breaking up of great fortunes holding the government bonds by inheritance & income taxes."[71]

Although Roosevelt's attack in 1906 had an effect, muckraking remained a major journalistic genre through 1917; then, as Americans went to fight overseas, war reporting became dominant for a time. The year 1917 also marks the end of an era because the tragedy of trench warfare in France was compounded by the Soviet seizure of power in Moscow, the fall-out from which would coat much of the 20th century. After the Bolshevik Revolution a few muckrakers, including John Spargo, distanced themselves from the blood that flowed and the red flag that signified the willingness to spill more. Others took a harder line; a contemporary remembered Lincoln Steffens "talking revolution and blood—and sucking the guts out of a chocolate eclair impaled on an upright fork."[72]

Four hundred years earlier, modern journalism had begun with the sound of Luther hammering on the cathedral door. In 1917 a new dispensation appeared to be underway; Steffens baptized the Russian Revolution, writing of how Petrograd mobs made him "think of the mobs that followed Jesus about." (Later he found the Exodus story a better vehicle and wrote *Moses in Red,* which attempted to prove that "not Lenin, but Nature required the excesses of the Russian revolution; or, if you please, God."[73]) For centuries much of American journalism had emphasized *restraint,* but Steffens would praise Soviet leaders—as Benjamin Bache had lauded the French revolutionaries—for their willingness to "lay out consciously and carry through ruthlessly" a program "to arrange the conditions of social living . . . to adjust the forces of economic life."[74]

Steffens' most famous (and often misquoted) remark was, upon returning from the Soviet Union, "I have gone over into the future, and it works."[75] From 1917 on, leading American writers would look to the Soviet Union—and later to China, Cuba, North Vietnam, or Nicaragua, as each revolution was successively discredited—for hints on how to change the world.[76] Steffens set the standard for those who wanted to make sure the future would work; when other radicals still thought Steffens soft, a playful child of the despised bourgeoisie "wandering among the social battlefields," he proved himself by engaging in "slander and character assassination" against anyone who stood in the way of "progress."[77]

Earlier journalists had pointed readers toward the Bible and, later, the Constitution; but after 1917, leading editors such as Oswald Garrison Villard argued that "There are plain masses seeking a journalistic Moses to clarify their minds, to give them a program of reconstruction."[78] Leading newspapers and magazines of the next seven decades would display the words of those who saw man as possessing unlimited potential that a strong and benevolent state could help to liberate, if only journalistic influence were brought to bear on the side of perceived righteousness. A journalism that emphasized the *oppression story* could once again achieve the muckraking heights as "Argus-eyed guardian of the people's rights, the omnipotent champion of the oppressed, the scourge of the oppressor, the light of the land, the greatest uplifting force in civilization."[79]

The story of those next seven decades could fill another book. But, briefly, what became most ironic during this period was the tendency of many journalists to apologize for and promote new forms of oppression, while claiming that they were fighting for liberty. In doing so, they often neglected the lessons in liberty provided by their courageous predecessors, and genuflected before a future that claimed to work but was in many ways a curious merger of the official and oppression stories. *Corruption story* journalists had viewed centralized government as part of the problem; *oppression story* journalists would see it as the center of the solution, the weapon that could force social changes and coerce America into utopia. American journalism, which had developed as an antiestablishment force, had become part of a new establishment that did not have the self-understanding to recognize itself as one.

A key question for the press, as the last decade of the 20th century began, was whether the best and brightest journalists would have the grace to look at themselves and say, with Edmund in *King Lear,* "The wheel is come full circle; I am here."

Appendix A: 16th-, 17th-, and 18th-Century Moral Tales

Before newspapers were an everyday occurrence in England, many news ballads sensationally covered current events while communicating biblical morality. The "ballads"—quickly composed, event-oriented songs printed on single sheets of paper and sold in the streets—apparently were everywhere. In the words of one historian:

> Ballads were not written for poetry. They were, in the main, the equivalent of modern newspapers, and it cannot well be denied that customarily they performed their function as creditably in verse as the average newspaper does in prose. Journalistic ballads outnumbered all other types. . . . In them are clearly reflected the lives and thoughts, the hopes and fears, the beliefs and amusements, of sixteenth and seventeenth century Englishmen.[1]

The ballads were on vastly different subjects, but they often had a common theological thrust. To cite a very early example, one report of a strange animal birth in 1562 first provided a description of the piglet whose head was shaped like that of a dolphin, and then gave "An Admonition unto the Reader":

> Let us knowe by these ugly sights,/ And eke consider well,/ That our God is the Lord of mights,/ Who rules both heaven and hell./ By whose strong hand these monsters here/ Were formed as ye see,/ That it mighte to the world appere,/ Almightie him to bee/ Who might also us men have formde/ After a straunge device.[2]

The emphasis on God's sovereignty in that stanza was followed by the corollary story of man's sinfulness in the next:

> And loke what great deformitie/ In bodies ye beholde;/ Much more is in our mindes truly,/ An hundred thousand folde./ So that we have great cause in deede,/ Our sinnes for to confesse,/ And eke to call to God with speede,/ The same for to redresse.

An account by another writer of that same incident drew a similar moral: "These straunge and monstrous thinges Almighty God sendeth amongest us, that we shuld not be forgetfull of his almighty power, nor unthankefull for his great mercies so plentifully poured upon us."[3]

Ballads frequently cited earthquakes as tokens of God's power. Within several days of an April 6, 1580 earthquake, five pamphlets or ballads about it were for sale on the streets. The titles tell the message: "A godly newe ballat moving us to repent by ye example of ye erthquake."[4] "Alarm for London and Londoners settinge forthe the thunderinge peales of Gods mercye." "A true and terrible example of Gods wrathe shewed by ye generall earthquake." (One title sounds as if it has rock 'n roll potential—"Quake, quake, it is tyme to quake. When towers and townes and all Doo shake.")

Fire reporting, then as now, was dramatic. In 1586 one report of a fire in the town of Beckles observed:

> The flame whereof increasing still/ The blustering windes did blowe,/ And into divers buildings by/ Disperst it to and fro;/ So kindling in most grievous fort,/ It waxed huge and hie;/ The river then was frozen, so/ No water they could come by.[5]

The balladeer-reporter went on to write that the fire was part of God's providence. That did not imply that the fire was necessarily punishment for the townsfolks' sins. It did suggest that the fire was a warning, and that residents should "Seeke not your neighbors lasting spoyle/ By greedy sute in lawe;/ Live not in discord and debate,/ Which doth destruction draw." Beckle was "a mirrour to all such/ That doth in pleasure stay." God's judgment could come at any time, and Englishmen should have their spiritual affairs in order.

During this period, for the first time in English-language publications, "news" began to be organized. Networks of reporters and publishers emerged, and timeliness became significant: Many ballads and pamphlets were published 2 days after the events took place, and reports of some executions were prepared largely in advance, like obituaries today, with only last-minute (literally) details added. The emphasis on telling a moral tale continued, however. A typical account of spousal murder concerned an innkeeper's wife becoming friendly with "a Person of ill fame and very dissolute liver . . . in a more familiar manner, than was convenient," and then conspiring with him to murder her husband"; the murderess eventually was executed.[6]

Publications were not afraid to be sensational. In 1624 a newsbook entitled *The crying Murther: Contayning the cruell and most horrible Butcher of Mr. Trat,* told of how four murderers,

> with their hands already smoking in his blood, did cut up his carcass, unbowel and quarter it; then did they burn his head and privy members, parboil his flesh and salt it up, that so the sudden stink and putrefaction being hindered, the murderers might the longer be free from [discovery].[7]

But the body was found "all saving the head and members, disposed in this manner and form following. His arms, legs, thighs, and bowels were powdered up into two earthen steens or pots in a lower room of the house . . ., the bulk of his carcass was placed in a vat or tub." The murderers were hanged, and "died obstinate and unrepenting sinners." The pamphlet's author was careful to say that his story was based on "intelligence which I have received from credible persons, engaged in their trial."

Writers saw an important purpose in such coverage. John Reynolds in 1622 had provided one of the fullest rationales for stories of crime and disaster when he wrote of his desire to help readers understand the dangers of "the bewitching World, the alluring Flesh, and the inticing Devill."[8] He listed items that should be viewed critically:

> Wealth, Riches, Dignities, Honours, Preferments, Sumptuous houses, perfumed Beds, Vessels of gold and silver, pompous Apparell, Delicious fare . . . Perfuming, Powdering, Crisping, Painting, Amorous kisses, Sweet smiles, Sugared speeches, Wanton embracings, and Lascivious dalliance. . . .

Reynolds argued that Satan would take advantage of whatever tendencies his careless readers might possess:

> Are we inclined to wantonnesse, and Lasciviousnesse, he will fit us with meanes and opportunity to accomplish our carnall desires: or are wee addicted to covetousness and honours, hee will either cause us to breake our hearts, or our necks, to obtaine it: for it is indifferent to him, either how or in what manner we inlarge and fill up the empty roomes of his vast and infernall kingdome. . . .[9]

Reynolds wrote of two ways to avoid citizenship in that infernal kingdom: Worshiping and praying to God, and learning from the errors of others. Journalism could play a crucial role in the latter task. Reynolds wrote that his accounts of evil thought leading to evil action were for our detestation, not for our imitation: Since it is a poynt of (true and happy) wisdome in all men to beware by other mens harmes; Reade it then with a full intent to profit thy selfe thereby, and so thou mayest boldly, and safely rest assured, that the sight of their sinnes and punishments, will prove the reformation of thine owne.[10]

Reynolds, like other journalists of his time, stressed a condemnation of sin and a proclamation of the need for repentance and future avoidance. His writing was democratic in coverage and style but not at all in theology; early journalists proposed not that each man should be an oracle unto himself, but that sin was real, that all were ensnared in it, and some captured by it. He wanted readers to avoid entangling alliances of the kind depicted in a ballad, *Murder upon Murder,* in which "a man of honest parentage" married "a filthy whore," who "sotted" his mind so that they lived a "vile loose life" and were "bent to cruelty."[11]

Other ballads presented what their writers perceived as the general mood of early 17th-century England. One composition by John Barker—"A Balade declaryng how neybourhed, love, and trew dealyng is gone"—lugubriously stated:

Now straunge it is to men of age,
The which they se before their face,
This world to be in such outrage,
It was never sene in so bad case.
Neibourhed nor love is none,
Trew dealyng now is fled and gone

Where shall one fynde a man to trust,
Alwaye to stande in tyme of neede?
The most parte now they are unjust,
Fayre in wordes, but false indeede.
Neybourhed nor love is none,
True dealyng now is fled and gone[12]

The ballad went on that way for 19 verses, but in the 20th gave the hope:

Graunt, oh God, for thy mercyes sake,
That neighbourhed and dealyng trewe
May once agayne our spirites awake,
That we our lyves may chaunge a-new;
Then neybourhed and love alone
May come agayne to every one.

Later in the century, the corruption story was carried on through ballads of domestic tragedy combined with pleas for repentance. For example, in 1661 the ballad "Misery to be lamented" reported that a man had been buried alive and was unable to get out of his coffin, but cried out so loud that people who heard his shouts dug up the coffin and opened it: "His Coffin opened was, wherein/ a dolefull sight they then beheld:/ With strugling he had bruis'd his skin,/ his head and eyes were sadly sweld." The conclusion was,

> Now let us all with one consent/ turn to the Lord with heart and mind:/ And of our grievous sins repent,/ that so we may God's mercy find,/ And to conclude to God let's call,/ from such a death Lord keep us all.[13]

By the last third of the 17th century, specific genres of sensational reporting were emerging. For example, "The Bloody Butcher," a ballad broadside of 1667, began with an exclamation about "What horrid execrable Crimes/ Possess us in these latter Times;/Not Pestilence, nor Sword, nor Fire,/ Will make us from our Sins retyre."[14] The report told of a husband and pregnant wife arguing about his adultery, and then:

> With a strong long sharp-poynted knife,/ Into the back he stabs his wife:/ Flesh of his flesh, bone of his bone,/ With one dead-doing blow is gone.
>
> She faltred, fainted, fell down dead,/ Upon the ground her bloud was shed;/ The little infant in the womb/ Received there both Life and Toomb.
>
> Then was he Apprehended, by/ Some Neighbours that did hear her cry/ Out Murther, murther, and for this,/ He judg'd and Executed is.
>
> Let this a warning be to those,/ Whose Passions are their greatest Foes . . ./ Return to God, reform your Lives,/ Men be not bitter to your wives.

The consistency of themes during this period is indicated by a similar story 30 years later, "The Murtherer Justly Condemned," that also spotlighted an adulterer who killed his wife:

> He had long been absent which made her suspect,/ Both her and his business he did much neglect,/ Which put her in passion, that streightway she went,/ To know by this usage what to her he meant.
>
> In Leaden-Hall Market she found him, and there/ The cause of her grief she did freely declare./ Though justly reproved, yet so Angry he grew,/ That at her with violence his Knife he then threw.[15]

The story continued with the man tried, found guilty, and awaiting hanging:

> His Drunken Debauchries now swarm in his mind,/ And how he to her and himself was unkind,/ By spending his money so idley on those,/ That Lewdly had brought him to trouble and woes,/ And though for Repentance it is not too late,/ Yet death now looks terrible on life's short date.

Finally, the practical application was rammed home:

> Thus let all Rash men well consider his fall,/ How innocence loudly for Vengeance do's call,/ And govern their passions that bring them to shame,/ For which when too late they themselves do much blame.

> Consider how Rashness brings troubles and fears,/ Shame, Ruin, and death, it oft for them prepares,/ Then let all be warn'd how they rashly proceed,/ Least trouble and anguish for them be decreed.

Hundreds of similar crime ballads were sold in the streets during this period. They typically showed a strong faith in biblical right and wrong and a stress on God's sovereignty, while at the same time claiming accuracy of reporting. "Sad News from Salisbury," for example, presented tragedies "incredible to believe, but that some who were in the same Storm are alive to justify the truth thereof."[16] That stress on eyewitnesses was important because the purpose of the tale was not mere amusement, but testimony to be taken as important only if true; the story was to be a "warning to all,/ Least greater Judgments on this land befall." The specific detail, rather than emphasizing the plight of nobles or gentlefolk, was thoroughly democratic:

> Collins the Taunton Carryer, people say,/ Upon the Douns did strangly loose his way,/ Two of his Passengers were starv'd with cold,/ A fearful Spectacle for to behold. . . .

> And this for truth report us plainly tells,/ The Carryer that belong'd to Bath and Wells,' His own dear Son was frozen unto death;/ And on the Downs did loose his dearest breath. . . .

> And thirty more in Sometshire were lost/ In this unusual Snow and cruel Frost,/ Who littel thought when they went out of door,/ Their wives & children they should see no more. . . .

Then came the crucial journalistic question, then as now—not just who, what, when, where, and how, but *why:*

> This judgment came from god's almighty hand/ For sins committed in our native land,/ Lord grant that it to us a warning be/ And teach us how to shun iniquitie.

> Our sins for vengeance do to Heaven cry,/ Yet we like sinners live in vanity,/ O grant that we our sinful lives may mend,/ That we may live with thee when life doth end.

> From storms & tempests Lord preserve us still,/ Teach us they holy laws for to fulfill,/ So shall we gainers be by loosing breath,/ And ride triumphant o're the second death.

Fires often provided the fuel for disaster stories, including a typical one entitled "A Sad and True Relation of a great fire."[17] The story began, "Give thanks, reyoyce all, you that are secure,/ No man doth know how long life may indure/ Regard dear hearts, at the truth the authour aims,/ Concerning those that suffer in fiery flames." The author, with superior artistry, then switched to point-of-view from a neighboring woman who, while nursing at night a sick child, saw the fire: "In the Merchants lower Rooms she espied,/ The Violent flames and then aloud she cryed/ Fire, Fire . . ." Other stanzas vividly described what was found in the wreckage, and then returned to the great story:

four lumps of flesh was after found./ About the bigness of a man's hand were they,/ As black as a Coal, and a skul or two there lay;/ O little did they think over night being merry,/ That before morn in fiery flames to fry. . . .

All you that are Masters of a family,/ Govern well your house and fear the God on high,/ For when to sleep that we do close our eyes,/ The Lord doth know whither ever we shall rise.

The emphasis on God's sovereignty was accompanied by a stress on his mercy. That was a theme especially of prisoner stories, which were often told in the first person. "Luke Hutton's Lamentation" included details of the crime (a woodcut showed one man with a knife at the other's stomach) and the prisoner's hanging at York, and ended with a prayer: "Lord Jesus forgive me, with mercy relieve me,/ Receive O sweet Saviour, my spirit unto thee."[18] Those dying of natural causes also had first-person accounts written about them. The title of one long one gave the essential detail: "The Godly Maid of Leicester. Being a true Relation of Elizabeth Streeton, who lying on her Death-bed, was wonderfully delivered from the Temptations of Satan, worth the noting of all that would live and die in the fear of God."[19] Her deathbed statement (assuming poetic license) was that

Christ doth ne'r forsake his Flock,/ who evermore on him depend,/ He was my Fortress and my Rock/ and brought my troubles to an end. . . ./ For I have fought a happy Flight,/ and overcome, by God's good Grace,/ The Divel in his power and might,/ and run with Comfort now my Race.

Suicides, however, were treated very differently. The title/lead of one ballad was,

The Devil's cruelty to Mankind, BEING A true Relation of the Life and Death of George Gibbs, a Sawyer by his Trade, who being many times tempted by the Divill to destroy himself, did on Fryday being the 7 of March 1663. Most cruelly Ripp up his own Belly, and pull'd out his Bowells and Guts, and cut them in pieces: to the Amazement of all the Beholders, the sorrow of his Friends, and the great grief of his Wife, being not long married: and both young People.[20]

The gruesome epic told how Gibbs lingered for 8 hours, and how neighbors realized the lesson: "Trust not too much to your own strength/ to God continual pray/Resist the Divil elce at length,/ hee'l lead you his Broad way."

Other genres, including "advice ballads," also emerged.[21] They too proceeded from a Christian worldview that acknowledged the ravages of sin and prescribed virtuous personal conduct, made possible by God's grace, as a way of overcoming evil.

The ballads performed a similar function in England's American colonies for a time; as in England, they often emphasized sensational events and tried to combine reporting and teaching. One note immediately under a headline said of the story that followed, "Very proper to be read by all Persons, but especially young People."[22] Crime coverage typically discussed the criminal's downfall: "No timely Warnings would he hear,/ From kind Reproofs he turn'd his Ear,/ Provoked God for to depart,/ And leave him to an harden'd Heart."[23] Warnings sometimes were explicit: "Oh! may the Fate of this young Man/ scarce turn'd of Twenty Three,/ A Warning prove to all our Youth,/ of high and low Degree."[24]

In the sense of carrying a message, these ballads were akin to sermons, and their conclusions often emphasized God's mercy: "So here we leave his pitious Case,/ In tender Arms of Sov'reign Grace,/ Altho' his Crimes are great and sore;/ Grace can abound and pardon more."[25] At the same time, the ballads insisted that they offered not parable but news account, and prided themselves on attribution and eyewitness testimony; for example, the end of one account of a fight with Indians has the reporter noting,

Thus I have summed up this tragick scene,/ As from their mouths it told to me has been;/ No alteration but in some expressions/ Us'd other words; then pardon such digressions,/ Since I us'd such only for sake of verse,/ Which might not less nor more than truth rehearse.[26]

By the 1720s in England, the old-style ballad/moral tale was beginning to receive sarcastic treatment. Daniel Defoe in 1722 noted in his preface to *Moll Flanders,*

there is not a wicked action in any part of it, but is first and last rendered unhappy and unfortunate; there is not a superlative villain brought upon the stage, but either he is brought to an unhappy end, or brought to be a penitent; there is not an ill thing mentioned but it is condemned, even in the relation. . . .[27]

But in the colonies, the excitement of the Great Awakening—that reinvigoration of the colonial church led by evangelist George Whitefield and theologian Jonathan Edwards during the 1730s—gave new impetus to biblical sensationalism. Benjamin Franklin wrote, "It seemed as if all the world was growing religious, so that one could not walk through the town in an evening without hearing psalms sung in different families of every street."[28]

Earthquakes, for example, received attention as—in the title of one ballad following a June, 1744, quake—*Tokens of God's Power and Wrath*. Through earthquakes, the ballad proposed, God showed power and then mercy: "Justly may we now stand amaz'd/ At GOD's abundant Grace,/ To think so base and vile a World/ Is not all on a Blaze."[29] When another earthquake struck in 1755, the *Boston News-Letter* reported 2 days after the quake that "the Inhabitants of the Town were, in general, put into great Consternation, fearing, every Moment, least they should be buried under their Houses; but, thro' the Divine Favour, no life was lost."[30] A ballad called the earthquake "A Solemn Warning to the World" and reported how "In Depth of Sleep, or Scenes of Guilt,/ Sinners securely lay;/ When sudden shook the tott'ring Ground,/ And threatned to give Way.[31]

Fire coverage also was reinvigorated. One fire that destroyed over 300 buildings was covered as "the Rebuke of God's Hand." The reporter gave the basic news and then explicitly tried to deal with the "why," observing that God's

> Judgments oftentimes he does retard,/ While we run on in Sin and don't regard;/ And when he sends them then we think He's hard:/ But pray examine, think on what's the Cause,/ Isn't it Contempt of his most righteous Laws?/ Then can we clear ourselves, aren't we to blame/ Who sin without Remorse, and cast off Shame/ And pay no Rev'rence to his holy Name?—/ This is the Cause He sent this Judgment down,/ This awful Desolation on the Town. . . ."[32]

Coverage of a crime story in 1756 and 1757 showed a tendency toward division of labor, with the newspapers increasingly providing short bits of news and the ballads presented more detail. The *Boston News-Letter* in 1756 succinctly reported that

> a sorrowful Affair happened at Watertown, one John Herrington and Paul Learned, scuffling together, the former struck a long Knife in the other's Back, which gave him a mortal wound, and died within two Hours after. Herrington we hear surrendered himself up to Justice.

Ballads that covered the same crime and eventual execution of Herrington made it a pointed story of God's mercy, with the convicted man first wondering whether his guilt is so great that God will not hear his prayers. Soon, however, he was shown to be praying, with the particular request that his life not pass in vain, but that he might become a symbol of God's grace: "Dispell the Mists that cloud my Mind,/ And all my Pangs abate;/ Give this Example to Mankind,/ Of Love and Grace compleat." The final verse of that ballad showed the victory, just prior to Harrington's execution: "Then shall this Truth be ever known,/ While God sustains this Frame;/ In me his boundless Mercy shone,/ And Goodness is his Name."[33]

Right up to the American revolution, ballads continued to emphasize both God's anger with sin and his mercy toward repentant sinners. One man about to be executed was depicted as praying to Christ, "Thou who did'st suffer Death and Shame,/ Such Rebels to restore:/ O! for they great and glorious Name,/ Accept one Rebel more."[34]

Appendix B: Journalism Historians and Religion

As the research behind this book suggests, all interpretive journalism has a religious or philosophical component. Any story that goes beyond "who/what/when/where/how" into "why" stirs up questions of meaning and causality. Those questions are essentially religious (or "world view," if we are scrupulous about restricting the term *religion* to beliefs pertaining to a deity). Therefore, historians *should* examine how presuppositions have influenced action, both in earlier times and in our own century as well; few, however, have. This appendix provides a brief overview of the oversights.

19TH-CENTURY INTERPRETATIONS

The tendency among journalism historians to stand apart from independent journalism's biblical base began early. American journalism's first two major historians, Isaiah Thomas and Frederic Hudson, were not Christian believers, and they tended to be embarrassed by the origins of American journalistic practice. Nevertheless, they did pay some attention to a historical record that in those days was too recent to forget.

Isaiah Thomas, author in 1810 of the massive *History of Printing in America,* worshipped liberty and economic progress. He saw America as the leading manifestation of both. He showed his commitment through courageous action as a leading Patriot printer and editor during the American Revolution. Thomas never showed much interest in the Bible; he had been apprenticed to a printer who cared little about Christianity and knew less.[1] (The apprentice may also have been understandably hostile to the Puritan heritage because his great grandfather was hanged as a witch.) Bored with catechisms, Thomas was in a rush to go on to things more exciting, in his case deism and an Enlightenment sense of having progressed "beyond" the Bible.[2]

Yet, Thomas' bias did not keep him from conscientiously recording specific detail concerning the religious connections of early printer/journalists. His listing of what was printed is valuable in itself. Titles such as "Speedy Repentance Urged," a news report/sermon about a murderer, "With certain Memorable Providences relating to some other murders," show practical applications of a Christian world view.[3] But Thomas went beyond the bare essentials to comment about the religious underpinnings of journalistic pioneers such as Samuel Kneeland,[4] Richard Draper,[5] and others. Thomas sympathetically portrayed men such as Bartholomew Green, first printer and second owner of the Boston *News-Letter,* and "a very humble and exemplary Christian" with a "tender sympathy to the poor and afflicted."[6]

Thomas' history was standard for many decades. At mid-century, Joseph T. Buckingham and James Parton wrote about some journalistic personalities,[7] but the second general history, Frederic Hudson's *Journalism in the United States from 1690 to 1872,* did not emerge until the Gilded Age.[8] Hudson, like Thomas, tended to identify journalistic progress with religious regress, but his book was also like Thomas' in that concern for accurate detail and recording of crucial documents often seemed to overcome bias. For example, Hudson reprinted the entire first (and only) issue of *Publick Occurrences,* allowing attentive readers to see the way editor Benjamin Harris' stress on God's sovereignty affected his coverage of news items. Hudson also reprinted Andrew Hamilton's masterful speech at the 1735 Zenger trial, allowing readers to see the biblical basis of the Zenger defense.[9] Hudson even provided an autobiographical sketch of editor Nathaniel Willis[10] and briefly gave the history of some of New York's Christian newspapers.[11]

The third general history written in the 19th century, S. N. D. North's *History and Present Condition of the Newspaper and Periodical Press of the United States,*[12] was far below those by Thomas and Hudson in that it had a purely materialist emphasis. The first two historians both spotlighted the role of individual editors and their choices, but North—who had been commissioned by the U.S. Census Bureau to study newspapers for the 1880 census—saw the growth of newspapers almost purely in terms of industrialization and new technology. With statistical tables replacing discussion of ideas at North's inn, there was no room for discussion of religion's impact.

EARLY 20TH-CENTURY WORKS

The first general history of journalism published in the 20th century, James Melvin Lee's *History of American Journalism* (1917), also reflected a developmental emphasis that ignored theological considerations.[13] It was methodologically similar to Thomas' century-old work in its tracing of printing's progress colony-by-colony (and territory-by-territory, and state-by-state, and so on, and so on). However, it lacked the patriot printer's fervor and pride. Lee apparently believed that "neutral" reporting was the highest journalistic calling. He was unable to appreciate journalists of an earlier age who saw world view context as vital. For example, Lee labeled the early 19th century—a time of great ideological debate in the press, with Christian-based publications dominant and editorial passion evident—as "the darkest period in the history of American journalism."[14]

George Henry Payne's *History of Journalism in the United States*,[15] published only 3 years after Lee's, showed appreciation of the courage of some early Christian journalists. For example, Payne quoted Benjamin Harris' declaration on being sentenced to prison in England for publishing a work openly critical of the King—"I hope God will give me patience to go through with it"—and wrote that, "There is something of the best of American journalism in that simple declaration."[16] Yet, although Payne praised "the democratic tendency that came with Christianity,"[17] he was conventional in his criticism of Puritanism,[18] and evidently viewed religion as a vestigial organ of the body politic.

The next author of a general journalism history, Willard Bleyer, wanted that organ surgically removed. In his *Main Currents of American Journalism* (1927), Bleyer equated "Church" with "restrictions on freedom of discussion,"[19] and ignored differences among church traditions. Bleyer, essentially a developmental historian, had the elite Progressive belief that the "unthinking masses" were ruled by emotion and primitive faith.[20] The goal of journalists, as members of the enlightened class, was to point the way to social reform. Bleyer wanted to make sure that future developments in journalism would reflect the high points of the progressive past: In the 1930s he argued for professional licensing of journalists and for legal requirements that newspapers be run in what was defined as the public interest.[21]

Some popular critics and historians of the 1920s and 1930s also fostered hostility to the idea of Christian influence in journalism history. Oswald Garrison Villard, in *Some Newspapers and Newspaper-Men*, attacked Christian belief and twisted Bible passages to promote an early version of liberation theology. Villard wrote that "There are plain masses seeking a journalistic Moses to clarify their minds, to give them a program of reconstruction, a moral issue through which to rebuild a broken-down society."[22] George Seldes similarly examined recent newspaper history and saw press, church, and "big business" embracing each other adulterously.[23]

Both academic and popular progressive historians more and more seemed to consider Christianity a conservative ally of the upper class, and therefore a reactionary foe of the masses' drive for equality. A new publication during the inter-war period, *Journalism Quarterly,* showed some of the same tendencies and (probably reflecting the lack of interest among journalism professors) ignored the Reformation origins of American journalism. However, one article did go on at great length about an early deistic editor.[24]

MID-CENTURY DEVELOPMENTAL INFLUENCES

Frank Luther Mott, the leading journalism historian of the 1940s and 1950s, expressed scorn for George Seldes' acceptance of inaccuracy. He wrote of one Seldes book that "the way to read our author is to forget about facts and concentrate on the gyrations of flashing mind and a violent set of emotions."[25] Mott showed, in his large, general text *American Journalism,*[26] that he never met a fact about journalism history he didn't like—and, therefore, the Christian heritage did receive some mention. Mott noted that from 1801 to 1833 "a phenomenon of the times was the 'religious newspaper,' a weekly journal which printed some secular news [and] often competed successfully with the secular papers. . . . Many of these papers were conducted with great vigor and ability."[27]

Mott, however, refused to see religious influences as in any way significant for the larger development of journalism, and thus left many important stories incomplete. For example, Mott wrote that in the *Courant* inoculation debate Episcopalians were lining up on one side and Calvinists such as the Mathers on the other—but Mott did not see, or did not explain, how journalistic visions grew out of theological distinctives.[28] He did not explain the role of religion in the Harris or Zenger episodes, or in many other controversies as well. In short, Mott deserves great credit for his perseverance in scholarship, but his developmental perspective led him to believe that as newspapers became more "professional" they would leave world views behind. Thus, his discussion of more recent decades ignored religion entirely, except to note the existence of some ghettoized churchly publications. The tendency was still to equate the dominant American religious heritage with suppression of thought and opposition to press freedom.

PROGRESSIVE/DEVELOPMENTAL SYNTHESIS

It is no wonder, given Mott's scholarship but density, that a new, simpler textbook of the 1950s, Edwin Emery's *The Press and America,* now in its sixth edition, was able to sweep the field.[29] *The Press and America* was widely accepted not only for its ease of presentation, but because the text's liberalism, materialism, and emphasis on class struggle fit perfectly with academic orthodoxy of recent decades. Power, the book informed students, is "grasped by one class at the expense of another."[30] Politics is a battle of "the rights of property versus the rights of the individual."[31] The American Revolution began because journalists and others saw "the need for a realignment of class power."[32] In one astounding paragraph about the Revolution. *The Press and America* five times brought in "class struggle . . . class conflict . . . class struggle . . . class leaders . . . a class insisting upon a greater share of control."[33] This struggle continued into the early twentieth century, when "crusaders for social justice" fought against "unrestricted economic individualism."[34]

The book's historical materialism included a treatment of religion as super-structure and material as base. *The Press and America* termed Puritan theology "religious double talk" and equated it with the antebellum slavery debate as "the basket in which all the differences of peoples, regions, and ideologies could be carried."[35] The few mentions of religion showed the authors accepting stereotypes that historians who took theology seriously long had discredited. For example, *The Press and America* equated Calvinism with a gospel of prosperity, in which money is the sign of "having passed through the eye of the needle into the circle of the elect."[36] (In reality, Calvinists frequently warned about the snares of wealth: "Riches are no part of your felicity," Richard Baxter wrote; "riches are nothing but plentiful provision for tempting corruptible flesh."[37])

The Press and America, influential because it was so widely used as a textbook, was one of many works that emphasized the relation of media and society. Books by Sidney Kobre also tried to take into account cultural forces, but in practice Christian influence received only minor attention in his books, and the attention it received was as negative as that in Emery. For example, Kobre wrote of the problems faced by those "who dared defy the wrath of the Puritan clergy and the royal governor," as if those were one force.[38]

The few *Journalism Quarterly* articles that touched on religious/historical aspects during the 1950s and 1960s often mixed progressivism with theological know-nothingism. This approach probably reflected the general ignorance of, or antipathy toward, Christianity among many professional historians.[39] For example, Howard H. Fogel in 1960 was amazed that Cotton Mather campaigned for a colonial charter following the downfall of royal governor Sir Edmund Andros: "His agreement and acceptance of the Charter and his subsequent fighting for it seems remarkable considering how limited the role of the clergy in the government's affairs would be."[40] That was not at all remarkable, because Reformation political theory required a limited role for the clergy in government, but Fogel was echoing the prejudice that a free press must have emerged in a battle against "theocracy."[41]

A few other articles published during the 1950s and 1960s also looked at journalism history and religion. Henry S. Stroupe, in "The Beginning of Religious Journalism in North Carolina, 1823–1865," related the Christian press to religious reawakening.[42] Elizabeth Barnes described religion's role in an early 19th-century magazine, the *Panoplist*.[43] John M. Havas gave background on *The Journal of Commerce*.[44] Robert Lee assessed the relationship of Yale College president Timothy Dwight and an early Christian publication, the Boston *Palladium*.[45] Donald F. Brod in 1965 examined press coverage of the Scopes trial four decades before, but missed major issues.[46] A book by Stroupe profiled 159 antebellum religious publications of the South Atlantic states.[47]

In addition, a few dissertations and monographs produced during the late 1960s and 1970s provided useful information about some specialized Protestant publications. William Jesse Stone, Jr., in "A Historical Survey of Leading Texas Denominational Newspapers: 1846–1861," noted that in many Texas antebellum issues "the 'news hole' content was often as much secular as sacred."[48] Alfred Roger Gobbel, in "The Christian Century: Its Editorial Policies and Positions, 1908–1966," examined that magazine's attempt to merge Christianity and liberalism.[49] Claude W. Summerlin, in "A History of Southern Baptist State Newspapers," narrated developments from 1802 through 1967.[50] Wesley Norton's published history of early 19th-century Midwest newspapers showed how they helped to shape public thought on a host of moral issues.[51] Robert W. Ross' *So It Was True: The American Protestant Press and the Nazi Persecution of the Jews*, showed that Protestant denominations publications reported news of Nazi atrocities, but could not quite grasp the full extent of depravity.[52]

Also worth noting are publications specializing in the Jewish and Catholic journalistic heritages in America. Two articles by Sidney Kobre on Mordecai Noah, and a biography of Noah published in 1936, were milestones before 1980.[53] In 1981, Jonathan D. Sarna produced a book-length examination of Noah's attempt to harmonize minority identity, national allegiance, and political editing.[54] Then came an intriguing article by Kathryn T. Theus on mid-19th-century Reform Jewish newspapers.[55] Other recent works deserving mention include Mary Lonan Reilly's examination of the history of the Catholic Press Association,[56] and M. R. Real's overview of specialized Catholic publications.[57] Robert Peel showed how the *Christian Science Monitor* was founded in response to sensational attacks on Mary Baker Eddy by *McClure's* and by Joseph Pulitzer's *World*.[58] In 1980, Harold H. Osmer's *U.S. Religious Journalism and the Korean War* examined the reaction of specialized religious publications to communism and containment.[59] A reference work, *Religious Periodicals in the United States*, profiled various publications.[60] Quentin J. Schultze has done fine work on Christian broadcasting; his recent article, "Evangelical Radio and the Rise of the Electronic Church, 1921–1948," showed how evangelical Christians, despite restrictive network and regulatory policies, built audiences through creative programming.[61]

These points of light were very welcome, but they still tended to examine what could be called *marginalized religion*. It was good to have information about publications *of* and *about* various groups, but only a few historians have been writing articles examining the impact of world views on the journalistic mainstream; their work is footnoted in various parts of this book. I do hope that my overview, as a whole, will encourage more detailed work on mainstream beliefs.

Journalism history textbooks, it should be noted, are not alone in having dropped down the memory hole Christianity's central role in American history. In 1986, a National Institute of Education study of 60 representative pre-college social studies textbooks found Christianity virtually excluded.[62] In books for Grades 1 through 4 that introduced children to an understanding of American society, researcher Paul Vitz and his associates found not a single word about Christianity. Fifth-grade history texts made it appear that religious life ceased to exist in America about a century ago. Fundamentalists were described as people who followed an ancient agricultural way of life. Pilgrims were defined as "people who took long trips." Some journalism history textbooks are more sophisticated but not different in kind. Should we laugh? Should we cry? No, we should get to work.

Appendix C: Methodological Notes

This book has narrated the history of three macrostories in American journalism from its European beginnings in the 16th and 17th century through 1917, when the impact of the Russian Revolution began to open up a new phase in journalistic perceptions. The coming together of the *official story* and the *oppression story* during recent decades is a phenomenon that needs more examination by both liberals and conservatives. But it is especially important that conservatives understand the historical significance of the *corruption story,* for there is danger that the right, in its battle against the capture of leading media by the left, will come to oppose investigation and exposure generally.

One of my goals in writing this book, therefore, has been to honor those who fought to establish the corruption story as journalistically valid; my hope is that in removing dirty bathwater and screaming babies we do not throw out the bathtub that some heroes of early journalism built. One of the most famous historical chapters of the New Testament—chapter 11 of Hebrews—describes the travails of "heroes of faith." We are told that "Some faced jeers and flogging, while still others were chained and put in prison. They were stoned, they were sawed in two, they were put to death by the sword." Those lines come near the end of a chapter that summarizes the stories of Abel, Noah, Abraham, Moses, and others whose names have come down to us, and concludes with praise for many unknown soldiers as well. The first line of chapter 12 then gives the practical application of the long account: "Therefore, since we are surrounded by such a great cloud of witnesses, let us throw off everything that hinders and the sin that so easily entangles, and let us run with perseverence the race marked out for us."

The early history of English and American journalism has its own great cloud of witnesses. Some were martyred in the belief that they should speak and write the truth revealed in the Bible, and in the faith that this truth would make them free. The names of some in the great cloud, and the means of their deaths, are included in the index. Other names in the index testify to the power of other world views; the index includes several references to technological developments, such as the "Hoe cylinder press," but the emphasis is on people, and the ideas that animated their lives.

This emphasis is deliberate. The traditional method of teaching history has involved storytelling about giants of the past whose lives provide lessons (of emulation or avoidance) for those in the classroom who will be the leaders of the future. There are dangers in the "great man" (or "great person") approach, but there are greater dangers when history is depersonalized. If we keep in mind the efforts of the past, we are more likely to realize our deep responsibility not only to those who come after us but to those who came before us. Furthermore, some of the difficulties of personal history can be overcome if we see journalists not as autonomous saints or sinners, but as proponents of macrostories that affected the way millions of readers and listeners viewed the world.

A narrative history of macrostory change intrinsically raises many methodological questions. After all, some researchers trained largely in quantitative methodology smell a rat unless there are numbers involved in a study. A quick way to deal with such objections is to counter them with the need to look for rats whether or not the numbers are present; just as seeing is not believing in an age of video wizards, so counting should not be believing at a time when statistical manipulation is rampant. But the question of numbers deserves something better than a flip reply; the introductions to two books published in 1988 presented deeper responses to potential critiques from those who demand numbers.

The first introduction, that of Charles Murray to his fine book *In Pursuit,* noted the old joke about a drunkard who drops his keys in one place but then looks for them under a streetlamp because "the light's better." As Murray then pointed out concerning analysis of social policy questions,

> We have looked where the light is, and for modern policy analysis the light consists of quantitative analysis. I do not say this altogether critically. Give a policy analyst variables that can be expressed in numbers, and he has at hand a powerful array of analytic tools to probe their meaning. The limitation—and it has become more and more confining over the years—is that so few of the interesting variables in the social sciences can be expressed in numbers. The more complicated the constructs one wants to examine, the less likely that they can be crammed within the quantitative paradigms.[1]

At a time when many communications researchers have fallen in love with quantitative analysis, Murray's point needs strong emphasis: The important questions in journalism cannot be dealt with satisfactorily through techniques of quantitative content analysis or survey research.

The other introductory note I like is a model defense of the qualitative approach. It was offered by Joshua Muravchik at the beginning of his monograph, *News Coverage of the Sandinista Revolution:*

> A more formal or quantitative method is often regarded as lending objectivity to a study, but in this case I think it would have had the opposite effect. . . . Any quantitative analysis would entail assigning news stories to categories that could be counted, categories like 'pro-Sandinista' and 'anti-Sandinista,' or more complex or sophisticated ones. But whatever the categories, the reader without access to my files would have no independent means of evaluating whether I had assigned stories fairly. In contrast with the common-sense discursive approach that I have employed, any skeptical reader can easily check to see whether I have quoted accurately and fairly or whether any of my generalizations are too broad.[2]

Similarly, I propose to anyone interested in further analysis of the macrostories: Crank the microfilm and see for yourself. It is good that, given justified concern about the potential plasticity of historical narrative, storytellers can only gain reader confidence the old-fashioned way: By earning it. It is good to treat even historians with a reputation for accuracy to the slogan of recent disarmament talks: "Trust, but verify." It is important to demand from writers considerable quotation and other specific detail to back up arguments, along with full footnoting so that fancy footwork can be examined, if necessary.

But those are not the only checks on subjectivity run amuck. The concept of "macrostory," which is based on the integration of existing ideas concerning "narrative framework" and "world view," provides a structure of analysis that allows us to see and keep records of the ways that world views interact with journalistic coverage.

Narrative framework (known to language patricians as "archetypal framework" and to plebians as "story formula") is something that every reporter learns on the job, if not before. Almost every thoughtful journalist has stories of how the lesson is taught; a good one was told by Robert Darnton, a reporter who later became a history professor. When he was a police beat novice on the *Newark Star Ledger* in 1959, Darnton wrote a straightforward story about a boy whose bicycle had been stolen in the park. When he showed the story to an older reporter, the veteran told him, "You can't write that sort of story straight," and proceeded (making up detail when useful) to show Darnton how a pro would handle the theft:

> Every week Billy put his twenty-five-cents allowance in his piggy bank. He wanted to buy a bike. Finally, the big day came. He chose a shiny red Schwinn, and took it out for a spin in the park. Every day for a week he rode proudly around the same

route. But yesterday three toughs jumped him in the middle of the park. They knocked him from the bike and ran off with it. Battered and bleeding, Billy trudged home to his father, George F. Wagner of 43 Elm Street. "Never mind, son," his dad said. "I'll buy you a new bike, and you can use it on a paper route to earn money to pay me back.[3]

Darnton, after finding facts to fit that formula, had his first byline, a front-page story. Soon the commissioner of parks announced that the park would have additional security, and neighbors were collecting money to buy Billy a new bike. As Darnton recounted, "I had struck several chords by manipulating stock sentiments and figures: the boy and his bike, piggy-bank savings, heartless bullies, the comforting father."[4]

The implications of "narrative framework" for concepts of journalistic objectivity were discussed intelligently by NYU professor Mitchell Stephens in his book published in 1988, *A History of News*. Stephens wrote that "journalists' supposed objectivity" is:

compromised by the narrative frameworks they impose on their stories—their decision, for example, on which combination of formulas a particular crime might be made to fit: woeful victim ("his life savings"), noble victim ("a former Boy Scout"), tearful relatives ("their only child"), twist of fate ("had his car not been in the shop"), awful irony ("scoffed at fear of crime"), despicable criminal ("despite the victim's pleas"), psychologically scarred criminal ("abandoned by his parents"), shocked acquaintances ("seemed such a quiet boy"), the wages of poverty ("unemployed for seven months"), the scourge of drugs ("to support his habit"), or the breakdown of societal values ("the fourth such crime in this month"). Most events provide sufficient facts to support a multiplicity of possible formulas; journalists choose among them.[5]

Stephens' point was good, but he did not follow through on the question of why journalists choose one narrative framework and not another. To go deeper, we need to understand the nature of "world view"; essentially, world views are clusters of convictions and values not verifiable by the means of natural science. Every person, whether religious or atheistic, has a world view. When astronomer Carl Sagan says there is only the cosmos and nothing beyond it, we need to ask him how he learned that. We will find that he did not discover that by peering through a telescope, but by certain assumptions or presuppositions that he brought *to* his telescope. Similarly when psychologist B. F. Skinner says that human beings are made solely of matter, and that we think with our bodies because bodies are all we are, we need to ask how he learned that. The answer he gives will have nothing at all to do with science; it is as much a matter of faith as anything Jerry Falwell says. The scientists who hold to these beliefs hold them sincerely, no doubt, and they often believe that those who do not agree with them are primitive or foolish or blinded by religious dogma—but they still hold them as matters of faith.

If this is true of "hard science," it is even more evident in that "social science" known as policy analysis. As Charles Murray has noted:

> Policy analysis is decisively affected by the analyst's conception of human nature. One may consider a government policy to be practical or impractical, safe or hazardous, only according to one's conception of what is good for humans, and that in turn has to be based on one's conclusions about the potentials and limitations of humans acting as social creatures.[6]

Journalistic coverage is similarly affected; to show that, we might look at several modes of coverage.

First, say a journalist is writing about foreign policy issues that include questions of disarmament treaties, defense spending, and so on. Journalists who believe that leaders across the world naturally want to avoid war but are forced into it through mistrust or institutional problems will emphasize attempts to change the institutional framework through restraining arms production, eliminating military alliances, deemphasizing nationalism, having more negotiations, and the like. This has been the predominant current framework within American journalism for many "in-depth" stories on such issues.

A journalist proceeding from a different view of human nature, however, might ask other questions: What if war is very natural, given man's greed for power? What if some leaders see war as a permissible way to gain more power, in the belief that they can achieve victory without overwhelming losses? Of course, history is full of mistaken calculations of that sort—dictators have a tendency to overrate their own power—but they may still plunge ahead unless restrained by the obvious power of their adversaries. Journalists who do not assume a benign human nature concerning warfare would emphasize inquiry into whether steps were being taken to raise the cost of war to potential aggressors, and whether those dictators might be overthrown by popular upheaval. For these journalists, the most important news would involve plans for military preparedness and alliances, specific evidence concerning the evil of dictators and the possibilities of overthrowing them, attempts to arouse the public, and so on.

Stories concerning domestic crime also are tied to world views. A journalist who believes that man is naturally good but is corrupted by societal pressures will also believe that criminals are often driven to their crimes by some external cause, often an institutional failure. Criminals are victims. They have been treated badly and have thus deviated from their true natures. They deserve sympathy, not punishment. Murder is due to circumstance; executions are thus unfair. Journalists with such beliefs will want to stress the socioeconomic "reasons" for crime. They will produce stories about reducing crime by spending more money on early childhood education so that potential criminals get off to a better start. We are seeing many such stories now.

On the other hand, those who see the committing of crimes as part of human nature, unless people are restrained by man's force or God's grace, will see the individual as responsible. They will emphasize the need to take hard steps to cut down on crime, and to pray for spiritual change. They will argue that crime must always lead to punishment, both because criminals deserve such a reward and because punishment is a powerful force in keeping people from doing what they want to do.

We might also look briefly—and all these glances are brief and simplifying— at stories concerning economic inequality. Some say that when there is inequality, government should try to end it; journalists who believe this will construct stories, in which people call for action of some sort; any inequalities are instances of wrong doing that should be exposed and challenged. On the other hand, those who see equality of process (e.g., a ban on discrimination by race) as essential, but do not demand equality of result, are likely to produce stories that emphasize individual entrepreneurship rather than societal "oppression."

World views are influential not only in coverage of political matters but in those soft features known as "lifestyle" stories. The *Austin American-Statesman,* for example, has regularly praised thinkers and writers who argue that life is best when we follow our natural instincts and are not "repressed"; the goal, as one article advised, should be to "follow your bliss." An alternate view suggests that we learn not to be ourselves, but to be better than ourselves; such a view, which pokes fun at our belief that whatever we want to do is right, does not receive much favorable press. Larry McMurtry noted even in the 1970s that:

> One seldom, nowadays, hears anyone described as 'a person of character.' The concept goes with an ideal of maturity, discipline and integration that strongly implies repression: people of character, after all, cannot do just anything, and an ability to do just about anything with just about anyone—in the name, perhaps, of Human Potential—is certainly one of the most *moderne* abilities.[7]

What is "character" to some is seen as "hang-up" by others.

These views of human nature tend to be consistent across the boundaries of particular issues: A journalist who sees aggression as something natural (and to be guarded against) in international relations is not likely to assume that crime arises merely from poverty. Nor is such a journalist likely to believe that it is generally best for desires to be met and restraints abolished. Such a journalist will not write from the assumption that people are naturally good but are oppressed by the institutions and other pressures around them.

The concept of *macrostory,* in short, cuts against recent ideas of journalistic objectivity by noting that reporters put news stories in narrative frameworks chosen in relation to world views.[8] However, the concept does not argue that there is no objective truth, nor does it argue that subjectivity reigns totally in modern journalism. It is important to distinguish between *obligatory* and *discretionary* coverage and writing. Obligatory stories are the occurrences that readers, within a particular media community and cultural framework, expect to see covered. Earthquakes, coach or car accidents, major fires and other local disasters, the death of kings and presidents, the doings of the rich and famous— all are grist for a local publication's mill, almost regardless of its editors' and reporters' world views.[9] But journalists can and do deviate from obligatory coverage in three ways. They cover obligatory stories but delve deeper, particularly by asking "why." They choose to cover stories that do not demand coverage but that support their world view concerns. Or they do both by covering discretionary stories in depth.

Any story that goes beyond obligatory coverage becomes highly dependent on journalistic world views. As John Corry of the *New York Times* has noted, "There are fewer rules of pure journalism here than journalists pretend, even to themselves. Journalists, especially big-time journalists, deal in attitudes and ideas as much as events."[10] That has been true throughout journalism history.

Appendix D: Defending the Corruption Story

Journalists who embraced the corruption macrostory sometimes had to defend themselves against arguments that exposure of wrong-doing would increase its incidence or corrupt general discourse. In August 1834, the Reverend J. R. McDowell, editor of a hard-hitting New York monthly appropriately titled *McDowell's Journal*—his motto was, "The world is our field, prevention is our aim"—printed a spirited justification of the biblical sensationalism he practiced. McDowell's discussion, more thorough than any others I have seen, provides valuable insights into the logic of some early crusading journalists, but to my knowledge it has never been reprinted. A few excerpts follow; for easier modern reading I have re-paragraphed some of McDowell's material and deleted some italics and other overly used attention-getting devices of the time.

SHALL LICENTIOUSNESS BE CONCEALED, OR EXPOSED?

This I apprehend is one great question before the community; and the final decision of it will doubtless constitute an interesting and important era in the history of this vice. It is assumed that the Bible is our only rule of Faith and Practice, and is a competent arbiter of the question.

First.—I propose for decision the general question: *Shall Vice and Sin be concealed, or exposed?* In deciding this question, I inquire, What does the Bible TEACH? and What does the Bible PRACTICE?

1. *What does the Bible TEACH?*

(1.) Cry aloud and *spare not;* lift up thy voice like a trumpet, and SHOW MY PEOPLE THEIR TRANSGRESSIONS, AND THE HOUSE OF JACOB THEIR SINS. (Isaiah 58:1) *Show my people their transgressions.*—He must tell them how very bad they really were . . . He must deal faithfully and plainly with them . . . God sees sin in his people, in the house of Jacob, and is displeased with it. They are often unapt and unwilling to see their own sins, and need to have them showed them, and to be told, *Thus and thus thou hast done.*

He must be vehement and in good earnest herein, must cry *aloud, and not spare;* not spare them, nor touch them with his reproofs, as if he were afraid of hurting them, but search the wound to the bottom, lay it bare to the bone; not spare himself or his own pains, but cry as loud as he can; though he spend his strength, and waste his spirits, though he get their ill will by it, and get himself into an ill name; yet he must not spare . . .

(2.) Son of Man, CAUSE JERUSALEM TO KNOW HER ABOMINATIONS. (Ezekiel 16:2) God not only commands Ezekiel to expose abominations, but details minutely the abominations to be made known. It will be recollected that we are now investigating the *general* precept of the Bible in regard to concealing, or exposing vice and sin. . . .

(5.) The Lord said moreover unto me, son of many, wilt though judge [plead for] Aholah and Aholibah? Yea, DECLARE UNTO THEM THEIR ABOMINATIONS. (Ezekiel 23:36) Please examine the whole chapter. In the 33d Chapter of Ezekiel is pointed out the duty of watchmen to blow the trumpet and warn the people of approaching danger. But it is in vain for a watchman to shout "Danger!" unless the people are distinctly told what the danger is. Certainly that was the uniform practice of the ancient prophets. And doubtless St. Paul approved of the same practice, for he says: Therefore watch, and remember that by the space of three years I *ceased not to warn every one night and day with tears.* (Acts 20:31)

And he also . . . commanded Titus to do so likewise (Titus 1:13) saying: "This witness is true; wherefore *rebuke them sharply,* that they may be sound in the faith". . . . Here then we have authority not only to *warn,* but to *rebuke,* and to rebuke *sharply.*" [Whether] we are to expose them (even were it possible thus to rebuke them and still conceal their vices) will appear more clearly under the second head.

(6.) If thy brother, the son of thy mother, or thy son or thy daughter, or the wife of thy bosom, or thy friend, which is as thine own soul, entice thee secretly, saying Let us go and serve other gods . . . neither shalt thou spare, neither shalt thou CONCEAL him . . . And all Israel shall hear, and *fear* and shall do no more any such wickedness as this is among you (Deuteronomy 13: 6-11). Hence it appears such idolators were to be made *public examples,* for the good of all.

(7.) *And have no fellowship with the unfruitful works of darkness, but rather reprove them.* (Ephesians 5:11) . . . Endeavor to expose their wickedness, and make the perpetrators *ashamed* of them . . . If it should be said that the perceptive duties that have been cited to expose vice and sin, have special or sole reference to the sins of the *church,* and not to those of the world, than I reply both the church and the world are under the same moral government of God—both are amenable to the same laws—both will stand at the same final Tribunal—and both will be either condemned or acquitted by the same general principles.

Moreover, St. Paul, particularly in the first chapter of the Romans, and the other apostles did expose and denounce the sins and vices of the *gentiles* as well as those of the *church*. And finally, it would be hard indeed to charge upon the church all the sins, and vices, and abominations that are exposed and condemned in the Bible. The precept therefore, has as much respect to the abominations of the *world,* as to those of the *church.* And as there is nothing in the Scriptures of an opposite spirit and import to the general scope of the passages quoted, we are forced to the conclusion that the BIBLE PRECEPT is, to DETECT, EXPOSE, and PUNISH VICE and SIN.

2. *What does the Bible PRACTICE?*

(1.) When Adam and Eve had eaten of the forbidden fruit and thus transgressed the commands of God, *they hid themselves, as vice and sin are wont to do.* Then what did God do? He went into the garden and sought for them saying "Adam where art thou?" And *detected, exposed,* and punished them.

(2.) When Cain committed fratricide, the Lord suffered him not to escape, but detected him, saying unto Cain, "Where is Abel thy brother?" "What hast thou done?" And thus did the Lord expose and severely punish Cain. Genesis 4: 8-14.

(3.) In like manner, was the wickedness done by Jacob's sons to their brother Joseph in selling him into Egypt, and then in lying to their father about his death— *detected and exposed.*

(4.) Another interesting illustration of the Bible practice is found in the case of Achan, whose theft so seriously troubled the armies of Israel. Showing very clearly God's utter abhorrence of concealed vice and sin, and his determination to have it detected, exposed, and punished . . .

(20.) In the book of Esther is a very interesting narrative of Haman's wicked devices against the Jews, and of his detection, exposure and punishment. "And when Haman saw that Mordecai bowed not, nor did him reverence, then was Haman full of wrath. And he thought scorn to lay hands on Mordecai alone; for they had showed him the people of Mordecai: wherefore Haman sought to destroy all the Jews that were throughout the whole kingdom of Ahasuerus, even the people of Mordecai." (Esther 3:5,6) But when the plot had advanced so far that the destruction of the people of Mordecai seemed inevitable, then the Lord saw fit to detect and expose the machinations of Haman. And cold indeed must be the heart that can read this story and not rejoice at the developments of the 7th chapter. And colder and harder still must be the heart that would advocate the concealment and protection of vice and crime, and sin. . . .

(27.) The 16th of Ezekiel is not the only chapter that exposes vice and sin. Among other chapters of the *same character,* we may mention—The fifty-ninth of Isaiah, the fourth of Hosea—see also the 1st, 2d and 3d.), the twenty-second of Ezekiel, and the Prophets generally, the twenty-third of Matthew, the first of Romans.

Of the twenty-third chapter of Ezekiel, Dr. Clark remarks, In this chapter there are many of what we would call indelicate expressions, [if the term "indelicate," is a form of *reproach,* query, if it is right in the sight of God for us thus to stigmatize his Holy Word!] because a parallel is run between *idolatry* and *prostitution,* and the circumstances of the latter illustrate the peculiarities of the former. Ezekiel was among the Jews, what *Juvenal* was among the Romans; a ROUGH REPROVER OF THE MOST ABOMINABLE VICES. THEY BOTH SPOKE OF THINGS AS THEY FOUND THEM; STRIPPED VICE NAKED, AND SCOURGED IT PUBLICLY. THE ORIGINAL IS STILL MORE ROUGH THAN THE TRANS-LATION.

(29.) See how God speaks of Licentiousness.—Will you denounce God as indecent? As collateral evidence and illustration of the Bible method of dealing with vice and sin, especially of *speaking* upon the subject of Licentiousness, let us examine some of the laws which God gave to Israel . . . "Moreover thou shalt not lie carnally with thy neighbor's wife to defile thyself with her. And thou shalt not let any of thy seed pass through the fire to Molech, neither shalt thou profane the name of thy God: I am the LORD. Thou shalt not lie with mankind, as with womankind; it is abomination. Neither shalt thou lie with any beast to defile thyself therewith . . ."

At this time when so many honest Christians are anxiously inquiring and seeking for light, and truth, and correct principles, and for the proper mode of speaking and conversing upon the subject of licentiousness, it is peculiarly interesting and important to know how God spake upon this subject: for true Christians will never hesitate to follow an example set by their Father in heaven. God's mode and style of speaking upon the subject I have exhibited in the selections indiscriminately made from all the sacred writings . . . It will be well for us not to become "wise above what is written." Shall we be "wiser than God?" "Shall any teach God knowledge?" (Job 21:22)

TAKE NOTICE: Not only did the allwise Jehovah speak in this style, and give these laws and statutes on the subject of Licentiousness, but he gave commandment, saying "thou shalt teach them diligently unto thy children, and shalt talk of them when thou sittest in thy house, and when thou walkest by the way, and when thou liest down, and when thou risest up." (Deuteronomy 6:6-9) . . .

And thou shalt teach them diligently unto thy children. Under all the Divine dispensations from the beginning, no duty is set higher, or more insisted on, than that of instructing children in the knowledge of religion. [And what is "the knowledge of religion," but the knowledge of vice and virtue, of sin and holiness, of evil and good, of wrong, and right?] . . . Christian parents are most expressly enjoined to "bring up their children in the nurture and admonition of the Lord;" and to the praise of young Timothy, as well as of those relations, who had been his instructors, it is said, "that from a child he had known the Holy Scriptures, able to make him wise unto salvation, through faith which is in Jesus Christ."

Now is it to be supposed that "young Timothy" was taught to omit, in his reading of the Scriptures, all those chapters that relate to licentiousness? Must "young Timothy" be kept in profound ignorance of this vice against which the Bible thunders so loudly? Is only a part of the Bible "profitable for doctrine, for reproof and for instruction in righteousness?" . . .

No concealment of vice at the final Judgment . . . O, the developments and disclosures of that awful day! "When God shall judge the SECRETS of men." (Romans 2:16) When every disgusting abomination shall be stripped naked, and vice in all its horrid deformity and odiousness shall be exposed to the assembled universe! Ah! whither will fastidiousness then flee—and how shall squeamishness veil her face? Will the rocks and the mountains afford a hiding place?

Let us think, speak, and act with sole reference to our final account. We are to give account of ourselves to God, and not to man. If duty requires the detection, exposure, and punishment of vice, we are not to inquire or regard what the world will say; our only concern is to know what God thinks, and what he will say. Hear the Lord Jesus—"What I tell you in darkness, that speak ye in light: and what ye hear in the ear, that preach ye upon the housetops. And fear not them that kill the body, but are not able to kill the soul; but rather fear him that is able to destroy both soul and body in hell." (Matthew 10:27,28)

Conclusion of the argument

Having adopted the Bible as our only Rule of Faith and Practice, and having ascertained, that it is both the Doctrine and the Practice of the Bible to expose vice and sin, and having also ascertained that licentiousness, which is one of the most flagrant and abominable of all vices, is not recognized by the Bible as an exception to the general rule of exposing vice and sin—It necessarily follows, THAT IT IS OUR DUTY TO EXPOSE LICENTIOUSNESS.

The code of criminal law proscribed by every civilized and christian government, requires the most diligent and energetic efforts to *detect, expose, and punish vice*. Look at the combination of wisdoms and power in the Legislative, the Judicial and the Executive departments of all our governments, both superior and subordinate, to effect these objects. It is only upon the detection and punishment of vice, that the peace and safety of society depend. Banish from the community the vigilance of a Police by day, and of a Watch by night—Deprive the constable of his staff, and the sheriff of his power—Demolish Bridewell and Jail, Penitentiary and Prison—Paralyze the strong arm of the law—Close every court of Judicature—in short, abolish the whole system of means and measures, or powers and functions, organized for the *detection, exposure, and punishment of vice*—And then shall you see commence the Reign of Terror and the Misrule of Anarchy. Then shall the assassin plunge the dirk and the dagger at noon-day, and blood shall deluge the land. . . .

Burglary and Burning, Riot and Rain, Pillage and Plunder, Death and Destruction shall become the watchwords of an infuriated mob. The domestic fireside, that sacred retreat of innocence and virtue, shall be invaded by *Lust and Rape,* and the dwelling place of a mother's purity and of a daughter's chastity, shall be converted into the Brothel and the House of Death. Order, Temperance, and Sobriety, shall be ingulfed in the whirlpool and confusion of bachanalian revelry, and midnight debauchery. The Sabbath shall no longer be sanctified by the church-going bell, by the prayers, and praises, and precepts of God's Holy Sanctuary, by the quiet devotions of the social circle, or the aspirations of calm retirement: but the Lord's Day shall become the grand Jubilee of Tumult and Banqueting, of Horse-racing and Gambling, of the Parade of Military and the Pageantry of Pride and Folly, of the Desolation of Error and the Havoc of Infidelity.

And yet all these horrors are but the inauspicious beginning of that Reign of Terror, and the Misrule of Anarchy, consequent upon the abolition of Penal Law, and the Concealment and protection of vice. Those therefore who oppose the detection and exposure of vice, must see that they are acting in opposition to the best interests of society, and to the collective wisdom and experience of legislators in every age of the world. *But this is not all:* Such opposers must find themselves acting in fearful opposition to the Precept and Practice of the Bible, and of the Bible's God.

Notes

INTRODUCTION

1. Roy Basler, ed., *The Collected Works of Abraham Lincoln* (Rutgers, 1953), vol. II, p. 385.

2. William Camden, *Annales* (London, 1625), book 3, p. 16. Stubbes' offending pamphlet is also available in some rare book libraries: See *The Discourie of a Gaping Gulf Whereinto England is like to be swallowed by another French marriage; if the Lord forbid not the banes, by letting her Majestie see the sin and punishment thereof* (London, 1579).

3. Ibid.

CHAPTER 1
UNNATURAL ACTS

1. Quoted often; the best brief, readily available summary of the conditions of Luther's time and his battle against indulgences is found in Roland Bainton, *Here I Stand* (New York, 1956).

2. Ibid, p. 61.

3. Margaret Aston, *The Fifteenth Century: The Prospect for Europe* (London, 1968), p. 76: "Printing was recognized as a new power and publicity came into its own."

4. This response came at the Diet of Worms when Archbishop of Trier Eck asked how opponents of Christianity would "exult to hear Christians discussing whether they have been wrong all these years. Martin . . . would you put your judgment above that of

154

so many famous men . . .? For a time the protection offered by Frederick was the only material force preserving Luther from many enemies who wished to kill him—yet Luther continued to criticize Frederick's prized relics collection. (Frederick, nevertheless, protected him, and in 1523 finally agreed not to exhibit his relic collection, but to place most of it in storage.)

5. Elizabeth Eisenstein, *The Printing Press as an Agent of Change* (Cambridge, England, 1980), vol. I, p. 426.

6. Ibid., p. 330.

7. Bainton, p. 63.

8. Luther advocated civil disobedience in some instances but was opposed to anarchistic revolution. If each person were to take justice into his own hands, he wrote, there would be "neither authority, nor government, nor order nor land, but only murder and bloodshed."

9. Bainton, p. 120.

10. Eisenstein, p. 304.

11. Quoted in Frederick Siebert, *Freedom of the Press in England, 1476–1776* (Urbana, Illinois, 1952), p. 45.

12. Henry VIII broke from Rome not on grounds of principle, as did Luther and Calvin, but in order to make himself the principal arbiter of theology, especially when it came to his own divorce of first wife Katharine of Aragon. Benjamin Hart suggested correctly that "to place the king at the head of the church was a far more oppressive and corrupting influence on Christianity than the pope in far-off Italy. The bishops, formerly responsible to the Roman authority, often served as an effective check on royal power. Now they were little more than a political arm of the state, used to stamp out religious dissent, which was seen as a threat to social order." (Benjamin Hart, *Faith and Freedom* (Dallas, 1988), p. 61)

13. Siebert, p. 49.

14. 34 and 35 Henry VIII, c. 1. The 1542–1543 law stated, "There shall be no annotations or preambles in Bibles or New Testaments in English. The Bible shall not be read in English in any church. No women or artificers, prentices, journeymen, servingmen of the degree of yeomen or under, husbandmen, nor labourers, shall read the New Testament in English. Nothing shall be taught or maintained contrary to the King's instructions. And if any spiritual person preach, teach, or maintain anything contrary to the King's instructions or determinations, made or to be made, and shall be thereof convict, he shall for his first offence recant, for his second abjure and bear a fagot, and for his third shall be adjudged an heretick, and be burned."

15. The Bible had to be carefully followed, and the interpretations of those who had studied it at length were not to be negligently disregarded. But in the end, neither individual consciences nor church leaders were to be in charge: The Bible was viewed as clear enough so that ordinary individuals could read it themselves and see its truths for themselves.

16. When Henry died in 1547 and his son Edward VI briefly took over, restrictions were eased, but when Mary assumed the throne upon Edward's death in 1553 and attempted to reassert Catholic dominance, freedom fled.

17. For more details see M. A. Shaaber, *Some Forerunners of the Newspaper in England* (New York, 1966), p. 76.

18. Ibid., p. 71.

19. See, for instance, *The complaynt of Veritie, made by John Bradford,* and *The*

wordes of Maister Hooper at his death were published in 1559, and *A briefe Treatise concerning the burnynge of Bucer and Phagius at Cambrydge* came out in 1562. These and others are cited in Shaaber, p. 77.

20. John Foxe, *Actes and monuments of matters most speciall and memorable, happenying in the church, with an universall history of the same,* 6th edition (London, 1610), pp. 586, 606, 609, 612, 946, 1033, 1423, 1527, 1547, 1738, etc. A much more readily accessible paperback edition, but without the woodcuts, is published as *Foxe's Book of Martyrs* (Springdale, PA, 1981).

21. Foxe was following the biblical tradition of the apostle Luke, who wrote at the beginning of his gospel that "I myself have carefully investigated everything from the beginning" in order to "write an orderly account" dependent not on speculation but on eyewitnesses.

22. *Foxe's Book of Martyrs,* op. cit., pp. 212–213.

23. Ibid, p. 213.

24. Ibid., pp. 309.

25. Ibid., pp. 351–387.

26. Ibid., loc. cit.

27. Ibid., pp. 201–202.

28. Miles Coverdale, ed., *Certain most godly, fruitful, and comfortable letters of such true saintes and holy martyrs of God, as in the late bloodye persecution here with in this realme, gave their lyues for the defence of Christes holy gospel: written in the tyme of theyr . . . imprysonment . . .* (London: John Day, 1564), p. ii.

29. The Stationers Company, a group of government-certified printers granted a publishing monopoly, sent out spies to determine each printer's number of orders, number of employees, and wages paid them. That information, along with identification of customers and works currently being published, allowed officials to make sure presses were not used for "seditious" purposes.

30. Siebert, pp. 91–92.

31. G. W. Prothero, *Select Statutes and other Constitutional Documents illustrative of the reigns of Elizabeth and James I* (Oxford, 1894), p. 400.

32. Ibid., pp. 427–428.

33. Leland Ryken, *Worldly Saints: The Puritans As They Really Were* (Grand Rapids, 1986), p. 124.

34. Patrick Collinson, *The Elizabethan Puritan Movement* (Berkeley, 1967), p. 380. The last word of that quotation, "simpletons," shows how the Puritan emphasis on Bible reading by everyone was folly to those who scorned democracy.

35. Jack Bartlett Rogers, *Scripture in the Westminster Confession* (Grand Rapids, 1967), p. 383.

36. Quoted in Ryken, p. 384.

37. Everett Emerson, ed., *English Puritanism from John Hooper to John Milton* (Durham, NC, 1968), p. 153.

38. Ryken, p. 105. The Puritans did at times fall into repetitive prolixity to make sure that their meaning was clear; sometimes their motto seemed to be "clarity, clarity, clarity," as a fuller quotation from Perkins indicates: "Preaching must be plain, perspicuous, and evident . . . It is a by-word among us: *It was a very plain sermon:* And I say again, *the plainer, the better*."

39. Ibid., pp. 105, 106.

CHAPTER 2
PERILS OF THE PURITAN PRESS

1. A Cologne publication, *Mercurius Gallobelgicus,* commenced publication in 1594 and continued semi-annually for four decades, but its summaries of diplomatic and military events and other news were in Latin, and the publication thus made no claim to popular appeal.

2. See Joseph Frank, *The Beginnings of the English Newspaper 1620–1660* (Cambridge, MA, 1961), p. 13.

3. *Boston Gazette,* June 2, 1755; cited in Jeffery A. Smith, *Printers and Press Freedom: The Ideology of Early American Journalism* (New York, 1988), p. 21.

4. Frank, p. 41.

5. Ibid., p. 80.

6. Ibid., p. 91.

7. There were errors, of course, and Puritan editors learned from hard experience that sources were not always reliable. Frank describes how the editor of one newspaper, *The True Informer* (1643–1646), observed that "Truth is the daughter of Time. Relations of Battels, fights, skirmishes, and other passages and proceedings of concernment are not alwaies to be taken or credited at the first hand, for that many times they are uncertaine, and the truth doth not so conspicuously appeare till a second or third relation" (p. 55). But the *goal* of truth-telling led to vigorous attempts to uncover the reality of events; in the words of Richard Sibbes, "Truth feareth nothing so much as concealment, and desireth nothing so much as clearly to be laid open to the view of all: when it is most naked, it is most lovely and powerful."

8. Hyder Rollin, *Cavalier and Puritan* (New York: University Press, 1923), p. 44. Average newspaper circulation was only 500, but copies were passed from hand to hand; most London males, and many females, were literate, and most read all or part of one of the weekly newspapers. In addition, one page ballads, customarily selling for a cent, also continued their practice of covering news events.

9. In 1642 Parliament decreed that "no person or persons shall Print, publish, or utter, any Booke or Pamphlet, false or scandalous, to the proceedings of the Houses of Parliament," but the emphasis was on falsehood, not embarrassment, and enforcement was largely absent. For additional perspective, see Frederick Siebert, *Freedom of the Press in England, 1476–1776* (Urbana, IL, 1952), p. 182.

10. Samuel Hartlib, *A description of the Famous Kingdom of Macaria* (London, 1641); quoted in Siebert, p. 192.

11. William Walwyn, *The Compassionate Samaritane* (London, 1644), p. A5.

12. Henry Robinson, *Liberty of Conscience* (London, 1644), p. 17.

13. John Milton, *Aeropagetica,* in many editions; here, in Douglas Bush, ed., *The Portable Milton* (New York, 1949), p. 199.

14. Ibid., loc. cit.

15. Quoted in Joseph Frank, *Cromwell's Press Agent: A Critical Biography of Marchamont Nedham, 1620–1678* (Latham, Md., 1980), p. 186.

16. *Mercurius Britanicus,* June 10–17, 1644.

17. Ibid., August 12–19, 1644.

18. Ibid., June 24–July 1, 1644.

19. Ibid., June 10–17, 1644.

20. Ibid., July 1–8, 1644.

21. Ibid., August 12–19, 1644.

22. Ibid.

23. Ibid.

24. Ibid., October 21–28, 1644.

25. Ibid., May 20–27, 1644.

26. Ibid., May 25–June 2, 1645.

27. Parliament, trying at that time to work out a compromise with King Charles, was not pleased when Nedham described the monarch as "a wilfull King . . . with a guilty Conscience, bloody Hands, a Heart full of broken Vowes and Protestations."

28. Quoted in Frank, *Nedham,* p. 100.

29. Francis Wortley, *Characters and Elegies* (London, 1646), p. 26.

30. Marchamont Nedham, *Independencie No Schism* (London, 1646), p. 40.

31. Rollin, p. 45.

32. See John Adair, *Founding Fathers* (Grand Rapids, MI 1986), p. 218.

33. *Mercurius Pragmaticus,* October 19–26, 1647.

34. Ibid., October 12–20, 1647.

35. Ibid., November 21–28, 1648.

36. Frank, *Nedham,* p. 45.

37. *Mercurius Pragmaticus,* October 5–12, 1647.

38. Marchamont Nedham, *Ding Dong* (London, 1648), pp. 1–2.

39. Marchamont Nedham, *A Short History of the English Rebellion* (London, 1661), p. 4.

40. Ibid., p. 7.

41. Ibid., pp. 11, 14.

42. Ibid., p. 31.

43. William Waller, *Vindication,* quoted in Adair, p. 220.

44. Frank, *The Beginnings of the English Newspaper,* p. 194.

45. Ibid., p. 185.

46. *Mercurius Pragmaticus,* p. 34.

47. Ibid., p. 37.

48. Marchamont Nedham, *The Great Feast at the Sheep-shearing of the City and Citizens, on the 7th of June last,* p. 6.

49. Marchamount Needham, *The Case of the Commonwealth of England, Stated, or The Equity, Utility, and Necessity, of a Submission to the present Government* (London, 1650).

50. Ibid., p. 40.

51. Ibid., p. 30.

52. Ibid., loc. cit.

53. Holles quoted in Adair, p. 220.

54. Nedham edited the *Mercurius Politicus* through the demise of the Cromwellian regime in 1660. From 1655 to 1660 he also edited *The Publick Intelligencer;* it appeared on Monday and *Politicus* on Thursday, with some pages duplicated.

55. Frank, *Nedham,* p. 207.

56. See, for example, *Publick Intelligencer,* July 5–12, 1658, execution of Edmond Stacy.

57. Marchamont Nedham, *The Excellencie of a Free State* (London: 1656), p. 45.

58. *Mercurius Politicus,* March, 1657.

59. Adair, p. 228.

60. Ibid., loc. cit.

61. Marchamont Nedham, *Interest will not Lie* (London, 1659).

62. Marchamont Nedham, *Newes From Brussels* (London, 1660).

63. *A Rope for Pol* (London, 1660).

64. Quoted in Frank, *Nedham,* p. 127.

65. Charles II executed many of those who had signed the death warrant for his father, and even hanged (by what was left of their necks) the semi-decayed corpses of Cromwell and two other leaders. But Nedham in 1647 and 1648 had opposed the execution and given aid and comfort to Charles I, and that twist evidently was remembered by Charles II.

66. Preamble of 13 & 14 Charles II, c. 33.

67. In 1664 the First Conventicle Act made it illegal for five or more people not of the same household to meet together for worship except in accordance with the Anglican liturgy. In 1665 the Five Mile Act forbade ejected ministers to come within 5 miles of any place where they had ministered, unless they would swear never to attempt "any alteration of government either in Church or State." In 1670 the Second Conventicle Act imposed heavier penalties on preachers or others who defied the law. Seizure and sale of Dissenters' goods was authorized, with one third of the revenue gained paid to informers.

68. 15 Charles II 1663, in *Howell's State Trials,* p. 513.

CHAPTER 3
PLANTING OF CORRUPTION STORY

1. Quoted in Leonard Levy, *Emergence of a Free Press* (New York, 1985), p. 18.

2. Ibid., pp. 19–20.

3. Charles M. Andrews, ed., *Narratives of the Insurrections, 1675–1690* (New York, 1915), p. 309.

4. Ibid.

5. During this period, walking the tightrope of reformation without revolution was akin to walking the plank. For example, in 1698 Philip Clark, although a member of the Maryland assembly, was sentenced to 6 months in jail for criticizing Governor Francis Nicholson. According to the governor's Council, Clark's criticism was incitement to rebellion not because he actually suggested such an activity, but because his critique would reduce the esteem in which the governor was held—and that was seen as the first step toward rebellion.

6. John Harvard's gift of books for a new college was important, but Harvard's founders had to overcome political as well as material obstacles: They were challenging royal authority. In England, the universities at Oxford and Cambridge were arms of the government, which had a monopoly on the granting of college diplomas; Harvard, however, awarded its first diplomas in 1642, without royal authorization. The timing, it turned out, was good: In 1642 a king besieged and eventually to be beheaded was in no position to assert his authority.

7. Quoted in Benjamin Hart, *Faith and Freedom* (Dallas, TX, 1988), p. 121.

8. Clyde Duniway, *The Development of Freedom of the Press in Massachusetts* (Cambridge, MA, 1906), pp. 34–35.

9. Samuel Danforth, *The City of Sodom Enquired Into* (Cambridge, MA, 1674), cited in David Nord, "Teleology and News: The Religious Roots of American Journalism, 1630–1730, paper presented to the History Division, Association for Education in Journalism and Mass Communication (AEJMC), Portland, OR, July, 1988, p. 8.

10. Cited in Isaiah Thomas, *History of Printing in America* (Worcester, MA, two volumes, 1810), I, 83.

11. Harry S. Stout, *The New England Soul: Preaching and Religious Culture in Colonial New England* (New York, 1986), p. 3.

12. Ibid. As Stout noted, "Twice on Sunday and often once during the week, every minister in New England delivered sermons lasting between one and two hours in length. Collectively over the entire span of the colonial period, sermons totalled over five million separate messages in a society whose population never exceeded one-half million. . . . The average weekly churchgoer in New England (and there were far more churchgoers than church members) listened to something like seven thousand sermons in a lifetime, totaling somewhere around fifteen thousand hours of concentrated listening." (pp. 3–4)

13. See Alice M. Baldwin, *The New England Clergy and the American Revolution* (New York, 1928), p. 4.

14. Studies show that most publications in New England in the seventeenth century were event oriented. David Nord's review of the seventeenth century titles listed in Charles Evans' *American Bibliography* shows that 426 of 777 (55%) were linked clearly to events. (Nord, p. 10)

15. Quoted in Stout, p. 77.

16. Cited in Nord, p. 12. Nord, an exception to the lack of interest among leading journalism historians in the religious roots of American journalism, pointed out correctly that "Increase Mather's publication record in the last quarter of the seventeenth century represents the first major flowering [of] indigenous American journalism."

17. *Some Meditations Concerning our Honourable Gentlemen and Fellow-Souldiers* (Boston, 1675).

18. Increase Mather, *A Brief History* . . . (Boston, 1676), included in *So Dreadfull a Judgment: Puritan Responses to King Philip's War, 1676–1677,* Richard Slotkin and James K. Folsom, eds., (Middletown, Conn. 1978), pp. 113, 119.

19. Ibid., p. 109. On another occasion colonial soldiers pursued Philip's army into a swamp but withdrew just as Philip was about to surrender. "The desperate Distress which the Enemy was in was unknown to us," Mather reported; rather than bewailing a lost opportunity, however, he wrote how "God saw that we were not yet fit for Deliverance" (p. 90).

20. Ibid., p. 92.

21. Ibid., p. 130.

22. Ibid., p. 140.

23. Ibid., pp. 176–177.

24. Ibid., pp. 191, 193.

25. Increase Mather, *An Essay for the Recording of Illustrious Providences* (Boston, 1684), preface.

26. Ibid.

27. Ibid.

28. Ibid.

29. Mather, *A Brief History* . . ., p. 125. Nord, in noting the protest of Robert Middlekauff that Mather's procedure was "not genuinely empirical," pointed out that "it is empirical in its way. The empirical data are the statements of the sources. Mather's method is the empiricism of the news reporter, not the scientist."

30. Mather wrote about not only political events but storms, earthquakes, and fires. He stated, in *Burnings Bewailed* (Boston, 1711), that all such events were "ordered by the Providence of God . . . When a fire is kindled among a people, it is the Lord that hath kindled it."

31. Nord, p. 11.

32. Increase Mather, *A Brief History* . . ., in Slotkin and Folsom, p. 81.

33. Cotton Mather, *Magnalia Christi Americana* (London, 1702), vol. II, p. 341.

34. Quoted in Barrett Wendell, *Cotton Mather* (New York, 1891), p. 46.

35. Wise was ordered to pay a fine of 50 pounds (the equivalent of about $5,000) and to post a bond for 1,000 pounds ($100,000) to guarantee his good behavior.

36. Kenneth Silverman, *The Life and Time of Cotton Mather* (New York, 1984), p. 74.

37. William and Mary's ascension was called the "Glorious Revolution," because the coup was militarily unresisted and the bloodshed of the English civil war was not repeated.

38. Duniway, pp. 67–68.

39. *A Short but Just Account of the Tryal of Benjamin Harris* . . . (London, 1679), p. 8.

40. Benjamin Harris, *A Relation of the Fearful Estate of Francis Spira* (London, 1683), p. 4.

41. Some details of his life, although not his theology, are provided in J. G. Muddiman, "Benjamin Harris, the First American Journalist," *Notes and Queries* 163 (1932), pp. 129–133, 147–150, 166–170, 223, and 273–274 (Muddiman's article was spread over several issues).

42. Harris, *Spira,* p. 11.

43. Ibid., p. 13.

44. See Carolyn Cline (Southwest Texas State University), "The Puritan Revolutionary: The Role of Cotton Mather in the Founding of *Publick Occurrences,*'" paper presented to AEJMC, p. 4.

45. *Publick Occurrences Both Foreign and Domestick,* September 25, 1690.

46. Ibid.

47. Ibid.

48. Ibid.

49. Ibid.

50. See Cline, op. cit.

51. One of the stories he produced, entitled "The Irreligious Life, and Miserable Death of Mr. George Edwards, who committed suicide on January 4, 1704," indicates the type of coverage of news events that Harris evidently would have developed in America, if he had been given the opportunity. Harris first described how "Edwards threw himself upon a Belief, that All Things came by Nature, and that what Christians call the Providence of God, was purely Accident and Chance." Then, ideas had consequences: "These Notions thus imbid'd, led him to a voluptuous and sensual Life; and consequently devoted him to an Atheistical Conversation." For years Edwards "continued to run on in Infidelity,

Impenitence, and Drunkenness. In his drink he was Mad, and out of it, in a melancholly despairing Condition. . . . Thus he hurry'd away his Precious Time, 'till his Estate became morgag'd, and his Affairs ran backwards; the thoughts of which, with the Horrors of Conscience for disowning his Maker, and living a prophane, debauch'd Life, threw him into extream Despair." Finally Edwards shot and killed himself: "Here was the dreadful End of his Atheism, and Infidelity, his Irreligion and Impiety. In this horrible manner did he cut off his Life and Hopes at one Blow, and, without any Fear of God, or Regard to the Good of his Soul, launch'd out into an unalterable Eternity." (included in sixth edition of Benjamin Harris, *A Relation of the Fearful Estate of Francis Spira* (London, 1718).

52. Chadwick Hansen, "Some of the Witches Were Guilty," in Marc Mappen, ed., *Witches and Historians* (Huntington, NY, 1980), p. 46.

53. See "Appendix: List of Known Witchcraft Cases in Seventeenth Century New England," in John Demos, *Entertaining Satan* (New York, 1982), pp. 401–409.

54. Quoted in Perry Miller, *The New England Mind: From Colony to Province* (Boston, 1953), p. 194. *The Return of Several Ministers*, a pamphlet of unknown authorship published in June 1692, made the same point.

55. Chadwick Hansen, *Witchcraft at Salem* (New York, 1969), argues that some of those executed probably did try to practice witchcraft, but others did not.

56. Mather made this offer in August 1692, while again stating that spectral evidence is fallacious.

57. Increase Mather's strong sense of God's sovereignty led him to state that it would be better for ten of the guilty to escape than for one innocent person to be put to death wrongly; he argued that if there is no convincing proof of a crime, God does not intend the perpetrator to be discovered.

58. Increase Mather, *Cases of Conscience* (Boston, 1692), p. 10.

59. Miller, p. 195.

60. "Command" was Mather's word for it.

61. Cotton Mather, *The Wonders of the Invisible World* (Boston, 1692), p. 1.

62. Miller, p. 191.

63. Quoted in Clyde Augustus Duniway, *The Development of Freedom of the Press in Massachusetts* (New York, 1905, reprinted 1969), p. 73.

64. The grounds for acquittal were technical, but the jury did pass up an opportunity to shut up a writer disliked by New England leaders.

65. Thomas Maule, *New-England Persecutors Mauled with their own Weapons* (New York, 1697).

66. *Boston News-Letter*, August 6, 1705.

67. Ibid., April 30, 1704.

68. *Ibid.*, July 24 and October 30, 1704.

69. Ibid., June 30, 1704.

70. Ibid., May 29, 1704; June 5, June 12, 19, 26, and July 3, 1704.

71. Mather, *The Voice of God in Stormy Winds* (Boston, 1704), quoted in Nord, p. 29.

72. Begun on December 21, 1719, by editor William Brooker, Campbell's successor as postmaster.

73. Perry Miller (p. 206) found excerpts in Mather's diaries of 1694 and 1696 that show him still churning about the "unheard of DELUSIONS" at Salem and the "Inextricable

Things we have met withal." Later, Mather continued to agonize about how "divers were condemned, against whom the chief evidence was found in the spectral exhibitions."

74. *Boston News-Letter,* July 24, 1721.

75. John B. Blake, "The Inoculation Controversy in Boston: 1721–1722," *New England Quarterly* 35 (December, 1952), p. 493.

76. Historians have given the *Courant* an anti-establishment reputation, because it opposed Cotton Mather, but that is an error; the "establishment," although united in religious belief, had become politically pluralistic.

77. Ironically, it was the bravery of Mather that resurrected tales of his former cravenness. As Perry Miller noted concerning the witchcraft trials, they were quickly forgotten at the time, and seen as just one more problem that temporarily overtook New England: "For twenty-eight years this cataclysm hardly appears on the record—until summoned from the deep by opponents of inoculation as a stick to beat the clergy for yet another 'delusion.' Only in 1721 does it begin to be that blot on New England's fame which has been enlarged, as much by friends as by foes, into its greatest disgrace." (Miller, p. 191).

CHAPTER 4
ESTABLISHMENT OF AMERICAN PRESS LIBERTY

1. *Boston News-Letter,* January 21, 1723.

2. Massachusetts had fewer political shocks during the second quarter of the 18th century, but "remarkable judgments" such as earthquakes still could cause excitement. In October 1727, a "horrid rumbling" and "weighty shaking" was felt throughout New England. Thomas Paine of Weymouth, Massachusetts, using good specific detail, reported that "the motion of the Earth was very great, like the waves of the sea. . . . The strongest Houses shook prodigiously and the tops of some Chimnees were thrown down." Aftershocks over the next 9 days, in Paine's words, "mightily kept up the Terror of it in the People, and drove them to all possible needs of Reformation." (Thomas Paine, *The Doctrine of Earthquakes* (Boston, 1728).) Seventeen news sermons about the earthquake were published.

3. *Boston New-Letter,* January 4, 1733.

4. Mark A. Noll, *Christians in the American Revolution* (Washington, 1977), noted that during this period the theological composition of the colonial population began to change, as Anglican state churches of the middle and southern colonies lost their hold on the populace. By the American Revolution, 75% of all colonists would be identified with denominations—Congregationalist, Presbyterian, Baptist, and German or Dutch Reformed—that had arisen from the Reformed and Puritan wing of European Protestantism (p. 30).

5. *American Weekly Mercury,* February 26, 1722.

6. *New York Weekly Journal,* November 12, 1733.

7. Ibid.

8. Ibid., December 31, 1733, p. 2; see also January 13, 1735, p. 3.

9. Ibid.

10. *Journal*, March 11, 1734, p. 2.

11. Jonathan Dickinson, *The Vanity of Human Institutions in the Worship of God* (New York, 1736), p. 11, and quoted in David Nord, "The Authority of Truth: Religion and the John Peter Zenger Case," *Journalism Quarterly*, Summer, 1985, p. 234.

12. Ibid., p. 31. Dickinson added, "If they without conviction submit to our opinions, they subject their consciences to human, and not to divine authority; and our requiring this of any is demanding a subjection to us, and not to Christ." In publishing such material, Zenger was spreading around ideas long current in New England; as minister Ebenezer Pemberton had argued in 1710, "kings and royal governors must govern themselves by unalterable Principles, and fixed Rules, and not by unaccountable humours, or arbitrary will . . . they take care that Righteous Laws be Enacted, none but such, and all such, as are necessary for the Safety of the Religion & Liberties of a People . . . [rulers] that are not skilful, thoughtful, vigilant and active to promote the Publick Safety and Happiness are not Gods but dead Idols."

13. James Alexander, *A Brief Narrative of the Case and Trial of John Peter Zenger*, Katz edition, p. 95.

14. The story of the trial is told in James Alexander, *A Brief Narrative of the Case and Trial of John Peter Zenger*, first published in 1736 and reprinted in several books including Livingston Rutherford, *John Peter Zenger, His Press, His Trial and a Bibliography of Zenger Imprints* (New York, 1904).

15. *The Press and America*, pp. 38, 44.

16. Alexander, op. cit.

17. *New York Journal*, December 31, 1733, p. 2; see also January 13, 1735, p. 3.

18. Alexander, op. cit. Hamilton's biblical references were frequent; he argued that, "If a libel is understood in the large and unlimited sense urged by Mr. Attorney, there is scarce a writing I know that may not be called a libel, or scarce any person safe from being called to account as a libeller: for Moses, meek as he was, libelled Cain; and who is it that has not libelled the devil?"

19. As David Nord (op. cit.) concluded in his excellent article, "Like the revival converts who asserted their right to interpret the law of God, the Zenger jury asserted the right of ordinary people to interpret the law of man. In both cases, the operative principle was not freedom, but truth. Andrew Hamilton, like a revival preacher, told the jurors that authority lay, not in them, but in truth. He did not ask them to condone individualism or to approve individual diversity of expression—only truth . . ."

20. *Maryland Gazette*, January 17, 1745.

21. *The Essential Rights and Liberties of Protestants* was signed "Philalethes," but Baldwin (p. 65) credited Williams and discussed possible attribution to other writers. This essay was following along George Whitefield's allowance for civil disobedience when he argued that laws "are good and obligatory when conformable to the laws of Christ and agreeable to the liberties of a free people; but when invented and compiled by men of little hearts and bigotted principles. . . . and when made use of only as ends to bind up the hands of a zealous few, they may be very legally broken." News sermon/pamphlets published during the years following the Zenger trial repeatedly distinguished between arbitrary and legal government. Restraint among all parties was vital, as Jared Elliot told Connecticut residents in 1738: "Arbitrary Despotick Government, is, When this Sovereign Power is directed by the Passions, Ignorance & Lust of them that Rule, And a Legal

Government is, When this Arbitrary & Sovereign Power puts itself under Restraints, and lays itself under Limitations."

Emphasis on literacy led to the idea that allegiance was not to persons but to written documents—the Bible, and laws based on the Bible (in England, those laws as a group made up the nation's constitutional framework).

22. Alice Baldwin, *The New England Clergy and the American Revolution* (New York, 1958), pp. 67–68.

23. Included in Williams Wells, ed., *The Life and Public Services of Samuel Adams* (New York, 1865–68), three vols, I, 22–23. Adams began his examination of questions concerning disobedience to government shortly after the Zenger case. The title of his master's thesis at Harvard in 1743, when Adams was 21, was "Whether it be lawful to resist the Supreme Magistrate, if the Commonwealth cannot be otherwise preserved." He maintained the affirmative, but no record of the thesis remains.

24. Ibid.

25. Donald Barr Chidsey, *The World of Samuel Adams* (Nashville, 1974), p. 9.

26. Quoted in Stewart Beach, *Samuel Adams: The Fateful Years, 1764–1776* (New York: 1965), p. 13.

27. Quoted in Pauline Maier, *The Old Revolutionaries* (New York, 1980), p. 37.

28. Ibid. p. 4.

29. Harry Cushing, ed., *The Writings of Samuel Adams,* 4 vols. (New York, 1904), vol. I, p. 33, and vol. III, p. 220.

30. Maier, p. 47.

31. Ibid., p. 7.

32. William Tudor, *The Life of James Otis* (Boston, 1823), pp. 274–75.

33. *Writings,* III, 284. Adams' willingness to emphasize emotional, human interest stories has bothered some historians who associate such techniques with propaganda. For example, John C. Miller's *Sam Adams, Pioneer in Propaganda* (Boston, 1936), is filled with hatred toward its protagonist.

34. *Boston Gazette,* January 21, 1771.

35. In 1988 politics, this might mean prison furloughs.

36. Ibid.

37. *Writings,* IV, 108.

38. *Boston Gazette,* January 21, 1771.

39. Ibid.

40. *Writings,* IV, 106–107. Adams realized extremely well the dangers of investigative journalism to the journalist; he noted that the writer who exposes does so "at the Risque of his own Reputation; for it is a thousand to one but those whose Craft he puts at Hazard, will give him the odious Epithets of suspicious dissatisfiable peevish quarrelsome &c."

41. Ibid., I, 10.

42. Ibid., I, 60.

43. Arthur M. Schlesinger, *Prelude to Independence* (New York, 1957), p. 22, tells this story.

44. *Boston Gazette,* April 4, 1768.

45. Ibid.

46. Ibid.

47. Ibid.

48. Ibid.
49. Adams, *Writings,* I, 27.
50. Ibid.
51. Ibid.
52. Ibid.
53. Ibid., I, 27–28.
54. See John W. Whitehead, *An American Dream* (Westchester, IL, 1987), p. 62.
55. John Lathrop, quoted in Baldwin, p. 181.
56. Ibid.
57. Stout, p. 7. As Stout noted, in prerevolutionary New England communications the terms "most often employed to justify resistance and to instill hope emanated from the Scriptures." John Locke was widely read, but his political ideas came out of the Bible and Reformation thought. (As Herbert Foster has noted, the citations in Locke's *Two Treatises of Government* "are almost entirely Calvinistic: Scripture seventy-nine times; seven Calvinists . . . one ex-Calvinist . . . and only one reference uninfected by Calvinism, the Scottish Catholic Barclay.")
58. *South-Carolina Gazette,* June 20, 1774.
59. *Pennsylvania Evening Post,* June 27, 1775.
60. *Virginia Gazette,* June 20, 1774.
61. *Norwich Packet,* November 6, 1775.
62. *Boston Evening Post,* November 4, 1765.
63. *Boston Gazette,* October 3, 1768.
64. *Boston Evening-Post,* June 16, 1770.
65. *Boston Gazette,* March 7, 1768.
66. *Massachusetts Spy,* October 8, 1772.
67. *Boston Gazette,* March 7, 1768, column signed "The True Patriot."
68. Stout, p. 6.
69. *The Melancholly Catastrophe* (Boston, 1774).
70. *Massachusetts Spy,* June 2, 1774. The reference is to David's lament concerning the death of King Saul.
71. Quoted in Hart, p. 262.
72. *Virginia Gazette,* December 8, 1775.
73. Maier, p. 3. Many historians have attacked Adams' beliefs and his methodology. John Eliot in 1807 called him "austere . . . rigid . . . opinionated." [*A Biographical Dictionary* (Salem, 1807), p. 7] James Hosmer in 1885 did not like the "sharp practice" that Adams as journalist sometimes used [Hosmer, *Samuel Adams* (Boston, 1885), pp. 68, 229, 368]. See Maier, pp. 11–16, for a discussion of 20th century historiographical trends.
74. Some historians have mistakenly assumed that references by Adams and his contemporaries to "Providence" meant a movement away from belief in a theistic God, when exactly the opposite is true: reference to God's Providence distinguished theists from deists who posited a clockwork universe, in which God created all but then went on vacation.
75. Samuel Adams, *An Oration Delivered at the State-House in Philadelphia, to a very Numerous Audience, on Thursday the 1st of August, 1776* (Philadelphia, 1776); reprinted in Wells, vol. III, p. 408.
76. Ibid.

77. Ibid.

78. Ibid.

CHAPTER 5
FIRST SURGE OF THE OPPRESSION STORY

1. Quoted in Schlesinger, p. 284.

2. Ibid., pp. 284–5.

3. *A brief account of the Execution of Elisha Thomas* (Portsmouth, N.H.: 1788).

4. *Connecticut Courant*, December 17, 1782.

5. Ibid.

6. *The Federalist* no. 10, available in many editions including Clinton Rossiter, ed., *The Federalist Papers* (New York, 1961), pp. 77–84.

7. Ibid., No. 6, pp. 53–60.

8. "Essays of Brutus" in Herbert J. Storing, ed., *The Anti-Federalist* (Chicago, 1985), pp. 112–113.

9. *The Federalist Papers,* op. cit., pp. 320–325.

10. Quoted in Leonard Levy, *Emergence of a Free Press* (New York, 1985), p. 200.

11. *Gazette,* January 14, 1790, quoted in Levy, p. 291.

12. Quoted in Louis Ingelhart, *Press Freedoms* (Westport, CT, 1987), p. 131.

13. Quoted in Levy, loc. cit.

14. James Billington, *Fire in the Minds of Men* (Princeton, 1980), p. 33: "Indeed, the emergence of dedicated, ideological revolutionaries in a traditional society (in Russia of the 1860s no less than in France of the 1790s) depended heavily on literate priests and seminarians becoming revolutionary journalists. . . . Journalism was the only income-producing profession practiced by Marx, Lenin, and many other leading revolutionaries during their long years of powerlessness and exile."

15. These and subsequent Rousseau quotations are from Paul Johnson, *Intellectuals* (London, 1988).

16. Billington, pp. 35, 62.

17. *The General Advertiser,* March 6, 1797.

18. *Aurora,* December 21 and 23, 1796.

19. Quoted in Walter Brasch and Dana Ulloth, *The Press and the State* (Lanham, Md., 1986), p. 104.

20. Hart, *Faith and Freedom,* pp. 307–308.

21. For an account sympathetic to Bache and his beliefs, see Bernard Fay, *The Two Franklins* (Boston, 1933), particularly pp. 264–361.

22. Quoted in Levy, p. 298.

23. Timothy Dwight, *The Nature, and Danger, of Infidel Philosophy* (Hartford, 1798), p. 9.

24. Thomas Paine became famous for his timely pamphlet *Common Sense* (1776), but by the 1790s Paine seemed a believer in his own infallibility; Paine's friend Etienne Dumont said of him, "He believed his book on the Rights of Man could take the place of all the books in the world and he said to me if it were in his power to demolish all the libraries in existence, he would do it so as to destroy all the errors of which they were the

depository—and with the Rights of Man begin a new chain of ideas and principles. He knew by heart all his writings and knew nothing else."

25. Quoted in James M. Lee, *History of American Journalism* (Boston, 1917), p. 101.

26. Ibid., p. 102.

27. Franklin made a perhaps-jocular suggestions as to what specifically the offended party should do: If a writer attacks your reputation, "break his head." If you cannot find him immediately, "waylay him in the night, attack him from behind, and give him a drubbing."

28. Ingelhart, p. 138.

29. Levy, p. 297.

30. See Aleine Austin, *Matthew Lyon* (University Park, Pa., 1981), pp. 108–109.

31. Lyon took his seat in the House on February 20, 1799. The Federalists obtained a 49–45 vote for expulsion, but that fell far short of the necessary two-thirds majority.

32. Speech of July 10, 1798, quoted in Levy, pp. 301–302.

33. George Hay, *An Essay on the Liberty of the Press* (Philadelphia, 1799; reprinted in Richmond, 1803), p. 25 (Richmond edition).

34. Harold Nelson, ed., *Freedom of the Press from Hamilton to the Warren Court* (Indianapolis, 1967), p. 119.

35. Ibid.

36. Quoted in Hart, p. 309.

37. Quoted in Howard Kenberry, *The Rise of Religious Journalism in the United States* (unpublished dissertation, University of Chicago, 1920), p. 20. Statistics are from the *American Almanac*, 1835.

38. Roberta Moore, *Development of Protestant Journalism in the United States, 1743–1850* (unpublished doctoral dissertation, Syracuse University, 1968), p. 237. There had been 37 newspapers in the 13 colonies in 1775. According to the 1835 *American Almanac*, the number of daily newspapers increased from 27 in 1810 to 90 in 1834.

39. Alexis de Tocqueville, *Democracy in America*, ed. J. P. Mayer, trans. George Lawrence (New York, 1969), p. 69.

40. Sketch of Willis' life in the *Boston Recorder*, October 21, 1858, p. 167.

41. Ibid., loc. cit.

42. Ibid., January 3, 1816.

43. Ibid.

44. Ibid.

45. Ibid., March 29, 1822.

46. Ibid.

47. Ibid., December 23, 1817.

48. Ibid., August 18, 1826. In this the *Recorder* anticipated de Tocqueville's observation that "Americans of all ages, all conditions, and all dispositions constantly form associations. . . . If it is proposed to inculcate some truth or to foster some feeling by the encouragement of a great example, they form a society. . . . what political power could ever [do what Americans voluntarily] perform every day with the assistance of the principle of association" (book 2, chapter 5).

49. *Lexington Western Monitor*, August 3, 1814.

50. *New York American*, March 3, 1819.

51. *Christian Disciple and Theological Review*, February, 1814, pp. 61–62. This

quotation and others from the War of 1812 era are found in William Gribbin, *The Churches Militant* (New Haven, 1973).

52. Ibid., August 21, 1813.

53. Claudius Buchanan, *Christian Researchers in Asia: with notices of the translation of the Scriptures into the Oriental languages* (Boston, 1811), p. 34.

54. *New Hampshire Patriot,* March 2, 1813.

55. *Niles' Weekly Register,* January 30, 1813.

56. *Columbian Phoenix,* November 28, 1812.

57. *Baltimore Patriot,* April 28, 1813.

58. *Boston Yankee,* January 23, 1815.

59. *Niles' Weekly Register,* October 30, 1813.

60. Leggett's columns are most readily accessible in William Leggett, *Democratick Editorials* (Indianapolis, 1984); here, p. 3.

61. Ibid., loc. cit.

62. Ibid., p. 11.

63. Ibid., loc. cit.

64. Ibid., loc. cit.

65. Ibid., p. 13.

66. See, for example, pages of the *Boston Recorder* throughout the 1830s and 1840s.

CHAPTER 6
GREAT DEBATES OF JOURNALISM

1. Established publications then as now had a tendency to become dull, with long sentences and elliptical statements at a time when punchy paragraphs were demanded. The classic statement of stodginess and literary arrogance was offered by the editor of a Christian magazine, *Spirit of the Pilgrims:* He announced that "extended and labored articles" were the best kind, and that readers "uninterested in communications of this nature may as well give up their subscription and proceed no farther with us." *Spirit of the Pilgrims* soon went out of business.

2. New York *Sun,* April 4, 1835, and cited by James Stanford Bradshaw, "George H. Wisner and the New York *Sun,*" *Journalism History* 6:4, Winter 1979–80, p. 118.

3. Ibid., May 13, 1834.

4. Ibid., May 19, 1834.

5. Ibid., April 21, 1834.

6. Ibid., July 4, 1834.

7. Ibid., September 2, 1833.

8. Bradshaw, p. 120.

9. *New York Herald,* July 27, 1836.

10. Quoted in Isaac Pray, *Memoirs of James Gordon Bennett and His Times* (New York, 1855), p. 276.

11. See *New York Herald,* December 14, 1838, and July 2, 1845. For other views see Mott, p. 237, and Don Seitz, *The James Gordon Bennetts* (Indianapolis, 1928), p. 83.

12. Unitarianism, the belief Calvin considered most dangerous to orthodox trinitarian

Christianity, arose in the center of the Calvinistic commonwealth, Massachusetts. This was both ironic and logical, because Unitarianism was a reaction against the Reformed world view with its concept of man's fallenness, its untamed God, and its doctrine of salvation based on God's sovereignty. Harvard itself became the Unitarian Vatican, with publishing enterprises (the influential *Monthly Anthology and Boston Review*) and supporters such as William Emerson, minister at the First Unitarian Church and father of Ralph Waldo, and William Tudor (Harvard, 1798), future editor of the influential *North American Review*.

13. Albert Brisbane, *Association* (New York, 1843), p. 209.

14. Ibid., p. 207.

15. When William Henry Harrison was elected president in 1840, Horace Greeley expected a pay-off. He had edited *The Log Cabin,* a major Whig campaign organ, and thought that Governor Seward would ask that the position of postmaster of New York be given to him. He did not get it, nor was he able to get anything in what he called "the great scramble of the swell mob of coon-minstrels and cider-suckers at Washington." Greeley complained that "no one of the whole crowd . . . had done so much toward General Harrison's nomination and election as yours respectfully," yet he was "not counted in." (Letter of November 11, 1854, quoted in Frederick Hudson, *Journalism in the United States, From 1690 to 1872* (New York, 1873), pp. 549–550.)

16. Greeley letter to B. F. Ransom, March 15, 1841, in Horace Greeley, *Autobiography* (New York, 1872), pp. 68–74.

17. Greeley, *Hints Toward Reforms* (New York, 1854), p. 86.

18. Quoted in Jeter Allen Isely, *Horace Greeley and the Republican Party, 1853–1861* (Princeton, 1947), p. 15.

19. Brisbane, p. 205.

20. William Harlan Hale, *Horace Greeley: Voice of the People* (New York, 1950), p. 99.

21. Brook Farm, which attracted for a time some leading literary lights, became the best known of the communes; Nathaniel Hawthorne's *The Blithedale Romance* shows his sarcastic reaction to Brook Farm.

22. Ibid., p. 105.

23. E. L. Godkin quoted in Mott, p. 277.

24. Hale, p. 299.

25. Quoted in James Lee, p. 405.

26. Ibid.

27. Because the 1840s was a decade of utopian hopes that in some ways paralleled the 1960s, some readers also would be excited by commune coverage.

28. Quoted in Charles Sotheran, *Horace Greeley and Other Pioneers of American Socialism* (New York, 1892), p. 193.

29. Ibid., p. 195.

30. *New York Tribune*, November 20, 1846.

31. *New York Courier and Enquirer*, November 23, 1846 (hereafter noted as *Courier*).

32. *Tribune*, November 26, 1846.

33. *Courier*, November 30, 1846.

34. *Tribune*, December 1, 1846.

35. *Courier*, December 8, 1846.

36. *Tribune*, December 10, 1846.

37. *Courier*, December 14, 1846.

38. *Tribune*, December 16, 1846.

39. *Courier*, December 24, 1846.

40. Ibid.

41. *Courier*, December 24, and *Tribune*, December 28, 1846.

42. Ibid.

43. *Courier*, January 6, 1847.

44. Ibid. Raymond went on to state that Greeley's "blunder is exactly that of the man who should expect a water-wheel, by turning, to produce the water which is from the first to turn it;—who should look to the motion of a watch for the creation of the main-spring, which alone can give it motion. It is precisely the error which the would-be inventors of Perpetual Motion have constantly committed. Can anything be more palpably impossible? And is not this defect *fatal* to the whole system?"

45. Ibid.

46. *Tribune*, January 13, 1847.

47. Ibid.

48. Ibid.

49. Ibid.

50. *Courier*, January 20, 1847.

51. Ibid.

52. Ibid.

53. *Tribune*, January 29, 1847.

54. Ibid.

55. *Courier*, February 10, 1847.

56. Ibid.

57. *Tribune*, February 17, and *Courier*, March 5, 1847.

58. *Courier*, January 20, 1847.

59. Ibid., March 5, 1847.

60. Ibid.

61. *Tribune*, March 12, 1847.

62. *Courier*, March 19, 1847. Raymond also argued that few people in the communes would do any work, but Greeley insisted that production would not be a problem if well organized; he anticipated Bellamy's industrial army of the 1880s by arguing, curiously, "What Organization may do to render the repulsive attractive is seen in the case of War and Armies. Intrinsically the most revolting employment that can be suggested to a man is that of maiming and butchering his fellow-men by the wholesale, and taking his chance of being maimed or butchered in turn. And yet millions are found to rush into it, take delight in it, spend their lives in it, in preference to peaceful and better rewarded avocations. And why? Because (I speak of the regular soldier, who makes war his life-long profession) rulers have given to war an Organization, which satisfies two of the senses—that of Hearing by Music, that of Sight by glittering uniforms, precision of movement, and beauty of array. In a few, Ambition is also excited, while to the mass the assurance of an unfailing though meager subsistence is proffered. By these simple expedients the imagination is led captive, and millions constantly enlisted to shoot and be shot at for an average of not more than sixpence per day.

"O that the governments of the world were wise enough, good enough to bestow one-half the effort and expenses on the Organization of Labor that they have devoted to the Organization of Slaughter!"

63. *Tribune,* March 26, 1847.

64. *Courier,* April 16, 1847.

65. Ibid. Raymond wrote concerning Greeley's Associationism, "The Trinity in which it pretends to believe, is resolved into a trinity of the 'active, passive, and neutral principles of life and order.' It gravely declares that by the 'Kingdom of Heaven' is meant Association."

66. Ibid.

67. Ibid.

68. Ibid.

69. Ibid.

70. *Tribune,* April 28, 1847.

71. *Courier,* May 20, 1847.

72. Ibid.

73. Ibid., March 5, 1847.

74. Ibid.

75. Ibid., April 16, 1847.

CHAPTER 7
IRREPRESSIBLE CONFLICT IN THE PRESS

1. One of the phalanxes Greeley had joined, Red Bank in New Jersey, lasted the longest: 12 years, 1843 to 1855.

2. *On Association,* p. 213.

3. Ibid., p. 212.

4. *New York Tribune,* April 10, 1845.

5. See Horace Greeley, *Hints Toward Reforms.*

6. Greeley did, however, continue to give space to Brisbane; in 1858 the *Tribune* provided room for Brisbane to promote a massive, 100,000-acre commune. (*New York Daily Tribune,* July 12, 14, 23, August 18, 20, 27, 1858.)

7. Hale, pp. 135–136. Those Greeley worked closely with included George Henry Evans, an apostle of Tom Paine and editor of the *Working Man's Advocate,* and Lewis Masquerier, an early socialist.

8. Horace's wife Mary also had her ways. Once, when she had become a supporter of what today would be called the "animal rights" movement, she met writer Margaret Fuller on the street one day, touched Fuller's kid gloves and began to scream, "Skin of a beast, skin of a beast." Mary was wearing silk, and Margaret Fuller had the presence of mind to begin yelling, "Entrails of a worm, entrails of a worm."

9. *New York Evening Post,* September 7 and 9, 1835; included in *Democratick Editorials,* pp. 203, 206.

10. Ibid., *loc. cit.*

11. Ibid., September 9, 1835, and p. 209.

12. Ibid., August 8, 1835, and p. 197.

13. From biographical information distributed by the Greater Alton/Twin Rivers Convention & Visitors' Bureau.

14. Plaque on the Lovejoy monument, Alton, IL, visited by the author.

15. Clay archives, University of Kentucky Library, and quoted in H. Edward Richardson, *Cassius Marcellus Clay* (Lexington, KY, 1976), p. 34.

16. *True American* prospectus, February 19, 1845.

17. *True American,* August 16, 1845.

18. Quoted in Richardson, p. 46.

19. Ibid., p. 47.

20. Muhammed Ali, originally named Cassius Clay, showed a lack of historical sense (and a different theology) by changing monikers because he "didn't want a slave name." Freedom of choice, of course, but the original Cassius Clay freed his own slaves and risked his life many times to help free others.

21. Clay archives, University of Kentucky library.

22. Clay's later years were not particularly distinguished except by a variety of philosophical delusions and rapscallion activities.

23. *New York Daily Tribune,* October 17, 1851. See also April 12.

24. Ibid., May 2, 1854.

25. Ibid., July 12, 1860.

26. Ibid., August 22, 1860.

27. Ibid., March 10 and 26, 1856, and June 27, 1859.

28. Isely, p. 131.

29. *Daily Tribune* from August, 1855 to March, 1856.

30. Isely, op. cit.

31. This account is based on Otto Scott, *The Secret Six* (New York, 1979), pp. 5–9.

32. *New York Daily Tribune,* May 20, June 1, 3, 5, 6, 9, 14, 17, 1856.

33. Ibid., April 5, 8, 1856; October 28, 1859.

34. Isely, p. 177.

35. Lydia Maria Child, "The Kansas Emigrants," *New York Daily Tribune,* October 23 to November 4, 1856.

36. See Lloyd Chiasson, "A Newspaper Analysis of the John Brown Raid," *American Journalism,* Spring, 1985, p. 30.

37. *New York Daily Tribune,* November 9, 1859.

38. Ibid., November 17 and 19, 1859.

39. Quoted in Isely, p. 266.

40. Ibid., p. 266. Greeley wavered in his intellectual stand for violence as real, large-scale violence came nearer. In November 1860, he wrote concerning states wishing to secede that "we shall be in favor of letting them go in peace. Then who is to fight? And what for?" (*Daily Tribune,* November 2.) It is not clear now whether Greeley was playing a dangerous game of "chicken," or whether he truly believed the south would not leave and that, if it did, the north would not pursue. Once the southern states did secede, the *Tribune* abruptly changed its policy. This might indicate that Greeley was bluffing in his coverage, and that once his bluff was called, he advocated what he all along felt would be necessary. But consistency was not Greeley's strong point, and it may be unnecessary to look for it in this case; Greeley wrote what he wanted when he wanted.

41. *New York Herald,* March 7, 1850, p. 2. Cited in Gary Whitby, "Economic Elements of Opposition To Abolition and Support of South by Bennett in the New York *Herald,*" *Journalism Quarterly,* Spring, 1988, p. 83.

42. Ibid.

43. *New York Herald,* October 20, December 10 and 22, 1859.

44. Ibid., November 26, 1860.

45. *New York World,* October 12, 1860.

46. Ibid., November 30, 1860.

47. Ibid.

48. Ibid.

49. Ibid.

50. Quoted in Llerena Friend, "Sam Houston," in H. Bailey Carroll et al, *Heroes of Texas* (Waco, 1966), p. 93.

51. Ibid., p. 92.

52. "Christian Patriotism" by Elbert S. Porter, in the *New York World,* December 1, 1860.

53. Ibid.

54. Ibid.

55. Even though some northern newspapers were more moderate, the *Tribune,* with its reach throughout the north and personification in Greeley, always seemed to be seen in the south as the embodiment of an aggressive northern spirit.

56. *Raleigh Register,* March 1, 1860.

57. See Howard C. Perkins, ed., *Northern Editorials on Secession,* I, pp. 88–92.

58. *Atlantic Monthly* CIII (May, 1909), p. 654.

59. George Talbot quoted in Isely, p. 54.

60. Ibid., p. 3.

61. *New York Daily Tribune,* April 7, 1858.

62. C. Vann Woodward, *The Burden of Southern History* (New York, 1961), pp. 63–68.

63. *New York World,* op. cit.

64. Charleston, Jacksonville, and Jackson newspapers, November 1860, quoted in Reynolds, p. 148.

65. *Richmond Dispatch,* January 6, 1860.

66. Ibid., January 26, 1861.

67. *Augusta Daily Constitutionalist,* December 7, 1860.

68. *Albany Patriot,* February 9, 1860.

69. Ibid., March 8, 1860.

70. May 19, 1860, letter, quoted in Donald E. Reynolds, *Editors Make War* (Nashville, 1966), p. 36.

71. Ibid., loc. cit.

72. *Hillsborough Recorder,* December 12, 1860.

73. *New York Herald,* January 29, 1861.

74. *New York Daily Tribune,* February 18 to 28, 1861.

75. Ibid., January 23 through 26, 1861.

76. Ibid., June 26 to July 4, 1861. One New York Greeley-watcher, James W. Nye, saw humor in the situation: "Imagine Greely [sic] booted & Spurred with Epaulets on his

Shoulders and with a whetted blade in his hands marching at the head of a column. . . . The idea of Greely turning warrior, is to ridiculus [sic] to be thought of."

77. Quoted by Thomas Keiser, " 'The Illinois Beast': One of Our Greatest Presidents," *Wall Street Journal,* February 11, 1988. Keiser's column was based on research by David Donald and Thomas Bailey.

78. Ibid.

79. James E. Pollard, *The Presidents and the Press* (New York, 1941), p. 352.

80. Quoted in George Fort Milton, *The Age of Hate: Andrew Johnson and the Radicals* (New York, 1930), p. 153. Milton also quotes other vengeful leaders, including Senator Benjamin Wade, who suggested that the north "hang ten or twelve of the worst of those fellows; perhaps, for full measure, I should make it thirteen, just a baker's dozen." (p. 56)

CHAPTER 8
OBSTACLES TO POWER

1. Frank Moore, *Life and Speeches of Andrew Johnson* (Boston, 1865), p. 471.

2. Ibid., p. 484.

3. Johnson quoted in Claude G. Bowers, *The Tragic Era* (New York, 1929), p. 41.

4. See William Harlan Hale, *Horace Greeley, Voice of the People* (New York, 1950), and Glynden Garlock Van Deusen, *Horace Greeley: Nineteenth Century Crusader* (Philadelphia, 1953).

5. C. Gregg Singer, *A Theological Interpretation of American History,* rev. ed. (Phillipsburgh, NJ, 1964), pp. 88–89.

6. Bowers, p. 109.

7. Ibid., loc. cit.

8. George Milton, *The Age of Hate* (New York, 1930), p. 357.

9. Ibid, p. 287.

10. Ibid., loc. cit.

11. *National Intelligencer,* February 23, 1866.

12. Gideon Welles, *Diary* (Boston, 1911), II, 432.

13. Ibid., loc. cit.

14. David Miller DeWitt, *The Impeachment and Trial of Andrew Johnson* (New York, 1903), p. 62.

15. Milton, p. 354.

16. Ibid., p. 359.

17. Ibid., loc. cit.

18. *New York Tribune,* February 26, 1866.

19. *New York Herald,* September 10, 1866.

20. Ibid., September 13, 1866.

21. David Ross Locke, *Swingin Round the Circle* (Boston, 1867), pp. 210–217.

22. *Cleveland Leader,* September 4, 1866.

23. Sarah Watts, *The Press and the Presidency* (New York, 1985), p. 211.

24. Ibid., loc. cit.

25. *New York Tribune*, September 6, 1866, and subsequent days.

26. *The Independent*, September 6, 1866.

27. Ibid.

28. Ibid., August 15, 1867.

29. *New York Tribune*, October 25, 1869.

30. Watts, p. 212.

31. Ibid., loc. cit.

32. *Congressional Globe*, January 3, 1867.

33. "The Public Situation," *The Independent*, September 19, 1867.

34. 1 Samuel 12:3.

35. *New York Tribune*, May 14, 18, 23, 1868.

36. *The Nation*, May 21, 1868.

37. Quoted in John F. Kennedy, *Profiles in Courage* (New York, 1963), p. 143.

38. Ibid., p. 148.

39. *New York Tribune*, May 14, 18, 23, 1868.

40. Ibid., September 2, 1868.

41. Albert Bigelow Paine, *Thomas Nast: His Period and His Pictures* (New York, 1904), p. 129.

42. Quoted in *New York World*, March 6, 1869.

43. Bowers, p. 284.

44. Ibid., loc. cit.

45. *New York Herald*, April 19, 1870.

46. Bowers, p. 355.

47. Ibid., loc. cit.

48. Quoted in *New York World*, February 8, 1873.

49. Paine, p. 270.

50. *New York Tribune*, December 5, 1872.

51. Hale, pp. 351–352.

52. November 13 statement quoted in Van Deusen, p. 423.

53. *New York Tribune*, April 7, 1877.

54. *The Nation*, April 5, 1877, p. 202.

55. Sumner said, "If we do not like the survival of the fittest, we have only one possible alternative, and that is the survival of the unfittest. The former is the law of civilization; the latter is the law of anti-civilization. We have our choice between the two, or we can go on, as in the past, vacillating between the two, but a third plan, the social desideratum—a plan for nourishing the unfittest and yet advancing civilization, no man will ever find." Christianity was that third plan, but Sumner found it wanting.

56. William Graham Sumner, *Folkways* (Boston, 1906), p. 65.

57. See Marvin Olasky, "Social Darwinism on the Editorial Page," *Journalism Quarterly*, Fall, 1988, pp. 420–424.

58. *Dallas Morning News*, November 15, 1887.

59. *Dallas Daily Times Herald*, January 29, 1891.

60. Ibid., January 17, 1891.

61. See *Proceedings of the Texas Press Association* from 1880 to 1900.

62. *Dallas Daily Times Herald*, January 30, 1891.

63. See Marvin Olasky, "Lenin, Grover Cleveland and Election Year Economics," *Countywide*, November 1, 1984.

64. Ibid.

65. Ibid.

66. Edmund Burke, *Reflections on the Revolution in France* (London, 1960), p. 44.

67. Icie F. Johnson, *William Rockhill Nelson and the Kansas City Star* (Kansas City, 1935), p. 81.

68. *Kansas City Star,* September 20, 1880.

69. Johnson, p. 61.

70. Ibid., p. 80.

71. "Where the Responsibility Rests," *Kansas City Star,* October 24, 1892.

72. Josephine Shaw Lowell, *Public Relief and Private Charity* (New York, 1884), p. 66.

73. Ibid., loc. cit.

74. Lowell's worldview also led her to emphasize effect on character: the problem with "outdoor relief," she wrote, is that "It fails to save the recipient of relief and community from moral harm, because human nature is so constituted that no man can receive as a gift what he should earn by his own labor without a moral deterioration . . ."

75. Many small newspapers came and went as the Greenback movement, along with political elements of the Granger and National Alliance farm movements, had their days in the sun. Most during the 1870–1900 period concentrated on useful ways to improve business and perhaps buy and sell in bulk to attain better prices; there may have been a thousand such newspapers, with circulation in the hundreds of thousands. Others appealed to envy and hatred.

76. Edward Bellamy, *Equality* (New York, 1897), p. 17.

77. Edward Bellamy, *Looking Backward* (Chicago, 1890), p. 276.

78. Ibid., loc. cit.

79. Richard Ely, *Social Aspects of Christianity* (New York, Thomas Crowell, 1895), pp. 24–25. This quotation is from Ely's second edition; the first edition was published in 1889.

80. Ibid., p. 92.

81. The book, published in a second edition in New York by Longmans, Green in 1895, was based on a series of eight lectures Fremantle delivered at Oxford in 1883. The lectures by Freeman, who was Canon of Canterbury and Fellow of Balliol College, Oxford, excited little attention either then or immediately upon their initial publication in 1885, but during the 1890s Ely's promotion of the book was extremely successful. By the middle of the decade, as Fremantle proudly noted, his work was "placed in the line of succession, reaching down from Aristotle's Politics . . ." (p. x)

82. Ibid, pp. 278–280.

83. Ibid., pp. 278–279.

84. Ibid., p. 281.

85. See Elizabeth Higgins, *Out of the West* (New York, 1902).

CHAPTER 9
OF MUCKRAKERS AND PRESIDENTS

1. One practical joke actually led Pulitzer into his career. Unsure about what to do upon his discharge from the cavalry, Pulitzer decided to move to where no one knew

German, so that he would be pushed into learning English to survive. He took the advice of a prankster who told him his best bet was St. Louis, but Pulitzer learned upon arrival that the city was a major German-language center, one "almost like the old country, there was so much German." He could not have moved forward so rapidly in journalism had he been in a community where German was not spoken, but in St. Louis Pulitzer was able to go to work on a St. Louis German-language newspaper, the *Westliche Post*.

2. See *St. Louis Post-Dispatch* front pages, e.g. August 18, 1882; September 8, 1882; June 25 to July 4, 1883.

3. Ibid., May 16, 1882.

4. Ibid., June 15 and July 24, 1880.

5. Julian Rammelkamp, *Pulitzer's Post-Dispatch, 1878–1888* (Princeton, 1967), p. 135.

6. *St. Louis Post-Dispatch*, June 29 and July 8, 1881.

7. Examples may be found in *New York World*, August 31 and September 8, 1883, and February 24 and September 2, 1884.

8. The *World* in 1898 seemed to have an "Enemy of the Month" club.

9. Robert Rutland, *The Newsmongers* (New York, 1973), p. 281. "Truth" for Pulitzer was not what it had been for John Peter Zenger, however; Zenger had called for individual responsibility before God, but Pulitzer demanded that all bow down to him. Wanting to be omnipresent, Pulitzer instructed his editors and reporters to spy on each other and send reports directly to him. He purposefully created overlapping authority so that he would have to be called in to break deadlocks. Pulitzer's system, according to one journalist, "produced in time a condition of suspicion, jealousy and hatred, a maelstrom of office politics that drove at least two editors to drink, one into suicide, a fourth into insanity."

10. Everyone told Pulitzer to be content, but he could not be. One reporter described how "when anything went wrong, and things seemed to go wrong with him very often, there would come from his office . . . a stream of profanity and filth." Pulitzer's friend and fellow newspaper editor Henry Watterson noted that "Absolute authority made Pulitzer a tyrant." Things became worse when Pulitzer gradually became blind during the 1890s. He called himself "the loneliest man in the world," but even his laudatory biographer noted that "the loneliness, although real, was instead the terrible isolation of the helpless megalomanic and egocentric . . ." Pulitzer was separated from his wife and children for most of his last 20 years because he wanted around him only "compliant attendants." His wife often wanted to join him, but Pulitzer raged at her, then complained that he had to eat dinner with "nobody at my table except paid employees."

11. William Salisbury, *The Career of a Journalist* (New York, 1908), pp. 146–147.

12. Allen Churchill, *Park Row*, p. 70.

13. Ibid., p. 87.

14. Frank Luther Mott, *American Journalism* (New York, 1941), p. 539.

15. Quoted in Ferdinand Lundberg, *Imperial Hearst* (New York, 1936).

16. Roy Everett Littlefield III, *William Randolph Hearst: His Role in American Progressivism* (Lanham, Md., 1980), p. 103.

17. Ibid., p. 153.

18. Ibid., p. xiii.

19. *Park Row*, p. 98.

20. Description by Thomas Beer quoted in Watts, p. 316.

21. Louis Wiley, "A Come-back from the *Times*," *Collier's*, May 13, 1911, p. 28.

22. *New York Journal*, March 3, 26, 1901.

23. *San Francisco Examiner*, March 25, 26, 1901.

24. *New York American*, March 2, 4, 10, 1904.

25. *New York Journal*, February 2, 1898.

26. San Francisco *Examiner*, March 8, 31, 1901.

27. *Park Row*, p. 81.

28. Ibid. There is little evidence from Hearst's conduct of his newspaper that he actually cared about people at all. In the 1890s, when Hearst and Pulitzer had a bidding war for journalistic talent, Hearst hired many away and fired fast. When some new hires then demanded ironclad contracts, they received them, but those who did not do what Hearst wanted were forced into resignation through humiliation: Senior reporters were turned into copy boys or men's-room attendants until they gave up. But some fought back. One caused the drains to clog every few hours by stuffing them with copies of the Journal; the business office gave in. Another announced loudly at the saloon that the humiliation was making his brain crack, he felt a strong pressure to set the city room afire. He also was paid off.

29. *New York Journal*, February 4, 1901.

30. The stories were apparently inaccurate but nevertheless pointed.

31. Mott, p. 541.

32. Even circulation stunts showed a lack of concern about consequences: Once, to boost sales, Hearst advertised a feature on "faithless husbands" by sending to wives throughout the city postcards suggesting they buy the *Journal* and learn the truth about their husbands; each postcard was signed cryptically, "A Friend." Gore Vidal, in his novel *Empire* (New York, 1987), gets at Hearst's conception of press power when he has one character see "herself creating a world that would be all hers, since she, like Hearst, would have reinvented all the players, giving them their dialogue, moving them in and out of wars: 'Remember the Maine' . . . She too could use a newspaper to change the world. She felt giddy with potentiality" (p. 100).

33. *New York Times*, February 14 and November 1, 1905.

34. Littlefield, p. 123.

35. See *Munsey's*, January 1900, for an example of the magazine's treatment of public utilities.

36. Quoted in C. C. Regier, *The Era of the Muckrakers* (Chapel Hill, 1932), p. 19.

37. Upton Sinclair, *The Industrial Republic* (New York, 1907), pp. 280–283.

38. Sinclair's *The Jungle* did not lead to changes in working conditions, but led to inspections and a temporary reduction of demand for American meat. Sinclair complained that his investigative journalism had merely "taken a few millions away from the packers and given them to the Junkers of East Prussia and to Paris bankers who were backing meat-packing enterprises in the Argentine." (Fuller, p. 168.)

39. See Floyd Dell, *Upton Sinclair* (New York, 1927).

40. See especially Sinclair's novel of the 1920s, *They Call Me Carpenter*.

41. Ray Stannard Baker, *American Chronicle: The Autobiography of Ray Stannard Baker* (New York, 1945), p. 33.

42. Ibid., p. 47.

43. Quoted in Robert C. Bannister, Jr., *Ray Stannard Baker: The Mind and Thought of a Progressive* (New York, 1966), p. 105.

44. Ibid., loc. cit.

45. Not much has changed in Berkeley during the past century.

46. The radical journalists were a media elite, as David M. Chalmers has noted in *The Social and Political Ideas of the Muckrakers* (New York, 1964). Chalmers noted that "In the decade between 1903 and 1912, nearly two thousand articles of a muckraking variety appeared in the popular magazines, complemented by editorials, cartoons, and serials. . . . But of this vast outpouring, close to a third were written by a small group of twelve men and one woman who concentrated on and professionalized this kind of journalism."

47. The leading muckrakers were not united in every way politically, but they tended to see themselves as a fraternity, with frequent meetings in the backroom of Considine's Saloon on Broadway near 42nd St., luncheon discussions every Wednesday at Luchow's restaurant, and membership in the Liberal Club (President Lincoln Steffens, Vice President Charles Russell) on East 19th St. Many worked together at *McClure's* and, later, the *American Magazine*.

48. Salisbury, p. 150.

49. See Oliver Carlson and Ernest Sutherland Bates, *Hearst* (New York, 1936), p. 111.

50. Chalmers, p. 97.

51. Steffens' article appeared in *American Magazine*, November, 1906; this assessment of Hearst is from *The Autobiography of Lincoln Steffens* (New York, 1931), p. 543.

52. Quoted in *Cosmopolitan*, October, 1936.

53. Theodore Roosevelt to McClure, October 4, 1905, Baker Papers, quoted in Harold S. Wilson, *McClure's Magazine and the Muckrakers* (Princeton, 1970), p. 179.

54. Swanberg, *Citizen Hearst*, p. 242.

55. Roosevelt to Ray Stannard Baker, April 9, 1906, Baker Papers, quoted in Wilson, p. 181.

56. *American Magazine*, May, 1906, p. 111.

57. "Sentiments on the Liberty of the Press," *American Weekly Mercury*, April 25, 1734.

58. Among these might have been a general public weariness with the muckraking proposals of Hearst and other journalistic "reformers." As H. L. Mencken noted, "Reform does not last. The reformer quickly loses his public. . . . This is what has happened over and over again in every large American city—Chicago, New York, St. Louis, Cincinnati, Pittsburgh, New Orleans, Baltimore, San Francisco, St. Paul, Kansas City. Every one of these places has had its melodramatic reform campaigns and its inevitable reactions. The people have leaped to the overthrow of bosses, and then wearied of the ensuing tedium." ("Newspaper Morals," *The Atlantic Monthly*, March, 1914, p. 293)

59. Only one historian on the left, to my knowledge, has given Hearst the praise he deserves—from that ideological perspective—for stirring up class hatred. Louis Fuller, *Crusaders for American Liberalism*, p. 132: "Hearst, more than any other man, was the absolute expression of all the blind need and ignorance and resentment which troubled the worker and farmer. He dived to the bottom of the reader's mind and stirred up the filth and despair that had lain so quiet before. . . . Hearst was steeped in mire. His long campaign against McKinley was virulent to the degree of insanity. But did McKinley really deserve much better treatment? It would have been splendid if another, more upright, more principled man than Hearst had been present to carry on the quasi-Socialist battle. But no such man existed."

60. Salisbury, p. 522.

61. Upton Sinclair, "The Muckrake Man," *The Independent*, September 3, 1908, pp. 517–519.

62. Ibid., loc. cit.

63. Ibid., loc. cit.

64. Ibid., loc. cit.

65. Salisbury, pp. 196–197.

66. Charles Russell, *Doing Us Good and Plenty* (New York, 1914), p. 156.

67. Baker's manuscript Notebook I, pp. 111–112, and J, pp. 107–128, quoted in Chalmers, pp. 69–70. Baker eventually decided not to join the Socialist Party; he continued to hug a liberal social gospel.

68. David Graham Phillips, *The Conflict* (New York, 1912), p. 62. The novel was published shortly after Phillips' death in 1911.

69. See also John Spargo, *The Spiritual Significance of Socialism* (New York, 1908); Spargo argued that only socialism would allow honest examination of the spiritual problems of life, because only then would the masses be freed from those who taught superstitution and fearful dogma.

70. *Collier's*, March, 1911, pp. 18–20.

71. William Allen White to Baker, August 28, 1913, Baker Papers, quoted in Wilson, p. 270.

72. See Marvin Olasky, *Prodigal Press* (Westchester, IL, 1988), p. 55.

73. Steffens to Upton Sinclair, May 19, 1926, quoted in Wilson, p. 307.

74. See the later chapters of Steffens' *Autobiography* for the full panorama of his tribute to the left and his attack on those of the right or center.

75. His statement is usually reported as, "I have seen the future, and it works."

76. Books that have documented these tendencies include James Crowl, *Angels in Stalin's Paradise* (Lanham, Md., 1982); Joshua Muravchik, *News Coverage of the Sandanista Revolution* (Washington, DC, 1988); many others.

77. See Steffens' *Autobiography*, and Justin Kaplan, *Lincoln Steffens* (New York, 1974).

78. Villard, *Some Newspapers and Newspaper-men* (New York: Knopf, 1923), p. 314. Villard wrote that the crusading journalist should provide "moral and spiritual leadership" but did not offer specifics. Villard's moral relativism was evident in his statement that journalists should "recall Isaiah's saying: 'The voice said, Cry.' And he said, 'What shall I cry?' But if he is true to his ideals he will always know what to say." In the Bible, of course, Isaiah had been told to emphasize God's sovereignty, not his own conceptions: "All men are like grass,/and all their glory is like the flowers of the field./ The grass withers and the flowers fall,/ because the breath of the Lord blows on them."

79. Salisbury, p. 231.

APPENDIX A

1. Hyder E. Rollins, ed., *A Pepysian Garland: Black–Letter Broadside Ballads of the Years 1595–1693* (Cambridge: Cambridge University Press, 1922), p. xi.

2. *A Collection of Seventy Nine Black–Letter Ballads and Broadsides, Printed in the*

Reign of Queen Elizabeth, Between the Years 1559 and 1597 (London: Joseph Lilly, 1867), pp. 45–47.

3. Anon, *The description of a monstrous pig, the which was farrowed at Hamsted* (London: Garat Dewes, 1562).

4. This and other titles cited in M. A. Shaaber, *Some Forerunners of the Newspaper in England* (New York: Octagon, 1966), p. 164.

5. *A Collection of Black-Letter Ballads,* pp. 81–84.

6. J. A. Sharpe, "Domestic Homicide in Early Modern England," *Historical Journal* 24, 1 (1981), pp. 42–43; cited in Mitchell Stephens, *A History of News* (New York, 1988), p. 111. Sharpe's collection of 25 ballads of spousal murder—13 reporting the murder of husbands, 12 the murder of wives—shows that they were moral tales concerning the outcome of adultery.

7. Quoted in Stephens, p. 113.

8. John Reynolds, *The Triumphs of Gods Revenge Against the crying and Execrable Sinne of (Wilfull and Premeditated) Murther* (London: Edward Griffin/William Lee, 1640), 2nd ed., p. ii; first published in 1622.

9. Ibid., loc. cit.

10. Ibid., p. 211.

11. Quoted in Stephens, p. 115.

12. John Barker, "A Balade declaryng how neybourhed, loue, and trew dealyng is gone" in *A Collection of Seventy-Nine BlackLetter Ballads and Broadsides* (London, 1867), p. 134.

13. Hyder Rollins, ed, *The Pack of Autolycus, or, Strange and Terrible News of Ghosts, Apparitions, Monstrous Births, Showers of Wheat, Judgments of God, and other Prodigious and Fearful Happenings as told in Broadside Ballads of the Years 1624–1693* (Cambridge, MA, 1927), pp. 68–74.

14. *The Euing Collection of English Broadside Ballads* (Glasgow, 1971), pp. 26–27.

15. Ibid., p. 360. The murder took place May 5, 1697.

16. Ibid., pp. 251–252. The storm struck on December 23, 1684.

17. *The Pack of Autolycus,* pp. 103–106.

18. Euing, pp. 298–299.

19. Ibid., pp. 198–199.

20. *The Pack of Autolycus,* pp. 122–125.

21. One ballad, "The Trappand Virgin," had as its secondary headline, "Take my advice while you are free,/ and young-men do not trust,/ They promise fare as fare can be,/ but mean what is unjust." The ballad began, "Come mourn with me you Leadies all,/ whom Young men have betrayed,/ I was belov'd of great and small,/ and thought a virtuous Maid:/ At length a Young-Man to me came/ and he did me much wrong,/ For he betray'd a harmless Maid/ with his deludeing Tongue./ Such vows and Protestations he did to me often use,/ With sights, and Sobs that pittyed me,/ so that I could not chuse/ But condescend to his desire." Promises of marriage were not fulfilled, and the betrayed maid concluded, "Take warning by me Maidens fair . . . When they have got what they desire/ their passion's at an End." There was also a word for men: "False hearted men where e're you be/ think not for to Escape,/ For what you gain by Treachery/ is next kinn to a Rape." (Euing, p. 577).

22. *Advice from the Dead to the Living; Or, a Solemn Warning to the World. Occasioned by the untimely Death of poor Julian, Who was Executed on Boston Neck, on*

Thursday the 22d of March, 1733, for the Murder of Mr. John Rogers of Pembroke, the 12th of September, 1733 (Boston, 1733).

23. Ibid.

24. *A Mournful POEM on the Death of John Ormsby and Matthew Cushing, who were appointed to be executed on Boston Neck, the 17th of October, 1734* (Boston, 1734).

25. Ibid.

26. *Narrative, or Poem, Giving an Account of the Hostile Actions of some Pagan Indians,* in Ola Elizabeth Winslow, *American Broadside Verse* (New Haven, 1930), p. 115.

27. Daniel Defoe, *Moll Flanders* (New York, 1978 edition), p. 30.

28. Hart, p. 220.

29. *Tokens of God's Power and Wrath* (Boston, 1744).

30. *Boston News-Letter,* November 20, 1755.

31. Jonathan Newland, *Earthquakes Improved: Or Solemn Warning to the World; by the tremendous EARTHQUAKE which appeared on Tuesday Morning the 18th of November 1755, between four and five o'Clock* (Boston: 1755). The ballad continued vividly: "See! how poor Wretches from their Beds/ Affrightedly arise,/ And to their clatt'ring Windows run,/ With Horror in their Eyes!/ Around them crack their shatter'd Walls,/ The Beams and Timber creak;/ And the Inhabitants amaz'd/ With dismal Out-crys shreak./ Buildings leap up, the Joints give Way,/ The crumbling Chimney groans;/ The loos'ned Bricks tost from on high/ Come thund'ring on the Stones."

32. *A Poem On the Rebuke of God's Hand In the Awful Desolation made by FIRE in the Town of Boston, On the 20th Day of March, 1760.*

33. *The Agonies of a Soul departing out of Time into Eternity* (Boston, 1757).

34. *The Dying Groans of Levi Ames* (Boston, 1773).

APPENDIX B

1. Isaiah Thomas, *The History of Printing in America, with a Biography of Printers and an Account of Newspapers,* 2nd Ed. (Albany, NY, 1874), vol. 1, p. xxiv. Masters were supposed to instruct their apprentices in matters theological as well as occupational, and Thomas reports that his master gave him "a weekly lesson . . . by rote merely." The master asked "the question from the catechism 'What are the decrees of God;' I answered I could not tell, and then, boy-like, asked him what they were. He read the answer from the book. I was of the opinion he knew as little about the matter as myself."

2. Ibid.

3. Ibid., vol. II, p. 332.

4. Ibid., vol. I, p. 109.

5. Ibid., p. 147.

6. Quoted from the *Boston News-Letter,* January 4, 1733.

7. Neither Buckingham [*Specimens of Newspaper Literature: With Personal Memoirs, Anecdotes, and Reminiscences,* (1850)], nor Parton [*The Life and Times of Benjamin Franklin* (1864)], provided any systematic examination.

8. Frederick Hudson, *Journalism in the United States from 1690 to 1872* (New York, 1873).

9. Ibid., p. 89.

10. Ibid., pp. 289–293.

11. Ibid., pp. 296–305.

12. S. N. D. North, *History and Present Condition* . . . (Washington, DC, 1884).

13. James Melvin Lee, *History of American Journalism* (Garden City, NY, 1917).

14. Ibid., p. 143.

15. George Henry Payne, *History of Journalism in the United States* (New York, 1920).

16. Ibid., p. 21. Payne also described Harris reading the Bible while on the ship taking him to Boston. Payne himself showed a liberal deism in writing of how "humanity could be led to reverence the Deity through the simple processes of Eternal Law, unfolding and unraveling man's liberty, equality and happiness." (p. 11).

17. Ibid., p. 2.

18. Ibid., p. 11.

19. Willard G. Bleyer, *Main Currents in the History of American Journalism* (Cambridge, 1927), p. 2.

20. Ibid., p. 2.

21. See Bleyer, "Journalism in the United States: 1933," *Journalism Quarterly* 10 (1933), pp. 296–301, and "Freedom of the Press and the New Deal," *Journalism Quarterly* 11 (1934), pp. 22–35.

22. Villard, *Some Newspapers and Newspaper-men* (New York, 1923), p. 314.

23. See George Seldes, *Lords of the Press* (New York, 1945).

24. For example, see Chester E. Jorgenson, "A Brand Flung at Colonial Orthodoxy," *Journalism Quarterly* 12 (1935), pp. 272–277. Jorgenson looked at what he saw as the positive side of colonial printer Samuel Keimer: In Keimer's deism "superstition has given place to science," and "Calvin's wrathful and petulant God" was no more. Jorgenson applauded Keimer for "extolling reasonableness rather than saintliness, nature rather than scripture, humanitarian service rather than the spiritual ascent of the individual . . ." (In this Jorgenson differed from Benjamin Franklin, quoted in Thomas, I, 233; Franklin sympathized with Keimer's expressed theology but observed that Keimer "was a great knave at heart, that he possessed no particular religion, but a little of all upon occasion.")

25. Review of *The Facts Are* in *Journalism Quarterly* 20 (December, 1943), pp. 335–336.

26. Frank Luther Mott, *American Journalism* (New York: Macmillan, 1950).

27. Ibid., p. 206.

28. Ibid., pp. 16–17.

29. Henry Ladd Smith was co-author of the first edition; Michael Emery is now co-author.

30. Michael Emery and Edwin Emery, *The Press and America*, sixth edition (Englewood Cliffs, N.J., 1988), p. 13.

31. Ibid., p. 106.

32. Ibid., p. 58.

33. Ibid., p. 47.

34. Ibid., p. 245.

35. Ibid., p. 146.

36. Ibid., p. 20.

37. Richard Baxter, *Chapters from a Christian Directory*, ed. Jeannette Tawney (London, 1925), p. 50.

38. Sidney Kobre, *Development of American Journalism* (Dubuque, 1969), p. 3; see also pp. 5, 6, 24, 154. Kobre did write two articles on the remarkable Jewish editor of the early nineteenth century, Mordecai Noah; see Kobre, "The Editor Who Freed Hostages," *Media History Digest* 1, 2 (1981), pp. 55–57, 60.

39. My co-authored book *Turning Point,* with Herbert Schlossberg (Westchester, IL, 1987), notes some recent examples of academic bias.

40. Howard H. Fogel, "Colonial Theocracy and a Secular Press," *Journalism Quarterly* 37 (Autumn, 1960), pp. 525–532. Fogel wrote that "A theocracy, by definition closed and narrow, does not favor an inquisitive mind" (p. 527)—but doesn't that depend on the type of theocracy, and on whether it is clericocratic or bibliocratic?

41. Ibid.

42. *North Carolina Historical Review* 30 (January, 1953), pp. 1–22.

43. Elizabeth Barnes, "The *Panoplist:* 19th-Century Religious Magazine," *Journalism Quarterly* 36 (Summer, 1959), pp. 321–325.

44. John M. Havas, "Commerce and Calvinism: The Journal of Commerce, 1827–1865," *Journalism Quarterly* 38 (Winter, 1961), pp. 84–86.

45. Robert E. Lee, "Timothy Dwight and the Boston *Palladium,*" *New England Quarterly* 35 (1962), pp. 229–239.

46. Donald F. Brod, "The Scopes Trial: A Look at Press Coverage after Forty Years," *Journalism Quarterly* 42 (Spring, 1965), pp. 219–227. Brod's dissertation, "Church, State, and Press: Twentieth-Century Episodes in the United States" (University of Minnesota, 1969), was a more extensive examination of the Scopes trial and three other events concerning church-state relations. For a different view of the Scopes trial, see my article "When World Views Collide: Journalists and the Great Monkey Trial," *American Journalism* 4 (1987), pp. 133–146.

47. Henry Smith Stroupe, *The Religious Press in the South Atlantic States, 1802–1865. An Annotated Bibliography with Historical Introduction and Notes* (Durham, NC, 1956).

48. William Jesse Stone, Jr., "A Historical Survey of Leading Texas Denominational Newspapers: 1846–1861," PhD. dissertation, The University of Texas, 1974.

49. Alfred Roger Gobbel, "The Christian Century: Its Editorial Policies and Positions, 1908–1966," PhD. dissertation, University of Illinois, 1967.

50. Claude W. Summerlin, "A History of Southern Baptist State Newspapers," PhD. dissertation, University of Missouri, 1968.

51. Wesley Norton, *Religious Newspapers in the Old Northwest to 1861: A History, Bibliography, and Record of Opinion* (Athens, 1977).

52. Robert W. Ross, *So It Was True* (Minneapolis, 1980).

53. Isaac Goldberg, *Major Noah, American-Jewish Pioneer* (Philadelphia, 1936).

54. Jonathan D. Sarna *Jacksonian Jew: The Two Worlds of Mordecai Noah* (New York, 1981).

55. Kathryn T. Theus, "From Orthodoxy to Reform: Assimilation and the Jewish-English Press of Mid-Nineteenth Century America," *American Journalism* 1, 2 (1984), pp. 15–26.

56. Mary Lonan Reilly, "A History of the Catholic Press Association 1911–1968," PhD. dissertation, Notre Dame University, 1970.

57. M. R. Real, "Trends in Structure and Policy in the American Catholic Press," *Journalism Quarterly* 52 (Spring, 1975), pp. 265–271.

58. Robert Peel, *Mary Baker Eddy: The Years of Authority* (New York: Holt, Rinehart,

Winston, 1977). Earlier works on the *Monitor* include Erwin D. Canham, *Commitment to Freedom: The Story of the Christian Science Monitor* (Boston: Houghton Mifflin, 1958) and John A. Klempner, "A Newspaper in Dissonance: The *Christian Science Monitor* Election Coverage, 1928 and 1960," Ph.D. dissertation, Michigan State University, 1960.

59. Harold H. Osmer, *U.S. Religious Journalism and the Korean War* (Washington, 1980).

60. Charles H. Lippy, ed., *Religious Periodicals in the United States* (Westport, Connecticut, 1986).

61. *Journal of Broadcasting & Electronic Media* 32 (Summer, 1988).

62. Paul Vitz, *Religion and Traditional Values in Public School Textbooks* (Washington, DC, 1986).

APPENDIX C

1. Charles Murray, *In Pursuit* (New York, 1988), p. 16.

2. Joshua Muravchik, *News Coverage of the Sandinista Revolution* (Washington, DC:, 1988), pp. 5–6.

3. Robert Darnton, "Writing News and Telling Stories," *Daedalus* 104, 2 (1975), pp. 190–191.

4. Ibid., loc. cit.

5. Mitchell Stephens, *A History of News* (New York, 1988), p. 264.

6. Murray, op. cit.

7. *Washington Monthly*, May 14, 1975, p. 14.

8. As *New York Times* editor Lester Markel has noted, "The reporter, the most objective reporter, collects fifty facts. Out of the fifty facts he selects twelve to include in his story (there is such a thing as space limitation). Thus he discards thirty-eight. This is Judgment Number One. Then the reporter or editor decides which of the facts shall be the first paragraph of the story, thus emphasizing one fact above the other eleven. This is Judgment Number Two. Then the editor decides whether the story shall be placed on Page One or Page Twelve; on Page One it will command many times the attention it would on page twelve. This is Judgment Number Three. This so-called factual presentation is thus subjected to three judgments, all of them most humanly and most ungodly made." [Markel was quoted in William Rivers, *The Opinionmakers* (Boston, 1965), p. 43.

9. Some variation occurs, but the *Austin American-Statesman* ran basic, who/what/ where/when articles about a girl killed crossing a highway, an airplane crash in Dallas, a hurricane closing in on Galveston, a major decision by the city council—and if there were other newspapers in Austin, they would have done the same.

10. John Corry, *TV News and the Dominant Culture* (Washington, 1986).

INDEX